CAMBRIDGE SOUTH ASIAN STUDIES

THE PEASANT AND THE RAJ

Studies in agrarian society and peasant rebellion in colonial India

CAMBRIDGE SOUTH ASIAN STUDIES

These monographs are published by the Syndics of Cambridge University Press in association with the Cambridge University Centre for South Asian Studies. The following books have been published in this series:

THE PEASANT AND THE RAJ

Studies in
agrarian society and peasant rebellion
in colonial India

ERIC STOKES

CAMBRIDGE UNIVERSITY PRESS

CAMBRIDGE

LONDON · NEW YORK · MELBOURNE

Published by the Syndics of the Cambridge University Press
The Pitt Building, Trumpington Street, Cambridge CB2 1RP
Bentley House, 200 Euston Road, London NW1 2DB
32 East 57th Street, New York, NY 10022, USA
296 Beaconsfield Parade, Middle Park, Melbourne 3206, Australia

First published 1978

Printed in Great Britain by
Western Printing Services Ltd, Bristol

Library of Congress Cataloguing in Publication Data

Stokes, Eric.
The peasant and the Raj.

(Cambridge South Asian studies; 23)
Includes bibliographical references and index.
1. Land tenure – India – History. 2. Peasantry –
India – History. 3. Peasant uprisings – India – History.
I. Title. II. Series.
HD875.S76   301.44'43'0954   77-77731
ISBN 0 521 21684 2

CONTENTS

80– 0213

MAPS

PREFACE

Most of the studies collected in this volume have already appeared in symposia or learned journals. Apart from the correction of the odd error and the addition of an occasional reference they have all been reproduced as they first appeared. Inevitably they exhibit some measure of intellectual progression. For example, the reader will observe that many of the studies of the 1857 uprising in the countryside were directed to criticising and amending Dr S. B. Chaudhuri's straightforward thesis that the rural areas rose as one man and that the principal cause was the loss of land rights to the urban moneylender and trader under the pressure of the British land revenue system. Instead my researches suggested that violence and rebellion were often fiercest and most protracted where land transfers were low and the hold of the moneylender weakest. Later studies acknowledge, however, that the mere transfer of proprietary title tells us little about its political, social and economic effects, which could vary enormously according to the strength and homogeneity of the political and lineage organisation of the peasantry. Similarly while in earlier essays the action of local communities was analysed (as it was by contemporary British officials) in terms of local caste subdivisions, there is increasing awareness that in the crisis of 1857 rural society did not abandon traditional political organisation structured along vertical cross-caste lines. Even among the Jats of the upper Ganges-Jumna Doab the *got* or maximal lineage was too dispersed to form a local territorial unit for political cooperation and action. Hence the importance of the local multicaste organisation of the *tappa* and *khap* as well as the still wider grouping of the *dharra* or faction. The Introduction seeks to put these matters in perspective.

I would like to express my acknowledgements to the editors and publishers of the following:

Paper 1: The Past and Present Society, Corpus Christi College, Oxford, England. This article first appeared in *Past and Present, a journal of historical studies*, no. 58 (February 1973).

Paper 2: First published in *Land Tenure and Peasant in South Asia*, ed. R. E. Frykenberg (Orient Longman 1977).

Paper 3: First published in *Modern Asian Studies*, 9, 4 (1975).

Paper 4: First published in *Indian Society and the Beginnings of Modernisation*, ed. C. H. Philips and Mary D. Wainwright, (School of Oriental and African Studies, London, 1976).

Paper 5: The Past and Present Society, Corpus Christi College, Oxford, England. This article first appeared in *Past and Present, a journal of historical studies*, no. 48 (August 1970).

Paper 6: First published in *Bengal Past and Present* (Diamond Jubilee Number 1967).

Paper 7: First published in *The Historical Journal*, XII, 4 (1969).

Paper 8: First published in *Elites in South Asia*, ed. E. R. Leach and S. N. Mukherjee (Cambridge 1970).

Paper 9: First published in *The Indian Economic and Social History Review*, XII, 2 (1975).

Paper 10: First published in *Bengal Past and Present*, 95, 1, no. 180 (1976).

Paper 12: First published in *South Asia*, no. 6 (1976).

Although in this form of intellectual inquiry I have been often ploughing something of a lonely furrow I have benefited enormously from the general climate of debate created by colleagues and pupils, whom it would be invidious to single out but some of whom are cited during the course of the book. In tending the fitful flame of authorship every writer is aware of the importance of domestic felicity and tolerance. To my wife and daughters, who have lived too long with a work they have known under the title of *The Pheasant and the Rat*, my gratitude goes deepest.

E.T.S.

St Catharine's College, Cambridge.

Introduction

To probe the nature of the 'traditional' agrarian order in which the vast bulk of the population of the Indian subcontinent was embraced, and to explore the extent to which rural society underwent fundamental alteration under colonial rule, forms the double-thread of inquiry linking these essays. Although events elsewhere in Asia, the practical concerns of development economists, and the rise of 'peasant studies' as an academic pursuit, have all combined to bring into fresh prominence the agrarian life of South Asia, it is remarkable how far thought and observation have been shorn of all but the most rudimentary historical dimension. The modern mind is the poorer in consequence, an impressive technical expertise being partnered all too often by a singular naiveté concerning the historic bases and continuities of the human society that it is planning to change. Doubtless the professional historian is himself much to blame for this condition, reluctant as he has been to put on the pair of good strong boots that Tawney declared to be an essential part of his equipment. Much of his difficulty has lain in the apparent complexity and technicality of Indian land systems and his despair at naturalising them among the common topics of historical discourse. Social anthropologists have long been preaching that complexity is the hallmark of pre-industrial rather than of industrial societies. But the complexity attending the manner in which land was held in the subcontinent was doubly compounded by the interlocking of land tenures with tax collection structures in an ancient order of civilisation. The British quickly added a further complication of their own. The force of subconscious ideology and the practical need to stabilise the tax system within an impersonal bureaucratic form of rule prompted them at the outset of colonial rule to introduce a modern form of private property right. How far the British

misunderstood and distorted South Asian society in consequence
has remained a matter of controversy. Certainly the British
believed that they were innovating. It was a fixed article of their
faith that, because the land tax imposed by rapacious native
governments had traditionally absorbed the entire economic rent,
effective private property in land had hitherto had no general
existence. Engels, echoing Marx, gave this belief vivid expression
in his aphorism that the key to the whole of the East lay in the
absence of private property in land.[1] Yet although the property
arising from the perpetual or long-term limitation of the land tax
was novel, the British proclaimed their purpose as being not to
overturn existing rights but to give amplification and legal certainty to rights that had hitherto remained vague and inchoate.
Modern critics have argued that a fundamental distortion of
Indian tenures was caused by the British inability to free themselves of the notion of an absolute and exclusive form of proprietorship when interests in land were traditionally multiple and
inexclusive.[2] Certainly British legal forms brusquely compressed
the overlapping and complex gradations of rural society into the
crude categories of landlord, tenant and labourer. Yet such critics
have believed too readily in British gullibility and imagined that
senior officials did not appreciate the discrepancy between British
law and Indian fact.

British revenue law – at least in northern India – was perfectly
clear that the novel private proprietary right it created lay not in
the land itself but in the right to levy revenue from it.[3] The existence of a separate and distinct customary right of physical
dominion, including the power to locate cultivators, plant groves,
sink wells, and in some areas control the waste, was never seriously
questioned. What the British attempted to do was to weld
the novel property attaching to the revenue-collecting right
(*malguzari*) to this primary right of dominion. But rendering the
revenue-collecting right compulsorily saleable, for default or in
satisfaction of decrees for debt, ensured that even where the right

[1] Engels to Marx, 6 June 1853, cited S. Avineri, *Karl Marx on Colonialism
and Modernization* (New York, 1969), p. 451.

[2] Cf. Walter C. Neale, *Economic Change in Rural India* (New Haven, Conn.,
1962), pp. 51 ff.

[3] Cf. James Cumming, c. 1820, 'The rights granted to the zamindars were
proprietary rights in the Circar [Government] share of the produce of the
land and not in the land itself', cited Rajat Ray, ' "Zamindars" and
"Jotedars" in Bengal', *Modern Asian Studies*, 9, no. 1 (1975), p. 87.

had been correctly lodged with those wielding primary dominion
there was no solder that could keep the two together. The malguzari right could all too readily become separated off as a form of
ground rental property leaving the physical control of the land in
the hands of others. It is still not always appreciated that in the
high volume of sales that characterised the new British revenue
systems in northern and central India it was for the most part
revenue rights that were being transferred and not land. Hence
the pattern of proprietary rights became little more than an index
of revenue payers and bore a steadily more distant relationship to
the distribution of operational holdings. The legal description of
society failed to fit the economic and sociological. Rural society
refused to be neatly segregated into the mutually exclusive roles
of landlord, tenant, and labourer, and doubled or trebled these
roles endlessly.[4] Hence the loss of the malguzari right was often
more a political than an economic fact. It is this degree of complication that is so frequently overlooked by those who have taken
too literally the introduction of an exclusive proprietary title.
Yet it vitally affects our understanding of the working structure
of rural society, of the causes of peasant violence, and above all,
of the larger question of the changes brought about by colonial
rule.

On this larger question informed opinion, whether of scholars
or practical administrators, has been traditionally divided, oscillating between the conviction of an India galvanised by Western
intrusion and the opposite notion of the changeless East. Papers 1
and 12 look at the long historical debate it has occasioned. In its
agrarian aspect the debate suffered a curious arrest, and from this
has sprung the shallowness of much contemporary discussion on
the historical side. What was the basic peasant tenure? In whose
hands lay the primary dominion of the soil? These questions,
which fired the train of discussion, appeared of vital practical
importance in the early decades of the nineteenth century when
the battle of land-revenue systems was being fought out. For the
answers determined the point in the tenurial scale at which the
'boon' of modern proprietary title was to be accorded – whether
at the level of the local magnate (the zamindari system), the joint-

---

[4] This was also true of ryotwar districts. Cf. the observation on the Bombay
presidency in I. J. Catanach, *Rural Credit in Western India* (Berkeley,
1970), p. 187: 'Many a cultivator was both landlord and tenant; he could
be landholder, tenant, and labourer as well.'

managing village notables (the *pattidari*, *mirasi*, or 'village zamin-dar' system), or the individual peasant holder (the ryotwari system). By the mid nineteenth century there was wide agreement that the coparcenary village community of joint-managing village notables had constituted the original tenure of Indian life, but that its derangement by the late eighteenth century over the greater part of the subcontinent had led to it being overlooked or set aside in the land-revenue systems of Bengal, Madras and Bombay. The independent momentum of administrative systems once under way ensured that there could be no going back. Yet the gathering belief in the historical primacy of the village community gave intellectual sanction to the currency of tenancy legislation which set in from the 1870s in northern India, and which sought to stabilise the position of those enjoying immediate and customary possessory dominion.

The academic elucidation of agrarian structure was given a decisive impetus by Maine's *Ancient Law* (1861) and more especi-ally his *Village Communities in East and West* (1871). Once in train the historical investigation of a state of society in which central power, seignorial jurisdiction, and quasi-manorial forms were observed to have overlaid coparcenary village communities, might have been expected to yield results fully as illuminating as those achieved by Maitland in his analogous study of the historical growth of English society published in *Domesday Book and Beyond* (1897). Yet it was not to be. Although Vinogradoff visited the Punjab in 1913 and put out a fascinating questionnaire, no European savant took up the subject.[5] The Indian subcontinent had to make do with the encyclopaedic labours and muddled thinking of Baden Henry Baden-Powell. Both academic and official interest then dried up, not to be revived again until our own day. By 1900 the historical character of land tenures seemed an increasingly sterile issue in the Indian official world where the British were being driven by political pressure to rely less and less on land revenue as a taxation source, and where the gathering weight of the agrarian problem was suggesting radical courses to cut away the dead incubus of the past. But the aborted nature of the discussion has left the contemporary agronomist and socio-logist curiously bereft of a solid historical foundation. Baden-

[5] H. A. L. Fisher (ed.), *The Collected Papers of Paul Vinogradoff* (Oxford, 1928), i, pp. 52–4.

Powell's *Land Systems of British India* (1892) and *The Indian Village Community* (1896) remain standard authorities nearly a century later and form the departure point for present-day scholarship.

Although without the intellectual force and clarity of Maitland, Baden-Powell was nevertheless responsible for an important revision of the concept of the Indian village community in which he followed very much the line of Maitland's argument.[6] So far from the coparcenary or joint village community being the original universal tenure, it was, he asserted, historically the exception and a later imposition over the severalty or ryotwar village which remained the norm. So, far from being general, the joint village was for the most part confined to northern and north-western India. Even then actual community of property was rare, the land usually being held in severalty and subject merely to joint responsibility and management in respect of the State revenue demand. Most types of joint village, Baden-Powell believed, had originated in local conquest or as a royal grant of revenue-collecting rights over ryotwar cultivators. Many of these grants were far from ancient. The proliferation of the grantee's kin within a few generations was sufficient to explain the progressive transformation of the tenure from single ownership (*zamindari khalis*) to joint undivided ownership (*zamindari mushtarka*) among his immediate descendants and then in the progress of time to division among the various branches (pattis) of the proprietary kin group. By this stage the group had become so enlarged that the profits on the revenue collected from subordinate cultivators no longer sufficed to support it. Part of the village lands would be taken into direct owner cultivation (*sir*) and held and cultivated in severalty. Subordinate cultivators would continue to pay their dues into a common treasury to be set against the revenue demand on the village as a whole. Any surplus or deficit would be distributed over pattis and individual pattidars on the basis of their ancestral share determined by their position in the genealogical table. So long as some land worked by subordinate 'tenant' cultivators remained common, the tenure was known as 'imperfect pattidari'. But ultimately, if in practice only occasionally, the entire village lands could be divided up among the pattidars,

---

[6] Cf. C. J. Dewey, 'Images of the Village Community', *Modern Asian Studies* 6, no. 3 (1972), pp. 320 ff.

either as their individual sir or as their individual 'rent property'. In revenue language this condition was known as 'perfect pattidari', the essential characteristic being that each patti and pattidar, despite the fact that all holding was now complete severalty, continued to meet the revenue demand on the basis of ancestral shares. When too great a discrepancy appeared between actual holdings and ancestral shares, the ancestral-share principle could itself be abandoned and a straight area rate on holdings (*bach* or *bigha-dam*) adopted in its place. The British called this *bhaiachara* or 'custom of the brotherhood'. Except for the survival of joint responsibility for the revenue demand on the village as a whole, the tenure was almost indistinguishable from ryotwar. The development cycle of tenures had reached its term and could be started anew only by the village falling again into single ownership as a result of fresh local conquest, state grant, or – under the British – of forced transfer for revenue default or mortgage foreclosure. These tenurial types were, of course, crude models and practice showed infinite modifications, especially when the separate pattis of a village or 'estate' were each held under different tenures. Although Baden-Powell adhered generally to the concept of a developmental cycle in tenures, he exempted bhaiachara. The term had been mistakenly used by British officials to indicate any joint tenure where the revenue was apportioned as a land or plough rate that did not follow the principle of ancestral shares. True bhaiachara, he believed, had an independent origin and did not spring as did all other forms of joint tenure from a political grant of overlordship, but stemmed from below as the result of the original tribal or clan colonisation of an empty tract. The rights divided among the colonists and their heirs were not the revenue payments of subordinate or conquered cultivators, but the virgin land itself. Yet apart from the vestigial right of the community to repartition the village lands Baden-Powell was unable in practice to distinguish this tenure from that in which the descendants of a single 'landlord' had come to occupy all the cultivated land themselves.

To the largely official audience for which he produced his books such fine distinctions must have seemed highly academic. With the practical desuetude of joint responsibility and the gathering pace of partitions the village communities were fast dissolving by the end of the nineteenth century into a form of either ryotwar or zamindari, according to the size of proprietary holding. Baden-Powell's plea for a census of village tenures in the Punjab and the N.W. Provinces and Oudh fell on deaf ears, and his emphasis on the essentially tribal character of true bhaiachara, exemplified by the Jats of Mathura district, must have seemed a crotchet on a par with the historical theory of the spread of Aryan institutions to which he chose to link it.

Papers 2, 3 and 10 together seek to show that in the evolution of modern agrarian structures these matters were far from academic, and that they influenced the local pattern of 'caste' and 'class' relationships in an important manner. Baden-Powell's insistence on the separate origin and nature of the bhaiachara tenure is upheld and defended. But the differentia from other tenures is sought in economic ecology. It is the contention of these studies that not only the major tenurial distinctions between the ryotwar and non-ryotwar forms of village, but also caste differentiation and social distance erected upon them, can be largely explained in their origin by the distinction between regions of secure and insecure agriculture and their corresponding contrasts in population density.

Only in regions of secure agriculture and heavy population was there sufficient competition to allow the equivalent of a landlord's rent to emerge. Only here was it worthwhile for a person or group to assert immediate physical dominion over land beyond his or its immediate cultivating needs. Village landlord forms were, therefore, confined in broad terms to areas such as the wet farming districts of Andhra and Tamilnadu, the coastal tracts of the Konkan and Gujarat in western India, or the Gangetic plain below Delhi. This did not mean that extensive cultivable waste might not exist in close proximity to densely populated regions, but the waste was of such a nature – for example, in Bengal or in the Himalayan terai of Gorakhpur and Saharanpur districts – as to require considerable capital for its clearance and settlement. So that peopling such areas often threw up village or supra-village landlord forms. In Hoshangabad district in the Narmada valley the colonisation of the wheat lands threw the malguzari and ultimately the landlord right into the hands of anyone of whatever caste or calling who could finance the colonists until the first full harvest was secured. There is a still more important qualification to the notion of the generation of landlord rents. It is not suggested that economic rents emerged under conditions of a free-market agriculture. Rental tribute was always extracted by extra-economic coercion, but at the village level it was only worthwhile asserting a monopoly of access to land over and above one's cultivating needs under conditions of relative land scarcity. Of course even where the man/land ratio was low the state itself could assert a practical monopoly over an area sufficiently extensive to extort tribute from all alike, or a local magnate class like the Bundela *thakurs* or the Ceded Districts *poligars* could levy protection rent over villages. But this was an overlord rather than landlord right, since it fell short of proprietary dominion itself. Within the village there remained an absence of landlord forms for there was no profit to be made in 'leasing out'. So long as arable land was freely available, wealth and pre-eminence lay in cattle, ploughs, and the numbers and labour power of the cultivating family.[7] Above all, privileged immunity from the full exaction of the state could be of the highest importance. Paper 2 argues that the structure of the ryotwar village with its characteristic apparatus of *ballotadars* or village officers and its dependence on petty 'service' tenures was the peculiar product of these conditions.

In practice the more successful forms of peasant agriculture appear to have emerged where owner-cultivator communities under ryotwar or bhaiachara forms obtained a novel security in their conditions of life.[8] This might result from the renewal of political and fiscal security and the reinvigoration of long-distance traffic in agricultural produce; but above all it was aided by the novel agricultural security springing from the extension of well and canal irrigation. In this respect the doubling of the sown area in the Punjab and Haryana between 1850 and 1925 to 30 million acres represented a remarkable episode of internal colonialisation.[9] Where conditions of insecure agriculture had originally produced

[7] On the enormous extent of cultivable waste in the ryotwar districts of Salem, Anantapur, Bellary, etc. cf. D. Kumar, *Land and Caste in South India* (Cambridge, 1965), p. 107.

[8] Biplab Dasgupta, *Agrarian Change and the New Technology in India* (UNRISD, Geneva, 1977) observes that 'the new technology of green revolution has so far been more successful in *ryotwar* areas [in which he includes Punjab. Haryana, and West U.P.] dominated by thrifty, hardworking peasant proprietors'.

[9] For expansion of cultivation of the Punjab, cf. S. S. Thornton, *The Punjab in Peace and War* (Edinburgh and London, 1904), p. 260; and also H. Calvert, *The Wealth and Welfare of the Punjab*, 2nd edn (Lahore, 1936), p. 156.

owner-cultivator rather than rentier-landlord tenures, there the novel security promoted a 'rich peasant' class which combined petty landlordism, moneylending and direct cultivation, and which was prominent by the 1880s among the Kunbi Patidars of Gujarat, the malguzars of the Narmada valley, and the village *maliks* of Haryana and the Punjab. These issues are touched upon in Papers 10 and 11.

In giving this degree of attention to nineteenth-century theorising on the Indian village community it is axiomatic to the argument that the 'ideological' context of debate contributed an important independent element to British land-revenue policy and to the transformation of Indian land tenures. This is not a popular view. Administrative policy has remained a comparatively neglected field for the historical scholar carried along by the post-War swing of interest away from transient imperialist superstructures to the inner workings of society. Older simplistic assumptions about the actions of ideas in modern South Asian history have deservedly been rejected. Few would now disagree that overt doctrine and covert presupposition had to work within the narrow constraints which were inherent in self-financing colonial autocracy and which allowed steadily diminishing room for manoeuvre. India was a country, as Kipling said, where the climate and the work were against playing bricks with words.[10] Yet British action cannot be reduced entirely to a near-sighted pragmatism. The role of theory is looked at afresh in Paper 4. It is not supposed that ideas found lodgement unless they converged with felt need, but that is very different from saying that they were mere rationalisations of material interests or otiose justifications of simple expediency. Some historians have argued that even where ideological assumptions were most deeply imbedded in the colonial institutional structure, that is to say in the legal system of private property rights in land, their effect was largely negated by limiting devices whenever they threatened to cause social upheaval or disorder. Such historians suggest that tenancy legislation was primarily introduced to keep the countryside quiet, even though its successive steps brought about a virtual 'transfer of ownership' to the cultivator.[11] Hence on this view, despite the

[10] R. Kipling, 'The Conversion of Aurelian McGoggin', *Plain Tales from the Hills* (London, 1965).
[11] Cf. Dietmar Rothermund, *The Phases of Indian Nationalism* (Bombay, 1970), p. 197.

aristocratic reaction in official thinking after the 1857 Revolt, the British were slowly forced to desert their larger landlord collaborators. Yet there is another side to the expiry of earlier hopes for a capitalist revolution in North Indian agriculture based on larger proprietary units.

As late as the 1860s Baird Smith pronounced freely transferable property rights in land as not merely the most effective means of attracting capital into agriculture but as the best form of famine insurance. The institution of village landlords (or malguzars) in the 1860s in a large part of the Central Provinces argued a continuing faith in building up a rural capitalist class. Yet by the 1870s there were few who believed that the monied classes would produce improving landlords or that many would turn into capitalist farmers. 'For it cannot be too clearly understood', wrote W. G. Pedder, a leading Bombay revenue official, 'that only in the dream of a visionary will the English agricultural system of large landlords, capitalist farmers of large farms, and peasant labourers for wage, ever be substituted for the *petite culture* of India.'[12] It was ironic that just at the point when the railway was opening up the countryside to new markets on an unprecedented scale British administrators should become increasingly apprehensive about the future. Their taskmasters were famine and agrarian indebtedness, which appeared in alarming form in the 1870s. Shrewder officials believed the two were interconnected. The new facilities of communication changed famine from a regional to a class problem and left the labouring class and small plot holders throughout the country exposed to starvation because of scarcity food prices.[13] To what extent was the small landholder undergoing gradual pauperisation? Pedder believed that the Deccan Riots of 1875 had shown that he was in serious danger of becoming 'the praedial serf of the money lender'. The frightening spectre which began to haunt officials was that not only would the increasing commercialisation of agriculture weaken the poorer peasant's defences against famine, but that the land would increasingly be starved of the capital that was essential for raising productivity. The threat of the moneylender took different shapes according to the land-revenue system in force. In the *mahalwari* region of

[12] W. G. Pedder, pamphlet, cited *Deccan Riots Commission Appx A Papers re Indebtedness of the Agricultural Classes in Bombay* (Bombay, 1876), pp. 139–40.
[13] B. M. Bhatia, *Famines in India, 1860–1965* (London, 1963), ch. i.

northern and central India there seemed a danger that the
moneylender would take over the proprietary title by the device of
mortgage foreclosure, and reduce the cultivating peasant 'owner'
to an impoverished tenant living from hand to mouth and practising an exhaustive agriculture. Here for officials like (Sir)
C. A. Elliott and Sir E. C. Buck the radical answer appeared to lie
in abolishing tenancy-at-will, prohibiting the sale of land for un-
secured debt and providing State loans for encumbered 'ancestral'
proprietors.[14] The vast mass of cultivators in the N.W. Provinces
and Oudh were already, however, classified legally as tenants, and
they proposed – unsuccessfully at the time – that all unprotected
tenants-at-will should be accorded occupancy status.[15] The upshot
of their proposals would have been to institute a ryotwar settlement by constituting the immediate cultivating holder the effective owner. Elliott and Buck were powerful voices on the 1880
Famine Commission, and, while their views were not given full
effect, the most important measures of tenancy legislation that
profoundly modified the original recognition of freehold title were
passed in the decade that followed. In all this it might be said
that there was no more than a return to the original hopes of
founding Indian agriculture on an owner-cultivator *petite culture*.
Yet the lowering of sights over the possibilities of introducing
capitalist farming was accompanied by doubts over the application of classical economic principles to the State land-revenue
demand. Paper 4 discusses the renewed influence of Richard
Jones' theory of peasant rents. Its effect was, firstly, to question
the validity of competition rents as a true measure of economic
rent, and, secondly, to throw doubt on the theory that saw
positive good in extracting a high proportion of rental assets as
State revenue. It was now felt that agricultural safety and progress depended on leaving as large a proportion of rent as possible
in the hands of the cultivating occupier. That did not mean a
permanent settlement which within a generation or two would
convert the revenue demand into a minor tax because of the
anticipated rise in prices. The demand had so to be pitched that
it did not allow the occupier to sublet and become a rent-receiver
who turned his land over to a tenant labourer with no capital or

[14] *Cawnpore Settlement Report 1878*, pp. 111 ff.
[15] *Famine Commission Report 1880, Parliamentary Papers 1881*, lxxi, pt i,
p. 493.

incentive for keeping it in good heart. Hence while politically-minded men like Cromer and Salisbury were anxious to keep land taxation low so that the incendiary speechifying of urban politicians should not set the countryside alight, there was a powerful school of administrative thought that believed in maintaining a full revenue demand at the modified level of at least one-half of the rental assets.

All legislative interposition seemed impotent so long as free trade in land allowed the moneylender to acquire proprietary title or the law allowed him to keep the cultivating owner and/or tenant a virtual debt serf. From the 1870s official opinion grew gradually obsessed by the problem of agrarian indebtedness until it found that prohibiting the transfer of title from 'agriculturalist' to 'non-agriculturalist' castes (by the Punjab Land Alienation Act of 1900 and the Bundelkhand Act of 1903) worked no miracle. How far was official opinion correct in seeing indebtedness as the chief cause of the absence of effective agricultural improvement and dynamic growth in Indian agriculture? Paper 11 examines this question in relation to part of central India. The answer suggests that while indebtedness was an important element in the rural economy it was in many ways as much a symptom as a cause of agrarian malaise. The paper points out (what was surmised at an early stage) that indebtedness so far from being a homogeneous problem masked a number of special situations.[16] Only those with a regular source of income and some form of security could obtain loans. The poor plot holder without tenant right, or the extremely poor area without significant production of cash crops, like Sholapur district in the Deccan, were at the bottom of the debtors' league.[17] Similarly large cultivating landholders were also low borrowers, being more often than not rural creditors themselves. The most heavily indebted areas and classes were the good soil tracts and the middle rank of comfortably-off peasant cultivators. In the Deccan, H. Woodward estimated in 1883 that this middle peasantry farming holdings of 50–100 acres formed 40% of cultivators (excluding labourers).[18] A high level of debt under such conditions signified not so much distress as the absence of continuous growth in the agricultural economy and high consumer

[16] *Fam. Comm. Rep. 1880*, pp. 22–3.
[17] On Sholapur, Report of H. Woodward, 10 August 1883, *Papers re Deccan Agriculturalists Relief Act* (Calcutta, 1897), i, p. 344.
[18] *Ibid.*, p. 336.

spending relative to productive investment. Yet, as a flourishing district like Hoshangabad (C.P.) showed, it was a burden that could periodically be worked off and then renewed as harvests and prices moved through their mysterious cycle of boom and slump. Debt was most insidious in congested areas like Bengal where it was so interwoven with the systems of rents and tenures, and where the moneylender was for the most part the zamindar and jotedar, that it could not be separated out as a distinct problem on its own.

Where indebtedness threw the cultivator into most serious dependence on the non-agriculturalist and fomented potential civil discord was in the agriculturally insecure tracts, or alternatively in densely settled pockets around district towns among the poorer tenant class. These were the special areas that caught the official eye and rendered it fearful. But it was the comparative unprogressiveness of rich and middle peasant agriculture that formed ultimately the most serious aspect of the agrarian problem. Here the ordinary settlement officer or even an authority like Darling had little picture of the larger setting within which the agricultural economy functioned. Paper 11 shows how areas like Bundelkhand or the Narmada valley could be picked up by the advancing market economy, put through a cash-crop boom and then left floundering in a condition that latter-day Marxists would perhaps describe as 'the development of underdevelopment'. The permanent loss of distant markets for cotton and wheat can be ascribed in part to the capriciousness of the central Indian rainfall coupled with the persistent scourge of *kans* grass. (As late as the 1950s it was an object of the Madhya Pradesh Five Year Plan to eradicate kans by tractor ploughing even in so flourishing a district as Hoshangabad.[19]) Yet what appears to have been more fundamental in turning enterprise wholeheartedly into agricultural production rather than investment in rent property, moneylending or middle-man marketing was the crude rate of net agricultural profits. Hanumantha Rao pointed out in Ferozepur district how the recent Green Revolution in the 1960s raised the net rate of profit (by the change from *desi* to high yielding wheat) from 6%

---

[19] Government of Nagpur, *The First Five Year Plan in Madhya Pradesh – An Appraisal* (Nagpur, [1954?], p. 17. The serious inroads made by *kans* after the period of distress, 1893–1900, are reported in *Hoshangabad S.R. 1913–18*, p. 16.

to 22%.[20] It has been the difficulty of sustaining a high rate of profit of that order for sufficiently long that makes Indian agrarian history so often the story of short-lived booms followed by long periods when the landholder diversifies his sources of income and puts his eggs into many baskets. Moreover in the varying fortunes of different regions there is something in the notion that the development of one region helped underdevelop the rest. Certainly the fall-back in the Narmada valley from the height of the wheat boom of the 1880s was part of the price to be paid for the success of the Lower Chenab and other canal colonies in the Punjab, though even there close observers were far from happy at the failure of the new *sirdars* to maximise cash-crop production and to abjure usury and subletting.[21]

The other major purpose of this collection is to examine the rural response to colonial rule as it was manifested in agrarian agitation and insurrection. The uprising in the countryside that formed so striking a part of the 'Mutiny' Revolt is the central focus of study. Paper 5 considers its general character, while Papers 6, 7 and 8 look at three separate areas in the Delhi-Agra region in some detail. They view in juxtaposition the action of the two local political forms – the autonomous village communities and the 'landlord estates'. In particular they seek to assess the effects of British revenue laws and of transfers of proprietary title on rural political affiliation in the hour of crisis. Such matters admit of a surprising degree of precision in some districts – especially in Saharanpur and Muzaffarnagar – so far as the statistical measurement of transfers or the incidence of the land-revenue demand are concerned. The analysis goes to show that economic rationality supplies the most consistent explanation of immediate response. Yet at the end of the day, when the tangible material interests have been quantified and weighed, these studies freely acknowledge that the rural response in 1857 cannot be read simply in terms of the material loss or gain experienced by an individual or community over the previous half century of British rule. For this was no 'possessive market society' in which the struggle for exis-

[20] Hanumantha Rao, *Technological Change and Distribution of Gains in Indian Agriculture* (Madras, 1975), p. 128.
[21] Basil Poff, unpublished seminar paper, 'Land Management and Modernization in a Punjab Canal Colony: Lyallpur 1890–1939', Institute of Commonwealth Studies, London University, 11 February 1975.

tence had been reduced to pure economic competition. It was one in which men still carried weapons at their side, expressive of the fact that Leviathan's shadow stopped short at the mud walls of the village. The varying gap between British revenue law and Indian sociological fact respecting interests in land measured the extent to which local political forms remained incompletely subdued by State authority. Title did not necessarily give or sustain possession. While a strong sense of rights over land prevailed, that right at the lowest level of effective occupation and physical dominion needed the constant support of extra-legal power. If local political consequence was thus important to economic strength, any reading of the response to 1857 in terms of 'have-nots' versus 'haves' takes on an extended dimension. Relative was more important than absolute deprivation, and the expression of material interests might take a predominantly political form. The groups which wielded local political influence most effectively – whether organised as a 'republican' league of village communities, or bound together more autocratically under a lineage head in a 'landlord estate' – are defined in these papers in caste terms; for these are the terms under which they appear in the British records. Caste affiliation was unquestionably important as a political bond, as was caste deference for securing acquiescence to land-control rights. Yet it supplies only an imperfect and in the end highly misleading key to political response in 1857. Contemporary and later attempts at interpreting the decision for hostility or collaboration in simplistic terms of a communal division between Muslims and Hindus, or a reaction determined by caste stereotype ('robber Gujar', 'industrious Jat', etc.) break upon the facts. For within these larger caste categories there emerged a bewildering absence of consistency of response when the uprising is viewed at large.

While the Jats of eastern Meerut district were foremost in 'loyalty' to the British, those of the western parts were notorious for their persistent rebellion.[22] Even within the sub-localities held solidly by a single landholding 'tribe' like the Jats, sharp variations occurred. After the early eviction of British authority Rohtak district (to the west of Delhi) was the scene of violent altercations which the British put down to internal feuding among the Jat clans. Modern writers continue to remark on Jat divisiveness,

[22] See below, pp. 184, 273–4.

attributing it to some constitutional propensity to factionalism.[23] What is overlooked is the root difficulty confronting the Jats in reconciling a social organisation based on extended kinship lineages with the maintenance of an effective territorial unit needed for immediate land control. Bhaiachara communities rested on the principle that all members of a brotherhood cultivated land directly and in severalty rather than formed landlord bodies. Hence constant dispersion and colonisation was the law of their being in the founding years, before the land had been fully staked out and before multiplying numbers had to be accommodated by subdivision of holdings, military service, or distant migration. Like the Boers an intense clannishness consorted with a marked divisiveness. The Jat's impatience of control extended to a reluctance to recognise the authority of even the village managers (*lambardars*) through whom he paid his revenue to the Government. Fission and dispersion thus deployed a clan in settlement groups over a wide area, often intermixed with the villages of other clans or castes. The result was a patchwork quilt of local groupings (*tappas*) in each of which members of one clan had obtained dominance.[24] Hence the tappa was a political and territorial rather than a purely kinship unit. As the Rohtak settlement officer wrote in 1839, it was 'a cluster of villages, owning the supremacy of one tuppadary village, generally the largest among them, and forming together a separate body corporate. The tuppa generally includes, without reference to caste, the villages surrounding the tuppadary mouzah [village]; and the connection may therefore be supposed to have found its origin in those disturbed times when small detached villages were unknown, and unions like these were necessary for the protection of even large communities.'[25] The tappas, dominated by members of a leading clan, together made up a clan area or *khap*, which consisted usually of contiguous tappas forming a solid block of territory around the parent village with a number of outlying ones beyond the ring fence.[26]

[23] Oscar Lewis, *Village Life in Northern India* (Urbana, 1958).
[24] Cf. map of *tappas* in *Rohtak S.R. 1873–79*.
[25] M. R. Gubbins, Settlement Report of Pergunnah Gohana, p. 57, in *Selections from Reports of Revision of Settlement under Regulation IX of 1833 in the Dehlie Territory No. 1* (Agra, 1846).
[26] Cf. M. C. Pradhan, *The Political Organization of the Jats of Northern India* (Oxford, 1966).

If caste was already compromised at the level of tappa and khap it was still more strikingly set aside at the higher level of political alignment. The area north west of Delhi was traditionally divided among the two Jat factions (*dharra*) of Haulania and Dehia. The factional split had originated apparently in the eighteenth century when the Ghatwals (or as they later proudly termed themselves, Malik) Jats of Ahulana near Gohana in Rohtak district led the fight to push back Rajput overlord pretensions and land-control rights in the area of rich soil (*bangar*) in the later Karnal district. The Ghatwals proved so successful that not only did they defiantly adopt the red turban but they also provoked the jealousy and alarm of the Dehia Jats settled about Sonepat. The latter thereupon formed a league of the defeated, which appears to have included not only the minor Jat clans of Huda and Latmar from Rohtak and the Jaglan Jats from Naultha in Karnal, but extended to embrace the Gujars and Tagas of Karnal and even the Mandhar Rajputs who held sway in the wild Nardak country where the Mughal rulers had traditionally hunted lion. The struggle ranged east of the Jumna into the upper Doab. In 1857 this factional division seems to have emerged anew. The Dehias had found British rule doubly bitter since the promise of the reopened West Jumna Canal which brought manifest prosperity to the Ghatwals of Ahulana brought them little but salination of their land and malaria causing impotency because of the faulty alignment of the Canal.[27] While the Ghatwals fought the Dehia faction they adopted an attitude of benevolent neutrality towards the British. Alone in the Rohtak district the *tahsili* or Government subdistrict offices at Gohana were preserved from harm. The Dehias were doubtless too intimidated by the presence of British forces along the Grand Trunk Road to venture upon much organised protest, but in Karnal to the north 'sixteen of the largest Jat villages in the Naultha *zail* refused to pay their revenue, drove out the Government village watchmen, joined in the disturbances in Rohtak district, went to Delhi whence they returned after an absence of 22 days, and threatened to attack the Collector's camp'.[28]

Across the Jumna in the rich western parganas of the upper Doab there was the same history of factional alignment. Sir

[27] D. Ibbetson, *Karnal S.R. 1872–80*, pp. 36–7, 82 *passim*.
[28] *Ibid.*, pp. 36–7.

Henry Elliot noted in the 1830s how the Ghatwals in Kandhla (which later became part of Muzaffarnagar district) held fewer villages but claimed superiority over the neighbouring Balian khap of Shikarpur and the Salaklain (or Des) khap centred on Baraut to the south (in the Meerut district) with their *chaurasi* of 84 villages. Their feuds had been perpetual in the times of the Marathas and Sikhs, the Balian and Salaklain Jats leaguing with the Kalsain Gujars and Sunbal Ranghars against the Ghatwal Jats and their allies from smaller Jat *gots*. In the disturbances of 1857 it was the Salaklain Jats from the Baraut area who under Shah and Suraj Mal's leadership did so much to aid the Delhi rebels with supplies, while the Balian khap contributed powerfully to the general rural uprising of September 1857 in western Muzaffarnagar when had not Delhi fallen to the British it looked as though it would have carried all before it.[29] Ibbetson observed how this movement of revolt was said to be linked to the Dehia faction west of the Jumna.[30]

Doutbless this internal divisiveness was fatal to the rebel cause, but it lights up the complex interplay of interests expressed variously in terms of land-control rights, caste, territorial and political affiliation. The story supplies a salutary cautionary note when attempts are made to read later peasant response in the twentieth century according to a simple economic stratification into rich, middle, and poor peasantry. Not that analysis of peasant action in terms of perceived material interest should be cast aside any more than it should for the events of 1857. Yet it remains no more than a heuristic device, a rough entrenching tool to dig up the buried past, and has to give place to more delicate and varied instruments once the outline of the treasure has been laid bare. Some general reflections on the analysis of later peasant movements are set out in the concluding Paper 12.

[29] Sir Henry Elliot, Settlement Book, I.O.R., MSS Eur. F. 56, fos. 109–10; Revenue Papers, MSS Eur. F. 60/B, fos. 419–21. For brief reference to Jat rising in Muzaffarnagar, see below, pp. 175 ff.
[30] D. Ibbetson, *Karnal S.R. 1872–80* p. 79.

I

The first century of British colonial rule in India: social revolution or social stagnation?

The science of history proceeds no doubt as the detailed criticism
of sociological generalisations, but of generalisations so rudimentary and so little analysed that they constitute primitive archetypal
images lurking in the background of the historian's consciousness
rather than a formed system of ideas. In South Asian studies such
images are the simple dichotomies of East and West, tradition and
modernity, continuity and change, status and contract, feudalism
and capitalism, caste and class; and the historian and social scien-
tist conduct their increasingly technical and sophisticated studies
in the form of an implicit critique of these conceptual polarities.
Nineteenth-century sociological thought, with its evolutionary and
therefore historical bias, founded itself squarely and unabashedly
upon such polarities, but today few read James Mill, or Hegel, or
Maine, or Lyall, or even, one suspects, Weber, on India. To strike
the primitive images into our consciousness there was needed a
synthesising mind of genius who could throw the sociological
generalisations of his time into memorable epigrammatic phrase
and fire them with political passion. That is one reason at least
why Marx's occasional journalism on India is still read and
pondered, even though his more academic studies have remained
neglected until quite recently.

Marx recognised that the pre-conditions of Western conquest
lay in Indian rather than in British society. His major premise
was the peculiar multi-cellular character of Indian society that
made it both highly resistant to change in its social and cultural

This is a slightly expanded version of a paper presented under the title
'The British in India' at the Past and Present Society's Annual Conference
in July 1971 on 'Conquest and Culture'. The paper was written for a non-
specialist audience.

aspects and *ipso facto* subject to constant political change and to conquest from without:

A country not only divided between the Mohammedan and Hindu, but between tribe and tribe, between caste and caste; a society whose framework was based on a sort of equilibrium, resulting from a general repulsion and constitutional exclusiveness between all its members. Such a country and such a society were they not the pre-destined prey of conquest?...Indian society has no history at all, at least no known history. What we call its history is but the history of the successive intruders who founded their empires on the passive basis of that unresisting and un-changing society.[1]

One of the most important consequences of this extreme com-partmentalism, which Marx described as 'the dissolution of society into stereotyped and disconnected atoms', was the discontinuity between the social base and the political superstructure. Parcelled out into a myriad of self-sufficient and self-governing village 'republics', each regulated internally by the institutions of caste, society was capable of ordering itself almost independently of superior political authority. The taproot of this self-sufficiency was economic, 'the domestic union of industrial and agricultural pursuits' within the village reinforced by the existence of tied industrial castes. These made otiose rural dependence on urban manufacture and its concomitants, an exchange economy and class differentiation, which had slowly eaten the heart out of Western feudalism.

The simplicity of the organization for production in these self-sufficing [village] communities that constantly reproduce themselves in the same form and when accidentally destroyed spring up again on the spot with the same name – this simplicity supplies the key to the secret of the unchangeableness of Asiatic societies, an unchange-ableness in such striking contrast with the constant dissolution and refounding of Asiatic states, and the never-ceasing changes of dynasty. The structure of the economic elements of society remains untouched by the storm clouds in the political sky.[2]

If compartmentalism was the keynote of the economic and social structure, 'oriental despotism' characterised its politics. Whether this arose as Marx believed primarily out of the need for a centralised bureaucratic authority to build and manage irriga-

[1] K. Marx, *New York Daily Tribune*, 8 Aug. 1853, cited in S. Avineri (ed.), *Karl Marx on Colonialism and Modernization* (New York, 1969), p. 132.
[2] K. Marx, *Capital* (1867), i, ch. 14, sect. 4, cited Avineri, *op. cit.*, pp. 40–1

tion works upon which agriculture depended, or whether it represented simply the systematisation of predatory military rule, is immaterial. But its consequence was the absorption by state taxation of the whole surplus produce of the soil beyond the bare subsistence needs of the cultivator. Hence private rent property in land and a stable allodial aristocracy based upon it never emerged.[3] Whatever magnate or gentry element existed owed its position to revokable state appointments and to stipends consisting of temporary grants or alienations of the public land revenue. In Weber's terminology the Indian nobility was prebendal, and feudal forms could not disguise its original and continuing dependence on state power and its lack of all enduring freestanding rights of its own. The same absence of class autonomy was true of what passed for the bourgeoisie. Given the self-sufficiency of the Indian village, its surplus production was not drawn out by the operations of an exchange economy resting on urban manufacture but had to be forcibly pumped out by the engine of taxation. These tax revenues were expended by the ruler and his satraps on luxury products supplied by the traders and craftsmen who gathered round the military encampments. And Indian towns rarely rose above this level.[4] They remained essentially artificial settlements, without an autonomous life of their own and above all, without a true burgher class possessing jurisdictional and political rights. The differentiation of society into classes did not occur, and the Western *Ständestaat* was not reproduced. Without the counterpoise of feudal 'estates' Asian government was by nature overcentralised and despotic, while its inherent instability prevented the growth of durable territorial states .[5]

The notion of 'oriental despotism' may be filled out from other nineteenth-century writers among whom it was a common theme. Sir Alfred Lyall, from whom Maine drew some of his later ideas, used it to explain the break-up of the Mughal empire and

[3] Marx merely shared the common assumption of his time in this respect. Cf. H. S. Maine, *Village Communities in the East and West*, 3rd edn (London, 1879), p. 179.

[4] It is noticeable that Maine held the same theory of Indian towns without the benefit of Marx; Maine, *op. cit.*, p. 119.

[5] This is a simplified thumb-nail sketch of Marx's ideas. For detailed critical treatment, see E. J. Hobsbawm's introduction to Karl Marx, *Pre-Capitalist Formations*, ed. E. J. Hobsbawm (London, 1964), and D. Thorner, 'Marx on India and the Asiatic Mode of Production', *Contributions to Indian Sociology*, ix (1966).

the rise of the British power. The Mughals he saw as merely the most recent and most successful of Indian rulers in planing flat the surface of political society and concentrating power in a top-heavy despotism at the centre. Hence when the centre crashed in the eighteenth century there was nothing to cushion its fall. In Lyall's words it was:

An era of chaos unprecedented even in the annals of Asiatic history, such an era as only follows the break up of a wide spreading despotic empire which has so carefully knocked out and cut away all internal or local stays and ties that its fall, when it comes, is a ruinous crash, and leaves a vast territory in a state of complete political dissolution...one important reason why the English so rapidly conquered was this, that the countries which fell into our hands had no nationalities, no long-seated ruling dynasties, or ancient aristocracies, that they had in fact no solid or permanent organisation of the kind, but were politically treasure trove, and at the disposal of the first who having found could keep.[6]

Lyall also found the source of political instability and the transience of political structures not in some special Asian propensity to despotism but in the Indian social structure. The historical evolution of Indian society had taken a peculiar direction. In Western Europe the tribal unit based on putative kinship had been dissolved into a multitude of nuclear families held together in political groupings based on land and territory, whether in the wide embrace of Roman imperial authority or later in smaller local lordships of feudalism. Out of these had emerged durable territorial states with a sense of nationality, and permanent political institutions capable of resisting the centripetal force of monarchy and hence of surviving the latter's temporary weakness or collapse. In India, however, 'religion seems to have stepped in as the tribal institutions dissolved, and to have strung all the kindred groups upon the great circle which we call caste', so that 'the trade, or the profession, or the common ritual becomes the bond of union instead of descent or political association'. Lyall thus arrives at the same conclusion regarding the discontinuity of the political and social systems.

This emphasis on caste as the prime datum is common to most non-Marxist writers. Marx poured scorn on the tendency to erect the social superstructure represented by caste into the principal

[6] A. C. Lyall, *Asiatic Studies*, 2nd edn (London, 1899), i, p. 204.

causal factor instead of looking to its economic base,[7] and Weber
was prepared to accept his explanation of the absence of social
change as 'due to the peculiar position of the artisan in the Indian
village – his dependence upon fixed payment in kind instead of
production for the market'.[8] But given Weber's notion that major
historical change was always the product of the independent con-
vergence of economic forces with an appropriate ideology, he
was led to give overriding emphasis to the role of religion in
ritualising the hierarchical occupational structure of caste and
preventing the institutionalisation of an egalitarian ethic essential
to a market economy.

Apart from this difference over the primacy of economic
causation, the nineteenth-century attempts to provide a grand
sociological framework displayed a broad agreement. Of course
they possess the bare starkness of caricature which is their value;
specialists in our own time work against the framework they
established, modifying, qualifying, sometimes refuting, but never
rendering them superfluous. Soviet historians have long since
retreated from the notion of the unchanging East and the dogma
of the absence of private property in land as the key to its history.
They recognise the development of an exchange economy and
mercantile capitalism from at least the seventeenth century onwards.[9] Oriental despotism, despite Wittfogel,[10] is too wide and
value-loaded a concept to survive as a working tool, but in a sense
the view it typifies persists in the school which sees changes in the
governmental superstructure rather than in the economic or social
base as the key to the emergence of nationalism. The political and
social as well as the economic self-sufficiency of the traditional

[7] K. Marx, *The German Ideology*, ed. R. Pascal (London, 1963), p. 30.
[8] Max Weber, *The Religion of India* (Glencoe, 1958), p. 111.
[9] Cf. V. I. Pavlov, *The Indian Capitalist Class* (New Delhi, 1964). Indian
Marxist historians have naturally been quicker to reject Marx's primitive
image of India before colonial rule. Irfan Habib has laboured to show that
a modified form of private property rights in land was fully established in
Mughal India; I. Habib, *The Agrarian System of Mughal India* (London,
1963). On merchant capitalism in Mughal India, see I. Habib, 'Potenti-
alities of Capitalist Development in the Economy of Mughal India', *Jl. Eco.
Hist.*, xxix, no. i (1969). His more recent work has sought to demonstrate
that so far from testifying to 'the unchangeableness of Asiatic Societies'
(Marx), Indian medieval history was characterised by significant technological innovation; I. Habib, Presidential Address to Medieval Section,
Indian History Congress Proceedings, 31st Session, Vanarasi, 1969 (Patna,
1970).
[10] K. Wittfogel, *Oriental Despotism* (New Haven, 1957).

Indian village is recognised as a dubious half-truth, but the village continues to form the unit for study of caste structure and change.

If Marx supplies a useful composite summary of the older socio-logical analysis, he also provides a convenient starting point for measuring the nature, extent and rate of change produced by colonial rule. He was torn by the desire to vilify it for its wanton destruction of indigenous society, for its crude plundering of Indian wealth, and its parasitic battening on the Indian economy; while at the same time he wished to demonstrate that it was the source of a profound modernising revolution. England has 'broken down the entire framework of Indian society, without any symp-toms of reconstitution yet appearing', Marx wrote in 1853, within four years of the centenary of Plassey. Previous conquerors had effected no more than political change, but England had struck at the heart of the social system – the Indian village. 'English interference...dissolved these small semi-barbarian communities by blowing up their economical basis, and thus produced the greatest, and, to speak the truth, the only *social* revolution ever heard of in Asia.' The instruments of the revolution had been English steam and English free trade, flooding India with cheap Lancashire textiles from 1810 onwards, and rupturing the domestic unity of agriculture and industry.

At the same time 'the work of regeneration' was just beginning to transpire 'through a heap of ruins', and its essence was the reversal of those specific characteristics that lay at the root of Asian stagnation. Marx listed its signs: (i) the unprecedented consolidation of the political unity of India, strengthened by the newly laid telegraph; (ii) railways ending village isolation and with the steamship linking India so closely to Europe that 'that once fabulous country will thus be actually annexed to the Western World'; (iii) economic development of the country in the interests of the English millocracy, the railway system being the forerunner of modern industry; (iv) modern industry arising to 'dissolve the hereditary divisions of labour, upon which rest the Indian castes, those decisive impediments to Indian progress and Indian power'; (v) the introduction of private property rights in land, instituted since the late eighteenth century; (vi) the emer-gence of a free press and education bringing into existence a new class of Indians imbued with European science and endowed with the requirements for government. All this led up to the fulfilment of colonialism's historic mission 'the laying of the material foundations of Western society in Asia'.[11] The interest of this analysis lies in the fact that Marx raises most of the points around which scholarly controversy has turned. At what date can the modernising impact of colonialisation be said to have begun? What was its precise nature? Was economic change primary, bringing in its train social change, or was economic change limited in scope and in its effects on society, and was not government itself through institutional agencies the only begetter of what little change did occur?

For a variety of reasons the older accounts tended to place emphasis on the abrupt transformation worked by the British conquest, whether like James Mill in order to castigate administrative error or like official spokesmen to puff up the British achievement. Marx was not entirely free from inconsistency in this respect. He saw an economic revolution in train from 1810, and an institutional revolution from 1793 following the Bengal Permanent Settlement and the introduction of private property rights in land; he recognised the importance of developments in education and a free press from at least the 1830s. Yet if anything current opinion goes much farther than his general conclusion that the work of modernisation had barely begun by 1857; its tendency is to minimise change of any sort, whether destructive or constructive.

The older accounts of the British conquest viewed the English East India Company as constrained to transform itself into a territorial power because of the insecurity caused by the collapse of the Mughal empire and the emergence of a rival European threat to its trading areas from the French. Having once stumbled into dominion over the Bengal territories in 1757, so the argument ran, the Company was driven steadily and reluctantly onward in its career of conquest by the military threat posed to its frontiers by the surviving Indian polities which commenced to modernise their armies with the aid of French mercenaries. From a more

<hr/>

[11] *New York Daily Tribune*, 25 June and 8 Aug. 1853, in Avineri, *Karl Marx*, pp. 93, 132 ff. It is interesting that Marx is still used by modern political scientists and social anthropologists to supply them with some of their critical assumptions. Cf. L. I. and S. H. Rudolph, *The Modernity of Tradition* (Chicago, 1967), pp. 17 ff.; Louis Dumont, *Homo Hierarchicus* (Paris, 1966), p. 275 (Paladin edn (London, 1972), p. 265).

modern viewpoint such an account gives insufficient weight to the breakaway movement of sub-imperialism on the part of the Company's servants, who like the conquistadors were the real founders of empire. The structure of the Company had always represented an uneasy equipoise between corporate and private interests; and in a situation in which the expansion of the Company's trade with Europe had levelled off, the practice of looking for political profits had commenced early in the eighteenth century. In Bengal, Company officials abused their duty-free import privilege in order to participate in the internal trade of Bengal and to sell the Company's pass or *dastak* to Indian traders. It was this situation that helped bring on the decisive clash of 1756–7 between the Bengal nawab and the British. The Plassey Revolution was the first English essay in private profiteering on a grandiose scale, and it opened the floodgates. The acquiescence of the Home Authorities was purchased on the strength of the argument, first advanced by Dupleix to his masters, that territorial dominion would pay all local establishment costs and yield a surplus tribute that would give the Company its annual shipment of Indian goods *gratis*. In practice the force of local sub-imperialism was such that the Company ran rapidly into the red, for not only were much of the Bengal revenues diverted into private pockets, but the pressure for civil and military posts, supply contracts, and the like, led to constant war and expansion.[12] These conditions soon left the Company a debtor to its own servants, and its annual shipment of goods to Europe became simply a means of remitting interest payments. The Company by the 1780s was little more than a shell for private interests, which themselves derived their wealth primarily from political profits (viz. the perquisites of office, legal or illegal). This reversion to primitive mercantilism, with force itself an economic power, meant that the political frontier between 1757 and 1818 was flung far ahead of the true economic frontier; and it was not until the 1860s that the two began to be brought into closer correspondence.[13]

The consequences of Plassey shaped the form of British overrule and the modes of culture contact. If the trading frontier lagged so far behind the political, it may seem surprising that the

---

[12] The best analysis of this process remains H. Furber, *John Company at Work*, 2nd edn (Cambridge, Mass., 1951).

[13] On the economic background, see P. J. Marshall, *Problems of Empire: Britain and India 1757–1813* (London, 1968), pp. 78 ff.

British eventually took as much as two-thirds of the subcontinent under their direct administration. Why within fifteen years of Plassey had they abandoned the device of the protectorate in Bengal, and why within thirty years had they so dismantled the traditional Bengal administration, making a clean sweep of not only the old Bengal political elite but of all but the meanest administrative official? Why did not they pursue the Dutch example in Java of effecting a minimal interference with the indigenous society, gearing its traditional tribute system to the production of export products like opium, indigo, and piece goods as tribute, and leaving the people as far as possible under their own chiefs, laws and land tenures? It used to be supposed that the answer lay in the contemporary Industrial Revolution which reversed the economic relationship with India and required the opening up of the country as a market and primary producer for British industry with all that this implied – a market society of legal equals under the rule of law, modern judicial and administrative institutions, private property rights in land, taxes reduced to fixed imposts in cash, and the general monetisation of the economy. J. S. Furnivall attributed the difference between Dutch and British colonial policy in Asia to the absence of an industrial export economy in the one case and its presence in the other,[14] and numerous historians have seen the early British land-revenue settlements in Bengal and Madras as direct responses to Britain's new market requirements.[15]

The evidence of British intentions lends little support to these views. Instead it suggests first and foremost an attempt to bring order and regulation to the decayed indigenous revenue systems. This was the real reason for what appeared to be the exceptionally rapid assumption of direct administrative responsibility and the abandonment of indirect rule through a protectorate system in all the populous regions of the subcontinent. The fact that India unlike Java possessed a tax system yielding huge sums in cash made this the key objective of policy. In order to maximise receipts the Company was driven increasingly to eliminate all intermediaries and, outside the Bengal territories, to undertake direct collection through an official bureaucracy whose subordinate rungs and

[14] Cf. J. S. Furnivall, *Colonial Policy and Practice* (Cambridge, 1948) and *Netherlands India* (Cambridge, 1939).
[15] Cf. Ramkrishna Mukherjee, *The Rise and Fall of the East India Company* (Berlin, 1958).

administrative practice (at the subdistrict level) were taken over from the pre-British rulers. The Company was forced willy-nilly both to intervene in government and yet remain an Asian power. Its purpose remained mercantilist, to wring a surplus from the Indian revenue sufficient to purchase its annual investment of Indian goods and (through the sale of state-monopolised opium) supply the silver required by the Canton treasury for the China tea trade. Greenberg has noted that not only in this way 'the surplus of the Indian revenues were thus sent home in teas from China', but that it was through this payments link with China that India was enabled to purchase the new textile manufactures of Lancashire and become one of the industry's major markets.[16] The situation did not alter fundamentally with the abolition of the Company's trading functions in 1834. Despite the banner of Free Trade it held aloft, Lancashire broke into the new markets of Asia with all the old-fashioned weapons of earlier mercantilism.[17]

If, therefore, the onset of modern economic relations was a much tardier and much less complete process than was at one time assumed, the same may be said to be true of the socio-cultural sphere. Although Cornwallis's attempt to inaugurate a 'regulated imperialism' from the 1780s necessitated the introduction of English administrative and judicial institutions at the superior level, the movement of anglicisation was strictly limited. On grounds of both policy and expediency the East India Company continued to act in many respects as an Indian ruler, striking its coinage with the image of the puppet emperor at Delhi, maintaining the use of Persian in official correspondence and in the law courts, administering Hindu and Muslim personal law, repressing Christian missionary activity and upholding the religious institutions of the country. Spear has argued that in the age of the nabobs in the later eighteenth century, when the residence of English women was uncommon enough to make liaisons with Indian women a normal practice, the new rulers showed every

16 M. Greenberg, *British Trade and the Opening of China* (Cambridge, 1951), p. 15. Also cf. K. N. Chaudhuri, 'India's Foreign Trade and the Cessation of the East India Company's Trading Activities, 1828–40', *Econ. Hist. Rev.*, 2nd ser., xix (1966).

17 Cf. K. N. Chaudhuri, *The Economic Development of India under the East India Company, 1814–58* (Cambridge, 1971). See also Peter Harnetty, *Imperialism and Free Trade: India and Lancashire in the Mid-Nineteenth Century* (Manchester, 1972).

sign of accommodating themselves to the culture and customs of their subjects, at least away from the seaport presidency towns of Bombay, Calcutta and Madras.[18] But the tendency was rapidly stultified by the psychological need of a conquering minority to preserve social distance; and that potent mixture of suppressed fear and open arrogance, which make up racialism, gained a firm ascendancy from Wellesley's time (1798–1805) as the British extended their power over the entire subcontinent. If 'respectability' made intermarriage socially unacceptable and Indian wives subject to ostracism by European society, cohabitation was practised down to the time that the steamer in the 1860s and 1870s began to redress the sex imbalance of the European population. By the 1880s, despite the occasional tragic *mésalliance* dealt with so idyllically in *Without Benefit of Clergy*, the 'Unknown Goddess' of Kipling's verses was indubitably white:

> Does the P & O bear you to meward, or, clad in short
> frocks in the West,
> Are you growing the charms that shall capture and
> torture the heart in my breast?

Even so, it must be remembered that, when in 1857 the cannon opened fire at Cawnpore (Kanpur) in the Mutiny, General Wheeler had an Indian Christian wife; and the place in which the European women and children were confined by Nana Sahib, before their massacre and mass burial in the well, was named the Bibigahr, or woman's house, where a European had been keeping his Indian mistress.

It is notoriously difficult to fix racial attitudes with precision, or to relate higher cultural and intellectual opinion to the world of everyday expediency. In the early decades of the nineteenth century the onset of the Evangelical-Utilitarian philistinism together with the emergence of a philosophy of economic development and modernisation transformed the Enlightenment's admiration of Oriental society into contempt, and the preservationist mentality of men like Warren Hastings gave place to the censorious prophets of Victorian improvement. But how far shifts in formal ideological attitudes run ahead of practice and what is their functional relation to it are problems we are far from resolving. The current tide has set firmly against regarding ideological attitudes as an

[18] Percival Spear, *The Nabobs* (Oxford, 1932).

accurate index of historical change or of allowing them any causal role.[19]

Indeed, it is the undue attention to formal statements of policy aims that, it is now argued, has grossly misled historians about the working practice of British rule. For these both unduly anticipate the introduction of modernising administration and exaggerate its power to alter society. Colonial rule is peculiarly subject to the distortions of bureaucratic structures, which mistake the report for the bullet, the plan for action, and what one clerk says to another for history. On this view the age of modernising reform which set in reputedly when Lord William Bentinck was appointed Governor-General in 1827 was a grand confidence trick. For all the paper planning at headquarters and the splendid periods of Macaulay's minutes on law reform and education, the British administration, it can be urged, had neither the financial means nor the technical instruments for a development programme. There was neither the requisite British or Indian capital investment nor the communications network of railways and telegraphs that could begin to change the face of the country within the framework of a *laissez-faire* economy. It is noticeable in fact that most of the plans for law reform, educational development and scientific revenue systems, were not translated into effective action until the 1860s when the railway system was laid down and India's foreign trade began to leap forward.

Except in the Western enclaves of Calcutta and Bombay, where urban growth stimulated an intelligentsia prepared to employ the new lights of Western learning to attempt syncretist cultural reform movements, and where new literary vernaculars like Bengali sprang to life, the indigenous cultures of India lingered on in the courts of the princes and pensioners. Languages like Urdu and old Marathi survived as the media of lower level administration; and the ostentatious government disavowal of Oriental studies in preference for English in 1835 had little immediate effect.

In keeping with this line of thought some historians in recent

---

[19] There is a large literature on the ideology of British colonialism in India. Cf. E. Stokes, *The English Utilitarians and India* (Oxford, 1959); G. D. Bearce, *British Attitudes Towards India 1784–1858* (Oxford, 1961); R. Guha, *A Rule of Property for Bengal* (La Haye, 1963); F. G. Hutchins, *The Illusion of Permanence: British Imperialism in India* (Princeton, 1967); R. Kumar, *Western India in the Nineteenth Century* (London, 1968); Clive Dewey, 'Images of the Village Community: a Study in Anglo Indian Ideology', *Modern Asian Studies*, vi (1972).

years have tended to reverse in their thinking the direction from which initiative and control emanated, and to see the British district officer as a prisoner if not a puppet of local social forces. Dependent on hereditary administrative cadres of Brahmins or Kayasths or Muslims, whose hold was not weakened until entry became regulated after 1860 by competition and educational qualification, the British officer was reduced to a game of blind man's buff. That at least is the burden of Frykenberg's account of Guntur district in Madras in the first half of the nineteenth century. Formal decisions as to whether the engagement for the land revenue should be made with large proprietary landholders (zamindars) or with small peasant landowners (ryots) of the dominant castes remained empty of meaning, since under either the zamindari or the ryotwar system the village was subject to the exactions of the same chain of hereditary office-holders and petty revenue collectors.[20] The British administrative systems for all their appearance as products of rival ideologies had to fit themselves to the frame of local society. James Mill and his early school of development economists had believed that, since all social strata above the peasant lived off disbursements of land revenue, the British had it in their power to shape society as they chose according to the type of land-revenue system they adopted. And Indian nationalist writers have strenuously kept alive the notion, first voiced by British administrators, that Indian society suffered in consequence wanton derangement from arbitrary decisions as to what social group should be vested with the novel form of proprietary right in land.[21] But in the intellectual sea-change of our times a number of Indian historians are now coming round to the view to which Baden-Powell lent his authority as long ago as the 1890s when the nationalist attack was first beginning to gather force. So far from being artificial constructions, the land-revenue systems, Baden-Powell maintained, were essentially practical

[20] R. E. Frykenberg, *Guntur District 1788–1848* (Oxford, 1965), pp. 67–8.
[21] The nationalist view of the effects of colonial rule on Indian society has a long historical pedigree and borrows heavily from arguments used in controversial policy debates by British administrators themselves. R. C. Dutt, *Economic History of India in the Victorian Age* (London, 1906); Radhakamal Mukerjee, *Land Problems of India* (London, 1933), and M. B. Nanavati and J. J. Anjaria, *The Indian Rural Problem* (Bombay, 1944) are among the more sober authorities on which much wilder generalisation has frequently been based. For a valuable summary and critique of orthodox nationalist view, see Dharma Kumar, *Land and Caste in South India* (Cambridge, 1965), pp. 186 ff.

adaptations to local circumstances; they had to be if they were to work at all.[22] Not only were there two sharply differing major types of village, but the village so far from being the unchanging republic of popular myth was an inegalitarian structure subject to constant vicissitudes and strains from within and without. Hence almost everywhere, not merely was the particular type of land controller dominant in a region recognised as the agency of revenue collection and *ipso facto* as landed proprietor – the large landholder in Bengal, the individual peasant landholder in the Madras and Bombay presidencies, the corporate village coparceners in the United Provinces and the Punjab; but also large exceptions were made within each system to allow for local variety. Consequently in the supposedly 'big landlord' settlement of the Bengal presidency the settlement in Midnapur district was made with some 3,000 petty landholders; in the opposing Madras system a third of the presidency was paradoxically left under substantial landlord settlement; outside the Deccan districts of the Bombay presidency the ryotwar system had to be modified to accommodate the joint and superior tenures that prevailed in Gujarat and the Konkan; in the United Provinces large landlord 'estates' were recognised in Oudh and elsewhere. Although in the districts where the ryotwar system was firmly imposed the joint tenure known as *mirasi* might have been dissolved by administrative action, this probably meant that it was already too decayed and exceptional to offer a positive basis upon which to found the revenue system.

The precise degree of interference with indigenous practice is impossible to determine; but what is clear is that irrespective of the legal recognition of tenures the British were scrupulous in avoiding interference with the social structure. For all the romantic notions of the Munro school, the 'peasant' with whom they dealt was of the elite landholding castes, and cultivated his land with the aid of inferior landless castes. In the Madras presidency the agrestic serf class, which amounted in some districts to as much as a fifth of the population, was left unfree under its traditional masters; and for all the formal legislation against slavery which Bentinck and Macaulay promoted, the British

22 B. H. Baden-Powell, *The Land Systems of British India* (Oxford, 1892), i, p. 244. Also B. H. Baden-Powell, *A Short Account of the Land Revenue... in British India*, 2nd edn (London, 1907), pp. 46–7; B. H. Baden-Powell, *The Indian Village Community* (London, 1896), pp. 430 ff.

district officers were generally careful to leave this issue to the
erosion of time.[23] For here landlord and labourer were rooted in
an institution more enduring than political and administrative
arrangement, the institution of caste. As in the sphere of race
relations the last word appeared to lie with local society irrespective of European intentions and attitudes. In the end the British,
it seemed, could only fit into the Indian social structure as yet one
more endogamous caste with their freedom of action severely
restricted.

Since the Lancashire textile invasion failed to blow up the
economic base of village self-sufficiency in any visible manner, as
Marx assumed it would, one might suppose that in the sphere of
institutional change decisive results would follow. The mere suppression of open violence and the introduction of Western-style
law courts seemed in themselves to spell revolution. Attention has
naturally fastened on the introduction of freely-alienable proprietary rights in land and the emergence of a land market. The
older school spoke freely of the agrarian revolution this had
caused, at least among the upper levels of landholding. Nowhere
was this more striking than in Bengal where the former zamindar
class apparently went to the wall within twenty years of Cornwallis's Permanent Settlement of 1793, and in their place the
quick-witted Calcutta banyans and monied men stepped in as
the main beneficiaries of British rule. But this simple picture dis-
solves in the light of modern examination. It is evident that the
century before Plassey was as much a period of rapid change in
landholding as the period that followed. Not only is there strong
evidence of men from commercial and literate castes during the
Mughal period making their way into landholding via official
office, mortgage and purchase, and of then acquiring ritual
kshatriya (warrior) status, but it is clear that on their displacement by men of similar origin under British rule the process was
in considerable measure repeated. The notion of rigid occupational caste stratification is clearly inapplicable; Bengal at least
approximated more closely to contemporary Western Europe,
where wealth and official service could in time be translated into
landed gentility. Although, therefore, old elites might appear to

---

[23] Dharma Kumar, *Land and Caste*, pp. 72 ff. Cf. N. E. Mukherjee and
R. E. Frykenberg, ch. 9 in R. E. Frykenberg (ed.), *Land Control and
Social Structure in Indian History* (Madison and London, 1969).

crumble, they prove on examination to have been far from old, and their successors to have been drawn largely from the same original social base.[24]

The only long-standing hereditary aristocracy were the petty Rajput rajas who were buttressed by their role as clan chiefs and who were scattered broadcast over northern and central India. Most of these suffered slow decay in an age which set a premium on managerial skills rather than fighting prowess. But that did not prevent a significant proportion from making the necessary adjustments and retaining their position as local notables. It is evident that the enormous volume of transfers of proprietary title in the first half of the nineteenth century in northern India represented for the most part circulation within existing dominant landholding castes at the petty proprietary level. The Rajput clans undoubtedly lost ground, mainly to Brahmins, and to a much smaller extent to urban trading castes. But actual eviction was rare, the dispossessed usually remaining as 'tenants' in what was *de facto* a sub-proprietary role. Urban capitalists were more interested in rent-receiving or in controlling the disposal of peasant-grown cash crops than in directly engaging in agriculture; so that the introduction of legal private property rights in land tended to lengthen the chain of intermediaries above the actual cultivator and left the peasant *petite culture* intact. Compulsory alienation of land in satisfaction of debt was recognised by the British as a drastic innovation on traditional practice, and official concern was being voiced at the extent of transfers under this head already by the 1850s.[25] Since, however, the peasant was not displaced (and it must be remembered that he himself was a member of the village elite controlling non-elite caste cultivators), it is often argued that he was reduced to the condition of a debt slave to the moneylender. The latter was thus in a position to siphon off the enhanced value of agricultural production brought about by the extension of the market.[26] But any such tendency for caste to turn into class division was frustrated by constant diffusion of roles

---

[24] See the contributions of B. S. Cohn and T. Raychaudhuri in Frykenberg (ed.), *op. cit.* Also N. K. Sinha, *Economic History of Bengal*, ii (Calcutta, 1962) pp. 179–80.

[25] P. H. M. van den Dungen, *The Punjab Tradition* (London, 1972), pp. 42 ff.

[26] This notion, which has been used *ad nauseam*, was first voiced by British administrators themselves, notably Sir George Wingate in 1852.

among the peasantry themselves, one man being able to combine the position of landlord, tenant, and petty moneylender. Before 1857 this degree of complication was only apparent in the over-crowded eastern districts of the present Uttar Pradesh, where fragmentation and parcellation of holdings was already far advanced.[27] For our immediate purpose it can be said that, although rural society must have undergone a profound change by the suppression of open violence and the turning of individual and group struggle into a battle for land rights through the courts, there was no complete structural change. British hopes of the emergence of capitalist agriculture, whether at the peasant or superior level, were disappointed, and the class stratification of rural society by legal revolution into landlord and tenant was never properly consummated.

This conclusion can be given a more general bearing. Of course there has been, and continues to be, a respectable body of historians, Marxist and non-Marxist, who accept the broad argument of nineteenth-century sociology that under colonial rule Indian society moved from status to contract, and from caste to class. Professor Misra has taken it as his principal assumption in his well-known, *The Indian Middle Classes* (1961), while Desai in *The Social Background of Indian Nationalism* and more recently S. N. Mukherjee have accepted the outlines of Marx's historiography as still valid.[28] But they are challenged increasingly by scholars who themselves are drawn equally from opposite ends of the political spectrum. These jointly conclude that the institutional and the economic 'inputs' of modernity were too feeble to blow apart the structure of Indian society and that the elastic, accommodating nature of the latter was adequate to contain them. Anil Seal, while acknowledging that between 1840 and 1886 India's foreign seaborne trade increased more than eightfold and played a vital role in the U.K. balance of payments, asserts that 'these changes were not sufficient to give India social classes based on economic categories. For the most part Indian traders remained as they had always been, men following their hereditary

---

27 Cf. Elizabeth Whitcombe, *Agrarian Conditions in Northern India*, i (Berkeley, 1972), pp. 143–4.
28 B. B. Misra, *The Indian Middle Classes* (Oxford, 1961); A. R. Desai, *The Social Background of Indian Nationalism* (Bombay, 1948); S. N. Mukherjee, 'Class, Caste and Politics in Calcutta, 1815–50' in E. R. Leach and S. N. Mukherjee (eds.), *Elites in South Asia* (Cambridge, 1970).

vocations in the traditional way, both unwilling and unable to break down those barriers inside their society which inhibited more active development.'[29] Hence nationalism did not come as the older school supposed by the prior emergence of a genuine modern middle-class or bourgeoisie thrown up by economic change. The Western-educated element which took up the modern political struggle against colonialism was an exotic, 'more the product of bureaucratic initiative than of economic change'. In the struggle among the literate castes, predominantly Muslim, Brahmin and Kayasth, for posts in government service and the related professions of law, education and journalism, one element, usually of aspirants rather than possessors, dropped the traditional Persian and Sanskrit learning and turned to English. From the mid nineteenth century this element came to man the middle and upper levels of the increasingly technical, legalistic, and bureaucratic machine that was the Raj; and from the 1880s slowly began to secure effective command of the channels of communication between the Raj and the millions of its subjects. The British thus became steadily more dependent on the modernistic section among their collaborators. In consequence, what is usually thought of as the history of the nationalist struggle was little more than the struggle of this section to extort from the British the loaves and fishes of political office and administrative place, followed by an unedifying scramble over the share-out. The ultimate victory of Congress should not be allowed to disguise the fact that what it represented was, on this view, not the victory of a new class but the lateral adjustment of an old elite.

The ineffectualness of the forces of economic change and the limitation of the impact of modernity to a small exotic sector are notions shared by Indian scholars for whom this interpretation of nationalism would appear insultingly cynical. Tapan Raychaudhuri and Bipan Chandra indignantly refute the view advanced recently by Morris D. Morris that the Indian economy experienced significant growth during the nineteenth century. Foreign capital investment merely 'meant the growth of enclaves, their linkage effects being confined to a minimum'.

The most striking feature of colonial economic development is the dichotomy between the traditional and modern – as also between the subsistence and non-subsistence sectors of the economy. The pre-

[29] A. Seal, *The Emergence of Indian Nationalism* (Cambridge, 1968), p. 34.

modern subsistence sector accounts for the stagnation of skill, technology, social organization and attitudes. In more extreme cases like Indonesia the colonial market economy grew up in total isolation from the subsistence sector, and at heavy cost to it. In the Indian case the picture was only somewhat different. Recent village studies reveal a marked pattern of socio-economic stagnation in rural India. So far as one can see there was hardly any significant change until after World War I, and very often, until after 1947.[30]

This attack on colonialism as an inhibiting, distorting influence on India's economic growth stems from a nationalist standpoint that views with suspicion Western historians' recent efforts to play down the importance of imperialism as an historical force. It borrows something from latter-day Marxist and Maoist theories which stress the parasitic role of colonialism, its political alliance with 'feudal' landlord elements, and the comprador character of the national bourgeoisie. In this latest Marxist version the reproduction of Western bourgeois society, thought by Marx as colonialism's historic mission, is seen to be necessarily stultified. Whatever the intellectual pedigree of their views, Indian economic historians tend to support Bipan Chandra's argument that the impact of colonialism in the nineteenth century resulted in 'an aborted modernization'. Although after 1860 India began to produce on a significant scale for the world market, this was effected without the mode of peasant agricultural production undergoing any fundamental change; the essentially parasitic structure of ownership, credit, and marketing, on their view, simply 'skimmed cash crops off the surface of an immobilized agrarian society'.[31]

The concept of a dual economy advanced by Boeke appears to provide a convenient way of acknowledging a measure of development on the one hand and denying its fertilising influence on the greater part of Indian society on the other. In India's case the

---

[30] T. Raychaudhuri, 'A Reinterpretation of Nineteenth Century Economic History', *Indian Soc. and Econ. Hist. Rev.*, v (1968), pp. 98–9; M. D. Morris, 'Towards a Reinterpretation of Nineteenth Century Economic History', *ibid.*, pp. 1–15. Also Morris, 'Trends and Tendencies in Indian Economic History', *ibid.*, pp. 319–88; Bipan Chandra, 'Reinterpretation of Nineteenth Century Economic History', *ibid.*, pp. 35–75. This important debate has been collected in M. D. Morris *et al.* (eds.), *Indian Economy in the Nineteenth Century: A Symposium* (Delhi: Indian Economic and Social History Association, Delhi School of Economics, 1969).

[31] Cited by D. Rothermund, *Phases of Indian Nationalism* (Bombay, 1970), p. 264, n. 19.

analogy with Indonesia cannot be pushed too far, yet the concept is valuable in that it recognises that the traditional sector was not totally insulated from the modern but underwent some measure of change. Simply because this change was not progressive but represents an adjustive capacity in traditional society to absorb external forces without structural alteration, it has been christened in suitable paradoxical terms. Boeke spoke of 'static expansion', and more recently Geertz of 'this peculiar pattern of changeless change'. Indeed it is Geertz's refinement of the concept under the term 'agricultural involution' which has produced the most subtle and sophisticated analysis so far developed.

In land tenure, in crop regime, in work organization, and in the less directly economic aspects of social structure. . .the village. . .faced the problems posed by a rising population, increased monetization, greater dependence on the market, mass labor organization, more intimate contact with bureaucratic government and the like, not by a dissolution of the traditional pattern into an individualistic 'rural proletarian' anomie, nor yet by a metamorphosis of it into a modern commercial farming community. Rather by means of a 'special kind of virtuosity', 'a sort of technical hair-splitting', it maintained the over-all outlines of that pattern while driving the elements of which it was composed to ever-higher degrees of ornate elaboration and Gothic intricacy. . .Perhaps the most trenchant phrase which has been coined to summarize what appears to have been the career of the Inner Indonesian village over the past century and a half is 'the advance towards vagueness'. The peculiarly passive social-change experience which. . .rural society has been obliged to endure seems to have induced in it an indeterminateness which did not so much transform traditional patterns as elasticize them. Such flaccid indeterminateness is highly functional to a society which is allowed to evade, absorb, and adapt but not really allowed to change.[32]

Something of this imagery has been carried over into the analysis of the Indian social system. For F. G. Bailey 'the more involute is a system of closed social stratification, the more inclined we are to call it a caste system'.[33] But involution obtains only in closed small-scale, face-to-face societies; hence it is the village which

---

[32] C. Geertz, *Agricultural Involution* (Berkeley, 1963), pp. 90, 102–3. For Boeke's concept of economic dualism, see J. H. Boeke, *The Structure of the Netherlands Indian Economy* (New York, 1942), and *Economics and Economic Policy of Dual Societies* (Haarlem, 1953).

[33] F. G. Bailey, 'Closed Social Stratification in India', *Archiv. Europ. Sociol.*, iv (1963), pp. 107–24.

'provides the boundary at which social relations turn in-wards' or involute. Reminiscent of Marx and nineteenth-century sociology, traditional India is regarded as composed of a myriad of self-sufficing village units, each of which was hier-archically stratified into endogamous caste groups whose mutual relations were those of cooperation rather than competition. 'The village', wrote Eric Miller, 'containing a cross-section of inter-dependent castes. . .was more or less self-subsistent', although in Kerala grouped politically in petty chiefdoms or kingdoms. But the cleavages in society were the vertical divisions of politics, not the horizontal divisions of caste. India was a giant Neapolitan ice cream cut vertically into an infinite number of small portions. 'The main structural cleavages were between territorial units – villages, chiefdoms, kingdoms – not between castes.'[34] It was these vertical divisions that colonial rule eventually destroyed or ren-dered porous by the enlargement of political and economic scale.

In place of countless small, relatively isolated, traditional political divisions, there are now emerging a few large political arenas which in this context we can take as the States of the Indian Union. Within these States various *jatis* (local sub-castes), which formerly were separated by being in different political systems, are now uniting. What were formerly caste categories are becoming groups.[35]

'Horizontal mobilisation' thus 'challenges the vertical solidarities and structures of traditional societies'. The formation of provincial caste associations is seen by the Rudolphs as the key to political mobilisation for the modern democratic system in India, and in this sense demonstrates 'the modernity of tradition'.[36] But the social anthropologists deny any such continuity of structure. Once castes start competing among one another, caste is coming to an end.

The caste society as a whole is, in Durkheim's sense, an organic system with each particular caste and sub-caste filling a distinctive functional role. It is a system of labour division from which the element of competition among the workers has been excluded. . . Wherever caste groups are seen to be acting as corporations in com-

---

[34] E. Miller, 'Village Structure in North Kerala', in M. N. Srinivas (ed.), *India's Villages* (Bombay, London, 1960), pp. 45–6.
[35] Bailey, *op. cit.*
[36] L. I. and S. H. Rudolph, *The Modernity of Tradition* (Chicago, 1975).

petition against like groups of *different* caste, then they are acting in defiance of caste principles.[37]

According to the social anthropologists the type of change associated with caste competition is relatively recent, going back in most cases no earlier than 1880 or 1900. But both this assumption and the assumption that such competition did not occur in pre-colonial India (upward mobility of individuals between caste groups being a different matter) are open to question. In southern India, where Christianity made its earliest and most rapid strides among the low caste groups, there was already pressure by the late 1820s among the Travancore Shanars against caste disabilities and in Pondicherry in 1833 from the Pallis. Yet other types of social conflict between right and left hand castes, which had occasioned quarrels in the eighteenth century died mysteriously away from the early nineteenth century. Here the action of the British administration in throwing open the acquisition of land-ownership rights enabled merchant and artisan communities to translate wealth much more readily into social status and muted rivalry with those castes with hereditary rights to land.[38]

There are also grounds for questioning the typicality of the areas from which Bailey and Miller drew their material for their concept of the tightly insulated village or chiefdom unit. Both highland Orissa and Kerala were outside the great agricultural plain areas that for centuries before the British had experienced large-scale political organisation. Bailey has argued that it was only on the encapsulation of the village society in the larger administrative unit that the need for middlemen or political brokers arose, and that this is the stuff of modern politics.[39] But in areas that had long lived under the hand of centralised power there was no such sharp discontinuity between the local social structure and the larger political superstructure. The role of political middlemen was traditionally performed by those local notables termed *taluqdars*, *zamindars* and *chaudhuris* (in the north), *deshmukhs* and *despandes* (in the west) or *nayakas* and *poligars* (in the south). It was a role contested by the officials of

[37] E. R. Leach in E. R. Leach (ed), *Aspects of Caste in South India, Ceylon and N.W. Pakistan* (Cambridge, 1962), pp. 5, 7.

[38] Brenda E. F. Beck, 'The Right-Left Division of South Indian Society', *Jl. of Asian Studies*, xxix (1970).

[39] F. G. Bailey, *Stratagems and Spoils* (Oxford, 1969), esp. ch. 8.

central power whether *amils*, *mamlatdars*, or *tahsildars*, who struggled to assert their own undivided authority but in the end struck up a *modus vivendi* with them. It is also evident that outside northern India, famous for its coparcenary village 're-publics', the typical Indian village was a body of discrete families held together by the headman, a semi-hereditary political appoint-ment but necessarily dependent for his tenure on the favour of the ruling power. Hence political isolation and self-sufficiency were an impossibility. Likewise the notion of the economic self-sufficiency of the village and its physical isolation have always been recognised as relative truths, but the very notions tend to belie the close web of communication which plain villages main-tained with surrounding areas, and the degree of movement and travel carried on by means of trade, pilgrimages and fairs.

If simple models based on atypical regions have too often coloured the thinking of social anthropologists, and continuities were more dominant than abrupt caesuras, has there been no significant alteration in the institution of caste? Has there been merely that elastic adaptation so noticeable in other spheres of life? Certainly it would be wrong to suppose that caste conflict constitutes the essential feature of modern politics any more than it did in the past. The reverse is the case. For the most part elite castes sustain the tradition Miller has postulated of the petty Nayar chiefdoms in what is now Kerala State: they compete among themselves and build up multi-caste factions vertically, drawing their followers from economic inferiors belonging mainly to the non-elite castes. To put the matter briefly and therefore crudely, caste competition as such is usually only to be found among middle and lower castes among which a prospering element has been denied political authority and social prestige commensurate with its economic success. This element then seeks to advance itself through the mobilisation of its poorer caste-fellows, but once it has achieved its objective it identifies itself with the elite circle into which it has broken, and politics resume their traditionally factional character.[40] Doubtless in the modern setting this means that the social composition of the elite is being steadily widened, but the overwhelming preponderance of the old elite castes in the modern elite has not been seriously affected.

[40] The best recent study is R. Kothari (ed.), *Caste in Indian Politics* (New Delhi, 1971).

But how far was the caste structure among the dominant landed elites weakened as a result of the dismantling of the subordinate local political organisations of the clan group? These were, of course, strongest among the coparcenary communities of Rajputs, Brahmins, Jats, Ahirs, and so forth that characterised North Indian land tenures, but they also had analogies elsewhere. It has recently been argued that the effect of a powerful centralised bureaucratic structure was to atomise relationships within society, particularly as a result of the extension of state-revenue collection and rental control to the individual peasant landholder. The local political substructures of *tappas*, at which level the state had traditionally come to terms with the dominant local structure, were gradually obliterated. The local clan, under its traditional heads (*rajas, rawats, raos,* or *chaudhuris*) was drained of all political authority, a process that seems to have advanced quite far within the first century of British rule.[41] Why then has the institution of caste survived? Why was the kinship group not narrowed to the immediate family and swallowed up within the homogeneity of the territorial state as in Europe? The usual answer is that endogamy has proved too strong a social practice, reinforced as Louis Dumont and his school would argue by the subjective notion underlying caste of ritual inequality between the 'clean' and the 'unclean'.[42] Yet without denying the force of religious and ideological sanctions, one can reasonably argue that social anthropologists working on India (as distinct from Ceylon) have curiously neglected the economic factor. True they have noted that the decline of the local kinship group has been compensated for by the strengthening of caste as an attributional category conferring upon an individual valuable status advantages, and so employment opportunities, in a society of enlarged scale. But almost no attention has been paid to the role of landed property. Now the constant fractionalisation of land rights through joint partition among heirs has traditionally forced out the less prosperous members of dominant landed castes into military and other service. The East India Company drew its high-caste Brahmin and Rajput sepoys precisely from those regions – southern Oudh, Benares, Shahabad – where through the proliferation of numbers the land-controlling lineages had been reduced to swollen bodies

[41] Richard G. Fox, *Kin, Clan, Raja, and Rule* (Berkeley, 1971).
[42] Louis Dumont, *Homo Hierarchicus.*

of co-sharers on petty holdings. But the pressure on land also had important internal effects. One has no need to go as far as Leach in asserting that 'the kinship system is just a way of talking about property relations' in order to recognise how vital the struggle to retain possession of the land has been in the maintenance of the corporate character of local caste systems.[43] A sample survey of 1951 showed that in Bihar Brahmins and Rajputs together, although comprising only 9·6% of the families surveyed, still made up 78·6% of landowners.[44] It is the tenacious hold of the dominant castes over the land, despite the numerous internal transfers and changes, that constitutes the great element of continuity. In 1886 D. T. Roberts, the settlement officer of Ballia district in the Benares region, summed up judiciously the effects of British rule:

> The dominion which these Rajputs and their attendant Brahmins then acquired (at the time of their original conquest) has been retained by them up to the present day, and an inquiry into the tenures of this district is mainly an enquiry into the legal forms under which this dominion is now exercised. Changes of government, changes of law, the progress of civilization, and the development of individual rights have affected more or less the distribution of the produce and the modes and extent of authority exercised over the land by the descendants of these colonists, but they still possess it. At once supple and tenacious, their connection with the soil has been indeed, regulated and defined, but neither weakened so much nor strengthened so much under British administration as it is usual to suppose.[45]

It has been said that the stark dichotomies of nineteenth-century sociological thought continue to haunt the recesses of our own thinking. Sociologists and economists are perhaps the most susceptible, unable to rid themselves in their search for precision of their proclivity to define change as necessarily absolute. Confronted by the economic and social transformation of Russia or Japan it is easy to designate as stagnation in India what the Victorians saw

[43] For this important controversy over the economic *raison d'être* of the kinship system, see the account in Meyer Fortes, *Kinship and the Social Order* (Chicago, 1969), pp. 294–302. Also E. R. Leach, *Pul Eliya: Village in Ceylon* (Cambridge, 1961) and G. Obeyesekere, *Land Tenure in Village Ceylon* (Cambridge, 1967).

[44] Cited by Ramashray Roy in Kothari, *Caste in Indian Politics*, pp. 231–2.

[45] D. T. Roberts, *Report on the Revision of Records...of Ballia District* (Allahabad, 1886).

as revolution. From the historian's viewpoint, the period that ran from Plassey in 1757 to the 'Mutiny' in 1857, and spanned the lifetime of the East India Company as an administrative power, is a relatively intelligible entity. It is possible to define within it the effect of the colonial impact by regarding change as occurring differentially – affecting the different regions, levels of society, and levels of administration at an uneven rate. Conquest decapitated the superior political elite, totally in the case of British India, and with more gradual effect in the protected states. The intermediate political elite, the local notables mentioned above, suffered less drastically and a minority were able to adjust to the new role of landowners. The administrative elite before 1857 suffered least, in many cases enriching themselves from office under the British and constituting a new landlord class. But by the 1850s the enlargement of political and economic scale effected by British district and provincial administration, by institutional changes in land-holding and by the expansion of cash-cropping, were (in northern India at least) beginning to produce novel strains. The British had reached the stage when, in the interests of a more advanced technical administration commensurate with a sophisticated property market in land, the subdistrict level of administration commanded by the old tahsildar class had to be invaded. A public service based on competitive entry by educational qualification was about to edge out the old system of subcontracting lower-level administration to traditional hereditary groups.[46] In similar fashion the British with their General Service Enlistment Act of 1856 and the use of greased cartridges for their new rifle threatened the monopoly of the traditional high-caste Rajput and Brahmin warrior castes in recruitment to the army, and resentment boiled over in the Mutiny of 1857. By the 1880s the dominance of the local notable, in town and more slowly in the country, was being effectively challenged by a new political broker, operating on the new enlarged scale. The 'modern' politician had arrived.

Under this notion of the slow, uneven, but progressive intensification of administrative and economic pressures, the village

---

[46] I am indebted to my colleague, Christopher Bayly of St Catharine's, Cambridge, for this idea; cf. C. A. Bayly, 'The Development of Political Organization in the Allahabad Locality, 1880–1925', University of Oxford D.Phil. thesis, 1970; and *The Local Roots of Indian Politics: Allahabad 1880–1920* (Oxford, 1975).

would be the last level to be directly invaded. That is not to say that through its external links it had not always been constantly subjected to change imposed from above, but until directly invaded it was the level most capable of absorbing it. In the first century of British rule the village was given external peace and high, unremitting taxation, conditions which created a major problem of adjustment for the village elite. The period saw the slow decline of warrior castes and the enhanced prosperity of thrifty, agricultural castes, the expansion of cultivation, the extension of cash-cropping, the gradual fragmentation and fractionalisation of landholdings, and a tighter dependence on the money-lender-graintrader. But none of these processes went far. It was the upper levels of society that took the full shock of conquest.[47]

In similar fashion, one may resolve some of the apparent contradictions concerning the character and purpose of British rule. The modernising impulse, so triumphantly proclaimed in the Bentinck-Macaulay period from Calcutta, was not the less real or significant because society in the Guntur district still appeared to be quite untouched by the transfer of power to British hands. And in this sense the study of British policy and its ideological background still retains its validity. But the differential rate of the colonial impact, and the uneven development of its own internal structure, gave it that air of paradox that Marx noted, at once free-trader and mercantilist, the fugleman of modernity and the latest of the predatory conquerors of Asia.

[47] Cf. K. A. Ballhatchet, *Social Policy and Social Change in Western India 1817–1830* (Oxford, 1957); Burton Stein, 'Integration of the Agrarian System in South India' in Frykenberg (ed.), *Land Control and Social Structure*, pp. 201–2; Imtiaz Husain, *Land Revenue Policy in North India* (Calcutta, New Delhi, 1967), pp. 170 ff.

2

Privileged land tenure in village India in the early nineteenth century

This paper poses two questions. Why was revenue-free or revenue-privileged tenure in the form of *inam* or *lakhiraj* land apparently far less extensive in northern than in other parts of India? What role did such tenure play at the village level?

Straight political and historical considerations doubtless supply part of the answer to the first question. The North felt the full weight of Muslim imperial power over a protracted period and so was precluded from the massive alienation of revenue-bearing land to Hindu temples that occurred in the far South. Even so, religious and charitable inam in the Madras presidency, when at last brought to book in the 1860s, proved to be only a quarter or so of total inam, the great bulk of which – that is, some three-fifths – was by this time classified as personal inam.[1] But allowing the historical argument its fullest scope, it may still be urged that the survival of extensive revenue-free or favourably rated land into the mid nineteenth century is to be explained by the particular form of the initial colonial impact rather than by endemic differences in the pre-colonial period. While settling at first with a heterogeneous mass of revenue-engagers (*malguzars*), the British in the North, in the Ceded and Conquered Provinces, recognised in effect only two superior tenures – the temporary revenue farm and the proprietary zamindari right (of which the *taluqdari* was merely a later refinement).[2] Privileged superior tenures like *jagirs*, *jaedads*, *mukararis*, *istumraris*, and the like, were bundled roughly into one of these two forms, and hence rapidly disappeared. Practice was different in other presidencies. Despite the

[1] *A Collection of Papers relating to the Inam Settlement of the Madras Presidency* (Madras, 1906), p. 17 (cited hereafter as *Papers re the Inam Settlement*), *Selections from the Records of the Madras Government*, new (revenue) ser., no. 1.

[2] Zamindari was not a superior, revenue-collecting tenure in this region as in Bengal, but designated actual and immediate proprietary dominion.

éclat of the ryotwari system, a considerable proportion of the
Deccan territories of the Bombay presidency was left as jagir and
so was classified as inam. In the Madras presidency a substantial
amount of intermediary privileged tenures – such as jagirs
belonging to relatives and dependents of great zamindars and
poligars – were left untouched, although the great part of
the superior tenures were subsumed under straight zamindari
tenure.

Allowing for the better survival of the upper privileged tenures
in the West and South of India – by 1900 almost half the 7·75
million acres of inam at Madras consisted of whole villages[3] – it
would still appear that at the village level inam played a much
more important role in the Bombay and Madras territories than
in the North. Why was this? Why should village inam have been
a minor feature in the North and a common occurrence elsewhere? How far were differences of basic tenure a decisive influence? Baden-Powell has rightly taught us to draw a sharp
distinction between the 'joint landlord' village of the North and
the ryotwar form prevailing elsewhere. The characteristic of the
one was the existence of a dominant body of kinsmen, exercising
the political and revenue management, claiming proprietary
dominion of the culturable waste, and enjoying an economic
superiority over other ryots by the levy of rental payments from
them in a quasi-landlord role. These rental payments might be
enjoyed in common or in severalty, or both, the joint character of
the tenure arising not from joint ownership but from joint management and joint responsibility for the revenue demand. The
characteristic of the ryotwar village, in contrast, was the existence
of a number of dominant office-holding families, one of which
traditionally exercised political and revenue control as village
head, subject to recognition by the ruling power. Government
levied the revenue demand in detail on the individual ryots
without the interposition of any joint landlord body and controlled
the renting out of the waste. The village elite clustered not around
landlord profits but around office and its perquisites. The key
offices were those of headman (*patel, reddi, kapu, naidu*) and
accountant (*karnam, kulkarni*); their perquisites were partly dues
in cash and kind (*haqs*) and partly in revenue-exempt or revenue-
privileged land (*manyam, wattandar inam*). In short, village

[3] *Imperial Gazetteer of India: Madras* (Calcutta, 1908), pp. 1–101.

service inam was integral to the ryotwar village. Baden-Powell had to admit at once that his models were too tightly drawn, that joint-landlord tenures in the form of *mirasi* right were widespread throughout western and southern India, and that conversely in the North the Mughal revenue system was constantly striving to get behind the landlord body and become ryotwar.[4] Allowing for some measure of geographical intermixture, how far were the two types mutually exclusive?

At first glance some forms of mirasi tenure in western and southern India look remarkably analogous to the joint tenures of the North. This is particularly true of the Tamil country where 'office mirasi', the property in village office and its perquisites, gave way to 'landed mirasi', that is, direct proprietary dominion over the land. Here there was a right not merely to engage for the Government revenue but also to appropriate a landlord's share of the produce (*tunduvaram*) from the subordinate ryots. Such mirasdars claimed joint ownership or control of the village, including the arable waste, and accepted joint responsibility for revenue payment. Landed mirasi could vary, as in northern India, between joint undivided tenure and complete severalty, the latter tending to prevail in mirasi villages south of the Coleroon River. Moreover, where landed mirasi was to be found, the system of village officers supported by office mirasi seems to have been weakest. In Tanjore, where a landlord's rent of a quarter of the produce was reported in 1818, *karnika* mirasi (the village accountant's proprietary haqs and inams) was nonexistent, as indeed was the office of headman itself. At the same time, the Madras Board of Revenue stated that in 'Tondai Mandalam [Chingleput and N. and S. Arcot] or anywhere east of the Payenghaut' the *patel* and his office were generally absent.[5] Apparently the internal structures of the ryotwar and the joint-landlord village could not coexist together.

Would it then be true to say that village inam appeared on a significant scale only where landed mirasi did not occur, or where it had been so reduced by overassessment as to be nugatory? There is a good deal to support this argument and its presupposition that inam was an escape mechanism for a village elite denied landlord

[4] B. H. Baden-Powell, *The Indian Village Community* (London, 1896), pp. 424 ff.
[5] Minute of the Board of Revenue, 5 Jan. 1818, para. 89, *Parliamentary Papers 1831–32*, 11, Appx, p. 425 (cited hereafter as *P.P.*).

profits or wilting under an excessive revenue demand. The existence of substantial landed mirasi in a region like Tanjore, which also had a fairly high amount of inam, does not confute this. For there is every reason to believe that landlord rights, which were here of a muted kind, were not characteristic of areas in which there was substantial inam. Landed mirasi in southern India conferred a much more limited landlord right than the joint tenure of northern India, and even in Tanjore was largely confined to the area under wet cultivation. Here the ruling power had always maintained a close involvement in the village through its provision of irrigation works and its collection of land revenue in kind. It also never surrendered its rights to interfere in the disposal of the waste. While personal inam was found on a moderately extensive scale in Tanjore, it is noticeable that two-thirds of such inam rested on *sanad* grants from the raja, that such grants consisted for the most part of entire villages, and that two-thirds of such villages were situated in the dry highland taluk of Pattukkotai, often paying a heavy *jodi* or quit-rent and clearly owing their origin to the raja's efforts to open up the waste.[6] In this sense they simply followed the pattern of other mirasi villages, not reckoned as inam, which had originated as *agraharams* for Brahman or Vellala colonists. Inam was, therefore, largely separate from the ordinary village structure; it was a device for encouraging colonisation rather than one to escape the revenue demand.

North of Tanjore, however, matters were different. Here the mirasi right, whether landed or office mirasi, was unsaleable and practically worthless, so Munro claimed, the weight of the revenue demand having left the mirasdar paying higher rates than the temporary cultivator. Yet it is a curious and undoubtedly significant feature that where mirasi had least value and the revenue demand bore down at its heaviest, there privileged tenure in the shape of inam or favourably rated land was often at its most extensive. This was particularly true of the Ceded Districts of Bellary and Cuddapah. Here according to A. D. Campbell, writing in 1831, alienations were so extensive that the lands liable to the payment of the Government revenue were little more than half 'or as 19 to 16 to those of which the entire Revenue has been alienated, in very small lots, by the Native Governments, chiefly to Brahmins or other individuals, on hereditary tenure denominated

[6] *Papers re the Inam Settlement*, p. 244.

Enam'.[7] It is true that a considerable portion of these alienations
was taken up by grants made by poligars to *kuttabadis* or military
and police peons in the hilly tracts. But village service inams
were twice as large again.[8] The *Bellary Gazetteer* states that this
formed the largest class of inam, amounting in 1862 to some
635,000 acres, or about one-sixth of the cultivated area. The
conditions under which it was acquired were described by William
Thackeray in 1807 in colourful terms. In the anarchy and plundering that prevailed from 1788 to 1799 'the Potail or the
Kurnum acted like a little prince in his own village...In most
parts of the Ceded Districts the Potail or head Rayet, and the
Kurnum, so peaceable in our other provinces, had become
captains of bandits garrisoning independent castles.'[9] In these
conditions one man's gain was another man's loss, and although
inam functioned to preserve a village elite, that elite was doubtless
subject to much internal revolution.

There was no doubt as to the function that inam was intended
to play at the village level. 'The possession of enam on such
favourable terms', wrote Campbell in 1831, 'enables the ryot
more easily to pay the revenue of the fields he holds which are
subject to public assessment.' Munro had noted earlier: 'The land
held by bramins under the denomination of dhirmadey is chiefly
cultivated by ryots who seldom pay the enaumdar more than a
fourth or a fifth of the rent. In many villages these enaums are
divided among the ryots, who allow the enaumdar only a small
quit-rent, and regard the rest as their own from long possession.'[10]

The historical conditions under which village inam appeared
are clearly important. It could swell to the monstrous size it
assumed in the Ceded Districts only when the authority of the
ruling power to control revenue alienations had largely slipped
away and the *poligars* felt strong enough to exercise such authority
themselves. With the prospect of tight bureaucratic rule ahead
there was every reason to secure and extend these encroachments
in the confused conditions following the British takeover in the
late eighteenth and early nineteenth century. They were far from

[7] *P.P. 1831–32*, 11, Appx, p. 45
[8] *Papers re the Inam Settlement*, p. 176.
[9] *The Bellary Gazetteer* (Madras, 1904), p. 176.
[10] A. D. Campbell, 'Paper on the Land Revenue of India', *P.P. 1831–32*,
11, Appx, p. 45; Thomas Munro, 'Report on the Ceded Districts, 26 July
1807', *P.P. 1812*, 7, 787.

confined to the Ceded Districts. In North Arcot and areas of the northern Circars like Rajahmundry such encroachments are well attested. In 1857 the Madras Government estimated service inam to comprise some 40% of total revenue alienated, although much of this was later to be classified as personal inam.[11]

There were contrasts and parallels in the Bombay territories. Elphinstone found that more than half the revenue of the new Deccan conquests acquired from the Peshwa was alienated in jagir (some 65 out of 115 lakhs) and much of this he felt bound to confirm. In 1835 Col. W. H. Sykes, wrote that in the Deccan the inam tenure was very extensive, pointing to 231 wholly alienated villages in the Poona collectorate and 581 partly alienated or *domala* villages in Ahmadnagar.[12] H. D. Robertson, the first Collector of Poona, put the figure higher in 1821, finding almost a quarter of the 1,200-odd villages held in inam and accounting for some one-third of the total revenue. Henry Pottinger in Ahmadnagar district found the same proportion of alienation. Yet curiously the Bombay Government reported in 1823 that there was but little alienated land in the Deccan and that investigation into the validity of titles was not likely to be attended with much advantage.[13] What appears to have been implied was that the vast bulk of inam, even when in the shape of *umuls* or a fixed percentage of the revenue in Government villages, was held as a form of jagir by superior tenure holders, but otherwise, apart from the wholly alienated villages, inam did not figure significantly. In Poona district Robertson estimated that the $317\frac{1}{2}$ wholly alienated villages carried an assessment (*tunkha*) of Rs. 3,13,776 while the assessment of the extraneous inam and mokassa and jagir umuls came to no more than Rs. 38,258.[14] It is possible that village service inam was not included in this figure, but it is unlikely that encroachments had swelled this unduly. As Gooddine argued, the fate of the village patels must have varied enormously

[11] *Papers re the Inam Settlement*, pp. 17 ff.
[12] W. H. Sykes, 'On the Land Tenures of the Deccan', *Journal of the Royal Asiatic Society*, 2 (1835) pp. 218–19.
[13] H. D. Robertson to Wm Chaplin, 10 Oct. 1821, *Selections of Papers from the Records of the East India House relating to the revenue, police, and criminal justice under the Company's government*, 4 vols. (London, 1820–6), 4, p. 425 (cited hereafter as *Papers at East India House*); Revenue Letter from Bombay, 5 Nov. 1823, para. 436, *P.P. 1831–32*, 11, Appx, p. 655.
[14] *Papers at East India House*, 4, p. 525.

under the pressures they encountered in the later Maratha period, but political conditions were not such as to make possible substantial enlargement of village inam even for those most favourably placed. Poona was too close. Where the patel was not depressed but extended his sway, he appears to have enlarged his financial perquisites by selling vacant miras land (*gatkul* miras) and inflating village expenses. Gooddine's celebrated study of 33 villages of the Patoda taluk of Ahmadnagar district was undertaken in the mid nineteenth century when admittedly circumstances had greatly changed and when for a lengthy period the patel's pickings had doubtless been pared right back. Gooddine's findings showed that in 1253 F.S. (A.D. 1845–6) the whole body of village officers, including the village servants, enjoyed fees and perquisites equivalent in value to 90% of the land-revenue collections. Of the total income of the village officers some 11% came from commission on the revenue collections, some 43% from revenue remissions on inam land, and some 46% from haqs or traditional dues. Of this total sum the patel families received something over 10%, but since there were some 284 patel families in the 33 villages, the share of each amounted to no more than Rs. 14-13-0 per annum.[15]

Inam was greatest at the extremities of the Peshwa's dominions both to north and south. When Goldsmid took over as superintendent of the revenue survey in the Southern Mahratta Country he was startled at the enormous proportion of land held in alienation in the Dharwar and Belgam collectorates. Besides whole clusters (*mahals*) of alienations, comprising 12 to 25 villages each, he found about 700 entire villages in the government portion claimed as inam. In the remaining 2,452 villages left to Government, there were minor alienations comprising some 60,000 estates, 'the share left for Government even in these its own villages, not averaging one-half thereof'.[16] Conditions at the time of British accession resembled those in the nearby Ceded Districts, but it is not clear how far village service inam was significant.

[15] R. N. Gooddine, 'Report on Deccan Village Communities', *Selections from the Records of the Bombay Government*, no. 4 (Bombay, 1852). For rights over waste and role of inam, see Hirshi Fukazawa, 'Land and Peasants in the Eighteenth Century Maratha Kingdom', *Hitotsubashi Journal of Economics*, 6, no. 1 (1965), pp. 32–61.

[16] 'Narrative of Bombay Inam Commission', *Sels. Recs. Bombay Govt.*, new ser., no. 132 (Bombay, 1879).

In some areas, like Badami in Dharwar, excessively high quit-rents on village service lands suggest that Maratha revenue farm-ing may have depressed the chief village officers, or in other places that the local petty notables (*desais* and *despandiyas*) had made good at their expense. But inam and privileged tenure clearly played an important part in the internal economy of the village. As in the Ceded Districts, these were devices to help meet the demand on the overassessed *chali* or land under permanent cultivation (in the Ceded Districts, *upanum*); and similarly the ryot was compelled to cultivate parcels of both the highly and the lowly assessed soils.

At the other geographical extremity, in Gujarat, the extent of alienated land was again enormous. In Kaira district, Elphinstone estimated that some $10\frac{1}{2}$ lakhs of revenue had been alienated, which must have represented something like 40% to 50% of the total revenue assets. In Broach, Monier Williams reported in 1821 that nearly one-third of the cultivated area was exempt. There were many outward similarities with the Southern Mahratta Country. Much of the alienated area was composed of entire villages under the control of former warrior chieftains or turbulent groups (*grassias* and *kolis*), who also held partial rights in many of the Government villages, Because of the excessive alienation of land even in the Government villages, the full revenue-bearing or *talpad* lands (or at least the most fertile soils in continuous cultiva-tion, known as *vaita*) carried a revenue rate that could go as high as Rs. 90 per bigha. So that again the ryot was compelled to hold a parcel of differently rated lands, among which the revenue-privileged inam land played a vital function in keeping him solvent. Yet the resemblance to conditions in the far south ceases at this point. For in much of Gujarat the patel was in the saddle. Securing the revenue farm he had largely succeeded in turning it into a form of *pattidari* property. Although there is some evidence that the patel families had extended their service inam (*pasaita*), as in the Nadiad pargana of Kaira district, they could look to more lucrative sources than inam or dipping their hand into the village expense account. Not only did they practise the illicit leasing out on mortgage of portions of the talpad, but their dominance was such that grassias and others had tamely to submit to the later reimposition of the full assessment on these lands, effectively cancelling out the mortgage interest. But of far greater significance was the development of the patel's office into a joint-landlord village structure in which the office-holding system characteristic of the ryotwar village withered away. In Broach, it is noticeable that the patel was the mere representative, or one of many muqaddam patel representatives, of the *bhagdars*, and according to Monier Williams he derived no profit and held no land as a reward for office.[17] In similar fashion the Kaira pattidars resisted the British attempt to foist village accountants upon them. Here are all the characteristics of coparcenary communities shedding their ryotwar integument. Why the village heads should have won out against the local baronage is to ask a question in political history, but that they should have managed to get so far in the development of joint-landlord villages can be more readily answered. Kaira moved even the dry-as-dust Alexander Rogers to write lyrically that 'there is no richer country in the Bombay Presidency, or probably in all Hindustan'.[18] Only in such regions of secure agriculture, with a high population-land ratio, could the joint-landlord form of tenure flourish and support the village elite with a landlord rent. Indeed, so far from being a recent innovation as Baden-Powell contended,[19] these semi-coparcenary communities encountered by the British in Gujarat may have represented the original tenure, according to Rogers. He was disposed to believe that in other parts like the Deccan it had been deranged by revenue-farming arrangements and oppression, and so had been transformed into ryotwari.[20]

This lengthy prolegomenon should serve to offer suggestions as to why formal privileged tenures at the village level were comparatively rare in the North. Not that there was no inam, or as it was called, *muafi* problem. Hastings, the Governor-General in 1815, noted that rent-free grants in the Ceded and Conquered Provinces amounted to 4,495,177 bighas, 'an extent exceeding the recorded area of the cultivated land in the largest of our Zillahs'.[21] Much of this was reckoned to be fraudulent. When the

---

[17] *P.P. 1831–32*, 11, Appx, p. 584.
[18] A. Rogers, *The Land Revenue of Bombay*, 2 vols. (London, 1892), 1, p. 103. On the re-emergence of joint landlord rights, cf. W. G. Pedder, 'Revenue Survey Assessment in Kaira Collectorate', *Sels. Recs. Bombay Govt.*, new ser., CXIV, pp. 2 ff.
[19] Baden-Powell, *The Indian Village Community*, pp. 387 ff.
[20] Rogers, *Land Revenue of Bombay*, 2, p. 9.
[21] *Selections from the Revenue Records of the N.W. Provinces, 1818–20* (Calcutta, 1866), p. 348.

British took over the Mathura (Muttra) district from Sindhia the greater portion of the *huzur* pargana was not assessed to revenue, having been alienated to the temples and religious institutions of this region sacred to Krishna and the *gopis*. Even in 1879, 9% of the district was *muafi*, the proportion rising in the huzur pargana to nearly a third. Much more provocative of official ire and cupidity were the muafi grants of the upper Doab and Rohilkhand region. In 1839 Edward Thornton could report that he had raised the revenue of the Saharanpur district by $1\frac{1}{4}$ lakhs in a single year through the resumption of muafi. Here the character of the muafidars was quite different:

Mafee parcels given by the Zemindars are rare; those that have been resumed were professedly the gift of Government, the Mafeedars were chiefly Mahomedans, and not of an agricultural class, and they resided chiefly in the Qusbahs or head Towns of the Pergunahs. Of the parcels that lay in the Villages the agricultural management was exercised by the Zemindars, and the Mafeedar held nothing more than the Government right. Of these the settlement has been made with the Zemindars. In the Qusbahs the Mafeedars held the agricultural management. . .The ex-Mafeedars were admitted to the settlement of the resumed land, and the Sudder Malgoozars were some from their party and some from the Zemindars of the old Khalsahs.[22]

The *milki* men, as the muafidars were known in Rohilkhand, fared no better, being castigated as late as 1874 by the settlement officer of Bijnaur as 'lazy, useless profligates, habitués of the bazaars of the larger towns'. By 1840 some 281,241 acres of muafi had been resumed in Rohilkhand, but in 1879 there still remained some 660,276 acres of rent-free land, only a small portion of which had been granted for Mutiny services.[23] Resumption was part of moral uplift.

Either the milki men. . .will have to reform their ways – lay aside their thin muslins, leave their couches, and discharge their favourites; gird up their loins, and exert themselves in the management of their plots, or they will have to make way for honester men. It is a strange collateral result. . .that the making these man pay their fair share of

[22] 'Saharanpur Settlement Report 1839', para. 46, in *Reports of the Revenue Settlement of the N.W. Provinces of the Bengal Presidency under Regulation IX, 1833* (Benares, 1862), 1, p. 112.

[23] L. Brennan, 'Agrarian Policy and its Effects on Landholders in Rohilkhand 1833–70', *University Studies in History*, 5 (1970), p. 10.

the Government land revenue will very sensibly reduce public prostitution of all sorts in the larger towns, notably in Nugeena.[24]

Muafi of this type could hardly be said to be an integral part of the village economy.

In the North it would seem that we are brought back to Baden-Powell's joint-landlord village as the basic model – a community composed essentially of a proprietary body of kinsmen whose representatives engaged for the Government revenue but who bore no taint of Government appointment as patels enjoying service inam and official haqs. But the vicissitudes to which this structure was subject should warn us against the notion of any fixed type. Indeed the distinction between landlord and ryotwari village could be worn thin to the point of obliteration. Given prolonged political turbulence, a large area of cultivable waste, and an oppressive revenue demand, the landlord village in the North could crumple almost beyond recognition. In much of the upper Doab and Rohilkhand in the early decades of the nineteenth century there was almost nothing in the shape of landlord rent to be derived from land control. The aim of the village elite consisted in securing more preferential revenue rates than outside or temporary cultivators. Failure in this aim under unremitting pressure could result in all ryots being forced down into an undifferentiated mass, except perhaps for the revenue managers who could become separated out as an office-holding elite, more the appointees of outside authority than the spokesmen of a common proprietary body.

As with the Deccan patel, so with his equivalent in the North, the muqaddam, the perquisites of office now became important. In the North such perquisites comprised exemption from assessment of the muqaddam's garden land, a percentage commission (varying from 2% to 5%) on the revenue collections, and the quiet embezzlement of village expenses. Vestiges of the old zamindari right might remain in the form of a zamindari allowance (*russoom*) of some 5%, but this could become confounded with the muqaddami allowance if the muqaddams were drawn from among the ranks of the old village zamindars. Where the former proprietary body had been set aside by a superior revenue farmer, jagirdar, or taluqdar, it might be given some compensation in the form of a small grant of *nankar* or revenue-free land, as was done

24 *Bijnaur Settlement Report 1874* (Allahabad, 1874), p. 77.

in the Sukrawah pargana of Farrukhabad after the jagirdar had dispossessed the Brahman zamindars of the villages of 'Suddurpoor and Beebeepoor'.[25] In such cases the taluqdar or *mukararidar* (holder of a privileged permanent revenue farm) might put in a muqaddam of his own choosing, emphasising the increasingly appointive nature of the office. In the village of 'Ummerpore' in the Meerut district the Gujar mukararidar, Raja Nain Singh, put in a Gujar cultivator as muqaddam over the heads of the old Tyagi proprietors. He was given 'the general management of the village, with authority to allot lands for cultivation, and to settle ryots. He received as mocuddumee two rupees per cent on the jummabundee, and two biswahs [rent-free] per bigah of zubtee [cash-crop] land, paying also less rent than other cultivators for the land he tilled.'[26]

In these circumstances, with a continuously high pitch of assessment, the only land of any value would be muafi. In 1832 in the Bareilly district in Rohilkhand, while the revenue engagement (malguzari) was selling for no more than one year's revenue, muafi fetched ten years' purchase. Boulderson, the settlement officer, thought that to talk of proprietary right for any but revenue-free land was a mockery:

The whole allowance of 25% on the gross rental is not a fraction more than will cover the ordinary village expenses and the chances of season. In point of fact there is no proprietor's rent throughout the country, where an estate is settled up to the Regulation mark, and the rent-roll is well ascertained. Government is indubitably the proprietor in the English sense of the word, and it is a mere farce to talk, up here at least, of proprietors in any other sense than that of Government officers for the collection of the revenue with a small remuneration for the trouble of collection.[27]

Yet where a village and its headman were not crushed by external pressures, the situation could encourage polarisation within the village community, Cavendish observed in Muzaffarnagar district in the early 1820s that 'in many villages. . .the headmen have made themselves farmers, that is, levying the full

25 'Settlement of Pergunnah Sukrawah, Zillah Furruckabad', *Selections from the Records of Government of the N.W. Provinces*, no. 22 (1848), p. 256.

26 Holt Mackenzie, Memo, 1826, *P.P. 1831–32*, 11, Appx, p. 254.

27 *Bareilly Settlement Report 1874* (Allahabad, 1874), p. 126.

Government share of the produce, and setting aside the right of their parceners to have a proportionate distribution of the assessed jumma, they have taken to themselves all the profit and loss on the engagement. This has also occurred in Delhi, where the mocuddums have been supported by powerful men.'[28] Thomas Fortescue, in his celebrated report of 1820 on the Delhi Territory, confirmed that the muqaddams were persons of much consequence in pre-British times, and that contention for the office was still eager.[29] John Lawrence found the same among the dry, thinly peopled tracts of the Rewari district, as did M. R. Gubbins in Rohtak in the late 1830s.[30] But here the principle of tribal union was so strong among the Jats and other communities that the ruling power had never managed to break into the village structure. Despite the region being one of precarious agriculture and more scarce in men and capital than land, so inhibiting the growth of joint-landlord forms, there was nothing comparable to the chain of state-dependent village officers that prevailed in much of western and southern India. The *bhaiachara* structure of the Jat villages was ryotwar except for the sense of tribal union which kept the ruling power at bay. The latter lay alongside the 'village republics', able to grant portions of its own revenue in superior privileged tenures but powerless to secure for them proprietary dominion. The settlement officer in Rohtak noted perceptively that the Nawabs of Jhajjar, Bahadurgarh, and (even the home of Indian cricket) Pataudi were not lords of the soil except in villages reclaimed from the waste and founded by themselves. Their tenures were in effect service jagirs of an unusual extent.[31] Inam at the village level had no role here.

In the eastern districts of what is now Uttar Pradesh, conditions offered a complete contrast. Here population pressed on resources, and the fertile soil was excellent for producing landlord-type villages and complex mahals. Privileged tenure was everything since only in those comparatively few instances in which the village landlord body was small and non-cultivating did the rental collections exceed the Government revenue demand, so yielding a true landlord rent. For the most part where the proprietary

[28] *P.P. 1831–32*, 11, Appx, p. 24.
[29] *Papers at East India House*, 3, pp. 401 ff.
[30] *Selections from Reports of the Revision of the Settlement under Regulation IX, 1833, in the Delhie Territory*, no. 1 (Agra, 1846).
[31] *Rohtak Settlement Report 1873–79* (Lahore, 1880), p. 109.

body cultivated part of the land themselves as home farms (*sir*), the object was rather to lower the rate on which the revenue fell on their own proprietary cultivation by shifting the burden on to the non-proprietary ryots. But if the proprietary body had proliferated so that the entire village lands were partitioned into sir, and subletting of the sir had fallen to a minimum, then the old ryotwari structure re-emerged. At this point the heads of the pattis, or lineage subdivisions, could readily constitute themselves as a new elite of managing proprietors. Thomason observed in the Sithwul taluqa of Azamgarh in the mid 1830s how the *lambardar* of each patti was rewarded with an allowance of Rs. 25 charged to village expenses, although he said such instances were rare 'because the other unauthorized advantages possessed by the [managing] proprietor have generally caused the office to be much an object of desire'.[32] With all the cultivating ryots being members of the proprietary body and paying an equal *bach* or revenue rate, the perquisites of office had once again become important. Privileged tenure by virtue of proprietary right having disappeared, privileged tenure by virtue of office takes its place for a new elite. At this juncture the state authorities might step in, and according to their disposition and power either put in their own officials and collect directly (*kham*) from each ryot, or support the managing proprietors with appointive village office, or indeed go so far as to vest the sole proprietary right in them. The latent power of tribal union among swollen and feud-ridden Rajput proprietary communities would usually deter the ruling power from the first course, although in order to collect a heavy demand it was the practice adopted among the turbulent thakurs of Mehrabad in the Shahjahanpur district of Rohilkhand.[33] The British followed one of the two latter courses. But either way, so long as the revenue demand ate deeply into agricultural profits, privileged tenure was fundamental to the land tenure system of the North.

Indian agriculture was characterised by a peasant *petite culture* in which the cultivating holding was often on an average no more than six acres, the amount of land that could be farmed directly

[32] 'Azamgarh Settlement Report 1839', in *Reps. Rev. Settl. N.W. Provs. Reg. IX, 1833* (Benares, 1862), 1, p. 31.
[33] *Ibid.*, 2, p. 7.

by a family using its own or tied labour.[34] This meant that even at
the village level the major source of additional income for a
village landholder of any substance was tributary or quasi-rental
receipts from his nondemesne or 'tenant' lands, rather than
ordinary agricultural profits won from direct farming of a large
holding.[35] Since the external revenue demand was tending constantly to absorb these rental receipts, privileged tenure was of
importance in assisting the village elite to maintain its economic
superiority. Where the ryotwari type of village prevailed, such
privileged tenure was formally separated out as inam, and appears
to have been most extensive where not only the revenue pressure
was severe but also where conditions made possible the enlargement of inam through private grants such as the transparent
fiction of transfers to Brahmans. At its greatest extent village inam
appears to have been partnered by much more substantial alienations of revenue rights in jagir (and other revenue-free or favoured
tenures) to superior landholders above the village level. This
usually occurred in regions distant from the centres of imperial or
state authority.[36]

By the beginning of the nineteenth century a long period of
disturbed political conditions and unstable central authority had
swelled inam to an unnatural extent. Even so, it provided no
permanent defence against a rapacious revenue demand since this
merely pitched up the rates on revenue-bearing land to extraordinary levels which could only be met through the simul-
taneous exploitation of specially low-rated land like inam. In such
circumstances inam might no longer provide a secure buttress of
privilege for the village elite. The other perquisites of office,
particularly traditional dues and the collection and management
of the revenue demand, might attain much greater significance.
The transformation of the patel into a petty revenue farmer could
work an internal revolution among the old elite, especially where

---

[34] Cf. *Aligarh Settlement Report 1882* (Allahabad, 1882), p. 50; and
Mainpuri Settlement Report 1875 (Allahabad, 1875), p. 88.
[35] Cf. Dharma Kumar, *Land and Caste in South India* (Cambridge, 1965),
pp. 20–3, 29.
[36] Cf. K. Haraksingh, 'The Revenue Administration of Sylhet District',
Ph.D. diss., Univ. of London, 1973, p. 31, where Lindsay formed the
impression in 1779 that 'not even one eighth of the district was revenue
paying, the rest being either jaghire, burmutre [brahmottra], muddut
muash, etc.'. On the amount of revenue-free land in Bengal, cf. A. M.
Waheeduzzaman, 'Land Resumption in Bengal 1819–1946', Ph.D. diss.,
Univ. of London, 1969, p. 171.

office had for long been a hereditary property whose rewards were fragmented among a host of co-sharers. The elevation of one man or family could occur amid the general depression of the old elite. Yet only where secure agriculture and pressure of population on land prevailed was there a possibility of landlord rents. Only there could there be a willingness to accept permanent responsibility for the revenue of the entire village lands. Only there could office mirasi be supplemented and overtaken by landed mirasi. Hence only there did village service cease to be of formal importance.

In the bulk of the ryotwari areas at the time of the British accession to power, the possession of office remained the key to economic superiority in the village. But whether this superiority was secured primarily through the possession of inam land or primarily through the direct financial gains of office and revenue management appears to have varied greatly and depended on the internal political configuration of the village elite and the distance of the area from central authority. In the Ahmadnagar and Poona districts, close to the centres of Maratha power, village inam appears to have been relatively unimportant. In contrast, in parts of the Madras Ceded Districts, like Bellary, it was at least one-sixth of the cultivated area. Yet even in the joint-landlord villages of northern India, where formal village service inam was confined to minor officials like village police and detectives (*goraits*),[37] privileged tenure remained of key importance. In a swollen proprietary body the compensatory advantages for bearing the revenue responsibility for the entire village lands were limited to social prestige and the enjoyment of reduced revenue rates on their proprietary sir or demesne land. Where the proprietary body encompassed almost the whole cultivating community as a result of lineage proliferation, as among some of the Rajput village communities of eastern Uttar Pradesh, or where by virtue of the special structure of bhaiachara communities, as in insecure tracts like much of the Delhi region, almost the entire village lands were regarded as sir, there many of the features of ryotwar village could be reproduced, particularly the importance of office and its perquisites.[38] As Baden-Powell was constrained

[37] E. A. Reade, Memo on Police and Auxiliaries, 4 Nov. 1857, *P.P. 1859* (2), 8, p. 810. Cf. also 'Note on the Remuneration of the Rural Police in the N.W. Provinces', *Sels. Recs. Govt. N.W. Provs.*, no. 4 (Allahabad, 1868), pp. 185 ff.

[38] For swollen Rajput communities in the Benares region, cf. *Jaunpur*

to acknowledge, the practical difference between the joint-land-lord and the ryotwari village could be worn to a shadow.[39] Hence the functional role of village service inam has to be assessed as simply one in the complex of variables that determined the distribution of economic power within the Indian village.

Settlement Report 1877–86 (Allahabad, 1886), p. 107 *passim*; *Ghazipur Settlement Report 1880–85* (Allahabad, 1886), p. 89 *passim*; *Ballia Settlement Report 1882–85* (Allahabad, 1886) *passim*. Also B. S. Cohn 'Structural Change in Indian Rural Society', in Robert E. Frykenberg (ed.), *Land Control and Social Structure in Indian History* (Madison, 1969); Richard G. Fox, *Kin, Clan, Raja & Rule* (Berkeley, 1971). Also see below, pp. 79 ff., 239 ff.

[39] Baden-Powell, *The Indian Village Community*, pp. 425–6, 429.

3

Agrarian society and the Pax Britannica in northern India in the early nineteenth century

It has been customary to view the effects of the British annexation of the Ceded and Conquered Provinces (1801–3) in terms of an abrupt caesura. Upon the whirling anarchy of the North Indian scene there suddenly fell the *Pax Britannica*. A political revolution was worked almost overnight. The tide of Sikh expansion was checked and turned back, Jat power penned in Bharatpur, Sindhia driven across the Chambal to his matchless rock citadel at Gwalior, and the Oudh nawabi stripped of its Doab, Rohilkhand and eastern districts. The second line of the political elite could not long survive this dismantling of the superior political structure. Although, at first, expediency impelled the use of large-scale intermediaries, the assertiveness of British rule and its hunger for revenue could tolerate no more than could the Mughals the existence of tall poppies along the principal strategic highway of its power between Benares and Delhi; and on their part the number of magnates capable of keeping their footing and making the rapid adjustment from warlordism to estate management were few indeed. Within two decades of 1801 a large proportion of the established magnates had been swept from the scene, and the remainder were finding that the sun of official favour had gone down while it was yet day. The *jagirdars* set up by Lake west of Delhi, the Gujar fiscal lordships of Nain Singh and Ram Dyal in the upper Doab, the Bargujar chieftaincies like that of Dundi Khan in the Aligarh and Bulandshahr districts, the Jat *taluqdar* Daya Ram, the Bangash nawabi of Farrukhabad, the Chandel raj of Sheorajpur in the Kanpur district or the Goshain adventurer, Himmat Bahadur's huge domain in Kanpur and Banda –

This paper was originally presented at the Director's study group on 'India: Society in War, 1795–1808', School of Oriental and African Studies, London, in 1974.

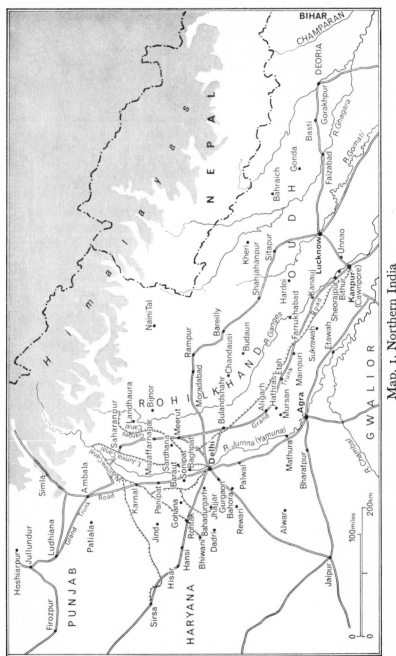

Map. 1. Northern India

all these had collapsed entirely or continued in a much attenuated existence. Even the quick-witted managerial entrepreneurs like Chaudhuri Udai Chand in Farrukhabad or Deokanundam Singh and the Benares raja in Allahabad, who strove to build up new fiscal domains out of the confusion, ignorance and corruption that flourished in the early years, found that after 1820 their teeth were drawn. The superior financial profitability and efficiency of direct administration ordained that wherever possible Government should enter into direct relations with the village.

Few tears were wasted on what were regarded not as pillars of traditional society but mushroom figures springing out of the dank soil of the eighteenth-century 'anarchy'. Yet what quickly troubled the British was the effect of Wellesley's impatient extension of the Bengal Regulations and the introduction of formal proprietary title to land during the period of temporary management through intermediaries. Had not the British damaged beyond repair the one stable institution that existed? Was it not true, as Holt Mackenzie was writing in 1819, that the immediate effect of the public sale of proprietary title for revenue default had been 'to disjoint the whole frame of the village societies, to deprive multitudes of rights of property which their families had held for ages; and to reduce a high-spirited class of men from the pride of independence to the situation of labourers on their paternal fields'?[1]

Such reflections were reinforced by Metcalfe with his contrasting picture of the still undamaged and unchanging village republics of the Delhi Territory which had lasted where nothing else had lasted and outlived the whirligig changes of dynasty and ruler; so that later generations came to believe with Marx that in traditional India 'the structure of the economic elements of society remains untouched by the storm clouds in the political sky'. How true in fact was Mackenzie's oft-quoted charge that, as a result of Wellesley's early administrative arrangements, 'in the landed property of the country a very extensive and melancholy revolution has been effected'?[2]

How correct is the notion that Wellesley rescued northern India from a destructive political anarchy only to subject the

---

[1] Holt Mackenzie, Memorandum, 1 July 1819, *Selections from the Revenue Records of the N.W. Provinces 1818–1820* (Calcutta, 1866) (cited hereafter as *Sels. Rev. Recs. N.W.P. 1818–20*) p. 117, para. 550.
[2] *Ibid.*, p. 98, para. 453.

immemorially stable and backward agrarian base to the disintegrative influences of modern legal property relationships, 'usury
capitalism', and commercial agriculture? Cohn endeavoured to
examine some of these questions in relation to the Benares region,
and his answers gave a sharp jolt to received notions. While he
detected some shift in the character and composition of the intermediate rural elite, he concluded that the Permanent Settlement
and expanded cash-crop production enabled superior land control
rights to be bought and sold without financial loss or physical
displacement of the village landholders.[3] But what of the rest of
the Ceded and Conquered Provinces, to which the Permanent
Settlement was not extended?

Contemporary British accounts of their condition after annexation painted a dark picture of the effects of misrule and constant
political instability. The Collector of Saharanpur and Muzaffarnagar was still writing in 1807 of the exhausted condition of the
district, while the Collector of Koil (Aligarh) spoke of 'the decline
of these once populous and flourishing Provinces', consequent on
the various political revolutions and revenue extortion through
which they had passed.[4] Welland, the Collector of Kanpur,
which had been subject to the exactions of the celebrated Oudh
revenue *amil*, Almas Khan, gave the blackest account in 1802:

> The subjects of this part of the country are in the most abject state
> of poverty. Let the face of the country be examined, and there will
> hardly be a manufacture found or an individual in such circum-
> stances as to afford the payment of a tax. The whole is one desolate
> waste, in which tyranny and oppression have hitherto universally
> prevailed.[5]

All this contrasted with early British bustle to get trade moving.
Henry Wellesley told his brother on 10 February 1803 that since
his project of opening the Jumna to navigation had become
known 'more than six hundred warehouses have been erected
at Allahabad, by merchants from Benares and the reserved
dominions of the Vizier; and Allahabad has already assumed the
appearance of a flourishing commercial capital'.[6]

---

[3] B. S. Cohn in R. E. Frykenberg (ed.), *Land Control and Social Structure
in Indian History* (Madison and London, 1969), esp. pp. 112–14.
[4] *Sels. Rev. Recs. N.W.P.* (Allahabad, 1873) (*Special Commission, etc.*) p. 337.
[5] Cited E. A. Atkinson, *Gazetteer N.W.P.*, vi, p. 91; also cf. Imtiaz Husain,
Land Revenue Policy in Northern India (Delhi, 1967), pp. 9–11.
[6] Henry Wellesley to Marquis Wellesley, 10 February 1803, *Parliamentary*

This image of a short step from darkness to light requires, of course, a great deal of shading. The distress from which the western districts were suffering at the time of British annexation had its origin in a much deeper scourge than war and fiscal oppression. Even as late as 1820 Fortescue was writing that the Delhi Territory had still not fully recovered from the terrible Chalisa – the great famine of 1783–4 – and that two hundred of the six hundred villages unpeopled by that disaster remained deserted.[7] In 1803–4 upper India was again afflicted by severe scarcity because of the failure of the rains. The notion that the local magnates who engaged in the constant spoiling warfare that swept the middle and upper Doab were simple military free-booters and predatory robber barons requires revision. Many of them were keenly aware of the inseparable connection between a high revenue and a high state of agriculture. Their advancement of *taqavi* loans was vital for the construction and maintenance of irrigation wells, and by this means the taluqdars of the Aligarh region in the famine conditions of 1803–4 kept their domains green oases in the parched plain. Not until the British had dis-mantled many of these smaller taluqs in the later 1830s and early 1840s, and the number of working wells fell off alarmingly in consequence, did they come belatedly to appreciate how impor-tant the magnate role had been.[8] In her jagir of Sardhana near Meerut the Begam Samru succeeded in collecting a fierce revenue demand from the sturdy Jat peasantry by using compulsion as well as credit advances to push cultivation of cash crops to their limit.[9] The same appears to have been true of the Agra district where under both Jat and Maratha rule a high revenue demand

---

Papers 1806–7, VII, p. 37. Wellesley's commercial hopes for Allahabad under British rule found their official epitaph 120 years later in the Census Report for 1923: 'it has long been notorious as a city which produces nothing except written matter, and imports even its waste-paper baskets'. *Census of India. U.P.*, XVI, pt 1, Report, p. 37.

[7] T. Fortescue, 'Report on the Revenue System of the Delhi Territory: 1820', para. 162, *Punjab Govt. Records*, I (Delhi Residency and Agency, 1807–57), p. 111.

[8] Husain, *Land Revenue Policy*, pp. 258–9; *Selections from the Records of Government, N.W. Provinces* (Agra, 1854), pt XVIII, art. 23, p. 345, 'Note on the Decrease in the Number of Wells in the Agra Division'.

[9] Report of T. C. Plowden, 16 March 1840, esp. para. 19. *Selections from the Reports of the Revenue Settlement of the N.W. Provinces under Regulation IX, 1833* (Benares, 1863) (cited hereafter as *Sels. Reps. Rev. N.W.P., Reg. IX, 1883*), II (2), p. 230.

had forced cultivation so that the collector could report in 1807 that no further great improvement could be expected.[10]

Constant political upheaval and military campaigning were far from incompatible with a substantial market sector in agriculture, demonstrated by the middle-distance traffic in cattle, sugar, cotton, indigo, opium, tobacco, wheat and salt. The financial advantages of establishing a commercial entrepôt for the sugar and rice of Rohilkhand as these made their way to supply the markets of Agra and Delhi were understood by the supposedly predatory Rohilla Pathans when they founded the mart of Chandausi in Moradabad district. Almas Khan, the notorious Oudh amil, had recognised the advantages of granting the European, R. Becher, a *mukarari* lease of the village of Dehwa in the Kanpur district in 1793 for the purpose of indigo cultivation. His example was followed by De Boigne and Perron in the Aligarh and Farrukhabad region who welcomed the setting up of a number of European indigo factories.[11]

Yet if the cruder images of the anarchy preceding British rule need correction, the older notion that agrarian society at the village level remained insulated from changes in the political world also requires re-examination. Sir Henry Elliot produced a well-known set of maps contrasting the state of zamindari possession in the North-Western Provinces in 1844 with that prevailing under Akbar in 1596.[12] It might be supposed that the extensive changes there recorded affected merely superior landholding rights. In a sense this is true. The most striking feature was the contraction of the area delineated as Rajput, most of the loss being incurred undoubtedly during the eighteenth century. British annexation partially and temporarily restored the position

---

[10] Atkinson, *Gaz. N.W.P.* vii, pp. 519–20, citing Mansel's settlement report, 1841; also Collector of Agra, 29 September 1807, *Sels. Rev. Recs. N.W.P. 1818–20*, p. 334.

[11] On the trade of the region, cf. H. Wellesley, 'Report on the Commerce of the Ceded Districts', 29 May 1802, Board's Collections, no. 2803, cited in Husain, *Land Revenue Policy*, p. 11. For a useful later account of traditional trading patterns, see N.W. Provinces Board of Revenue Proceedings, 6 October 1840, no. 47. For Becher's lease, see Board of Commissioners Ceded & Conquered Provinces Proceedings, 30 November 1806, no. 26. On European indigo production under de Boigne and Perron, Atkinson, *Gaz. N.W.P.*, ii, p. 472.

[12] Sir H. M. Elliot, *Memoirs of the History, Folk Lore, and Distribution of Races of the N.W. Provinces, of India*, ed. John Beames, 2 vols (London, 1869), ii, p. 202.

by re-exposing Rajput rights in the Rohilkhand districts and elsewhere once the control of intermediaries and revenue farmers had
been discontinued. Yet political change carried deeper.

It was most intense, of course, when it was accompanied by, or
took the form of, colonisation. When the power of the Bharatpur
raja was riding high, fighting immigrant clans of Jats encroached
into the Karnal/Panipat, Mathura, Agra, and Aligarh districts,
usually at the expense of Rajput groups.[13] But such a political
umbrella was too fragile and short-lived for substantial displacement to be effected. In Aligarh it was noted that 'the Jats of the
eastern parganahs are chiefly those who settled in the district
during its usurpation by the Bhartpur raja towards the end of the
last century. They do not seem to have settled and multiplied in
the way that the [long-settled] western Jats have done, and are
altogether not so prosperous.'[14] The most important changes at
the village level appear to have been those wrought by the superior
landholders attempting to consolidate their dominion won by the
sword or imperial grant. The collapse of the central Mughal power
had inevitably set up a process of feverish petty state-building
and the villages bore its full weight. The triple pillars of political
power in the countryside were the revenue-collecting right, zamindari possession, and lineage status. A local notable might start
with one or more of these attributes but to make himself secure he
needed to possess at the least the first two. In a substantial raj a
number of villages might be set aside as revenue-free *nankar* for
the raja, but to place his power and income on unequivocal
foundations he needed to introduce his dependants or officials as
the dominant village elite. To obtain zamindari possession could
well involve the total expulsion or extirpation of those holding the
existing right, which carried with it the immediate proprietary
control of the village lands, the right to locate cultivators, to dig
wells, to plant groves, and to let out the waste. Hence so far from
the transfer of the rights of village *maliks* being a British innovation, it was integral to the internal processes of 'traditional'

[13] Cf. Maps v and vi given in Denzil Ibbetson's *Karnal Settlement Report
1872–80* (Allahabad, 1883, vol. 2.

[14] Atkinson, *Gaz. N.W.P.*, ii, p. 397. Irfan Habib, using Elliot's maps, argues
that 'a great extension of Jat *zamindari*, particularly in the middle Doab'
occurred. Irfan Habib, *The Agrarian System of Mughal India, 1556–1707*
(Bombay, 1963), p. 341; but according to Whiteway's settlement report on
Muttra (Mathura), 1879, and Thornton's and W. H. Smith's reports on
Aligarh, 1839 and 1882, the main Jat occupation was very much older.

politics.[15] The British innovation was to make such rights alienable under due process of modern law.

Forced transfer looked harshest where the two parties enjoyed no common kinship heritage, as with the Benares raj built up in the later eighteenth century. 'The powerful Balwant Singh reduced the administrative and fiscal powers of the local kin brotherhoods and successfully removed all traces of economic and political precedence from internal lineage organization...In 1832, when the British investigated the subordinate rights of village zamindars, they found their powers surviving in only 600 out of 2,000 estates. Earlier in 1790, Duncan speculated that of 5,000 zamindars in the Benares province, 2,000 had been ejected by successive rajas.'[16] The precise degree of displacement is not clear. Fox writes as though the aim of the raja was simply to place the village elite on a level with the other landholding raiyats by setting aside the former's revenue and managerial powers and collecting *kham*. And Cohn has suggested that the change was more one of legal nomenclature than actual displacement or dispossession, the old elite surviving in a *de facto* position of local dominance.[17]

This was far from always being the case. The petty state-building process among the Jats of the Aligarh district was illustrated by the rise of the Mursan raj during the eighteenth century. According to John Thornton's inquiries of 1834, the head of the Tenwa Jats first gained a measure of supremacy in his lineage of tappa Jewar and then acquired revenue farming rights in the surrounding region. Ultimately the raja had managed to displace all traces of the proprietary *biswadars* in one-third of the villages of the Mursan pargana, and Thornton felt bound to recognise these as belonging to the raja in full zamindari right. Much the same occurred in the Mainpuri raj, although in Edmonstone's investigations, as in Thornton's, one feels the results were prejudged by prevailing revenue policy.[18] The Bara raj (of Allahabad

---

[15] It is one of the signal merits of Richard G. Fox's *Kin, Clan, Raja and Rule* (Berkeley, 1971) to have pointed this out afresh.

[16] *Ibid.*, pp. 116–17, citing *Jaunpur S.R. 1877–86* (Allahabad, 1886), p. 147.

[17] Cohn in Frykenberg, *Land Control*, pp. 112–13.

[18] Cf. J. Thornton, report on Mursan, *Reps. Rev. Settl. N.W.P., Reg IX, 1833*, I, pp. 248 ff; and N. B. Edmonstone, report on Mainpuri, *ibid*; also cf. Paper 8, pp. 190 ff., 203 ff., below; Fox, *Kin, Clan, Raja and Rule*, pp. 71, 96. In Somna the Jadon Rajput, Thakur Jai Ram Singh obtained the grant of a *taluqa* from Perron and left the Chauhan Rajput village zamindars in possession under a sublease, but when he died in 1825, his

district was carved out of Rewa State in equally drastic fashion. According to Sir Richard Temple, the Lal family began to acquire control of a number of villages in the eighteenth century by standing as security for the revenue or advancing loans for the purpose. When they had gained sufficiently strong footing they resorted to open force until, 'having universally reduced the resident [thakur] proprietors, the Lals succeeded in expelling them altogether, and introducing their own dependants'.[19] Fittingly, on British annexation the Bara raj was swallowed by the Benares raja who was only persuaded to disgorge it in 1831. The violent appropriation of zamindari rights to secure a local basis of power continued in the protected state of Oudh. Here, near Unao, across the river from Kanpur, Jussa Singh of Bangermau inaugurated a reign of terror; 'dividing the pargana between himself and his cousin...he set to work to stamp out every vestige of a former right. The villagers he turned out received the choice of service or death if he caught them. The majority fled and not until annexation [in 1856] did they venture to return to their homes.'[20]

Once the magnate elements came to appreciate that under British rule their tenure could be rendered secure only if they could show proof of zamindari title, many of them redoubled their efforts towards this end. In that sense the advent of British power probably accelerated tendencies already at work. It was not always possible to procure the immediate eviction of the old proprietary body, but the managerial right could first be transferred. In the village of 'Ummurpore' in the Meerut district, the Gujar chief, Nain Singh, put in a Gujar cultivator as muqaddam over the heads of the old Tyagi proprietors, and gave him 'the general management of the village, with authority to allot lands for cultivation, and to settle ryots'.[21] Nearby, exploiting a thin layer of Jat settlement in the Puth and Sayana parganas near the

---

three sons resorted to open eviction; 'in a short time there was not a trace of an old zamindar in the taluka. The original proprietors were deprived of all their remaining privileges, and were not even allowed to reside within the limits of the estate.' *Aligarh S.R. 1882* (Allahabad, 1882), p. 23.

[19] 'Report on the Moquddumee Biswahdaree Settlement of Pergunnah Barah, Zillah Allahabad', by R. Temple, 9 December 1850, *Sels. Rec. Govt. N.W.P.* (Agra, 1856), pt xxvii, art. 15, pp. 400 ff.

[20] *Unao S.R. 1867* (Lucknow, 1867), pp. 136–7.

[21] Holt Mackenzie, Memorandum 19 October 1826, *Sels. Rev. Recs. N.W.P., 1822–33*, p. 85.

Ganges, the ancestors of Fateh Singh had constructed the Kuchchesar raj out of revenue farming rights. His father, Ramdhan Singh, had extorted the zamindari rights in a number of villages 'by the exercise of the most rigorous and cold-blooded barbarity', according to Sir H. M. Elliot's information. When Ramdham Singh died in 1815, a European official was sent into the pargana and

ordered all present to stand in two divisions, one representing the mokuddums and inferior tenants, the other the claimants of the proprietary right. Most from fear of Futteh Sing, or apprehension of causing an increase of juma by disputed title, and others, through total ignorance of the consequences which would ensue by not having their names enrolled, stood on the side of the mokuddums, and offered no opposition to Futteh Sing's admission. The consequence was that he got recorded as zamindar in almost every instance, and remains as such in all those villages from which he has not been ousted by the Special Commission.[22]

The intensification of expropriation is to be seen vividly in the small pargana of Sukrawah which was granted in jagir to Amin-ud-daulah by the nawab of Farrukhabad well before British rule. From 1789 Amin-ud-daulah made every effort to reduce the rights of the landholders. Playing off the Brahmin Chaudhuri family and the Ahirs against the four different Rajput subcastes who each held a few villages, he finally managed to triumph over all, turning the engine of the newly established British courts to his ends. 'Under demands for revenue he by the agency of the courts, caused the houses and orchards of them [the Ahirs] and the [Gaur] Thakoors of Dhoondownee to be sold and himself bought them.' Having expelled the Ahirs he destroyed their fort and pulled down the *thakurs'* houses.[23] It was significant that the smouldering resentments caused by Amin-ud-daulah should have lasted long after his death in 1826 and prompted the Secretary to Government in 1844 to quote Lord Hastings' revenue minute of 21 September 1815. Here Hastings had expressed his conviction that the most serious damage to the rights of the village maliks had occurred in jagirs and revenue farms. 'In Burdwan, in Behar, in Cawnpore, and indeed wherever there may have existed extensive landed property at the mercy of individuals, whether in farm,

[22] *Sels. Rev. Reps. Reg. IX, 1833, N.W.P.*, II, pp. 171–2.
[23] *Sels. Recs. Govt. N.W.P.* (Agra, 1848), I, pt IV, no. XXII, 'Settlement of Pergunnah Sukrawah, Zillah Farruckabad', pp. 245 ff.

in jagheer, in talook, or in zemindaree of the higher class, the complaints of the village zamindars have crowded in upon me without number.'[24]

While the activities of the longer-established and more traditional-style taluqdar may well have effected more profound changes in village tenures, it was the new men who caught the British eye. The enormities practised in Kanpur moved T. C. Robertson in 1818 to call for an official inquiry that resulted in the establishment of the Mofussil Special Commission in 1821 charged with the task of repairing the damage. Agriculturally a rich and populous district, Kanpur had attracted a considerable volume of 'hot money' from Muslim officials in Oudh, much of it being invested speculatively in revenue management rights in the nearby British districts. Robertson was clear that much more than rights above the village level had been affected. A man like Ahmad Baksh, who, from the menial post of nazir to the collector, had within a year acquired estates bearing a *jama* of some Rs. 57,000 did not merely obtain his profits from a collusive lowering of the assessment by his nephew, the tahsildar. He bore down on the village maliks. The Commission believed that, despite the numerous changes of ruler in the previous century, 'the village maliks, the most valuable part of the population, or to speak more clearly, the heads of the agricultural communities located in the different villages, appear up to the acquisition of the country by the British Government to have remained undisturbed'. Their profits had hitherto been secured by a lower rate of assessment on their *sir* or personal lands, the Government demand being met mainly from the ryoti or tenant land. When the village was now transferred to an outsider 'regarding himself as landlord, according to our European notion of landed property, what a revolution must ensue!' The new proprietor could normally obtain the customary 15% profit on the revenue engagement by resuming that of the old 'proprietors', that is, by making their sir bear a full rate of assessment and equating them with their 'tenants'. The common lands of the village (*shamilat*) also suffered invasion by 'the newly-created zamindars, who have all a propensity to cutting down mango topes, and appropriating to themselves tanks, wells and grazing lands'. Yet Robertson was candid enough to admit

[24] *Ibid.*, pp. 245–6. The whole minute is given in *Sels. Rev. Recs. N.W.P., 1818–20*, paras, 138–9, p. 341.

that these acts met constant resistance. The new zamindar was 'very seldom. . .so imprudent as to live within the village he has acquired', but employed an agent 'who, backed by the authority of Government, is able to realize revenue, and seize upon everything visible and tangible'. But 'with the interior domestic economy of the village he dare not, however, for his life interfere. . .[and] possesses no influence but what the fear of the Darogah inspires'. The resulting disorder led inevitably to the appointment of *chaukidars* recruited usually from the criminal Bowriah caste who were notorious for fomenting thievish conspiracies of the dispossessed and lent colour to the charge that this was a rule under which sweepers flourished. There was no greater contrast than the peaceableness of the Sheorajpur pargana, still in possession of its original Chandel chiefs, and Ghatampur, which had fallen almost entirely into Ahmad Baksh's hands, and where now chaukidars swarmed and theft was rife.[25]

Internal derangement of village tenures could go further. Where the British entered directly into engagements with the village maliks (variously denominated biswadars, pattidars, muqaddams, village zamindars, etc.) one or more powerful men among the village elite could obtain the proprietary title by getting their names entered on the Government books to the exclusion of their brethren. R. Cavendish, who wrote some of the most informative reports on agrarian society in his settlement reports of the mid 1820s, was convinced from his own contrasting experience in Muzaffarnagar and the Palwal and Bahora parganas of the Delhi Territory that extensive alterations of this kind had occurred.

In the Regulation Provinces the rights and interests of the agriculturalists are unknown, the Moccudums, Lumbardars, Malicks, etc. have usurped the right of their brethren, have been converted by the connivance or corruption of the Native Officers into Farmers and Malicks (sole proprietors) of the 20 biswas or whole village; and have been armed with some persons for realising the rents of their estates as Collectors. . .There, many of the Moquddums have begun as farmers, have changed the bhaeechareh or coparcenary tenure into a farm, treat the brethren as tenants, and their object is to oust all who dispute their assumed power.[26]

25 T. C. Robertson's report, 9 September 1820, *Sels. Rev. Recs. N.W.P.* (Allahabad, 1873) 1 (Special Commission, etc.).
26 R. Cavendish, 'Report on Pergunnah Borah [pargana Bahora]', 20 May 1826, and on Palwal, 4 December 1826; Board's Collections, 1215, no. 30955, fo. 1564 and no. 30956, fo. 1736.

In the Muzaffarnagar district Cavendish had observed that 'in many villages. . .the headmen have made themselves farmers, that is, levying the full Government share of the produce, and setting aside the right of their parceners to have a proportionate distribution of the assessed jumma, they have taken to themselves all the profit and loss on the engagement'.[27] This had not generally occurred in the Delhi Territory where the village communities had been preserved. He gave three main reasons: firstly, the much heavier revenue assessment there left the revenue farmer little profit and so no inducement to acquire the proprietary title; secondly, the public sale of title for revenue default had not been introduced; and thirdly, the absence of the apparatus of zillah courts had allowed overassessed peasants to abscond and resume possession without difficulty and at the same time had kept out the race of court officers and hangers-on who had illicitly acquired farming and zamindari rights in the Regulation districts.

There was a good deal of resounding generalisation in the remarks of men like Cavendish and Holt Mackenzie who were given to detailed observation but who lived in an age which still spoke in absolutes and superlatives. In their more guarded moments they recognised that there were limits to the changes that legal and fiscal weapons could effect. Cavendish admitted that *bhaiachara* villages had not in general been crushed out in the Regulation districts, and that 'a majority still preserve their rights', even though the muqaddams abused their authority by inflating the village expenses account (*malba*) and embezzling the surplus.[28] In the next breath after stating dramatically that the immediate effect of public sale had been 'to disjoint the whole frame of the village societies', Holt Mackenzie had acknowledged that the reason the change had not affected the public tranquillity more widely was probably because the purchasers had not yet ventured on the full exercise of the rights they supposed themselves to possess. Doubtless they were restrained either by dread of desertion or resistance, or were awaiting the term of the legal limitation of suits to expire when they would be exempt from inquiry as to how their property had been acquired.[29]

[27] Cited Holt Mackenzie, 19 October 1826, *Sels. Rev. Recs. N.W.P. 1822–33*, p. 87.

[28] R. Cavendish, report on Palwal, Board's Collections, 1215, fo. 1804.

[29] Holt Mackenzie, Memorandum, 1 July 1819, paras. 550–1, *Sels. Rev. Recs. N.W.P. 1818–20*, p. 117.

Clearly the main breakwater against change was agrarian society itself, especially when organised into that system of a clan community of proprietary cultivators of which the bhaiachara tenure was the overt expression. Richard Fox has performed an important service in renewing the attack on the old shibboleth of an essential discontinuity between the state structure and the village community, and in demonstrating that the former reacted powerfully on the latter in the pre-British period. Yet he has gone so far as to leave little in the formation of land tenures that is not derivative from political action except the effect of one variable, human reproduction, particularly the lineage proliferation of local conquerors or state-appointed magnates. To him, the dense clan communities holding in the jointly-managed severalty known as bhaiachara were the end product of a developmental cycle. By this point in the cycle the lineage founder's descendants had multiplied and been driven close to the soil, while the political authority of the raja which had separated out at an early stage had itself been obliterated by superior state power. A really powerful state authority could then reduce all to ryotwari. One would logically infer that so far from government, particularly a foreign state power like the British, being helplessly in the grip of local society and obliged to conform its administrative and revenue arrangements to a predetermined mould, we have returned to the concept of Asiatic despotism. The state has theoretically the power, which James Mill believed indeed the land-revenue system gave the British, to shape local society to its own exigencies.

But were land tenures so ductile as Fox supposes? Were they all strung along a single continuum from zamindari, through pattidari and bhaiachara to ryotwar, and dependent simply on two variables – the size of the landholding lineage and the extent of internal lineage stratification due to political forces? In making these assumptions Fox has been bold enough to say that Baden-Powell was wrong in believing that true bhaiachara had an independent tribal origin instead of being the product of mere lineage proliferation of the families of chiefs or revenue grantees, and the steady progress of tenures through the continuum.[30] Yet

---

[30] Fox, *Kin, Clan, Raja and Rule*, pp. 59 ff, 119 ff. *Bhaiachara* has suffered from want of clear definition. For revenue officers it was the system in which village communities apportioned the revenue burden according to actual possession rather than by ancestral shares. But, as Ibbetson insisted, the sense of ancestral right was never entirely abandoned and remained in

Fox drew most of his examples from the eastern districts of the U.P., and even there failed to note how rare real bhaiachara communities were. It is true that in the angle between the Ghagara and the Ganges, Rajput clan communities clustered thickly. Originally, Rajput conquering bands appear to have established themselves along the course of rivers from which they dominated areas of secure agriculture as well as river traffic. In the Benares region many had multiplied into swollen brother-hoods, forming nearly 15% of the population (compared with the general district average of some 8% or 9%) and taking as much as 50% or more of their village lands into their own direct cultivation as sir. Even though, however, they had abandoned the pattidari principle of ancestral shares and paid their revenue by an equal rate or bach according to the extent of their individual family holding, they did not form bhaiachara communities properly so-called. For all his apparent muddle-headedness on the issue, Baden-Powell's instinct did not play him false. The hall-mark of the true bhaiachara tenure was, indeed, that it was tribal, that practically all cultivators belonged to a single clan or tribe, that all held at equal rates and almost all shared in the proprietary management. A territory occupied by a small conquering lineage could become bhaiachara in its village land tenures only if it inter-mingled with or extirpated the existing inhabitants and only if it depended in no way on a tributary 'tenant' class.

There was a double barrier to this occurring, the one social and the other economic, but both in the end springing from a single ecological constraint. A conquering elite would tend to hold itself aloof from a subject population for so long as it could sustain an overlord or squireen role, and for so long as its numbers controlled more land than was required for their own subsistence. The main-tenance of a gentry status necessitated stricter marriage rules which imposed a brake on a lineage's proliferation and helped perpetuate its minority position. As Charles Elliott said of the Rathors of Shamsabad East pargana in Farrukhabad district,

his view an important constituent element of bhaiachara communities; Ibbetson, *Karnal S.R. 1872–80*, pp. 95 ff. In practice, profits from the common land, etc. might continue to be apportioned on ancestral shares, and other uses made of the ancestral principle, so that, given the infinite variety of methods, the larger proportion of such villages were classified as imperfect *pattidari*. The real test of approximation to bhaiachara was the extent to which the cultivating and the proprietary body coincided.

they were 'too aristocratic and exclusive to breed fast'.[31] Yet the overriding constraint preventing assimilation dwelt in the fact that agriculture was sufficiently secure in the eastern districts for population to press on the soil, for tributary rent to emerge, and for social differentiation to be reinforced by economics.

No doubt the minute subdivision of landed rights, the reduction of proprietary coparceners to cultivators working their small plots of sir without even the agency of *shikmi* sub-tenants, and the adoption of the bighadam method of revenue apportionment – all these features which were more fully recorded in the 1880s in all the eastern districts, give the impression of overswollen brotherhoods in no way different from bhaiachara, or indeed ryotwar. In 1886, P. C. Wheeler, the settlement officer of Jaunpur, could comment:

The village community, which Sir Charles Metcalfe in sentences of historic fame declared to be phoenix-like and indestructible by outward force, has in these parts destroyed itself. There is no corporate body. There is no absorption of the individual in the group. The unit is now the individual and not the village. That status must succumb to contract is no new truth. The tribe gives place to the clan, the clan to the village, the village to the family, and the family to the individual.[32]

Moreover, the pressure of population and the proliferation of the higher castes into the tenancy ranks had made cultivating possession more valuable than the proprietary right, rents stagnating while the value of agricultural produce mounted. To all appearances the Chhattri and thakur had been reduced to simple peasants. Yet such appearances are deceptive in two respects. Firstly, even in the densest communities a single Chhattri *got* never comprised a majority of the population. In the celebrated Lakhnessar pargana of Ballia the Sengar Rajputs formed only 15% of the population. It is evident that even if subletting of sir was minimal the main work of cultivation was carried on by an agricultural labouring class paying labour rents. Secondly, attention has been too much monopolised by the Chhattri clan communities, which, despite their historic importance, had long ceased

[31] *Farrukhabad S.R. 1875* (Allahabad, 1875), Rent Rate Reports, p. 55.
[32] *Jaunpur S.R. 1877–86* (Allahabad, 1886), p. 78. On the absence of *shikmi* sub-tenants on *sir* in communities having a multitude of sharers, cf. the 100 villages of 'Cohn's' Dobhi *taluq* of the Karakat tahsil, Cohn in Frykenberg, *Land Control*, p. 107.

to monopolise land control, except in Ballia.[33] Dispossession had been a constant process. As Wheeler noted in Jaunpur:

> In one point there is no change, viz., that the area occupied by the Rajputs (who originally acquired the whole district when they drove out the Bhars) is steadily diminishing. Three hundred years ago they owned all but a very small portion of the district, whilst now they are in possession of very little more than two-fifths.[34]

The Rajputs had been driven back closer to the limits of their actual cultivating possession. Even so, they still owned more land than they cultivated either as holders of sir or as tenants. Their cultivating rights were not separately recorded but in Azamgarh, as late as 1908, it was observed that Chhattris together with Bhuinhars, were still 'owning half its area and cultivating at least one third'.[35]

But more important than the extent of the Chhattri grip on the land was its variability. Because the strong clan communities created some of the major problems of revenue administration and police, they attracted a disproportionate amount of official attention, and have subsequently mesmerised historians. So far from being universal they were the real element of 'Asiatic exceptionalism'. There is every reason to believe that the Chhattri population bunched at these points, forming what were deemed bhaiachara tenures, while their settlement elsewhere was of a much lighter and more lordly nature.[36] Irvine observed in Ghazipur that the high district average for sir of nearly 32% of the cultivation was caused by some 264 bighadam villages and a few other large *mahals* in which the number of co-sharers was enormous, and the sir rate ran to 80%.[37] The general pattern was not one of peasant proprietors, but of a petty landlord class driven close to the soil but still continuing to exploit it largely through

---

[33] In the four districts of Benares, Ghazipur, Jaunpur and Ballia, Chhattris owned in 1886 some 41% of the land, their hold varying from a quarter in Ghazipur to three-quarters in Ballia; Orders of Government, Resolution, 15 June 1889, p. 8, printed as Appendix to *Ghazipur S.R. 1880–85* (Allahabad, 1886), and to the remaining district settlement reports of similar date.

[34] *Jaunpur S.R. 1877–86*, p. 56.

[35] *Azamgarh S.R. 1908*, p. 8.

[36] Of the 62,114 recorded Chhattri landholders in Jaunpur, 41,470 were to be found in Karakat tahsil where the famous Dobhi taluqa was situated. Yet rather less than a quarter of Chhattri land lay in Karakat tahsil. *Jaunpur S.R.*, Appx, no. 11.

[37] *Ghazipur S.R. 1880–85*, p. 89.

lower caste sub-tenants or labourers. It was a situation that in 1854 was observed by the Collector of Azamgarh to have caused a high rate of transfer of proprietary titles:

I attribute the frequency of transfers generally, especially in this district to the great subdivision of landed property, creating a very large class of zemindars, too proud to work, and too poor to live on their profits...The number of sharers is enormous, the complication of rights great. In the case of cultivating communities, where the proprietors and cultivators are identical, and are of an industrious and unpretending class, the large number of the proprietors paying revenue under a system of joint responsibility, is no disadvantage. On the contrary I have found it to work admirably. But here there are vast numbers of zemindars over the tenantry, not themselves mere proprietary cultivators paying as revenue a mitigated rent, but men who consider themselves of a superior, and are generally of an unthrifty class and who expect to live as zemindars on their profits.[38]

Fox has assumed that bhaiachara was the basic tenure, representing 'both the oldest and youngest tenurial form'. Since ryotwar was never realised, he saw bhaiachara in northern India as denoting the bottom dead centre of the developmental cycle, the point to which tenures tended to gravitate and from which zamindari arose anew.[39] Yet true bhaiachara was in fact the most recalcitrant of tenurial forms. It was, of course, the so-called bhaiachara clan communities of the Dobhi Raghubansis and the Lakhnessar Sengars that were almost the sole examples of successful resistance to the levelling policy of the Benares raja and later of revenue farmers under the British.[40] But the apparent malleability of tenures in the eastern districts was more a reflection of the fact that true bhaiachara was for the most part absent. The landholding castes, whether Chhattri, Bhuinhar or Brahmin, remained essentially a petty gentry living on rental or labour tribute.

[38] G. Campbell, Officiating Collector, Azamgarh, 29 November 1854, *Sels. Recs. Govt. N.W.P.* iv (Allahabad, 1868), pp. 350–1.
[39] Fox, *Kin, Clan, Raja and Rule*, p. 122.
[40] The Dobhi villages were formally classified as 'jamabandi mahals in the incomplete pattidari form', *Jaunpur S.R. 1877–86*, p. 74. Bhaiachara was rare. In Ghazipur only 264 of the 2,599 villages were bighadam, which settlement officers equated with bhaiachara. Of 4,625 estates or *jamabandi mahals* in Jaunpur only 82 were classified as bhaiachara, *ibid.*, p. 72. This was the situation, of course, after a century of British rule under which sale and partition had tended to dissolve pattidari or bhaiachara into some form of zamindari.

Their numbers were rarely such that a lineage chief or mushroom taluqdar could not ultimately displace or subordinate them and establish his own descendants as the proprietary elite.[41] The revenue farmers who secured ennoblement as the rajas of Benares and Jaunpur (Sheolal Dube) operated on a front too wide and fast-moving to establish roots in this fashion, and once they had secured recognition to zamindari titles under the Permanent Settlement, the incentive to establish local residence and immediate proprietary control was gone. Even so, they caused a great deal of disturbance of existing rights, if little actual displacement. Lord Hastings in his revenue minute of 1815 drew particular attention to the derangement caused by the Benares raja and other promoted revenue farmers, and as late as 1873, Wilton Oldham was calling for the annulment of all sales for revenue default between 1795 and 1830.[42] The area settled direct by Duncan, supposedly with the village zamindars, did not escape. His subtle distinction between the pattadars who were to hold the settlement and the pattidars who had proprietary interests was lost upon the country. As Lumsden, the Ballia Commissioner in 1887, wrote: 'Speaking generally all Rajputs were zamindars alike, but on the conversion of zamindars into proprietors only, the Sengar Rajputs of Lakhnessar succeeded in becoming, all of them, proprietors of their holdings. In other parganas the leading families contracted for the Government revenue and these only became proprietors. The other Rajputs and Brahmins retained their holdings at the customary rates and became fixed rate tenants.'[43] Yet this was no painless process. There was no record of rights for more than forty years and 'the great boon of the permanent settlement' was 'cast like pennies into the crowd to be

[41] The Dobhi Raghubansis numbered some 14,500 in a district population of 1,203,000, *District Gaz. U.P.*, xxviii, Jaunpur (1908), p. 80. The Lakhnesar Sengars were merely 8,538 in a pargana population of 52,733, *Ballia S.R. 1882–85* (Allahabad, 1886), p. 71. These were the densely-settled communities; ordinary proprietary bodies were very much smaller.

[42] Hasting's remarks are cited in the account of the revenue history of the old Benares province in *Jaunpur S.R. 1877–86*, p. 161. It is noticeable that Sheolal Dube did succeed not in ousting the old proprietors but in locating inferior cultivators in the turbulent Badlapur taluq of Jaunpur, Cohn in Frykenberg, *Land Control*, pp. 110–11. For Wilton Oldham's demand, see W. Oldham, *Tenant Right and Auction Sales in Ghazeepoor and the Province of Benares* (Privately printed, Dublin, 1873), p. 9.

[43] *Ballia S.R.*, p. 4. How this was carried out where no strong clan system survived is to be seen in the Ballia pargana which was broken up into a number of small taluqs and settlements made with local petty notables.

grabbed and fought over'. The year 1775 was fixed as the date prior to which possession alone was the criterion of right: 'for the rest the zamindars were left to fight it out among themselves. This they proceeded to do in the most literal fashion, and it has ever been the custom in Ballia to initiate civil proceedings concerning the possession of land by a fight with lathis.'[44] Simply because resistance was so effective in the taluqs held by strong clan communities, to which Cohn devoted his attention, it is hardly possible to follow him without reservation in his general conclusion that 'the majority of individuals, families, and lineages who "lost" land between 1795 and 1885 retained their positions, economically, politically, and socially *within* the local areas in which they had held rights as zamindars'.[45]

The true bhaiachara tenure was the product not of secure agriculture and high population density, but the reverse. It was to be found *par excellence* in the Delhi Territory and Bundelkhand. Over most of the Rohtak district, for example, the land was held by a single cultivating 'tribe', the Jats, who in 1839 formed as much as 80% of the Gohana pargana.[46] The bhaiachara tenure was almost universal, not necessarily in the strict definition 'in which possession is the measure of right in all lands', but in the sense that almost all cultivators were 'proprietors', paid the same revenue rates, and belonged to the single farmer caste of Jat. Indeed, the structure of caste itself and the absence of marked social and economic stratification reflected the environment. The loose marital customs of the Jats, their practice of *karewa* or widow remarriage, and their habit of adopting strangers, were doubtless the product of a situation in which land was permanently abundant and hands scarce. In such conditions there was no possibility of rental tribute or the existence of a tenant class. As late as the 1880s the British settlement officers were looking for competition rents in vain and finding 82% of cultivating possession held by owners.[47] Moreover, the peasant proprietary did not make use of a predial labour class. In the 1820s G. R. Campbell was describing Jat villages in which there was but a single family of Chamars practising their hereditary occupation of skinning

[44] *Ballia S.R.*, p. 20.
[45] Cohn in Frykenberg, *Land Control*, p. 89.
[46] M. R. Gubbins, 'Report on Pergunnah Gohana', 29 October 1839, para. 24, *Sel. Reps. Rev. Settl. Reg. IX, 1833 Delhie Territory*, no. 1, p. 81.
[47] *Punjab Gazetteers. Rohtak District 1883–4*, p. 73.

dead cattle and tanning hides. Here was a community structure that defied invasion from without and subversion from within. Men like Metcalfe and Cavendish had attributed the absence of a tenurial upheaval in the Delhi Territory to the absence of public sale for revenue default and of other such institutional innovations; but there was in practice no question of the revenue farmer transforming himself into zamindar. Here the bhaiachara tenure refused to budge along the path of the developmental cycle. It was observed of the border chiefs recognised by Lake, like the nawabs of Jhajjar and Bahdurgarh (Dadri), that they were

not lords of the soil. The grants of their territories were in reality mere service jagirs of an unusually large extent. No doubt the rulers were absolute owners in estates which they had reclaimed from the waste and founded themselves; but the grant in no way affected the status of the villagers of the estate then existing, who remained owners of the soil, as they had been for centuries before. Their right was never contested by the Nawabs; and the people sold and mortgaged lands as freely under their rule as under our Government, and they were entered as proprietors of the soil in their Settlement Records as in ours.[48]

The 'tribal' nature of the bhaiachara tenure would appear to have been not the product of some innate sociological peculiarity of the Jats, but simply the result of the physical environment. In Edmund Leach's phrase, the constraints of economics were prior to the constraints of morality and law. When the British came to observe the tenures of Haryana, they encountered a land still in process of recolonisation after the Chalisa famine. Conditions were to alter. The area of secure agriculture was to be greatly extended by the West Jumna Canal, but even so, the proportion of the cultivation protected by well and canal irrigation in Rohtak district remained in 1880 only 13%. While in the secure tracts the villages grew crowded, Chamar labour grew more common, and social and economic differentiation became more marked, the district as a whole was still constrained by nature into bhaiachara tenurial forms.[49]

Bundelkhand was the other region of uncertain rainfall and scanty population where the bhaiachara tenure prevailed. Yet here it would seem that the effect of the introduction in 1805 of

[48] *Rohtak District Gaz.*, p. 84.
[49] *Ibid.*, pp. 125, 128 and Table XV.

the Bengal Regulations and the machinery of public sale realised all the fears that Metcalfe expressed if such processes had been introduced into the Delhi Territory. By 1817 Scott Waring, the Collector, had been importuning the authorities so often on the derangement of tenures which had occurred that he confessed himself 'quite tired of the subject, and have little reason to hope that the Board [of Commissioners] have not been so long ago'.[50] At one level the process of mutation followed the well-tried practices that characterised Kanpur and the eastern districts. The early tahsildars, usually Muslim officials, appropriated enormous areas in revenue farm and then succeeded in having themselves recorded as proprietors. But the devolution of superior revenue management rights did not of itself mean tenurial derangement. Revenue farmers were frequently resorted to in the Delhi Territory, and as late as 1838 John Lawrence was commenting favourably on their employment in the Rewari pargana of Gurgaon.[51] For here there appeared no danger of their establishing any right to proprietary control. There was, however, a danger not entirely absent from the Delhi Territory; this was the practice of one or more members of the village elite subleasing the revenue farm on his own account. The nearer the tenure approached to ryotwari because of a high revenue demand and the absence of rental profits, the more the village elite had to rely on the perquisites of office and the detailed revenue management.[52] Waring commented extensively on the internal subversion of village constitutions caused by such practices. The revenue management right of a village was often so onerous and unremunerative that the village farmers frequently agreed to transfer it to the large speculative revenue farmers in return for privileged rent-free tenures for themselves. Bundelkhand was an area, which although generally poor and backward, exhibited very considerable variety. In the black *mar* soils in which cotton was grown in

[50] E. S. Waring, 14 April 1817, *Sels. Rev. Recs. N.W.P. 1818–20*, p. 235.

[51] J. Lawrence, 'Report on Pergunnah Rewaree', 22 July 1838, para. 35, *Sels. Reps. Rev. Settl. Reg IX, 1833, in the Delhie Territory*, no. 1 (Agra, 1846), pp. 14–15. Fortescue also put up a spirited defence of village revenue farmers or *kutkunadars* in 1820. *Punjab Govt. Records*, i, pp. 92–4.

[52] I have dealt with this point in a paper delivered at the xxixth Congress of Orientalists in Paris, July 1973, entitled 'Privileged Land Tenure in India in the Early Nineteenth Century', in R. E. Frykenberg (ed.), *Land Tenure and Peasant in South Asia* (New Delhi, 1977), see Paper 2.

the Banda, Pailani and part of the Augasi tahsils, cash crops and a strong element of commercial agriculture made their appearance, although later blighted by the cotton crash of the 1820s.[53] Hence it is difficult to generalise widely. Clearly there existed favoured areas where rental profits were obtainable, and the proprietary right had economic meaning. There was a further complication. The dominant landholding class consisted of Rajput clans, in which the Bais, Gaur and Dikhit gots were prominent. Although these formed cultivating communities, many of which, particularly on the banks of the Jumna, formed large brotherhoods, the extent of Rajput land control appears to have considerably exceeded their cultivating possession at the time of cession to the British. Cadell in his celebrated and voluminous settlement report of Banda in 1881 estimated that at cession Hindu Rajputs held two-thirds of the district; by 1878 their proprietary rights extended over little more than a third. Now in fact the area to which their proprietary holdings were reduced coincided almost exactly with the area they still held in cultivating possession. In other words, at cession Rajput groups were probably non-cultivating proprietors in half of their land and their losses precisely matched this extent.[54] There was no comparison with the Jats of Rohtak, where in the round the limits of proprietary and cultivating possession had always coincided, though, of course, individual gots like the Ghatwals (or Maliks) could enjoy a more favoured position. Hence despite conditions favouring bhaiachara communities Bundelkhand was not exempt from tenurial change.[55] Much of it occurred during the period of Wauchope's collectorate between 1808 and 1812, when over a fifth of the villages were subject to transfer and the tahsildar of Augasi 'was allowed to acquire under the transparent screen of his son's name a territory extending to 150 square miles'. As with Kanpur, it will be found that notwithstanding British lamentations in the later nineteenth century over the alarming amount of land passing into the ownership of the moneylending and trading

[53] A. Siddiqi, *Agrarian Change in a Northern Indian State: Uttar Pradesh, 1819–33* (Oxford, 1973), pp. 154 ff.
[54] *Banda S.R. 1881* (Allahabad, 1881), pp. 31, 35, 37.
[55] The formal definition of bhaiachara is surrounded by the same difficulties in Banda as elsewhere. By 1878 there were only 25 out of the 890 estates classified as such. Cadell stated that the most common tenure in the early period of British administration was the imperfect pattidari and bhaiachara.

classes, a major part of the land transfer occurred in fact in the early period of British administration, and the beneficiaries, so far from being bankers and traders, were men who had made their way through official office. Certainly in Banda between 1805 and 1840 the principal gainers were the Muslim officials of the early days.[56]

There was one area in the Doab where the contrasting tenurial systems met. In Mathura and Aligarh districts the celebrated 'republican' bhaiachara Jat communities of Nohjhil lived cheek by jowl with the Jat lineage taluqs of Mursan, Biswan, Kanka, Kajraut and Gorai, and Jat conquest taluqs like Hathras where the village zamindars were Rajput. Further inland from the Jumna and running into the British districts of Eta and Agra were pure single zamindari estates lacking all caste homogeneity. In 1831 J. G. Deedes commented perceptively on the contrast: In the parganas bordering the Jumna – Nohjhil, Mat, Soni, Raya, Saidabad, and Khandauli – the tenures were 'strictly byacharra or putteedaree' while inland – in Jalesar, Secundra Rao, and Ferozebad – they were 'with few exceptions as strictly zamindaree':

The cultivating ryots in the former pergunnahs are also the proprietors of the soil so far that they are the descendants of the original ryots from whom the amils of the pergunnahs collected the rents directly, without the intervention of any middle-men. In the latter pergunnahs the corresponding class of ryots i.e. the original breakers up of the soil, would seem to have almost passed away, and the tenures of the zemindars, who may in the first instance have been mere village farmers or middle-men between the Government and the ryots, are now of infinitely higher antiquity than those of the resident cultivators on their estates.

Deedes said he had met with no more than two or three cases to which these observations did not apply. In those cases where the stock of the original ryots still occupied their ancestral fields, the zamindar usually resided in an adjoining village and had continued to be the revenue farmer of the estate.

In byachara estates the proprietary community, who are at the same time the cultivators, are connected by blood, being all descendants from a common stock. In zemindaree villages the connection is nearly that which in European countries subsists between the land-

[56] *Banda S.R.*, p. 31.

lord and his tenantry, a large farmer and the cottagers who reside on and cultivate his farm on short leases. In byachara estates I am aware of no grades among the brotherhood further than the official importance which the engaging mocuddum enjoys, and that which superior wealth and intelligence must always give: the common assamee who cultivates as a tenant-at-will under a putteedar can hardly be said to form a part of the community. So in zemindaree estates I know of no intermediate grade between the village landlord and his near relatives who hold their trifling seer farms on favourable rates, and his cultivating tenants-at-will of *various castes* and *tribes*, except, indeed, in those extensive zemindarees or talooqas formed of many distinct villages: and underlet to mucuddums or thekadars [peasant revenue farmers], as the land tenures may be byachara or zemindaree. I should consider the recognized owner of a talooqa composed of byachara villages as more in the light of an hereditary revenue farmer, and not at liberty to exercise such an immediate interference with the cultivators as the talooqdar who has acquired a recognized property in a number of zemindaree villages by ousting or supplanting the original zemindars.[57]

Here almost all the tenurial possibilities had been exhausted. The eighteenth-century *Sturm und Drang* had added to their variety, and the imposition of the *Pax Britannica* for a time confirmed and accelerated existing tendencies. The quick-witted officials and revenue farmers who made such striking gains in the early years of British administration were simply a new species of taluqdar employing state power rather than placing sole reliance on their own military forces. Such power could still effect tenurial change down even to the village level. But the limitation it encountered was the local kinship system which at first by open resistance and increasingly by itself invoking the state power through the civil courts set limits to intrusive change. Yet only in a few localities was the kinship system so strongly entrenched that it embraced a tribal form exhibiting both homogeneity and territorial compactness as well as extended scale. Throughout most of the Doab, society was already too multi-layered to attain this form. The fissional tendency of all clans once they numbered 15,000 or so made for migration and dispersion. The Rajput constantly sought thakur status, and the existence of subordinate tenant and predial labour castes made even the Jat by choice a landlord and employer. Only in some places had this urge been checked by

[57] J. G. Deedes, Collector of Saidabad, 25 July 1831, *Sels. Rev. Recs. N.W.P. 1822–33*, pp. 328–9.

lack of opportunity for expansion, by security needs, and by attachment to the ancestral homestead so that the result was minutely partitioned proprietorship in the village lands. Even so, the true bhaiachara tenure was rare, that is to say, a tenure in which the entire agricultural society apart from the service castes belonged to a single group bound in the web of kinship, and which made no use of a subordinate tenantry or tied labour class. The nearer it was attained, the less malleable the tenure. But its comparative rarity left most of the country open to tenurial change. Not only in caste terms was the composition of agrarian society multi-layered; it was segmented into a patchwork quilt, so that adjacent villages might be held by different landholding clans and castes and even the separate pattis within a village. So far from change pursuing the path of a developmental cycle through lineage proliferation, change was effected precisely through the constant interruption of the cycle. Once a lineage had proliferated to form a compact body of cultivators it had effectively insulated itself against change. More usually, the counteracting tendencies towards dispersion or restriction of numbers left it open to displacement by conquest or reduction to a privileged subordinate status. Hence the patchwork. The only conditions in which a developmental cycle of tenures could occur was in a homogeneous clan territory, where a ruling lineage might emerge – as that of the Tenwa Jat, Nandram, in Mursan – and as easily be reassimilated when it declined or was overthrown. This remained always the exception and not the rule, though in eastern Oudh it was more frequently encountered. Yet even then, a ruling lineage could only push its kinsmen into village zamindari rights if there were rental profits to be obtained, that is to say, where population was already pressing on the soil, and conditions making for a subordinate tenantry and tribute labour were in existence. The absence of all evidence of a developmental cycle occurring in the Delhi Territory of Haryana demonstrated the absence of such conditions. Here the inability of rajas, jagirdars, and revenue farmers to break into the true bhaiachara brotherhoods gave rise to Metcalfe's eloquent theory of the indestructibility of the Indian village community.

Yet if in the end the structure of agrarian society rather than British institutional innovation was determinant, it has to be acknowledged that the weight of the British revenue demand helped, ironically, to preserve bhaiachara and imperfect pattidari forms not only in the Delhi Territory but also in much of the upper Doab forming the Conquered Provinces. In the Ceded Provinces the manner in which the already heavy demand was enhanced does not at a superficial glance appear so immoderate, rising steadily from 140 lakhs in 1803 to 178 lakhs in 1818. Yet in the Conquered Provinces, comprising Bundelkhand and the entire Doab upwards of Agra, the assessment was screwed up from 36 lakhs in 1805 to 118 lakhs in 1818. Delhi was separately assessed, rising from 7 lakhs to 17 lakhs over the same period. Not all this demand could be collected, but it was the western districts above Agra, including Rohilkhand, that fell most heavily into deficit. Of the 65 lakhs outstanding in 1818 at the end of fourteen seasons, 47 lakhs were due from this region.[58] It was strong *prima facie* evidence that the shoe pinched hardest here. The revenue officers in Rohilkhand and the upper Doab were convinced that the severity of the demand left no room for proprietary profits. In the village of Burleh in Muzaffarnagar, Holt Mackenzie observed that 'the weight of the Government assessment appears to have levelled all distinctions', and in 1832, S. Boulderson commented ruefully that in Rohilkhand it was 'a mere farce to talk, up here at least, of proprietors in any other sense than that of Government officers for the collection of the revenue with a small remuneration for the trouble of collection'.[59]

The co-sharing tenurial brotherhoods were the response to adversity, to the *peine forte et dure* inflicted by man and nature over the centuries. Whatever relaxation was afforded to them by the *Pax Britannica*, the British revenue demands imposed on Delhi and the western districts kept the brotherhoods banded together and ensured that for a space their existence would be prolonged. To the peasant schooled to fatalistic endurance the implacable destinies that ruled his world had not altered their nature but stood forth as of old in the guise of both Destroyer and Preserver.

[58] *Sels. Rev. Recs. N.W.P. 1818–20*, pp. 156–62.
[59] Holt Mackenzie, *Sels. Rev. Recs. N.W.P. 1822–33*, p. 87; S. Boulderson, cited in *Bareilly S.R. 1874*, p. 126.

4

The land-revenue systems of the North-Western Provinces and Bombay Deccan 1830–80: ideology and the official mind

The gap between profession and performance, between intention and achievement, is so wide in the first phase of conscious modern-isation that historians have traditionally sought to explain it away. The British were deflected from their initial purposes, they argue, because of insistent problems of external and internal security which beset them between 1836 and 1860. Outside the ring fence, the Afghan war, the annexation of Sind, the Sikh wars, the Burmese war, the Persian expedition; within, the Gwalior rebel-lion, the Bundela rising, the Sonthal disturbances, and finally the crisis of the Mutiny – these, we are told, absorbed the attention and financial resources that might have been devoted to economic development and administrative reform. Hence the twenty to thirty year delay between Bentinck's education resolution of 1835 and its translation into effective action, between Macaulay's published draft of 1837 and the passing of the Indian Penal Code in 1860, between Bentinck's paper plans and the actuality of rapid steam and rail communication in the 1870s. Today we look more cynically at statements of grandiose planning objectives. In the absence of capital investment from overseas what prospects of success were truly within the reach of a colonial government which, with the abolition of the East India Company's com-mercial functions in 1834, was finally stripped of those direct powers of intervention in the economy which it had previously wielded through bulk government purchasing of commodities?[1] In 1861 at the end of the first modernising phase, J. W. B. Money in *Java, or How to Manage a Colony* pointed out the much

---

[1] Cf. the regret later expressed by the board of revenue at the decline of cotton cultivation following the ending of the Company's investment and the winding up of the commercial residency in Bundelkhand; *Selections from the Records of Government N.W. Provinces*, iv, pt xxxvii (Allahabad, 1862), pp. 66 ff.

greater comparative success of the Dutch in furthering material development because of the direct exercise of such commercial functions by the State. Indeed one may share something of the suspicion harboured by the European mercantile community concerning the dominance of non-commercial objectives over British official policy. By the complete separation of government from commerce there was serious danger of reinforcing those retrogressive tendencies that Schumpeter was later to define as the true essence of imperialism. That is to say, the separation of functions confirmed the isolation of the power apparatus and encouraged it to pursue its own autonomous goals. As a military machine insatiable for revenue its constant tendency had been overextension of dominion and an obsessive concern for external security at the expense of internal development. It is not implausible to suggest that this remained a pervasive if concealed official attitude at the higher political level for much longer than is usually allowed, and that the Bentinck period constituted only a brief interruption of the prevailing mood whose representative figures remained Ellenborough and Palmerston. Indeed nothing could be more ironic than the fact that Palmerston's celebrated formulation of 'the imperialism of free trade' – 'It is the business of government to open and secure the roads for the merchant' – should have been uttered in order to nerve Auckland to plunge still deeper into the Central Asian wastelands where the prospects for British commerce were negligible.[2]

Whether economic development or the pursuit of power formed the first priority of the 'official mind' in its upper reaches was a speculative issue contrasted with the immediate financial exigencies of the Raj over which there could be no dispute. For on any reckoning these exigencies imposed the severest constraints on what direct governmental action could effect in promoting modernisation, even in the restricted sphere in which it was now allowed to function. In Bentinck's time the North-Western Provinces were quickly marked out as possessing the most aggressive and modernising of Indian provincial administrations; yet R. M. Bird, one of its formative minds, had no illusions as to

---

[2] Palmerston to Auckland, 22 Jan. 1841; cited R. Robinson and J. A. Gallagher, *Africa and the Victorians* (London, 1961), p. 5. Palmerston elaborated on the dictum and held out extravagant hopes of trade beyond the Indus, *Parliamentary Debates.* LXV (1842), cols. 1262 ff. How far this was his real motive is another matter.

where priorities lay. In his own words the British government from its nature and position had been, was, and must be an expensive government to India:

the Government must draw from the country as large an income as its resources can be safely made to bear. The necessity of keeping up a large Army for external defence and to deter the disaffected from, or repress attempts at internal treachery and tumult, it is enough to mention. I myself very conscientiously believe that the future good of India depends on the continuance of British rule. But in order to do the very good which I trust Britain is destined to effect for India she must for a long time continue to press on the resources of India.[3]

Given the pressure for free trade from European mercantile interests there could be no question of easing the burden of taxation on the land by a system of high revenue tariffs on internal and external commerce. Ironically the British were compelled to outdo traditional Indian governments in their reliance upon land revenue. How then could such iron financial constraints be reconciled with the extravagant hopes for modernisation and economic development that characterised the 1820s and 1830s? One answer lay in the rent doctrine which James Mill worked so hard to promulgate and enforce. It may be as well briefly to rehearse its argument. So long as the public revenue of a country could be raised from the 'unearned increment' of rent, taxation had no effect on profits, wages or prices and hence in no way interfered with economic growth. In India there was every case, therefore, for sustaining a heavy land-revenue demand on the condition that it was kept within the limits prescribed by political economy. Now this might seem merely to be making a virtue of necessity, but the policy of siphoning off the 'agricultural surplus' for capital formation and development purposes by a high tax on rent (or net produce) has found much to commend it in the experience of Japan and the teaching of modern development economists.[4] Despite the doubts and qualifications contemporaries voiced over its theoretical and practical applicability to Indian

[3] R. M. Bird, Minute, 31 Jan. 1840, para. 15; N.W. Provinces Board of Revenue Proceedings, Range 222/68, 31 Jan. 1840.
[4] Cf. H. T. Oshima, 'Meiji Fiscal Policy and Agricultural Progress', in W. W. Lockwood (ed.), *The State and Economic Enterprise in Japan* (Princeton, 1965). Ursula Hicks, *Development from Below* (Oxford, 1961), p. 330. R. M. Bird, *Taxing Agricultural Land in Developing Countries* (Cambridge, Mass., 1974).

conditions, the rent doctrine was enshrined as the official theory of the land revenue and was never formally discarded. While James Mill's views on the desirability of absorbing the entire natural rental of the soil in taxation were never accepted, the land revenue was authoritatively stated to be a share of the rent. The proportion was steadily lowered, from nine-tenths (or more strictly ten-elevenths) in the first two decades of the nineteenth century, to two-thirds in 1833, half in 1855, and two-fifths in 1925; so that eventually even in the ryotwar provinces of Madras and Bombay it was deemed politic to disown the eminent domain of the State over the land and acknowledge that the Indian land revenue was simply a tax and not a form of rent.

Adherence to the rent doctrine was the product of official fiat from on high. James Mill's notion of absorbing the whole rent so as to prevent private rent property from emerging received little countenance, but the doctrine that the assessment must be fixed on the soil according to its differential fertility, and not levied on the particular crop as a share of the gross produce, ranged behind it the powerful interests of Lancashire, whose spokesmen made constant complaint that cotton cultivation was being unfairly taxed. Despatch after despatch issued from London in the 1820s and 1830s enforcing the correct assessment principle, eventually becoming so peremptory that Auckland's government in 1838 promised absolute and immediate compliance. The home authorities believed that henceforth they had a cast-iron defence against any charge that the heavy pitch of the assessment or the mode of assessment was damaging India's economic growth, and in evidence before the Commons committee on the growth of cotton in 1848 the East India Company's witnesses were able to silence their critics triumphantly by brandishing the rent doctrine. The laggard Madras government was brought sharply into line when it set about revising its ryotwar system in 1855, the proposal to base the demand on a proportion of the gross produce calling forth from London another authoritative lesson in political economy.[5]

Yet the gap between theory and practice in the land revenue system yawns so widely that – discounting the possibility of official hypocrisy – the impression of double-think and double-speak as a

[5] For a more extended account, see Stokes, *The English Utilitarians and India* (Oxford, 1959), pp. 81–139.

defining characteristic of the official mind of the time is power-fully reinforced. Even in the scattered attempts in the 1820s to calculate rent as the net produce (by measuring out-turn and costs of producion on different soils) the theoretical criterion was em-ployed as no more than a check on the assessment and a means of equalising its distribution. As James Mill was the first to acknow-ledge the overall revenue demand was fixed primarily on a settle-ment officer's judgement of what an area or village could reason-ably pay in the light of its past revenue history. In the revised systems of the 1830s in both Bombay and the N.W. Provinces the pragmatic method in fixing the assessment was still further strengthened, the element of greater scientific precision being reserved for the survey of the holdings area and the classification of soil qualities. In Bombay all attempt at proportioning the assess-ment to natural rent was explicitly abandoned; in the N.W. Provinces competition tenant-at-will payments were allowed only a minor role in the calculation of the so-called rental assets. Yet paradoxically George Wingate even more emphatically than James Thomason remained convinced of the correctness of the rent theory and of its applicability to the Indian land revenue.[6]

The discrepancy manifest on the practical side also obtruded in the realm of theory. In 1831, in the same year as James Mill, the Company's chief executive officer, was making his authorita-tive affirmation of the applicability of the Ricardian rent theory to India, Richard Jones published his *Essay on the Distribution of Wealth*. For his work on peasant rents Jones was appointed Malthus' successor as Professor of Political Economy at Hailey-bury in 1835. His ideas represented an important and disturbing challenge to the classical economic teaching. In the Ricardian formulation capital employed at the margin of cultivation merely returned the wages of labour and ordinary rate of profit; it was the differential increment earned by all other soils of superior fertility that constituted rent. Rent rose as poorer soils were brought into cultivation and was determined by the cost of pro-duction at the margin and not by competition. What regulated the position of the margin was the relative proportion between capital and population. Now Jones argued that this classical analysis had relevance only to a capitalist system of farming where labour, capital, and ownership of land had been separated out

[6] *Ibid.*, pp. 127–8.

as distinct factors and possessed complete mobility. Peasant rents were differently determined since there was no capitalist farmer intervening between the labourer and the landlord. In India the peasant was a subsistence farmer in the position of a labourer forced to raise his wages from the soil or starve. Where the State, by virtue of a high land-revenue demand, was in effect a universal landlord, or where population pressure created competition among ryots for land, the whole of the produce could be exacted as rent except for the ryot's bare subsistence. Under these conditions peasant agriculture was kept confined to the better soils and yielded negligible profits, the only source of capital accumulation and economic growth. As J. S. Mill later explained the contrast:

The effect, therefore of this [cottier] tenure is to bring the principle of population to act directly on the land, and not, as in England, on capital. Rent, in this state of things, depends on the proportion between population and land. As the land is a fixed quantity, while the population has an unlimited power of increase; unless something checks that increase, the competition for land soon forces up rent to the highest point, consistent with keeping the population alive. The effects, therefore, of cottier tenure depend on the extent to which the capacity of the population to increase is controlled, either by custom, by individual prudence, or by starvation and disease.[7]

Despite his recognition of the importance of Jones' theory of peasant rents J. S. Mill as late as 1858 (in his defence of the East India Company) could reiterate his father's argument that so long as the land revenue was kept within the limits of rent the economy was left unaffected:

Where the original right of the State to the land of the country has been reserved, and its natural, but no more than its natural, rent made available to meet the public expenditure, the people may be said to be so far untaxed: because the Government only takes from them as a tax, what they would have otherwise have paid as a rent to a private landlord. This proposition undoubtedly requires modification in the case of a ryot or peasant cultivating his own land; but even in his case, if the Government demand does not exceed the amount which the land could pay as rent if let to a solvent tenant (that is, the price of its peculiar advantages of fertility or situation), the Government only reserves to itself, instead of conceding to the

[7] J. S. Mill, *Principles of Political Economy*, 5th edn (London, 1862), i, p. 368.

cultivator, the profit of a kind of natural monopoly, leaving to him the same reward of his labour and capital which is obtained by the remainder of the industrious population. Any amount whatever of revenue, therefore, derived from the rent of land, cannot be regarded, generally speaking, as a burthen on the tax-paying community.[8]

Now it is true that whatever assessment was laid upon land under a system of cottier tenancy, all soils above the margin of cultivation would still theoretically yield a differential increment constituting a type of rent. But this would be far from a 'natural rent' if the assessment were excessive. Even if marginal land were zero-rated and the assessment was duly graduated to allow for soil and other advantages, rent measured from the margin would exceed 'natural rent' since marginal cultivation would yield only a bare subsistence return instead of 'normal' wages plus the ordinary rate of profit on capital. Equally, if competition rents were taken as the measure of 'natural rent' the result would be erroneous and excessive, unless the 'solvent tenant' spoken of by Mill were a capitalist farmer, a possibility he had ruled out by definition.

This ambiguity surrounding the concept of rent in peasant agriculture was reflected in the writings of lesser apologists of the Indian revenue system. John Thornton's celebrated account of the *mahalwar* system of the North-Western Provinces in the *Calcutta Review* of 1849 is typical. When the East India Company furnished information on the revenue system for the defence of its charter in 1853 Thornton's article was reprinted in the massive parliamentary blue-book devoted to the subject:

Those who assert that the cotton and sugar of India are kept out of European markets by the pressure of the land-tax must be entirely ignorant of the nature of that tax...It is acknowledged on all hands that rent, as generated and regulated in England produces no effect on the price of agricultural produce. That price is influenced from time to time by the demand as compared with the supply, but is determined in the long run by the expense of production on the worst soils; and it is the value of this produce thus fixed which enables the better soils to yield rent. It is the same in India; although it is true, as Professor Jones has shown, that the conditions attaching to the

[8] [J. S. Mill], *Memorandum of the Improvements in the Administration of India during the Last Thirty Years* (London, 1858), cited Stokes, *English Utilitarians*, pp. 136–7.

amount and origin of rent are not precisely the same here as in England. The only difference between the principles which regulate the price of raw produce in the two countries is this: in England, the average price must be such as to afford the usual wages to the labourer, and the usual profits of stock to the farmer, upon the least productive lands, which the wants of the nation require to be kept in cultivation. In India, the labourer and the farmer are generally the same individual; there is no fixed standard for the rate of wages or of profits; and the mass of the people, having no resource except agriculture, are more liable to undue exaction than elsewhere. Still the price of produce must at least be such as to enable the cultivator to subsist, and to replace the little capital necessary for his operations. In both countries there are lands which are barely fertile enough to fulfil these respective conditions. . .and such land can, therefore, yield little or no rent. In neither can the rent, which the superior fertility of other lands enables them to yield, in any way influence the price of produce, this having been already determined on other grounds.

Thornton omitted entirely to deal with the argument that 'undue exaction' by the State could lead to ryot rents in excess of the economic rent, thus affecting the cost of production and the selling price, and so checking output. He cheerfully concluded:

If, then, the fact of the payment of rent (it matters not whether to the Government or a private proprietor) can in no degree affect the price of raw produce, it is still more certain that the demand by the state of only a portion of the natural rent can exercise no such influence. It has been seen that the revenue is limited in the North-Western Provinces to about two-thirds of the gross rent, and that it is often much less.[9]

Jones' argument had been neatly shuffled off, the applicability of the classical rent theory to India tacitly assumed, and the claim boldly asserted that the land revenue demand fell under two-thirds of the economic rent.

The adoption of this posture was the more extraordinary in that – as Wingate and Goldsmid observed – the pragmatic element in fixing the revenue was dominant, and assessment practice of the North-Western Provinces differed little in this respect from the Bombay system in which all pretence at employing a theoretical criterion had been expressly abandoned. For the North-Western Provinces 'aggregate-to-detail' method started out by fixing a provisional revenue demand on a homogeneous tract as a whole.

[9] *Parliamentary Papers 1852–3*, lxxv, p. 484.

According to Thornton's account there were three ways of doing this. By far the most important was to review the tract's revenue history over the previous twenty years so that the settlement officer was able to judge within narrow limits what his future demand should be. The second way of arriving at an overall figure was to examine the revenue history of each constituent village, especially if the tract exhibited considerable internal variety in this respect. From what appeared to be on a comparative view a fair assessment for each village or 'estate' (*mahal*) an aggregate sum could be fixed for the tract as a whole. The third mode was 'by inquiring into the prevalent rates of rent, or into the rate at which the revenue falls on the particular villages known to be fairly assessed. These rates when applied to the pergunnah area will give a proximate rental or jumma for the whole'.[10] Having decided on an aggregate *jama* or revenue demand, the sum was then distributed over individual villages. The simplest method was to strike revenue rates for each main soil quality and see how these fell on each village. When, however, average rent rates had also been calculated and a pargana rental formed from them, the revenue rates would be framed in the same proportion as the pargana jama bore to the pargana rental. The use of rent rates was not indispensable, Thornton acknowledged, and chief reliance continued to be placed on the careful distribution of an overall sum that was determined on general considerations. Even then there was an ambiguity in employing the concept of rent against which Metcalfe had long ago inveighed: 'We make a jumble between revenue and rent, when the plain intelligible thing to be ascertained is the Government share of the produce.'[11] For the term 'gross rental assets' had long been used to denote the aggregate revenue payments of subordinate cultivators together with a proportionate addition for owner cultivation (*sir*). Such a meaning of rental assets was very different from the full letting value of the entire holdings areas as calculated from competition rates paid in the portion held by *pahi* and *ghair maurusi* (tenant-at-will) cultivators on annual agreements. Thornton rather hesitantly acknowledged that the most satisfactory method was to frame the assessment of an estate on 'the actual rents paid by the cultivators

---

[10] *Ibid.*, p. 364.
[11] C. T. Metcalfe, Minute, 7 Nov. 1830; *Selections from the Revenue Records N.W. Provinces 1822–1823* (Allahabad, 1872), p. 214.

to the proprietors, or at least. . .the rate at which these rents are calculated'. But even then the typicality of such rates would need to be tested against the average rates in the pargana to see whether the assessment fell too lightly or too heavily.

The problems in following out the official plan of settlement were to be seen in Agra where G. C. Mansel did his best to observe the board of revenue's injunctions. In the parliamentary blue-book of 1853 his settlement report was printed along with Edward Thornton's on Muzaffarnagar presumably in order to supply illustrations of the most approved practice. Mansel's first step was to decide straight away on a total demand for the district purely on general considerations of its recent revenue history; in fact he chose a mean figure mid-way between those of the two previous settlements, thus giving an overall reduction. In the Ferozebad pargana he made every effort to work the board's system of pargana rent assets and deduced revenue rates. Having marked off the pargana into four tracts (*chaks*) of differing degrees of productiveness, he drew out specimen rent rates for six soil qualities (further subdivided into irrigated and unirrigated) from an analysis of several estates in average and superior cultivation. In three chaks the revenue was simply deduced as two-thirds of the rent rates, and in the poorest chak at one half. Mansel was lucky to find that the jama obtained by these revenue rates apparently corresponded closely to those obtained by distributing his assumed demand. Yet it was evident that in the other parganas the method failed to work. Here meaningful average rent rates proved impossible to ascertain, so that he fell back on distributing the old demand as an acre rate on the cultivation of each village and comparing it with the acre rate of a test village known to be fairly assessed.

In Saharanpur Edward Thornton calculated rent rates for different soils by an elaborate conversion of grain payments, but he fixed the demand as an overall sum and 'deduced' his revenue rates from it irrespective of the rent rates, except to use the ratio they bore to one another on different soils to establish the corresponding ratio of the revenue rates. In Muzaffarnagar he was bolder and derived his revenue directly from ascertained average rent rates, simply by making a deduction of 35%. Yet the application of these rates was far from automatic, and the final demand on an estate was adjusted according to the percentage of highly

manured soil (*meesun*) and the extent of the cultivable waste.[12]
Edmondstone followed a largely similar procedure in Mainpuri,
first arriving at a pargana demand, deducing revenue rates from
it, and then comparing the results of the application of these rates
to those arrived at by ascertaining average rent rates and deducting 30% and 35% from them.[13] This was the most general and
approved method. Some settlement officers, like C. Allen in the
Jalesur pargana of Mathura (Muttra), were punctilious in observing the fiction of landlord and tenant, refusing to interfere in the
settlement of subordinate cultivators' payments.[14] Yet in an over-
assessed district like Kanpur (Cawnpore) the notion that the
cultivators' payments represented some sort of free will bargain
with the *malguzars* had 'not infrequently' to be jettisoned.
H. Rose found that even the lowest rent rates were often not
sufficiently moderate to allow him to deduce fair revenue rates
from them. In these cases he 'discarded the rent rates entirely,
and fixed my revenue rates with reference to those which had
been found applicable in similar divisions of this or neighbouring
districts'.[15] In Bareilly the young J. W. Muir found that rent rates
were 'only useful as a check on the general revenue rates [deduced
from a provisional aggregate demand], which from all the experience I have had I consider a much more safe and useful standard
for the purpose of assessment'.[16] From his study of the settlement
of a portion of Gorakhpur John Rosselli has concluded: 'The
impression is hard to resist that even so meticulous and hard-
driving an officer as Armstrong used rent theory language as a
conventional front while he used traditional rough and ready
means to get the work of settlement done.'[17]

---

[12] *Reports of the Revenue Settlement of the N.W. Provinces under Regulation IX, 1833* (Benares, 1862), i, pp. 67 ff, 126 ff.
[13] *Ibid.*, ii, pt 1 (Benares, 1863), pp. 110 ff.
[14] *Ibid.*, p. 85.
[15] *Ibid.*, p. 368.
[16] *Ibid.*, i, 575.
[17] John Rosselli, 'Theory and Practice in N. India', *Indian Economic and
Social History Review*, 8 (1971) pp. 141–2. It should be said that not
only was Gorakhpur untypical as a district, but that Armstrong's work
was carried out between 1829 and 1834 when the detailed methods of
Regulation VII, 1822, had become discredited and before the board's
circular orders prescribing the use of average or standard rent rates had
been promulgated in 1835. Other historians who have questioned the
influence of the rent theory on revenue policy and practice have confined
their attention to settlements carried out under Regulation VII, 1822,
rather than under Regulation IX, 1833; cf. Imtiaz Husain, *Land Revenue*

There was nothing new about calculating what the British called gross rent, and the board's system blended imperceptibly into older traditional practice. The tahsildar, the *kanungo* or the *peishkar* had always submitted their *douls, nikasis,* and *jamabandis* to estimate the gross receipts of the revenue-engagers (malguzars), and the method of using average village and pargana rent rates to frame these estimates was also well-established. What was new was the generalisation of rates over much larger groups of villages. The chief purpose of rent and revenue rates lay in achieving greater equality in the incidence of the demand for similarly-circumstanced villages rather than to found the assessment on novel theoretical principles. They also permitted a vast acceleration in settlement procedure compared with the old village-by-village settlement pursued before Regulation IX, 1833.

Yet the board of revenue were insistent that they had not reverted to haphazard conjecture for framing the assessment, and claimed instead to be more truly scientific than their predecessors who had favoured ascertaining rent by calculations of output and costs of production. The assessment procedure, they argued, in 1839, proceeded systematically: firstly, an accurate survey and classification; secondly, 'there is a rate of rent as carefully deduced and applied to the area as the nature of such an operation will admit'; thirdly, a classification of different villages formed on the ascertainment of the rates of rent and productive powers of each class; fourthly, a reference to past records and general information; fifthly, a deduction of rental and jama from the comparison of all these particulars; sixthly, a comparison of this jama with that hitherto demanded; and seventhly a distribution of the newly assessed jama in detail on each *mauza.* 'What the Board wish to establish is that it is not the mere ascertainment of insulated facts [*viz.* net produce calculations], however laboriously sought after, and accurately ascertained, that will give true

---

Policy in N. India – The Ceded and Conquered Provinces, 1801–33 (Calcutta and New Delhi, 1967), pp. 151 ff., 251 ff. A. Siddiqi 'Agrarian Depression in Uttar Pradesh, 1828–33', *I.E.S.H.R.*, 6 (1969), p. 177. A. Siddiqi, *Agrarian Change in a North Indian State* (Oxford, 1973), pp. 182 ff. The depreciation of the importance of the 'net produce' criterion can be carried too far. The board of revenue described it as 'one favourite method of proceeding under the former settlement [of Reg. VII, 1822]' *Circular Order by the Sudder Board of Revenue N.W. Provinces on the Subject of Settlements* (Calcutta, 1839), p. 28, para. iii (I.O.R., List 56(90)).

results; but these facts must be collated, and the conclusion tested on true statistic and economic principles before they can afford a safe guide to political arrangements.'[18] For all its readiness 'to force on notice the existing state of things, not to force the introduction of a new state', the official mind claimed all the lights of modern scientific method and principle for the revenue system. Simply because it was appreciated that modern economic theory could not be translated directly into practice we must not, therefore, conclude that ideology did not remain an important ingredient in official thinking.

The notion that tradition and modernity could be harmoniously blended was the leitmotif of James Thomason's political philosophy. He was the architect of the finished system of the northwest and gave it codified form in his *Directions for Revenue Officers*. Speaking at the opening of the Benares New College in 1853, Thomason pointed to the work of Principal Ballantyne in grafting English on to Hindu philosophy:

In following this course he acted in consonance with the whole character of our administration in this country. We have not swept over the country like a torrent, destroying all that it found, and leaving nothing but what itself deposited. Our course has rather been that of a gently swelling inundation, which leaves the former surface undisturbed and spreads over it a richer mould, from which the vegetation may derive a new verdure, and a landscape that was unknown before. Such has been our course in the Civil Administration. In our systems of Police, of Civil and Criminal Justice and of Revenue management, we first examined the existing systems, retained whatever of them we found to be right and just, and then engrafted on this basis new maxims derived from our Institutions. And thus we have succeeded in forming a system which is generally admitted to have been easy in its operation, and happy in its effect.[19]

This happy eclecticism extended to the theory of the revenue and involved an unconscious sleight of hand. In his authoritative *Directions for Settlement Officers* Thomason had stated that it was desirable that government should not demand more than two-thirds of the net produce. 'By net produce is meant the surplus which the estate may yield, after deducting the expenses of cultivation, including the profits of stock and wages of labour, and this, in an estate held entirely by cultivating proprietors will

[18] *Ibid.*, paras. 108–103.
[19] *Sels. Recs. Govt. N.W.P.*, 2nd ser. i, pt i (1868).

be the profit on their seer cultivation, but in an estate held by a non-cultivating proprietor, and leased out to cultivators of asamees, paying at a known rate, will be the gross rental' (para 52). Having thus defined the net produce or rent in terms of the classical rent theory he had without *arrière pensée* equated it with the aggregate of actual cultivators' payments. In para. 73 he further shifted or widened the definition: 'The value assumed at average rent rates is what has been called net produce in para. 52, and is the amount the estate is supposed to yield to the owner. The value assumed at deduced revenue rates. . .is the portion of the above net produce which the Government is entitled to claim, and should be formed by deducting one third from the total.' From actual receipts Thomason had proceeded to rental or letting value using average rates, a shift that could imply the potential value of the land according to competition tenant-at-will rates. To crown his eclecticism, in the prefatory *Directions for Revenue Officers* (August, 1849) Thomason adopted Jones' definition of rent and explicitly referred to his authority: 'By net produce or rent is meant the ryot or produce rent, paid by labourers, raising their wages from the soil.'[20]

Thomason's subtle and careful mind was able to commute easily between the world of Western legal categories and the complex polymorphic structures of Indian agrarian society. But the act of translation implied a surgical violence of which Thomason was unaware or accepted with a clinical fatalism. One of the chief features of the mouzawar or more strictly mahalwar system of the North-Western Provinces, he claimed, was that 'it professes to alter nothing, but only to maintain and place on record what it finds to exist'. Yet from the very act of definition sprang the feature of the system which he acknowledged that the people least understood, and yet was essential to the attainment of the objects contemplated by the system. This was the compulsory alienation of landed property in satisfaction of private debt under a civil court decree or in liquidation of the land-revenue demand. 'Abstractedly considered, this is the just and necessary result of the definite property in land which is created by the system, but it is a process unknown to the Native Governments from the very absence of the recognition of all fixed rights.'[21]

20 *P.P. 1852–3*, lxxv, p. 5.
21 *Ibid.*, p. 9.

When talking of 'property' Thomason was employing the conventional double-speak of British legal and administrative terminology in conflating the revenue-engagement right or malguzari title with physical dominion over the land and its cultivators. Up until the Mutiny, however, the legal connotation of 'landlord' had effective reference only to the first of these attributes. Even so, transfers of the malguzari title caused mounting concern. Before Thomason became Lieutenant-Governor in 1843 the administration had shown little hesitation in bringing titles to public sale for revenue arrears despite all the official lamentations over sales ever since the early decades. The sale process was resorted to for the purpose not merely of bringing the *taluqs* of Etawah and elsewhere tumbling down but was also regarded as a healthy discipline for improving village communities. In Aligarh district between 1839 and 1848 title to some 95,000 acres was transferred by compulsory revenue process, more than a tenth of the cultivated area.[22] Thomason sought to moderate and assuage the harsher aspects of change, multiplying directives to minimise compulsory transfer and the legal dissolution of joint responsibility among village coparceners. But the problem was soon outstripped by the far greater volume of transfers created by mortgage foreclosure and decrees for the satisfaction of private debt. In 1854 the board of revenue commented: 'In no country in the world probably do landed tenures so certainly, constantly and extensively change hands. These mutations are effecting a rapid and complete revolution in the position of the ancient proprietors of the soil.'[23] Over this issue the British administration was to remain hopelessly divided and no remedial action was taken. In 1850 John Thornton, as revenue secretary, boasted of the advantage which the North-Western Provinces enjoyed over the Bombay ryotwar system in that it allowed 'the formation of large landed properties, the intermixture of which with smaller holdings is considered to be most desirable by the staunchest advocates of peasant proprietorship. . .In these provinces when a man has gained a few thousand rupees by trade or otherwise, he can easily lay it out in the purchase of entire villages, or of large shares of contiguous estates, and this is the mode in which much of the accumulated

22 E. A. Atkinson, *Gazetteer N.W.P.*, ii (Allahabad, 1875), p. 466.
23 *Report by Sudder Board of Revenue on Revenue Administration of N.W.P. 1852–53* (Agra, 1854) (I.O.R. L5.V. pt 1), para. 14, p. 5.

capital of the country is annually invested.'[24] The formal inquiries made to collectors in 1854 concerning the extent of transfer to non-agricultural classes revealed apprehension about the strengthening grip of the moneylender, but faith in freedom of contract burned too strongly for any substantial body of opinion to emerge in favour of restricting the power of alienation. Renewed inquiries in 1859 after the Mutiny upheaval produced no different result.[25] It was recognised that to speak of land changing hands was largely a fiction and that transfer of title simply stripped the owner of his revenue-collecting rights over subordinate cultivators and left him in cultivating occupancy of his former home-farm or *sir*. The danger was that an increasing body of agricultural proprietors would be reduced to a condition of tenancy in subordination to men of capital. Yet this was regarded as no unmixed evil. The famine of 1860–1 demonstrated, according to Baird Smith, the importance of the insurance provided by a vast mass of valuable and freely convertible proprietary titles.[26] His prescription of a permanent settlement to raise property values still higher found an answering echo in a wide range of administrative opinion which felt that after so much turmoil the land needed rest. A tax which fell as a minimum at half the rental assets, and pressed on a single section of the community, could not be permitted to increase, urged Baird Smith. There was every prospect that with a permanent settlement land would rise from its average level in 1861 of four to five years purchase of the government revenue to something like ten or twelve times that standard. Capital would then accumulate in the hands of the agricultural classes instead of merely in those of the moneylending and commercial classes.

The strains inherent in revenue policy were contained during the pre-Mutiny period. That was because no single one threatened to burst through the system's integument. The formal legal structure ran far ahead of reality, and fundamental change came slow and late. It was once supposed that Bentinck's administrative and revenue reforms ended the long era of fumbling experiment and ushered in a period of rapid and continuous progress. It is now clear that it was not until the end of the

24 *P.P. 1852–3*, lxxv, p. 442.
25 'Inquiry into the Frequency of Transfer of Proprietary Titles', *Sels. Recs. Govt. N.W.P.*, iv (Agra, 1854). 'Correspondence Regarding the Law of Land Sale', *Sels. Recs. Govt. India*, no. clv (Calcutta, 1879).
26 R. Baird Smith, Report on Famine of 1860–1 in the N.W.P., *P.P. 1862*, xl.

1840s, when recurrent famine and severe revenue pressure were put behind, that progress became at all rapid and visible. From 1849 grain prices after oscillating since 1820 around a stationary mean at length assumed a pronounced and sustained upward trend.[27] Land values, or rather the values of malguzari titles, which were reckoned at no more than one and a third years' purchase of the revenue as late as 1837, had risen to three and a half years by 1848, and some five by 1861. Expansion of the cultivated area at last leapt ahead.[28] In view of the relative lateness of these developments administrative attention could remain almost exclusively centred on proprietary (or malguzari) rights, on the relative claims of taluqdars and village *pattidars*, and on the problems of undue transfer to non-agriculturalists. The underlying base made up of the mass of cultivating holders was not called into question. According to formal law the malguzar was a landlord drawing rents from his tenants. In practice he was more often than not a superior village agriculturalist in receipt of customary revenue payments from the other cultivators, the balance of which he used to reduce or eliminate the revenue demand on his own cultivating holding. R. M. Bird had sought in 1832 to give legal fixity to cultivators' payments for the term of settlement, but this had been rejected by Bentinck and his councillors on grounds of the impropriety of interfering between landlord and tenant. Yet the settlement record comprised in the jamabandi and reinforced by the weight of custom proved sufficient to secure the objects for which Bird had contended.[29]

It was in this way that so many of the crucial issues of principle had been kept happily suppressed. Thomason's codes sought to express the truth that assessment and tenurial practice were imperfect approximations to an ideal type which might one day be realised when custom had given way to contract as the basis of society. The first decisive shock which exposed the contradictions

[27] For histogram of Farrukhabad grain prices, and price graph of Bareilly, Agra, Ghaziabad, and Allahabad markets, *Permanent and Temporary Settlements N.W.P.* (Allahabad, 1872), pp. 64a–65a, 144a–145a.

[28] For Bombay see below, note 48. N.W.P. figures for the expansion of cultivation are much more approximate, cf. Auckland Colvin, *Memorandum on the Revision of Land Revenue Settlements in N.W.P.* (Calcutta, 1872), Appx iii.

[29] Colvin, *op. cit.*, p. 90. An account of R. M. Bird's attempt in 1832 to secure fixing of cultivators' rents by law is given in Imtiaz Husain, *Land Revenue Policy*, pp. 197 ff.

of the Thomasonian compromise came not so much from the Mutiny and the temporary pro-aristocratic reaction that followed as from the great price rise of the later 1860s. The latter threw official policy into sharp reverse over the idea of a permanent settlement which had only a few years previously found acceptance in the highest quarters. Robert Knight's campaign in *The Indian Economist* against the wanton sacrifice of the just rights of the State in the revised settlements of the North-Western Provinces came at a time when the post-Mutiny financial crisis was biting hardest. The upshot was a major review by Auckland Colvin, the revenue secretary of the North-Western Provinces, into the whole question of permanent and temporary settlements and into the *raison d'être* of the revised settlements. The documents which he assembled in two substantial memoranda of 1870 and 1872 constituted a rigorous post-mortem on the first age of modernisation.[30]

It was Colvin's object to steer a course between the still powerful advocate of a permanent settlement and the even more vociferous Knight school behind which the government of India, and notably Sir John Strachey, had largely ranged themselves. In doing so he sought to reaffirm the validity of the rent theory and yet demonstrate that it could not be allowed to operate freely in practice. The statistics which he collated from the results of the revised settlements available to him brought out three salient facts: a massive expansion of the cultivated area of some 31% during the previous thirty to thirty-five years; a rapid but recent rise in agricultural prices; and conversely a remarkable sluggishness in the movement of 'rents'. It was the last feature which attracted most attention. Le Poer Wynne, who had carried out the revised settlement of Saharanpur, struck out in the pages of the *Calcutta Review* (No. ci (1870)) in defence of the principle of a permanent settlement. To do so it seemed necessary to refute the applicability of classical rent theory, and it was to Richard Jones' authority that he naturally turned. If rents in India, argued Wynne, had followed the classical model they would have risen with the advance of the margin of cultivation. The stagnation of rents in these circumstances was a demonstration that they were

---

[30] Colvin, *Memo*, and also *Perm. and Temp. Settls.* (Allahabad, 1873). For another minute by Colvin refuting Strachey's criticism, *Sels. Recs. Govt. N.W.P.*, 2nd ser., iv, no. 3 (Allahabad, 1871), pp. 294 ff.

regulated by the ratio of population to land and not by differential productivity produced by irrigation on better lands or by the extension of cultivation into poorer soils, or even by the rise of prices of agricultural produce. This conviction that classical rent theory had failed to operate found support among a large number of revenue officials. Commenting on the total failure of rent-rates to increase in the Serouli pargana despite a 44% increase in prices and a 47% increase in cultivation, the settlement officer of Bareilly wrote:

I expressly defend myself from political economists by stating that I allow that rents on the old lands ought to have risen largely; but there are no hulkabundee schools, and the Thakoor Zemindars and Brahmin cultivators have not yet studied Ricardo and Mill. I can only take facts as they are, and leave to others the consideration of what ought to have taken place, but didn't.[31]

Yet most officials were much more impressed by the validity of what was in effect Jones' theory of ryot rents than his analysis of cottier tenures. So-called rents, they found, followed rather than determined the revenue demand. A. B. Patterson in Fatehpur wrote in January 1872 that 'the standard of rent in every district during the 30 years of settlement was chiefly determined by the severity or lightness of the revenue and to comparatively small extent by the productive powers of the land'. In Aligarh, W. H. Smith reported that 'up to this time revenue has had more to do with rent than anything else; in other words heavy revenue means high rents, and vice versa, light revenue is generally accompanied with low rents. . .settlement proceedings seem to me to give the impetus to the general rise'. W. S. Halsey, the Collector of Kanpur, emphasised likewise that 'the rent rates per se have no connection with, or bear any proportion to the produce of the land; that they are the result of the Government demand. . .The whole ability and energy of the settlement staff was engrossed in ascertaining what they called rent-rates, but what I call contribution rates; and it is only now, when we find the whole district so rack-rented – the people cannot be worse off – that we discover the land revenue so far from being the rental of the Government property is a forced contribution from the occupant thereof.'[32]

[31] Cited Colvin, *Memo*, p. 121.
[32] *Perm. and Temp. Settls.*, pp. 49a, 72a, 198a.

This was to concede handsomely Richard Jones' central argument: 'The existence and progress of rents under the ryot system', Jones had said, 'is in no degree dependent upon the existence of different qualities of soil, or different returns to the stock and labour employed on each.' Given the monopoly over 'the machinery of the earth' the sovereign could determine the share of the produce to be left to the ryot at his own discretion. Yet the constant tendency to take an excessive share impoverished the ryot and injured the sources of all agricultural improvement and growth.[33]

Here was a powerful argument that reversed the notion that the immediate cultivator's payments increasingly represented the 'natural rent' and could be used as an objective criterion from which to frame the government demand. It totally contradicted John Thornton's claim, made in 1849, when he was attempting to refute Jones, that in the non-ryotwar areas 'the amount of rent paid by the actual cultivators, when not limited by special circumstances, is regulated by natural causes, with which the revenue paid to the state has no connexion'.[34] If in fact revenue rates determined the rent rates levied by the 'landlord' on the cultivator, then to the school advocating a permanent settlement the one hope for agricultural improvement lay in lightening the state demand on the landlord.

These views went too far for Colvin but he was prepared to acknowledge that 'what we now know as rents. . .were as a rule the old revenue rates formerly used as the basis of the Government assessment, but made over from henceforth to the men on whom we have conferred proprietary rights. These men received them in great measure stereotyped as revenue rates, by custom, and the idea of flexible competition rents was as unfamiliar to them as to those whom we declared their tenants.'[35] The reason why in most cases rent rates had not kept pace with the increase in prices, cultivation, and irrigation lay in the strength of custom and in the understanding, formalised in the jamabandi statement for each village, that the cultivator's 'tenant' payments would remain undisturbed with the proprietor's revenue payments for

[33] Richard Jones, *An Essay on the Distribution of Wealth* (London, 1831), p. 140.
[34] J. Thornton, 'The Settlement of the N.W. Provinces', *Calcutta Review* (1849), cited *P.P. 1852–3*, lxxv, p. 484.
[35] Colvin, *Memo*, p. 109.

the whole twenty- or thirty-year term of the settlement. Only for 'tenant-at-will' (pahi and ghair maurusi) cultivators had rents been readily enhanced, but their rising level was threatening to dissolve the customary nature of all other rents. Whatever the truth of Jones' theories it was wrong to suppose that according to them the progress of peasant rents was unaffected by the classical stimuli of increased prices and greater differential productivity. 'Men under peasant tenures having nothing else to live on, must live on the land, and must pay for it. But it does not follow that what they pay bears at no period any proportion to the quality of the land and is regulated solely by their numbers.'[36] Colvin's practical conclusion was that it was right and appropriate for the State to take a fair share of the increased rental value of the soil and not commit itself to a permanent assessment. At the same time it was evident that revenue could not be raised proportionately to the enhanced value of the produce, as Knight had maintained, lest 'in attempting to raise the land revenue, we may find ourselves raising the people'.[37] How was rental value to be adjudged for assessment purposes? Was it the valuation obtained by the competition rate levied on low caste tenants-at-will or *shikmi* tenants working a proprietor's home farm? This was the extreme logic of the classical rent theory which equated free contract rents with 'true' or 'natural' rents. Colvin accepted that once the cake of custom had been broken through rents could rise as a result of the two causes postulated by Jones – an increase in produce or its value, or an increase in the ratio of the produce taken by the landlord. Only the former was a legitimate source of an enhanced revenue demand, but there was no practical way of distinguishing the first cause of increase from the second.[38] There could be no going back to the former methods practised under Regulation VII, 1822, of 'wide and minute enquiries as to the out-turn of produce, and the cost, or profits, of production'. 'The experience gained by the assessing officer must guide him as to what are *true* rents' and the test must be empirical: 'the rents selected must be representative rents; not necessarily the average rents at present existing; but those which there are sufficient grounds for believing represent the average to which on the settle-

---

[36] Colvin, Note, *Perm. and Temp. Settls.*, p. 14b.
[37] Colvin, *Memo*, pp. 130–1.
[38] Colvin, Note, *Perm. and Temp. Settls.*, p. 15b.

ment being declared, the rents generally will be raised.'[39] Colvin clung to the notion that a legitimate and objective criterion could still be found in 'the existence of a great mass of recognised and unquestioned rents'.

Charles Elliott in Farrukhabad hungered equally for such an objective criterion. 'What a Settlement Officer wants is a real guide or check, independent of his preconceived ideas – a result which he cannot manipulate or tamper with, but which is worked out, as it were by machinery, and is uninfluenced by his consciousness.' Yet he had to confess that 'my soil-rates were not independent guides like these, but the reflex of my own preconceived views; they were an oracle given out by a priestess whose strings I pulled'.[40] Indeed while viewing rent-rates as objective criteria Colvin himself was the first to insist that they could not be left to find their own level. Once the hold of custom was gone the cottier principle would be brought into unimpeded play. Competition rents had already eroded the customary base and British legislation (Act X, 1859, in particular) was now introducing a modern landlord-tenant relationship into almost all cultivator payments. J. S. Mill in his *Principles of Political Economy* was quite clear on the necessary interposition of the State. 'Rent paid by a capitalist who farms for profit, and not for bread, may safely be abandoned to competition; rent paid by labourers cannot... Peasant rents ought never to be arbitrary, never at the discretion of the landlord: either by custom or law it is imperatively necessary that they should be fixed.'[41] There was no need to revert to Mill's authority. R. M. Bird had stated the case in 1832 for the settlement officer to fix all rents for the term of settlement, and Colvin proposed to revive his plan. Bird had proposed to exclude tenant-at-will rents from protection but to put a ring of steel around all others. Colvin was silent on this point, but others were not. Charles Elliott in Hoshangabad in 1866 had recognised all cultivators as occupancy tenants, and in the wake of the 1877–8 Famine he and Edward Buck proposed making this a general rule throughout the North-Western Provinces. By so doing, as C. P. Carmichael pointed out, the one independent criterion of assessment, the tenant-at-will competition rent, would have been

---

[39] Colvin, *Memo*, p. 60.
[40] Cited Colvin, *Memo*, p. 33.
[41] Mill, *Principles of Political Economy*, p. 403.

abolished and a ryotwar settlement implemented. Buck openly
avowed the latter as his aim.[42]

What this elaborate post-mortem on 'the first age of modernisation' reveals is that the position over the classical rent theory had
been altered profoundly. In the 1830s the rent theory could be
readily accepted as an explanation of the land revenue because its
realisation remained a distant ideal like Macaulay's and Trevel-
yan's political liberalism. By the 1860s and 1870s the technique
of soil classification and survey and above all the movement of
tenant-at-will rents made possible an assessment framed much
more strictly on ascertained rental assets; yet the applicability of
the classical rent theory was called much more gravely into question. Colvin warned that its enforcement threatened an agrarian
explosion. But there were also theoretical objections. Jones' teaching as manifested in Mill's *Principles*, had made competition rents
suspect as a measure of 'natural' rent. Still more did the analysis
of cottier and ryot rents challenge the landlord-tenant assumptions on which the North-Western Provinces administration had
elected to build a form of peasant capitalism. That did not mean
that rent theory was abandoned. Its hold among a generation
much more deeply versed in political economy had become more
powerful than ever, but it was Jones' influence, reinforced by
J. S. Mill's authority, that was now paramount.

The classical theory had been introduced into the North-
Western Provinces in a confused form. The decision to collect the
land revenue through an intermediary class had been taken
almost at the outset of British administration, and although
Hastings in 1815 had reaffirmed the superior claims of the village
zamindars, the decision inevitably introduced the form if not the
immediate substance of landlordism. Even rent theorists like Holt
Mackenzie had approved of the measure on the grounds that the
private rent property resulting from the limitation of the government demand should not be frittered away among a mass of needy
cultivators.[43] Later administrators, as we have seen, argued the
desirability of stimulating peasant capitalism by interlacing it
with larger 'properties' and encouraging the injection of capital
from the urban trading classes. Inevitably this school, represented

[42] Report of Famine Commission, Appx 1, *P.P. 1881*, lxxi, pt i, pp. 493, 503.
[43] Holt Mackenzie, Memo, 19 Oct. 1826, paras. 509–11; *Sels. Rev. Recs.
N.W.P. 1822–1833*. Also Stokes, *English Utilitarians and India*, pp. 112–
13.

by John Thornton and others, looked to consolidating proprietary rather than tenant right. All this departed from James Mill's formula of absorbing the entire natural rent as revenue and so preventing the emergence of private rent property completely. Even so, before Act X of 1859 the demand of the 'landlord' on the 'tenant' was limited by the settlement record. The one contract payment, the tenant-at-will rate, acquired, as a result, a sacrocanct status equating it with the 'true rent'. 'I think no one will presume to question the maxim', C. P. Carmichael could write by 1879, 'that the rack rent of the day is the one perfect standard by which all other rents should be adjusted.'[44]

This complication was absent in the Bombay Deccan where the State remained theoretically the universal landlord and all attempts to discover 'true rent' (other than occasional tests of out-turn and costs of production) had been abandoned. Yet when the question of a permanent redemption of the land revenue was referred to Sir George Wingate, he took the opportunity in 1868 of issuing the most fulsome *confessio fidei* in the validity of the classical rent theory and cited J. S. Mill at length on the suitability of rent as a source of taxation.[45] Despite the lack of any practical measuring rod Wingate claimed that his assessment remained a share of natural rent. Unlike his predecessor, Keith Pringle, he had aimed at securing an equal return to the cultivator irrespective of soil qualities rather than relinquish to him a private rent that varied according to the productivity of the soil he happened to cultivate. The need to revise the thirty-year Deccan settlement on its expiry in the mid 1860s brought up the absence of any theoretical criterion of assessment anew. To raise the revenue demand in line with the increase in prices meant enhancements of such magnitude that the Bombay government felt constrained to order reductions. Even so, Auckland Colvin was staggered at the results, which gave, for example, a 199% increase in the Bhimthari taluka over the first decade of the old settlement and an immediate increase over the last year of settlement of 68%.[46] Although the Bombay government rejected his criticism Colvin found, as a member of the Deccan Riots Enquiry Commission in 1876, that such large revised settlements could not be absolved

[44] *P.P. 1881*, lxxi, pt 1, p. 503.
[45] Cited Stokes, *English Utilitarians*, pp. 136–7.
[46] Auckland Colvin, Report of Deccan Riots Commission, *P.P. 1878*, lviii, pp. 392–3.

from blame in creating the predisposing conditions for agrarian unrest. Colvin's views found support from one of the ablest of the senior Bombay officials, W. G. Pedder. Like Colvin he clung to the fundamental verities of the classical rent theory and its corrollary, opposition to a permanent settlement. It was 'essential for the good financial administration of India that the State revenue shall rise in proportion to the natural "unearned increment" of rent which occurs in all progressive states'. At the same time in order to defend the doctrine and moderate the demand on the peasant, Pedder shifted the definition of rent in line with the argument of Jones and Mill on cottier tenures. Pedder accepted that 'the rents paid by peasants cultivating for subsistence, as in India, are regulated quite differently from rents paid by capitalist farmers cultivating for profit as in England. . .what regulates the capitalist farmer's rent is the ordinary rate of profit; what regulates the peasant cultivator's rent (not being a customary but a competition rent) is the ordinary cost of his subsistence – in other words, his "ordinary standard of comfort"; and the means of at least supplying him with a subsistence of the ordinary standard of comfort is what Wingate's principle of assessment leaves him.' The success of Wingate's work was to be seen, claimed Pedder, in the fact that cultivation had expanded ahead of population and revenue; 'each cultivator must, therefore, have a larger quantity of produce'.[47]

Here was a novel twist. In combating the proposition that the government demand should rise in line with prices, Pedder claimed that the rise in rental assets had been correspondingly less because of the enhancement of the subsistence wage of the cultivator. His conclusion was that the assessment should be pitched so as to leave the largest share of rent with the cultivator as was consistent with the latter retaining it and not allowing it to pass into the hands of a rack-renting private landlord. This was the same argument that had been advanced by Elliott and Buck in the North-Western Provinces for giving all cultivators occupancy rights and abolishing the tenant-at-will. So far from even the peasant landlord being looked upon favourably as a petty rural capitalist and the hope of agricultural growth he now stood condemned. For when the land was worked under him by men with no better status than tenants-at-will, it was subjected in practice to

[47] *Ibid.*, pp. 373–5.

an exhausting agriculture by cultivators living from hand to mouth without resources to invest in improvement or to withstand famine. James Mill's contention that as the one source of capital accumulation the immediate cultivator should be protected by having the demand fixed upon him, was now reinforced by all that Jones and sober experience had taught.

By the 1870s the British knew that they stood at a great divide in their administration of the peasant. Looking back it was evident that the revenue systems set up by Wingate and Bird had been accompanied by a remarkable expansion of the cultivated area but this had left only the smallest margin of arable waste remaining. In the Bombay Deccan in 1838 50% of arable land was reckoned to be waste; in 1871 only 1%. Population increased during the thirty-year settlement by $39\frac{1}{2}$%. In 1838 land was unsaleable; by the end of the settlement it was fetching from 10 to 52 times its assessment.[48] Yet this achievement had come late, and was principally to be dated from 1850. Before then in both Bombay and the North-Western Provinces there had often been heavy balances in arrears. Colvin noted that the assessments made under Regulation IX, 1833, broke down in the whole or parts of 14 districts in the North-Western Provinces. The vast progress that Strachey and others had seen as flowing directly from the Regulation IX settlements was *post hoc, propter hoc.* 'It owed its existence to the margin of culturable land, and not to the tender mercies of a 60 per cent settlement.'[49] It had also been accompanied in the North by a huge volume of transfers of proprietary title and an ominous increase in rural indebtedness. The plight of the Deccan peasant in the latter respect was duly highlighted by all those who feared that this would prove the Achilles heel of British endeavour, and doubtless they exaggerated the portents of the trifling disturbances of 1875 to try to secure direct state intervention to check the evil.[50] The one tangible achievement was the rise in the living standard, and this was an achievement incapable of measurement and readily disputed. Pedder was certain of the rise in the Bombay presidency. District

---

[48] Resolution of Govt. of Bombay, 30 Aug. 1875, cited 'Correspondence re Law of Land Sale', *Sels. Recs. Govt. India*, no. clv (Calcutta, 1879), p. 429.
[49] Colvin, Memo on Revision of Settlement, *Sels. Recs. Govt. N.W.P.*, 2nd ser., iv, no. 3 (Allahabad, 1871), p. 309.
[50] Neil Charlesworth, 'The Myth of the Deccan Riots of 1875', *Modern Asian Studies*, 6 (1972), pp. 401–21, esp. pp. 417 ff.

officials in the western portion of the North-Western Provinces also commented upon it. In Etah it was a 'standing joke now among the better classes to say that the labourer has got as much jewellery as the farmer'.[51] In 1872 S. M. Moens was likewise impressed by the immense improvement in living standards in Bareilly over the past thirty or forty years. Then the cultivator lived in abject poverty; metal cooking utensils had been rare, clothes scanty. Now every man had a good stock, food was more abundant and of good quality, and many kept travelling carts. From Kanpur eastwards the reports were far less optimistic, and H. S. Reid, one of the closest observers of peasant life, said he could discern no improvement in a densely-settled district like Azamgarh. Yet even Moens was impressed by the precariousness of the enhanced living standards. For the mass of cultivators he believed had been reduced to the status of métayers or crop sharers who borrowed their seed grain; only one-third, he estimated, were independent while the rest lived from hand to mouth. 'A considerable portion of the rent fund is thus intercepted by the mahajun with his tremendous rates of interest. The cost of cultivation is increased, and less is available for rent.' In his Jonesian definition he anticipated Pedder in the Deccan. 'We have not yet come to pure competition rents, and the ultimate limit of rent is the surplus of the produce of the land after the deduction of such wages as will maintain the labourer in the standard of comfort which has become habitual to his class.[52] But since the costs of cultivation had risen by the increase in the standard of comfort and by the increased amount paid in interest (owing to the price rise), cultivators' rents could not keep pace with prices, and the assessment had to be moderated accordingly.

This concern for the defence of the living standard won in the period of rapid expansion of cultivation became a dominant note. Charles Elliott believed that his investigation into twenty sample villages in Farrukhabad district showed conclusively the falsity of the claim that the cultivator would flourish equally as well without as with legal protection. Not only had the occupancy (maurusi) tenant survived on the land where his unprotected tenant-at-will (ghair maurusi) brother or heir had been swept off, but he was 50% better off in cattle, clothing, and possessions.

[51] R. T. Hobart, cited *Perm. and Temp. Settls.*, p. 128a.
[52] S. M. Moens, in *ibid.*, p. 175a.

If these facts become generally known it will hardly be possible in future for any one to declare that the theories of political economy – so far as they bear on the advantages to the people of the *petite culture* – look very well on paper, but do not bear the test of actual experiment. Here, as with all true theories, the logic of facts agrees with the logic of the closet.[53]

Not everyone among the British officials by any means agreed with Elliott and Buck. Reid in Azamgarh felt the village proprietors' interests deserved attention. Their growing numbers pressed them nearer the soil but they found themselves unable to gain possession of land on which occupancy rights had become established, and had to take up land as tenants-at-will in other villages. It was not until 1926 that tenancy-at-will was finally ended, but the Famine Commission Report of 1880–1 was sufficiently influenced by the body of opinion represented by Elliott (who drafted the report) for tenant right from henceforth to be steadily buttressed and the tenant transformed into a subproprietor.

The first age of modernisation gave to northern and western India the rent theory and a settlement system purporting to give it embodiment. These foundations stood firm during the remainder of the nineteenth century. What changed were the objects they were expected to achieve. James Mill had seen the land revenue as the grand means of exempting India from taxation and so promoting maximum economic growth; hence he had stood for a high proportion of natural rent to be taken as revenue. The cultivator was to be left with no portion of the natural rent, since the normal rate of profit on his stock would be a sufficient motive for capital accumulation. Private rent property merely led to parasitism and idle consumption rather than capital saving. Jones' theory of peasant rents did not displace the overall classical rent theory. Colvin and Pedder like Thomason and Wingate before them still adhered to the advantages of a substantial portion of the natural rent being taken as revenue. But progress was now to be measured from the peasant wage which it was only possible to raise by according him a greater portion of rent as Jones had defined it, and recommended.[54] Hence the proportion

[53] C A. Elliott in *Sels. Recs. Govt. N.W.P.*, 2nd ser., ii, no. 4 (Allahabad, 1869), p. 417.
[54] Jones' view was that the only way to raise production under peasant tenures was to lower rents and he criticised the Indian authorities for not

to be taken as revenue had to be lowered and the immediate cultivator allowed to become a sub-proprietor. Although Jones had urged that to lower the rent ratio was in the end to raise rents because of the increased production so stimulated, the new mood looked to other sources than the land for much of the state revenue. The hopes for peasant capitalism withered – except perhaps in exceptional areas like the Punjab, Gujarat and the deltaic areas of Madras – and the sheer survival of the ordinary cultivator in face of the scourge of debt, disease, and famine became the uppermost concern. The rent doctrine as James Mill had expounded it no longer held the high ground of policy. There remained a generation of administrators who were still its convinced adherents in its altered and chastened form, and they worked to perfect the work of their predecessors. But when the next round of settlement revision came in the 1890s and early 1900s their voices were to be drowned by R. C. Dutt and the Congress. Significantly it was Curzon who wrote the epitaph of the rent doctrine in what was intended as its grand defence in his polemical *Land Revenue Policy of the Indian Government* (1902). If internal capital formation was to be accomplished by the State, politics ensured that it would not come from the land.

An older and wiser man had detected the spell of abstract economic doctrine over the administrative mind and foreseen its ultimate demise. In 1875, from the detached heights of the India Office, Salisbury penned one of his characteristic *fin de siècle* minutes in connection with the prolonged revision of the Madras ryotwar system:

the essential point is that the language used should be understood by those to whom it is addressed. Now it is our function to address Indian officials – and speaking of the generation now coming into office – their vocabulary is derived with more or less fidelity from the writings of political economists. To the modern Indian statesman the refined distinctions of the economical school are a solid living reality, from which he can as little separate his thoughts as from his

---

doing so: 'when once either the exactions of landlords, or of the state, or indeed any other circumstances, have reduced a peasant tenantry to penury, the same difficulty constantly opposes itself to the commencement of improvement. No one is willing to make, no one ordinarily thinks of making, a direct sacrifice of revenue, for the purpose of augmenting their actual means; and nothing short of that will enable them to start.'; Jones, *Essay on the Distribution of Wealth*, p. 174.

mother tongue. To us it may seem indifferent whether we call a payment revenue or rent, so we get the money; but it is not indifferent
by what name we call it in his hearing. If we say that it is rent, he
will hold the Government in strictness entitled to all that remains
after wages and profits have been paid...If we persuade him that it
is revenue, he will note the vast disproportion of its incidence compared to that of other taxes...I prefer the latter tendency to the
former. So far as it is possible to change the Indian system, it is
desirable that the cultivator should pay a smaller proportion of the
whole national charge. It is not in itself a thrifty policy to draw the
mass of revenue from the rural districts, where capital is scarce,
sparing the towns, where it is often redundant and runs to waste in
luxury...As India must be bled the lancet should be directed to the
parts where the blood is congested, or at least sufficient, and not to
those which are already feeble from the want of it...At the same
time I think we may fairly discourage any scientific refinements in
the work of assessment, which are a natural exercise of the intellect
in highly cultivated officers, but which worry the ryot, distribute the
burden of the State with needless inequality, and impose a costly
machinery on the State.[55]

A century later the land-revenue systems still stand as the
ruined works of time, cumbering the ground but with their
strength clean departed. Doubtless Salisbury as a broad-acred
man might have viewed the outcome with a wry satisfaction.
But the development economists are beginning to have other
ideas.[56] Time's whirligig may yet bring back the first age of
modernisation to favour and rescue for a while the obscure and
rebarbative labours of early settlement officers from death's date-
less night.

[55] Lord Salisbury, Minute, 20 April 1875; *P.P. 1881*, lxxi, pt i, pp. 468–9.
Salisbury's metaphor on the necessity of bleeding India, was not allowed
to die by nationalist writers: cf. R. C. Dutt, *Open Letter to Lord Curzon
on Famines and Land Assessments* (London, 1900). Appx; W. Digby,
Prosperous British India (London, 1901), p. 197; Dadabhai Naoroji,
Poverty and Un-British Rule in India (London, 1901), pp. 280 ff.
[56] Cf. a brief survey of the question of reviving land taxation and of recent
writing on the subject in Deepak Lal, 'The Agrarian Question', *South
Asian Review*, 8 (1975), pp. 389–400.

5

Traditional resistance movements and Afro-Asian nationalism: the context of the 1857 Mutiny Rebellion in India

Two distinct, though not necessarily opposing, interpretations dominate historical writing on nationalism in the Third World: the elder which is the elitist, and the newer which, for convenience, may be designated the populist. Whatever its emotive origins in the writings of the Fanon school, the newer interpretation has been pioneered for modern historical scholarship by work on those regions, notably East and Central Africa and the Congo, where the roots of the modern-educated elite and modern-style politics are shallowest. Here the telescoped nature of political development has made it credible to argue a historical connection between modern political activities and traditional resistance movements and even to assert the existence of a permanent, underlying 'ur-nationalism' which manifested its hostility to the European presence in a distinct series of historical forms.[1] These forms were at first regarded as superseding one another in temporal succession as self-contained historical stages: firstly 'primary resistance', the hostile reaction of the unmodified tribal forms; then 'secondary resistance', the muter protest of millenarian movements, welfare associations, independent churches, and trade unions; and finally the emergence of modern political parties. On the old view only for this last stage could nationalism be regarded as a valid descriptive term.

The most recent school of East African historians has come, however, to see the process more as a logical progression than as

[1] Cf. the writings of T. O. Ranger, esp. 'Connexions between "Primary Resistance" Movements and Modern Mass Nationalism in East and Central Africa', *Jl. Hist.*, IX (1968); 'African Reaction to the Imposition of Colonial Rule in East and Central Africa', in *Colonialism in Africa 1870–1960*, ed. L. H. Gann and P. Duignan, i (Cambridge, 1969). J. D. Hargreaves has extended the notion to West Africa; cf. 'West African States and the European Conquest', in *Colonialism in Africa 1870–1960*.

one of strict temporal sequence, each stage or 'moment' representing an enlargement of scale in the expression of African political consciousness. The stages can, therefore, overlap, or, indeed, run in parallel. Given uneven development among regions and ethnic groups, primary resistance can still be occurring in one region while another is far advanced with secondary, so that a stimulus in one region can be imparted by imitation or rivalry to another until a whole territory becomes caught in the political ferment. More significantly, as part of a logical rather than temporal sequence each stage is not obliterated but rather 'sublated' or incorporated by its successor (in the manner of the Platonic dialectic) so that each retains a vital role in the make-up of present-day nationalism. Indeed, the earlier stages of primary and secondary resistance, the tribal structure of the one and the enlargement of scale of the other, have more to contribute to mass commitment than the articulation and organisation of the power elite on a territory-wide basis which modern nationalist political activity achieves.

John Lonsdale, as I understand him, retains a stronger emphasis on chronological sequence than Terence Ranger since he attributes greater importance to objective alterations in the social and political structure than to the progress of subjective awareness.[2] On the elite side of the argument he clings more strongly to the role of intergenerational competition among the elite leadership, which he relates directly to the increasingly disproportional access of each generation to modern education on the one hand and chiefly office on the other. But his major chronological emphasis is on the role of economic and governmentally induced change in effecting mass involvement. For it is not elite competition but the introduction of cash-crop agriculture and the transformation of tribesman into peasant that produces the fundamental revolution. The older leadership gets shouldered aside as prices, marketing arrangements and, above all, control of land tenure and agricultural practice bring the grower into direct relations with the central government and its bureaucracy. Lonsdale is thus able, in a more distinctively historical manner, to establish a connection between the progress of subjective awareness (from diffuse, to local, to central focus) and dateable steps in the enlargement of political scale. The populist

[2] J. M. Lonsdale, 'Some Origins of Nationalism in East Africa', *Jl. Afr. Hist.*, IX (1968).

and elitist aspects can be seen to run in parallel, and consequently the older notion of tracing the nationalist movement
downwards through a series of competing elite groups, each successively commanding a wider circle of support than its rival and
predecessor, can be fitted in perfectly harmoniously with the idea
of a populist ground swell rising to meet them.

Now the elite groups which claim the historian's attention are
composed of those 'modernists' or 'traditionalists' who act essentially as brokers (or link men or communicators in Lonsdale's
terminology) between the indigenous society and modernity as
symbolised by the white man. Classified for long under the am-
biguous term of 'collaborating classes' they require somewhat
closer analysis.

The essence of the Robinson-Gallagher reinterpretation of the
place of the imperial factor in the colonial equation was to stress
its constant tendency towards economy of effort, thereby rele-
gating it to a minimal variable just sufficient to overbalance
countervailing local forces.[3] The politics of collaboration follow
of necessity, but the nature of the relationship is easily miscon-
ceived. It is as false to interpret the 'collaborating class' as a
dependent compradore 'quisling' element as it is to suppose (on
Frykenberg's model of Guntur district) that it hoisted itself into
the saddle and rode the blinkered imperial war-horse as it chose.[4]
No such stable relationship of one-way dependency could survive
in any event because of the constantly changing nature of the
colonial equation. Historically the equation was struck initially
under conditions of relative equality with traditional rulers avid
for the benefits of trade and technology. Whether Bengal nawabs,
Egyptian khedives, Zanzibar sultans, Ngoni or Ndebele chiefs,
they sooner or later found themselves caught between the upper
and nether millstones they had set in motion. The more successfully they had promoted intercourse with modernity and aggrand-
ised their own internal position, the more surely they found they
had worked their own undoing as the modernising process slipped

---

[3] J. Gallagher and R. Robinson, 'The Partition of Africa', *New Cambridge
Modern History*, xi: *Africa and the Victorians* (London, 1961); 'The
Imperialism of Free Trade', *Econ. Hist. Rev.*, 2nd ser., vi (1953–4);
R. Robinson, 'The Official Mind of Imperialism', *Historians in Tropical
Africa* (University College of Rhodesia and Nyasaland, Salisbury, 1962).

[4] R. Frykenberg, *Guntur District 1788–1848: A History of Local Influence
and Central Authority in South India* (London, 1965).

from their control. To achieve their initial purpose or even to defend their autonomy, they needed to retain the monopoly of communication with the West. But in Western eyes successful commercial take-off now made them increasingly inefficient and uneconomic both as political brokers and as guarantors of internal security. Their initial success, which enabled them to centralise authority, had bred disaffection among traditionalist elements and a climate of frustrated expectation and ambition among more progressive elements. The 'imperial factor' came to recognise that the retention of its own freedom of manoeuvre depended upon it not allowing itself to fall captive to a single collaborating element. In consequence it felt constrained both to exert pressure on the traditional rulers to render them more dependent and more pliable for its purposes, and at the same time raise up other clients and allies as counterweights. As with every subsequent collaborating elite, the traditional rulers came under pressure from above and beneath. When the position finally became intolerable they usually caved in to one pressure in order to resist the other reckoned more formidable. This situation has come to be designated the 'local crisis', when the traditional ruler has to choose between throwing himself on the neck of the Westerner in total dependence or joining forces with the xenophobic elements in a desperate bid to oust him.

Such a bid it is customary to dub an instance of primary resistance, that is, a traditional society's act of violent defiance, from which usually follows the imposition of colonial rule in response. Pacification may result in the formation of a fresh collaborating class or set of communicators. But it is already clear that this will be no unified, homogeneous body. The necessities of the imperial factor and the facts of regional, ethnic and economic compartmentalism will insist that it will be no more than a shifting, imprecise classificatory group recruited from traditional and modern elements prepared to fill certain intermediary roles under the colonial umbrella. These elites will move into and out of collaboration according to the success with which they ride the downward and upward pressures that constantly threaten them with displacement. In practice under colonial rule most traditional elites collaborate themselves out of existence rather than risk again the perils of violent protest, for when eventually faced by displacement from above they find themselves long since bereft of support from below. Hence the ultimate fate of Indian princes and landed magnates or African chiefs and sultans. In practice again, though many quasi-traditional regimes were exceptionally long lived, it is obvious that the processes of modernity will set up a constant tendency to displace traditional by more modern elites. The crises of colonial history are crises of displacement; but they are not simply inter-elite conflicts, for they are mediated through the imperial factor upon which they rain invective and riot as a means of authenticating their claims to alter the distribution of official favour.

From this account it is evident that on first contact, cooperation is a more usual response than hostility, and true primary resistance a comparative rarity. Much of what passes for primary resistance occurs at the onset of the 'local crisis' when the first phase of collaboration has gone sour. The internal configuration of society has already been altered by the yeast of modernity, so that the 'local crisis' is always as much an internal as an external one and reflects the strains of dislocation and displacement. Even highly cohesive and isolated societies like the Ndebele will be found on closer examination to follow this pattern.[5] Primary resistance abstractly defined, connotes the forcible, instinctual attempt of an unmodified traditional structure to extrude a foreign body. In Tanganyika John Iliffe has shown that relatively few polities reacted in such purely negative and irrational terms to German penetration.[6] Most attempted to tread the path of coexistence and to exploit the German presence for their own ends. Even the Hehe were drawn into war, it would seem, only because the Germans had espoused rival peoples who were attempting to recover territory on the Iringa plateau from which the Hehe had evicted them twenty years earlier. The Bushiri rising on the coast in 1888 was anything but a blind xenophobic reaction to first contact with the West. The Zanzibar sultanate had for decades been strengthening its grip on the coast and beating down rival Arab groups with the newly won power gained from collaboration politics with the British. Finally caving in completely to joint Anglo-German pressure from above it was met inevitably by

[5] Cf. R. Brown, 'Aspects of the Scramble for Matabeleland' in E. Stokes and R Brown (eds.), *The Zambesian Past* (Manchester, 1966).

[6] J. Iliffe, *Tanganyika under German Rule 1905–1912* (Cambridge, 1969). Also, 'The Organization of the Maji Maji Rebellion', *Jl. Afr. Hist.*, VIII (1967).

resistance from dissident elements who had escaped Omani centralisation and now were threatened with total displacement.

If initial resistance was only sporadic and rarely primary in the purist sense, the general wave of violence that swept southern Tanganyika in 1905 was of a very different character. At least that is the main burden of Iliffe's argument. He uses the term 'post-pacification revolt' to describe it and to distinguish it from primary resistance. A number of important features enforce this distinction. Firstly, while primary resistance engages only the power structure of traditional societies, post-pacification revolt engages the total society, the traditional power structure having been removed or profoundly modified. New forms of leadership will therefore emerge, one of which will stem from a religious ideology and strive for both mass commitment and enlargement of scale to overcome the disadvantage of compartmentalism. But the inescapable facts of compartmentalism and of uneven development will ensure that a general revolt is bound to be a loose uprising of heterogeneous units bound together only in a common hatred of Western rule. Ideology will express that hatred and supply the link that produces concert, but the fight will resolve itself into a series of local conflicts in which the leadership will vary according to the uneven pattern of development.

On the Tanganyika coast it was the south-east region that provided the precise conjuncture of circumstance needed to touch off revolutionary violence – the beginnings of profound social change, a cult centre for the ideology, and an immediate intolerable grievance. Although this was far from being the most developed area of Tanganyika in economic terms, Iliffe argues that economic change had already begun to transform tribesman into peasant. Compulsory cotton cultivation at absurdly low prices produced a crisis of displacement in which the population forsook the leadership of its collaborating chiefs either for their local headmen or for *hongo*, the religious emissaries who brought the *maji* that could supposedly render a man immune from the white man's bullets. Peasant rebellion would have been too short-lived and sporadic had it not been for the charismatic leadership of the hongo. But further west where direct government pressure on the individual had hardly been felt, revolt followed more nearly the pattern of primary resistance, except for the religious contagion that touched it off. Here, especially among the Ngoni the tribal structure was much more strongly developed and preserved, and here in the crisis of displacement the chiefs, whose collaboration with the Germans had been more limited, caved in to popular pressure and led their peoples into rebellion. There were certain limiting features. Revolt was confined to the southern portion of Tanganyika. Although Iliffe calls it 'a great crisis of commitment', he acknowledged that not all peoples in the south rebelled and that some leaders and groups proved active loyalists and supplied the nucleus of the post-revolt collaborating elite.

In the largest sense Iliffe sees Maji Maji as a watershed between two distinct phases, the 'age of diplomacy' and the 'age of improvement'. The first rested on a 'local compromise' of limited commitment on both sides, in which a traditional chief offered collaboration in return for meeting certain minimal German requirements. The second age saw the collapse of this local compromise, the introduction of close administration and the raising-up of a less traditionalist-minded collaborating elite to promote economic development.

What is noticeable in all this is that it presents early prototypes of the elements which Lonsdale uses to analyse the final phase of nationalist growth in the period after 1945. Again, in a crude sense all the three major phases are contained in embryo in Maji Maji – the Ngoni still representing a measure of 'primary resistance', the Maji cult itself a type of 'secondary resistance', and the peasant rising the final mass nationalist phase. What this suggests is that the history of a colonial territory can be read as a continuum separated into a number of distinct phases, each one of which contains the same basic analytical elements. The 'mix' of these elements at any phase will vary, however, both in their geographical distribution and their overall proportions. In these terms it appears valid to connect early resistance movements with their nationalist successors and to weave the seamless historical web between them.

Historical analysis of the Indian subcontinent has been preoccupied with the modern phase led by the modern urban elite. The elitist interpretation has been worked out by Anil Seal with considerable subtlety.[7] Although he is concerned with the emer-

---

[7] Anil Seal, *The Emergence of Indian Nationalism. Competition and Collaboration in the Late Nineteenth Century* (Cambridge, 1968).

gence of modern political organisation and explains this with the model of Pareto's circulation of elites in mind, he does not make the mistake of supposing that the 'collaborating class' is drawn exclusively from the ranks of a single social group, namely the Western educated. For this would be to leave the imperial factor the latter's prisoner and stripped of all initiative. He recognises that uneven development meant that over a large part of the subcontinent the 'collaborators' were recruited from the traditional elites, that the British sought constantly to prevent any single group from capturing the channels of communication, and that they actively assisted the competition of elites by their search for a counterpoise to any group that grew too strong. The elitist explanation for the period with which he deals is a convincing one, so long as it is remembered that it stops short before the phase of mass politics and that he is only concerned with the fortunes of groups who register themselves in the formal political arena and have some direct relevance to all-India organisations. He frankly accepts that the ideology and economics of peasant involvement lay beyond the activating power of professional politicians, and that the widening, downward spiral of elite competition was incapable by itself of bringing the masses into politics.

In Seal's schema economic change has no part, unless it be the negative one that inability to live off landed income forces the elite castes to look increasingly to government employment. Modernisation means little more than the growth and sophistication of the state bureaucracy but this was sufficient to produce a crisis of displacement between the modern-educated and the older elites. The direct impact of economic change on social structure and the direct effect of British administrative measures are discounted. There is no groundswell from below. Yet here other historians have already faintly begun to suggest that these matters cannot be left altogether out of account. Ravinder Kumar's thesis that the rise of a 'rich peasant' class lay behind the rise of the non-Brahmin movement in Maharahstra; Gerald Barrier's and Gordon Johnson's connection of the Punjab take-off into politics with the agrarian legislation of 1900 to contain peasant discontent, the tenancy legislation of the same year in the United Provinces when the British were compelled to desert the landlord alliance, so forcing even the conservative elite into politics; the political accelerator effect that Broomfield and more recently Francis

Robinson have attributed to price inflation at least a decade before the First World War; all these are indicators that the direct action of both governments and economic forces on society was of major importance even in the age of tea-party politics between 1885 and 1905. Finally, that other force which focuses material discontents and effects mass commitment, the ideology of religion, was not slumbering. Doubtless there was a quieter period in many regions in the 1870s but the self-congratulation of Sir Alfred Lyall's administration at the dying away of communal strife in the U.P. proved in fact to mark the beginning of increasingly bitter grass-roots violence from the 1890s onwards, an embarrassment to the respectable classes and their political leaders but history's hint that the tinder of mass politics was drying slowly in the sun.[8]

If nevertheless it has been natural for the elitist interpretation to dominate the study of the formative phase of nationalism, it must be said that it has left the general conspectus of the subcontinent's history in the colonial period in a sorry state. Either a large degree of discontinuity between the traditionalist and modern phases has to be accepted, or the analysis of the past has to be wholly subordinated to discovering modern trace elements. In any event the traditional 'sector' is regarded as performing a passive, wasting role, bound sooner or later to fall down the 'trap door of history' except for the small but vital element capable of adjusting itself into modernity. Traditional resistance movements, of which the Great Rebellion of 1857 was in a sense the last and greatest, seem futile affairs comparable to the 'romantic, reactionary struggles against the facts, the passionate protest of societies which were shocked by a new age of change and would not be comforted', that Robinson and Gallagher saw in so many early African resistance movements. The political mythologising that

---

[8] R. Kumar, *Western India in the Nineteenth Century* (London, 1968); N. G. Barrier, *The Punjab Land Alienation Act:* 'The Punjab Disturbances of 1907', *Modern Asian Studies*, i (1967); J. H. Broomfield, *Elite Politics in a Plural Society* (Berkeley, 1968), p. 33; Francis Robinson, 'The Two Nations: the U.P. Muslims and the Transformation of Indian Politics in the U.P. 1905–22', unpublished Prize Fellowship dissertation, Trinity College, Cambridge, 1969; Mrs J. Rizvi, 'Muslim Politics and Government Policy: Studies in the Development of Muslim Organization and its Social Background in North India and Bengal between 1885 and 1917', Cambridge Univ. Ph.D. thesis, 1969; for communal disturbances in the U.P. *Administration of the N.W. Provinces and Oudh April 1882–Nov. 1887* (under Sir A. C. Lyall) (Allahabad, 1887), p. 113.

has gone on since Savarkar's day has been generally so crude as to reinforce academic scepticism on the proto-nationalist character of 1857; and in the latest round of this dusty controversy R. C. Majumdar's Johnsonian refutation has largely silenced S. B. Chaudhuri's attempt to lend professional respectability to the concept of a first freedom struggle.[9]

The mode of release from the mental cramp into which the historiography of pre-nationalist India has become set would seem to lie in the pursuit of the line of analysis that has yielded such stimulating results for Africa, especially in view of the incomparably richer documentary material available. The essence of that approach is the postulate that early resistance movements and modern nationalism do not differ *toto caelo* but that they have certain analytical elements in common. It assumes that these movements have moved beyond the category of primary resistance, and that they will be crises both of elite displacement and of mass commitment. Like Maji Maji, 1857 bears all the outward signs of a 'post-pacification revolt', that is, one that falls between the 'primary resistance' of the formal power apparatus of traditional society and the 'secondary resistance' of enlarged scale through pacific secular and religious associations (caste *sabhas*, Arya Samaj, etc.). The formal power superstructure having been wholly or partially dismantled at pacification, colonial rule engages society more directly and evokes in consequence a more widespread reaction should a revolutionary conjuncture occur. But the reaction will be a rally of heterogeneous elements, reflecting compartmentalism and uneven development, and held together loosely by an anti-foreigner sentiment expressed in the form of religious ideology. It will be partial, involving only part of the colonial territory and portions of the population. It will split society and bear some of the characteristics of civil war.

Iliffe says that 'Maji Maji as a mass movement, originated in peasant grievances, was then sanctified and extended by prophetic religion, and finally crumbled as crisis compelled reliance on fundamental loyalties to kin and tribe.' The description could be applied quite plausibly to the 1857 Great Rebellion, although the two sets of phenomena are in their particularity worlds apart.

[9] R. C. Majumdar, *The Sepoy Mutiny and the Revolt of 1857*, 2nd edn (Calcutta, 1963); S. B. Chaudhuri, *Civil Rebellion in the Indian Mutinies* (Calcutta, 1957); V. D. Savarkar, *The Indian War of Independence of 1857* (London, 1909).

Peasant grievances in this context imply a combined action of economic and governmental pressure strong enough to induce decisive social change and the displacement of traditional leadership. Such stark, absolute contrasts find no place in India, that land of half-tones and the long revolution, and no sudden transformation from subsistence to cash agriculture, or from tribal to peasant society is to be observed. The question is rather at what point quantitative becomes qualitative change and the intensification of economic and governmental pressures becomes revolutionary. And here again one is not starting from older simplistic views that held there to be some objective threshhold of tolerability beyond which a society would explode and blow away the power structure from below. Even for East Africa Iliffe admits that pressure on the people was greater elsewhere, and that a peculiar conjuncture of circumstance was necessary to produce revolutionary violence. The conjuncture in northern India in 1857 was formed by the defection of the lower-level collaborators, namely a high-caste peasant mercenary army, inflamed by an intolerable religious grievance, threatened with slow displacement by lower castes and outsiders, and recruited from regions undergoing recent political and economic dislocation. This did not mean that military mutiny and rural rebellion were concerted. Only rarely are there signs of this occurring. The military system already provided a supra-caste and supra-communal organisation so that the mutineers looked at once for outside political leadership from traditional sources to enable them to act on the enlarged political scale necessary to meet the British counter-attack. Consequently the sepoys made no attempt to lead rural revolt but concentrated themselves in the three urban centres of Delhi, Lucknow and Kanpur (Cawnpore). With the breakdown of British authority in the districts peasant grievances were the first to assert themselves, peasant disturbances being particularly marked in the Doab region between the Ganges and the Jumna. Only in the case of Muslim communities, however, was any vivid attempt made to generalise such outbreaks by means of a prophetic religion, the *jihads* of Maulvi Liaquat Ali of Allahabad and Maulvi Ahmad Ullah of Faizabad, being the best known. Usually the religious appeal was directed at a higher level where it intertwined with political leadership. Religion formed the chief rallying cry of the proclamations put out in the names of the Delhi Emperor, the

King of Oudh, Nana Sahib, and Khan Bahadur Khan of Rohilk-hand; but in order to overcome Hindu-Muslim divisiveness it had to be couched in terms of the destructive threat Christianity offered to the two major faiths, and so lost its millenarian edge.

The peasant risings were complex affairs. Naturally they mirrored peasant resentment at social displacement caused by their loss of land control to 'new men' or urban moneylending castes, but the toughest peasant resistance came from groups that had been the most successful in warding off this particular threat. Here excessive, differential taxation appears to have been a major grievance, whether among the backward Pandir Rajputs and Batar Gujars of Saharanpur district, or the advanced cash-crop Jat farmers of western Meerut and north-eastern Mathura. Such groups enjoyed strong 'democratic' clan structures and could the more readily disown superior traditional leadership like, for instance, that of the collaborating Gujar house of Landhaura in Saharanpur or of the Jat raja of Mursan in Aligarh. But where the same castes were less democratically organised the crisis of displacement was evident in the way in which local leaders sprang up and proclaimed themselves rajas, like the celebrated Devi Singh of Tappa Raya in Mathura, or the Gujar Kadam Singh of Parikshitgarh (Parrichatgarh) near Meerut. Yet their scale and power were too slight on their own and they either remained isolated or, more usually, were swallowed up in larger movements, whether of collaborating or hostile magnate elements. The latter, as always, were slowest to declare themselves, but their action was decisive. Although they kept forts and armed retainers none of them had passed untouched by fifty years of British overrule and many had parvenu origins. Military lordship and lineage head-ship had inevitably had to give place in large measure to rent-receiving and 'estate-management'. But magnate power and influence were strong enough to carry the superior peasant castes with them, and the disposition of districts for hostility, collaboration or prevarication was determined accordingly. While fierce peasant rebellion in Mathura and Aligarh could be brought under control and the revenue collected for their British overlords by collaborating rajas, the hostility of the Mainpuri and Etah rajas could take much more placid districts into the opposite camp. This did not mean that traditional political units necessarily moved *en bloc* or that they did not suffer from splinter movements (as among the Chauhan Rajputs of Mainpuri or the Bais Rajputs in Unao and Rae Bareli who purportedly raised 40,000 sepoys from their numbers). But generally leadership fell into the hands of landlords and lineage heads. Only a small handful of these were fit or willing to look beyond their local horizon, even in Oudh where the magnate levies formed the bulk of the rebel forces. Compartmentalism remained the order of the day. Only when a local magnate was forcibly tipped out of his district by British military action was he constrained to enlarge his political horizon, so that Kunwar Singh, Nawab Ali Bahadur of Banda, Beni Madho Singh of Shankarpur, or better known figures like Tatia Topi and the Rani of Jhansi only became 'national' leaders at the point when revolt was already half-defeated. But in this way compartmentalism was partially overcome and a war of collaborative manoeuvre inaugurated.

More significantly, the 1857 Indian Revolt ended up, like Maji Maji, in a last-ditch stand by the diehard elements of Indian society. In the old British districts of the Gangetic plain, where Mughal and British bureaucracy had long since levelled the surface of political society and where the British peace had deprived the conjuncture of social status and land control of its political cement, the response to 1857 can be plotted in the material terms of loss or gain of land-control rights.[10] But elsewhere this explanation clearly does not apply. The diehard elements have to be treated in other terms. In the celebrated controversy over the Oudh proclamation which declared a formal confiscation of proprietary rights in the land, Canning, the Governor-General, was quick to refute Outram's assertion that the rebellion of the magnates (*taluqdars*) sprang from the injustice of the land-revenue settlement of 1856. He was able to point to a

---

[10] E. Brodkin, in *Jl. of Asian Studies*, xxviii (1969), maintains that in the Rohilkhand districts the Rohillas as moneylenders were net gainers of land; and hence their rebellion sprang from political rather than economic deprivation. Their aim, says Brodkin, was to recover their political independence, of which Warren Hastings had been instrumental in depriving them in 1774. But Brodkin does not appear to have taken sufficiently into account the hordes of a down-at-heel Rohilla warrior class which Bishop Heber had spoken of as a serious political danger as early as 1824. This 'declining gentry' element is too marked a feature of Muslim communities in the Western U.P. to be disregarded. Cf. *Rampur State Gazetteer* (Allahabad, 1911), p. 104; *Bijnaur Settlement Report* (Allahabad, 1874), p. 77; *Police Administration Reports N.W.P. 1870*, 21B (I am indebted to Dr Peter Musgrave for this last reference).

number of taluqdars who in a material sense had demonstrably benefited from British rule but who were proving most inveterate in resistance. Significantly these were almost entirely drawn from the northernmost Oudh districts (Gonda, Bahraich and Kheri) where they had managed to fend off the patrimonial bureaucratic centralism of the Lucknow Nawabs and had built up revenue-estates from a traditional dynastic base. Canning was acute enough to see that the source of their hostility lay in the loss of their powers of military lordship and jurisdiction. No doubt this motive operated in the conduct of other Oudh taluqdars, but the more prominent of these like Man Sing, or Rana Beni Madho, or Hanwant Singh of Kalakankar, had also suffered the excision of many villages from their 'estates'. Amongst the northern taluqdars one may reasonably postulate a large element of 'delayed primary resistance' in their response. For here the traditional political superstructure of the Rajput raj had still to be dismantled and reacted violently when British power sought to effect what earlier nawab or local governor (*nazim*) had failed to accomplish.[11]

It was appropriate that the flame of Rebellion was last to be quenched in Central India where centralising bureaucracy, whether Mughal or British, had made least headway and where in Iliffe's terminology British rule was still engaged in the transition from the era of 'diplomacy' to the era of 'improvement'. It is true that the British hand had begun to fall heavily on a large state like Gwalior, where using the ruler as the instrument of centralisation it had ended the old system of revenue-farming. Such material changes rankled among those who counselled the young maharajah to throw off the British yoke in the mad June days of 1857.[12] But, unlike the Ngoni chiefs of Tanganyika, the major princes were too tamed to rebel, and the uprising took the form of a challenge to their authority in which political rather than economic motives were paramount.

In Rajpootana and the Central Indian Agency, the form taken by

---

11 For the Canning-Outram controversy, documents are given in *Freedom Struggle in Uttar Pradesh*, ed. S. A. Rizvi, M. I. Bhargava (Information Dept. U.P., Lucknow, 1958), II, pp. 332–8. For northern *taluqdars*, *Oudh Gazetteer* (1877), entries under Gonda and Bahraich. Nationalist historians were quick to note this point. Cf. [V. D. Savarkar], *The Indian War of Independence of 1857*, by an Indian Nationalist (London, 1909), pp. 326–7.
12 *Freedom Struggle*, III, p. 181. Also K. L. Srivastava, *The Revolt of 1857 in Central India – Malwa* (Bombay, 1966), pp. 64–5.

the anarchy which had resulted from the absence of the power that keeps the peace, has almost universally been the rebellion of the feudatories, the thakoors, and hereditary nobles against their liege chiefs. Throughout all this country a feudal system prevails, and everywhere the result has been the same.[13]

Here was the crisis of displacement, whether directed against collaborating prince or British officialdom, and as the Saugor Deputy Commissioner expostulated, could not be explained in terms of financial deprivation.[14]

What is remarkable in Central India is the manner in which resistance was kept alive long after the British presence had been re-established and the principal leaders of revolt had submitted. Bitter experience had at length made plain the appropriate formula for colonial rebellion; a long war in which the larger forces were employed in a wide-ranging tip-and-run strategy while local resistance was directed to guerrilla action. After the British recapture of Lucknow in March 1858 the 'national' leaders like Tatia Topi, Rao Sahib and Firuz Shah demonstrated the relative effectiveness of such a strategy, but deprived of an 'active sanctuary' into which they could retire they had given up the struggle by 1860. Guerrilla fighting went on long after in the jungle country of Chanderi and western Hamirpur. Here the Bundela *thakurs* would seem to have been driven by a combination of economic and political motives. That great engine of change, the British land-revenue system, had in Hamirpur worked the familiar cycle of forced sales and auction purchases by outsiders, followed by the forcible ousting of the latter when order collapsed in 1857. But in other districts the agricultural communities had been readily pacified on British reoccupation. In Hamirpur and eastern Jhansi resistance was brought to no such abrupt end but tailed off insensibly into dacoity, 'the form of crime', according to the *District Gazetteer*, 'to which the Bundela Rajput always reverts when pressed by hard times if the alertness of the authorities is in the least relaxed'. For in a region where uncertain rainfall rendered agriculture always a hazardous speculation, the thakur had never been tamed to peasant agriculture and the submission to central administrative control this usually

[13] 'Narrative of Progress of Events' 9 Jan., 1858, *Parliamentary Papers 1857–8*, xliv, pt 4, pp. 1089–90.
[14] *P.P. 1857–8*, xliv, pt 3, p. 528.

involved. At his local level he was in effect manifesting a 'delayed primary resistance' to the final loss of his political autonomy. In a sense that is not unduly strained one may say that as the English-tongued *évolués* of Calcutta, Bombay and Madras were deliberating on the formation of the Indian National Congress in the early 1880s, the last shots of the 1857 Struggle were still ringing out in the jungles of Hamirpur.[15]

In practice, of course, types of resistance cannot be so neatly distinguished and each fitted into its appropriate geographical compartment. For one thing the region of the Gangetic plain where British administration had functioned for more than half a century contained pockets where the indigenous political structures had been only partially dismantled. The resistance of the Rajput rajas of the Jumna (Yamuna) ravine country of Etawah or of the powerful clan communities of Sengar and Kausik Rajputs that dwelled in the inaccessible angle of the Ganges and the Ghagara north-east of Benares must be regarded as more political than economic. As was said of the Sengar pargana of Lakhnessar in the Ballia district it was 'a terra *incognita*, which had yet to be subjected to British rule'.[16] In some measure the same can be said of failing magnates or peasant communities that had been brought under closer British administrative control but been unable or unwilling to respond to the economic opportunities of 'estate-management' and cash-crop agriculture and clung all the more readily to lordship and status. Here there were undoubted grievances against the material hardship caused by the British system, whether on account of the anti-taluqdar settlement of 1840 in Mainpuri or the oppressive assessment levied on the Batar Gujar clan communities of south-western Saharanpur. But rebellion cannot be predicated directly from material loss. It was by no means true that those who lost the most rebelled the most, so that one is forced to resort to some theory of relative rather than absolute deprivation. That is, subjective attachment to a traditional status and way of life seems in these cases to have been paramount. It was loss of lordship rights rather than loss of

---

[15] On protracted rebellion and later dacoity in Hamirpur district, cf. *Freedom Struggle*, III, pp. 620 ff.; *District Gazetteers of U.P.*, XXII, Hamirpur, ed. D. I. Drake-Brockman (Allahabad, 1909), p. 160.

[16] Commissioner of Benares, 18 April 1856, cited B. S. Cohn, 'Structural Change in Indian Rural Society' in R. E. Frykenberg (ed.), *Land Control and Social Structure in Indian History* (Madison, 1969), p. 98.

income that appears to have been the major grievance of the Mainpuri house; loss of consequence rather than actual loss of land to the moneylender that motivated the Batar Gujars.

But of larger significance is the character of the general response in the Doab region. While the 'backward' groups may be described in terms of Wolf's 'closed peasant corporation', that 'will tend to fight off changes and innovations as potential threats to the internal order that it strives to maintain',[17] what of the generality of peasant communities, where substantial transfer of 'proprietary' rights had occurred? How far had they been drawn into an open market economy and subjected to the forces of 'merchant and usury capitalism'? Here the evidence is thin and uncollated, and generalisations drawn from it for a whole territory are necessarily of the crudest and most tentative kind. Even so, there would seem good reason to question the notion that the bulk of the rural population had been brought directly under economic pressures, and responded accordingly in 1857.

Transfers were most numerous where villages or 'estates were held not by extended lineages in clan communities (*bhaiachara*) living for the most part off agricultural profits from their own home farm (*sir*) but by small groups of co-owners (in zamindari or imperfect *pattidari* tenure) relying principally on 'rental' payments from various grades of subordinate cultivators. The inadequate nature of the statistics makes it impossible to analyse the transfers so as to speak with any certainty on the actuality underlying the apparently enormous changes in the 'ownership' or land-control pattern, under which in the Aligarh district, for example, nominally half the cultivated acreage changed hands in two decades before 1860. It is evident that a fair proportion must have represented internal transfers within the same landholding caste, and in this sense the elaborate British process of recording rights and enforcing them through the courts could be exploited by interested parties to pursue the old factional struggle for internal predominance within the village that in pre-British days had been more readily settled through open force. While 1857 provided an opportunity for the aggrieved to settle scores incurred

[17] Eric Wolf, *Peasants* (paperback edn, Indiana, N.J., 1966), p. 86; and Wolf, 'Closed Corporate Peasant Communities in Mesoamerica and Central Java', *Southwestern Jl. of Anthropology*, xiii (1957); and also Eric Wolf, 'Types of Latin-American Peasantry', *American Anthropologist*, LVII (1955), pp. 452–71.

under this head by force, it was naturally their eviction of 'outsiders' that attracted attention, especially where the latter were auction purchasers of 'estates' compulsorily sold up for revenue default, or were patently 'urban capitalists' of the *bania* and moneylending castes. The profitability of landlord rights before 1857 in an era of notorious overassessment must often have been questionable, and in the Bundelkhand region outsiders could burn their fingers in spectacular fashion.[18] As Auckland Colvin's splendid analysis of 1872 made clear 'rent rates' held steady at a more or less customary level before 1860, so that the high revenue demand and the rent-receiver's profit had to be met principally from fresh land being taken under the plough.[19] It is arguable, however, that the motive for acquiring land rights in this period was not rental profit. The record of rights and the enforcement of legal process for debt had the effect of extending an individual co-sharer's credit with the moneylender who in many instances was also the grain dealer. High assessment and enlarged market opportunity may well have increased the proportion of agricultural production devoted to cash-cropping. Hence the foreclosure of mortgage or the purchase of auctioned estates by the bania castes may have been carried out with the primary aim of securing enhanced control over the grain producer, enabling the bania all the more surely to buy cheap and sell dear. Since the transfer of title rarely led to the physical displacement of resident proprietors (though they could be totally shorn of their rights in other villages) the result would be to leave them in an impoverished 'managerial' role, like the Sayyids of eastern Muzaffarnagar who lost their zamindari rights to urban moneylenders on a prodigious scale.[20]

Cohn has argued that in fact no material loss need have occurred, 'as it would appear theoretically possible that there was enough enhanced value in agriculture for the former *zamindars* to profit along with the auction purchasers'.[21] But Cohn was

[18] Report on the Settlement of Humeerpoor, February 1842, in *Reports on the Revenue Settlements of the N.W. Provinces under Regulation IX, 1833*, II, pt II (Benares, 1863), p. 792.
[19] Auckland Colvin, *Memorandum on the Revision of Land Revenue Settlements, N.W. Provinces* (Calcutta, 1872), pp. 109 ff.
[20] See below, pp. 179–80. For *bania* control of land for the purposes of the grain trade, cf. Sir H. M. Elliot's notes on Allahabad district: India Office Library, MSS. Eur. F. 60/A, fos. 53–5.
[21] Cohn in Frykenberg, *Land Control*, p. 113.

writing of the Benares region where the land revenue had been settled permanently at a comparatively low figure and there was no question of overassessment making the revenue-engaging right unprofitable. It would be hard to extend this hypothesis to the rest of the North-West Provinces; but in so far as it was true it would mean that the general eviction of auction purchasers in 1857 was prompted by non-economic considerations. Assuming, however, that the transfer of land rights involved some material loss, and was not compensated by a share of rental income from fresh cultivation, it is likely that the former proprietors alone suffered, since subordinate cultivators' payments remained stable. By the nature of the proprietary tenures, the losers would tend to be drawn from the upper peasant and squireen ranks. The subordinate cultivators would appear to have had no direct economic grievance. Where therefore they followed the superior land-controlling castes into violence in 1857, they probably acted in response to traditional ties of allegiance. And the same must be said in large measure of the former village zamindars themselves. For often it was the case that where land transfers were most voluminous there a collaborating magnate element elevated itself out of the losing agricultural castes, and held the villages quiet despite their heavy loss. Yet if this were true of eastern Muzaffarnagar and Aligarh, things were very different in other districts where the transfer process failed to throw up such a class and the zamindari rights passed to a considerable extent into the hands of absentee urban owners. Heavy transfers in Kanpur (Cawnpore) and Banda districts followed this latter pattern, with the consequence that the agents of the new proprietors were at once evicted in 1857 and British administrative control thrown off completely. The inference would seem to be that novel economic forces had not penetrated rural society to an extent sufficient to bring about a total crisis of displacement in terms of socio-political leadership. One would suppose that on an analytical view the same could be said of the limited social effects of the abrupt introduction of cash-crop cotton cultivation by administrative fiat in the Rufiji complex on the Tanganyikan coast after 1900. The conditions for peasant nationalism had yet to be created.

The process by which social relations were decisively modified by economic action forms the history of the six or seven decades that followed the Great Rebellion. The chain of traditional leadership had to be worn to breaking point at the two decisive links, that connecting the small rent-receiving zamindar with the magnate or large 'estate' owner, and that connecting the small zamindar with the subordinate cultivators. This was accomplished by a steady divergence of economic interest, effected, on the one hand, by the introduction of competition rents from the 1860s and the fight of the 'tenantry' to obtain occupancy rights and fixed rents, and on the other, by the struggle for survival of the small zamindar against rising prices, stagnant rents, and constant partition among heirs.[22] The process was accompanied by all the manifestations of secondary resistance, local societies organised vertically in a hierarchy of deference being slowly displaced by horizontal provincial-wide associations of caste and interest groups acting competitively. This was the setting for the introduction of modern political organisation and the rise of popular nationalism.[23]

To trace out the course of these changes is to recognise that 1857 stands firmly in a historical continuum. Not of course that it was the direct product of social forces blowing off the political crust but rather a fortuitous conjuncture that laid these forces bare. Like 1848 in Europe – despite obvious disparities – it was an uprising *sans issue* that could catch a society moving into the early stages of modernisation when the state was powerful to disturb but not control, and before its security system had been brought up to date by railways, modern police and armed forces, and the general disarmament of the population. Yet when all is said, in the world of historical understanding 1857 like 1848 remains a date to be conjured with.

[22] See below, pp. 210 ff.
[23] Cf. C. A. Bayly, 'The Development of Political Organization in the Allahabad Locality, 1880–1925', Oxford Univ. D.Phil. thesis, 1970; and also Bayly, *The Local Roots of Indian Politics: Allahabad 1880–1920* (Oxford, 1975).

6

Nawab Walidad Khan and the 1857 Struggle in the Bulandshahr district

The major historical problem presented by the events of 1857 concerns the process by which military mutiny was converted into civil rebellion. Some of the key features of the process stand out immediately – the capture of key urban centres by the mutineers, an autonomous peasant *jacquerie* in the countryside, and the linking of the two by political leadership supplied from the magnate class. Bulandshahr district provides an interesting case-study of at least the two latter features. Close to the epicentre of disturbance at Meerut and bordering on Delhi, it commanded the line of communication with the Central Doab and Rohilkhand and so took the full force of the first shock wave. In its pattern of landed tenures and revenue settlement it was fairly evenly divided between an eastern portion dominated by large landlord estates and a western half where jointly owned individual village estates were more common. And it was this pattern which rendered revolt potentially more formidable. In Meerut district to the north the elements of popular disturbance were stronger, embracing not merely Gujar, Rangar, and Rajput peasant communities but also the better organised Jat clan colonies of northern Baghpat, Baraut, Chhaprauli, Kutana, and Barnawa parganas. But Meerut district lacked large-scale landlordism with the notable exception of the Jat raja of Kuchchesar in the extreme south-east whose estates properly formed part of the Bulandshahr landlord complex. In consequence there was lacking the political leadership which could weld heterogeneous elements together and generalise revolt beyond its immediate local and caste origins.

In Bulandshahr the movement of popular revolt was less sustained but it found leadership in the landlord tracts of the eastern portion of the district, principally in the person of Nawab

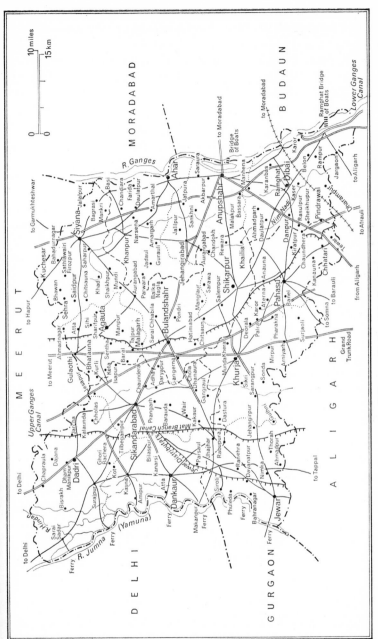

Map 2. Bulandshahr district

Mohammed Walidad Khan of Malagarh. For a time it looked as though he might build up an extensive power in the upper Doab. William Muir, head of the improvised intelligence service at Agra, mirrored official fears. Although as a civilian committed to exculpating the civil authorities by tireless iteration that 'the character of the affair is that of a Military mutiny – a struggle between the Government and the Soldiers, and not between the Government and the People', he and Colvin, the Lieutenant-Governor, were sufficiently alarmed at Walidad's activities by late July to press for a major change in strategy in order to deal with him: 'The mischief done by the country being from week to week organized against us, and the affair being thus not only of a mutinous Army, but of a generally hostile *population, is of a very serious character.*'[1] Like so many leaders of the 1857 rising Walidad remains a shadowy figure. J. W. Sherer met him in Agra shortly before the outbreak, and afterwards supposed he must have been engaged in plotting it:

During my stay at Agra Wulleedad Khan, who afterwards gave much trouble at his own town, Boolundshuhr, got an introduction to me, and called two or three times. He was then, as was known afterwards, plotting against our Government amongst the Mahomedans of Agra, and I suppose made up to me in the hopes of hearing from me what Harrington and men in his position thought in the crisis. I remember one day saying that the misapprehension in the Army was very extraordinary, and Wulleedad answered, 'But it is of no importance. What could revolted Sepoys do? A soldier untrue to his salt is not a formidable enemy.' When we finally parted, he said he hoped sooner or later the Government (Sircar) would send me to Boolundshuhr. It was very odd that he should have taken the trouble to talk in this false way. I can only suppose he wished to create a favourable impression of loyalty, as a string to his bow in case of accidents.[2]

Walidad had every motive for striking out as a revolutionary leader. On the death of his father, Bahadur Khan, in 1824, the British authorities had whittled down the family property by revoking

<hr />

[1] Muir to Brig.-Gen. Wilson, 25 August 1857, W. Muir, *Records of the Intelligence Department during the Mutiny*, (London, 1902) I, p. 144. The italicized words were underscored by Colvin. Cf. Colvin to Gov. Gen., 24 August 1857; *Freedom Struggle in Uttar Pradesh*, ed. S. A. A. Rizvi and M. L. Bhargava (Information Dept. U.P., Lucknow, 1960), v, pp. 858–9. Hereafter referred to as *F.S.U.P.*

[2] J. W. Sherer, *Havelock's March to Cawnpore*, n.d. pp. 18–19.

the lease of 36 villages in pargana Agauta. A compensatory life pension of Rs. 1,000 was made to Walidad, then a minor, leaving him with an estate of 20 entire villages and shares in 24 others, not a large patrimony for one with such considerable pretensions.[3] He never ceased to agitate for the reversion of the Agauta *taluq*, and Sir George Harvey selected him as the prime example of the man of ancient family with a grievance to nurse, the victim of British revenue policy and the law's delays. His case, wrote Harvey with some exaggeration, had been heard by every Resident of Delhi since the time of Ochterlony and by almost every Governor General in Council. 'The last decision, intended to be definitive, was by Sir Charles (late Lord) Metcalfe. and yet being a family quarrel it had been periodically re-opened, and was hardly closed finally when I held the office of Agent in 1855; and still rankled in the minds of many of the family'.[4]

In 1852 Walidad married his niece to Prince Mirza Jawan Bakht and so became connected with the royal house.[5] At the time of the Meerut sepoys' irruption into Delhi on the historic morning of 11 May 1857, Walidad was probably in or near the city. At all events he was quickly summoned into Bahadur Shah's presence on 13 May, and by 16 May the newswriter was reporting that he was to be sent across the Jumna to establish government on the other side because of the anarchy and misrule caused by the Gujars.[6] On 17 May, before he had apparently set off, he addressed a petition to the King concerning the administration of 'Ilaqa Doab, District Bulanshahr' to which he had been

---

[3] *Statistical Descriptive and Historical Account of the North Western Provinces of India*, ed. Edwin T. Atkinson, III, Meerut Division, pt II (Allahabad, 1876), pp. 64, 168. Referred to hereafter as *Gaz.*
Walidad's estate in 1857 was composed as follows:
    Pargana Baran Dowlatgarh and 12 mouzas share in Dhakouli and 10 mouzas.
    Pargana Agauta Neemchana and 5 mouzas share in Malagarh and 9 mouzas.
    Pargana Sikandrabaad Asadi and 3 mouzas.
C. Currie to F. Williams, 21 September 1858; Post-Mutiny Records, Commissioner Meerut, Special (Revenue) File. U.P. State Archives, Allahabad.
[4] G. F. Harvey, Commissioner Agra Division, Narrative of Events, pp. 41–2; cited *F.S.U.P.* (1957), I, pp. 264–5.
[5] *F.S.U.P.*, I, p. 87. The Gazetteer states it was Walidad's sister's daughter: *Gaz. op. cit.* p. 168.
[6] *F.S.U.P.*, I, pp. 981, 986. Walidad stated, however, on June 1857 that he had been at Delhi for the last two months; *ibid.*, v, p. 54.

appointed *Subah.* The terms are significant. Promising to remit the revenues to the King and dispatch recruits for the royal army, he was granted in return the *jagir* held by his father, power to raise troops on his own account, and a promise of assistance from the royal army 'at the time of necessity'.[7]

The Delhi regime was clearly anxious to draw upon the surrounding countryside for money and men and was worried that Gujar disorders might frustrate these hopes. The Gujars were thickly settled in the Yamuna (Jumna) and Hindan *khadir*, especially in the Dadri, Dankaur, and Sikandarabad parganas of the Bulandshahr district across the river from Delhi. Their immediate instinct on the news of the Meerut outbreak was plunder, but they were neither devoid of economic grievance nor innocent of political motive. In Dadri where they were considerable landholders their losses had been considerable, possibly amounting to something over a quarter of their holdings during the currency of the 1839–59 settlement. In Dankaur where at the end of the settlement they still held 48 of the 114 villages in the pargana, the 18 entire villages alienated during the period were said to be those 'chiefly belonging to Gujars'.[8] Their sharp demise from political consequence under the British must also have continued to rankle. At the outset of British rule three great Gujar chiefs, Ramdayal Singh, Nain Singh, and Ajit Singh held a large part of the upper Doab on fixed revenue farm (*mukarari*), but their descendants had suffered a catastrophic decline into obscurity and indigence.

The Gujars rose in the Sikandarabad area on 12 May 1857, pillaging and plundering along the roads, burning the rest houses and destroying the telegraph wire. During the evening Turnbull, the retiring Magistrate, and Alfred Lyall, then a newly joined civilian, galloped over from Bulandshahr, ten miles distant, to restore some semblance of order. Within the next few days by the aid of a contingent of the 9th Native Infantry they gathered in some 46 Gujar prisoners and took them back for incarceration in Bulandshahr gaol.[9] A week later the arrival of a mutinied regiment from the east threw Sikandarabad again into confusion. Walidad

[7] *Ibid.,* v, pp. 51–3.
[8] *Gaz.,* pp. 132–4, 138, 140.
[9] Narrative of Events by Brand Sapte, cited Kuar Lachman Singh, *Historical and Statistical Memoir of Zila Bulandshahar* Allahabad, 1874), p. 25. A. C. Lyall to his father, 12–15 May 1857: Lyall Papers, MSS. Eur. F. 132/3, India Office Library.

appears to have stopped at Dadri on his way from Delhi to Malagarh and decided to make use of the Gujar disturbances for his own purposes. At least there seems no reason to discredit the Crown witnesses who later alleged that Walidad entered into concert with the Gujar leaders at Dadri.[10] Certainly they were too fractured into small groups to acknowledge a single leader of their own. Hereditary right belonged to the grandsons of Ajit Singh who had been the mukararidar of the Dadri region. These were Bishun Singh and Bhagwan Singh of Dadri, who according to the British indictment 'raised the whole of the Pergunnah on the Jumna'.[11] Other Gujar leaders were thrown up spontaneously by the crisis. Such were Umrao Singh, zamindar of Kutaira (pargana Dadri), and Mullick Singh of Koonab (p. Dadri), who set themselves up as self-styled rajas, or Surjit Goojur an 'Officer' of the rebels and 'ringleader of the plunder of Dunpour' (Dunkour? i.e. Dankaur). Srivabansi Rai Vakil later deposed that Walidad 'and the Goojurs of Dadree, and Bishun Singh and Bhagwant Singh, and Umrao Singh, etc., meeting together, plotted the destruction of the Government'.[12]

It is not clear whether Walidad incited the huge Gujar attack of 21 May on the civil station of Bulandshahr. It appears to have been led by Umrao Singh with the double object of plundering the treasury and releasing the Gujar prisoners from the gaol, and coincided with the arrival from Aligarh of the headquarters of the mutinied 9th N. I. at Khurja (12 miles south). Deserted by their own contingent of the 9th N. I. as well as their Irregular Cavalry and collectorate *sowars*, the British officials were forced to quit.[13] For four days the town and civil station were given over to Gujar plundering until the Sirmoor battalion of Gurkhas arrived to clear it and allow the officials, led by Brand Sapte, the Magistrate, to resume control on 26 May. On that day Walidad reached his fort at Malagarh, which lay some 4 miles north of Bulandshahr and commanded the road to Hapur and Meerut. He still delayed declaring himself openly, acknowledging to Sapte that he had been deputed by the King as Subah of the

---

[10] Depositions of Quazi Kamalullin, Munshi Lachman Sarup, and Shrivabansi Rai Vakil; cited *F.S.U.P.*, v, pp. 40–51.

[11] List of persons eminent for disloyalty in Bulandshahr district; Commr. Meerut, Dept. XII, Special File 79/1858.

[12] *Ibid.*, p. 48.

[13] A. C. Lyall to his father, 1 June 1857: Lyall Papers MSS. Eur. F. 132/3.

Bulandshahr and Aligarh districts, but excusing himself on the grounds that only in this way could he have obtained a pretext to leave Delhi.[14] Although the district was rapidly falling into disorder, none of the principal landholders had stirred against the British. Indeed they had responded at the outset to Sapte's requisition for men at arms to help maintain order, especially Rao Gulab Singh, the Jat raja of Kuchchesar, Mahmud Ali Khan of Chhatari, Murad Ali Khan of Pahasu, Lachman Singh of Shikarpur, and even Abdul Latif Khan of Khanpur. Crown witnesses later alleged that Walidad instigated the Gujar sack of Sikandarabad that took place on 29 May, the day after the Gurkha force left the district to join Wilson's army at Ghaziabad.[15] By all accounts it was a fearful affair, and thousands of refugees came flocking into Bulandshahr. Sapte argued that he was unable to defend Sikandarabad because his forces were tied down by Walidad's armed presence so close to Bulandshahr. He appears to have ordered Walidad to send his troopers against the Gujars and obtained a show of compliance, but by 8 June Sapte had information that Walidad was assembling the Gujars at Baral (3 miles from Malagarh) in preparation for an attack on Bulandshahr. He dealt a stern warning that he would answer with his life and property if trouble ensued, at the same time making a sortie towards Malagarh. Walidad made a truculent reply but still did not disavow allegiance.[16]

In the end he stumbled rather than entered boldly into rebellion. On 10 June, confronted by the desertion of almost the whole of his guard of 75 irregular cavalrymen on the news of the arrival at Khurja of a large body of mutineers of the Oudh Irregular Cavalry, Sapte withdrew his small band 12 miles north to Gulaothi, returning to Bulandshahr next day when he learned that the mutineers at Khurja had moved towards Delhi. In the interval Walidad's forces under Mohd. Ismail Khan had, however, taken possession of the civil station in the name of the British Government. Sapte's account of the clash that followed suggests

---

[14] Umrao Singh's leadership of the attack on Bulandshahr of 21 May is attested by Munshi Lachman Sarup; *F.S.U.P.*, v, p. 44. Other details from Sapte's Narrative, cited K. L. Singh, *Memoir of Zila Bulandshahar*, p. 30.

[15] *Ibid.*, pp. 42, 45.

[16] Walidad Khan to Magistrate, Bulandshahr, 8 June 1857; *F.S.U.P.*, v, pp. 53–5.

that his small contingent was led deliberately into a trap, but undoubtedly the British forced the issue by taking the offensive when there was delay in giving them peaceful admission into the town.[17] They were decisively worsted and retired northwards, leaving Walidad in control.

The die was now cast, but Walidad's report of his success that day (11 June) showed little elation. He had brought with him a small band of Ghazis and mutineers and had unearthed half a dozen guns, but was in desperate need of trained troops and artillery.[18] The Gujars had given him useful aid but they were little better than an armed rabble and could not stand against regular forces. Even so, they were an important ancillary for a time, especially those of the Nadwasia clan drawn from his own pargana Agauta. Dwelling in the 12 villages known as 'nadwasa Barah', their leader Ayman Singh immediately cast in his lot with Walidad who acknowledged to the King the 'immense assistance' he had received 'from Ayman Googer and his tribe generally' in the actions which followed against the British between 11 and 22 June.[19] After that date Walidad was powerfully reinforced by the adherence of the mutinied Bareilly Brigade, but as late as 29 July when he was attacked at Gulaothi his army of 400 cavalry and 600 infantry was backed by 'about 1,000 insurgent Gujars and Rajputs'.[20]

Ayman Singh followed Walidad into Rohilkhand when the latter had to flee after the British recapture of Delhi in late September 1857, but generally the Gujars proved equivocal allies. Indeed, in the disturbed Hapur tahsil we are told 'on one occasion it was only with the assistance of the generally disloyal Gujars that the tahsildar was able to bring in his collections in safety from Datiyana'.[21] The Sikandarabad Gujars were a much

---

[17] Sapte, cited K. L. Singh, *Memoir of Zila Bulandshahar*, pp. 31–2. Lyall also at the time believed that a trap had been set (Lyall to father, 14 June [1857]), but later wrote on Ismail Khan's behalf stating he had now rejected this view (holograph copy of official letter, undated, unaddressed, MSS. Eur. F. 132/3).

[18] Walidad Khan to Bahadur Shah, 18 Shawwal 1273 (11 June 1857); *F.S.U.P.*, v, pp. 55–6. Walidad speaks of applications for troops and artillery that had gone unanswered hitherto, which suggests that he had been committed to rebellion for some time.

[19] Commr. Meerut, Dept. XII, Special File 79/1858. Cf. Singh, *Memoir of Zila Bulandshahar*, p. 178, *Gaz.*, pp. 104–5.

[20] *Gaz.*, p. 335.

[21] *Ibid.*

earlier and more serious embarrassment. Delhi naturally expected Walidad to consolidate his hold on this region which marched with that under its direct sway centred on Ghaziabad and comprised most of the Loni, Jalalabad and Dasna parganas of the Meerut district.[22] Although at one stage he sent a detachment to Sikandarabad under Mohd. Amin Khan and Mirza Ahmad Beg, Walidad confessed his powerlessness to prevent the continued looting of the town in view of the British threat to the north of Malagarh. 'No traveller can pass safely between Ghaziabad and Sikandarabad', he freely acknowledged, 'Gujars and other country folk of this neighbourhood have raised their heads. . .they have plundered and killed all the people of Sikandarabad, burnt their houses and carried away all their belongings on carts.'[23] Walidad used these conditions as evidence of his need for troops and artillery from Delhi, but they also threw a question mark over his capacity to assume the role of successor authority to the British. Inayet Ullah of the Baluch family of Chanderu was soon writing to the King offering to restore order in Sikandarabad and collect revenue from the pargana in the hope that he would be restored to his grandfather's title of Nassiruddaula and be made tahsildar and *kotwal*. And in August the King would appear to have agreed to the request.[24]

Even in the Agauta pargana, where the Gujars under Aiman Singh served loyally and where they were joined by the *batisa* (32 villages) of Muslim Chauhans that had formed the taluq of his father, Walidad ran into serious difficulties. The tide of popular revolt provoked its own counter-revolution. What prompted Jat resistance is obscure. Although they appear to have been gaining land in the Hapur tahsil, there is no evidence that the Jats had at this period made any significant acquisitions in Agauta pargana. By 1865, however, when the Chauhans 'had lost most of their

---

[22] Gujar villagers in the Ghaziabad area appear to have paid revenue to the King; Muir, I, p. 129.

[23] Letter of Walidad Khan to the King (n.d. from internal evidence c. 18 June 1859); *F.S.U.P.*, v, p. 66.

[24] Petitions of Inayet Ullah Khan to the King, 10, 23 July and 4 August 1857. Lord Lake had conferred the title on Inayet's grandfather. Inayet seems to have escaped punishment. At the outbreak of disturbances Sapte offered him permanent employ on condition of furnishing a troop of mounted men. In 1874 K. Lachman Singh recorded the family as owning some 15 villages in the Chanderu area: K. L. Singh, *Memoir of Zila Bulandshahar*, pp. 195–6.

villages by private sale or mortgage, [and] the Gujars by confiscation for rebellion', the Jats are recorded as possessing 26
villages out of some 90 in the pargana.[25] There may well have
been some traditional caste rivalry running back into the pre-
Mutiny decades. Alternatively, there may have been influences
from above. Just as the Chauhans heeded the call of their hereditary taluqdar, Walidad Khan, so the Jats of Bhutona, Sehra and
Saidpur may well have responded to the lead of the neighbouring
Jat raja, Rao Gulab Singh, with his huge taluq of some 270
villages. Or perhaps the efforts to collect revenue of Walidad's
agents, like Ghulam Haider Khan, touched off their anger.
Whatever the cause Jat resistance reaching out from Bhutona had
a critical effect.[26] Of a much more stubborn and cohesive character than Gujar insurgency, it proved indomitable not only against
the Bareilly Brigade which reinforced Walidad on 23 June but
also against the powerful Jhansi Brigade sent from Delhi in
response to Walidad's urgent request toward the end of August.
Khushi Ram, one of the Jat headmen of Bhutona, later made an
important contribution to the final suppression of the revolt after
the British had recovered the district at the end of September.
Appointed kotwal of Anupshahr and permitted to raise a force of
200 matchlockmen, he did yeoman service for his foreign masters,
holding the line of the Ganges against all rebel attempts to force
the passage of the river from Rohilkhand.[27] It was small wonder
that the British filled the ranks of the new district police with Jats
rather than rely on Gujars such as the brothers, Hatan Singh and
Bahadur Singh, who had been *jemedar chaukidars* of Khurja and
had deserted their posts to join the rebellion.[28]

[25] Charles Currie, *Bulandshahr Settlement Report 1865*. Also *Gaz.*, p.
105.
[26] Cf. Lyall to his sister Sybilla, 14 March 1858; MSS. Eur. F. 132/3:
'The Jâts are of Sikh origin, held by us, the Goojurs by the Maho-
metans. This, however, was nominal in reality every man was fighting
for his own hand. However it was grand fun. I shall never forget when
we routed Wulleedad Khan on the auspicious 18th of June, and let
loose the Jâts on the Goojurs. Seven villages were taken and sacked
that day by the victorious Jâts and the black smoke of the burning
hamlets spread terror through the country.'
Also Lyall to his father, 30 August 1857.
[27] On Bhutona Jats and services of Khushi Ram, cf. C. Currie to F. Williams,
26 June 1858, Commr. Meerut, Dept XII, Special (Revenue) File
59/1858.
[28] List of persons eminent for disloyalty in Bulandshahr Commr. Meerut,
Dept. XII, Special File 79/1858.

The most serious obstacle Walidad encountered was not, however, the opposition of the Jat peasantry. The attitude of the large landholders proved a much more decisive stumbling-block. On 21 June when he had been driven back at Gulaothi and felt in desperate straits (the Bareilly mutineers did not join him until two days later) he wrote bitterly to the King: 'The fact is that all the nobles (Raees) of this district have conspired with the Britishers and they are bent upon showing allegiance to the infidels (Kaffar). Although a battle is impending between me and the infidels, none of the nobles has come forward to my assistance, nor did they send any man.'[29] Walidad was overstating the case, or rather expressing the truth that a rebel can never allow his cause to stand still and that he that was not with him was against him. For the most part Walidad could complain of no more than a malevolent neutrality; the British found few active collaborators among the magnates. Even Rao Gulab Singh of Kuchchesar did little more than keep quiet in his domains until the British reoccupied the district.[30]

The pattern of magnate response was complex. While preparing to admit exceptions and qualifications the British hankered after a simplistic explanation of the revolt and found it in the theory of a general Muslim conspiracy.[31] The exceptions and qualifications were the adhesion of turbulent classes like the Gujars, and the isolated instance of Muslim 'loyalty' like that displayed by the Chhatari and Pahasu branches of the Lalkhani Bargujars. Charles Currie at least made some sort of analysis on these lines:

As a general rule with the exception of the Rajpoot Mahomedan Raees of Chuttaree, Danpoor, Pahasoo, and Dhurrumpoor, the Mussulmen throughout the district joined the rebels, heart and soul. Some few of the richer and wiser played a double game. The Jats for the most part sided with the British Government and kept quiet. The Rajpoots in most parts of the District and the Goojurs throughout the whole District took advantage of the times to plunder, and commit all kinds of atrocities. The Pergunnahs of Syanah, Ahar,

---

[29] Walidad Khan to Bahadur Shah, 28 Shawwal 1273 (21 June 1857) *transl:* Walidad Khan's letters, no. 19: U.P. State Archives, Allahabad.

[30] B. Sapte to F. Williams, 17 March 1858: Commr. Meerut, Dept. XII, Special (Revenue), File 58/1858.

[31] Cf. Lyall to father 30 August 1857 'the whole insurrection is a great Mahomedan conspiracy, and...the sepoys are merely tools in the hands of the Mussulmans'. Cf. R. C. Majundar, *The Sepoy Mutiny and the Revolt of 1857*, pp. 398 ff.

Anoopshahr, Dibhaee and Jawur suffered least. With the exception of the disturbances created by the Goojurs, Gourwa and Galoti Rajpoots, Meas and Rajpoots inhabiting the Grand Trunk Road in Pergunnahs Burn and Agoutah, the principal disturbances were caused by men of influence either quarrelling among themselves, or rising against the Government.[32]

The magnates, having most to lose, were last to move. Popular disturbance followed by defection of the local police establishments had first unseated British control in the countryside. Compelled to rely on their small, doubtful contingents of native infantry and on irregular levies raised by the magnates, the British found that while ready to repress popular disturbance these would not face the mutinied regiments coming in from the east after 19 May. Their last instrument of coercion having crumbled in their hand, the British quitted. Only then did the question of large-scale magnate defection arise, a pattern observable in other regions if we accept Professor Majumdar's interpretation.[33]

For the magnates the key problem was that of a successor authority to the British, more substantial ones being concerned to prevent a revolution that would upset the existing balance of social and economic power among them. Such a revolution naturally made its strongest appeal to the declining and the deprived, both among gentry and peasantry. But the fact that these elements were Muslim, whether the Sayyid and Sheikh squireens of Shikapur, or the Gahlot and Chauhan Rajput peasant communities, is to a large degree incidental. Although historic links with Mughal Delhi and the call of the faith were doubtless potent ideological factors, it would be safer, generally speaking, to regard Islam as a communal and political division rather than a religious one, and to see the broad separation of 1857 occurring in economic terms between the haves and have-nots. The split among the Bulandhshahr magnate class can certainly be read in such a way. The Muslim Bargujar Lalkhani family divided exactly in this fashion, the haves being represented by the Chhatari and Pahasu rais, and the have-nots by Mazhur Ali and Rahim Ali of Khylea. Similarly the sated Kuchchesar raja kept on the British side while the Hindu Rani Chauhan of Anupshahr ousted the

[32] C. Currie to W. Lowe. 20 November 1858; N.W. Provinces Revenue Proceedings, no. 293 of 23 April 1859 (Range 221/22).
[33] R. C. Majumdar, *The Sepoy Mutiny and the Revolt of 1857*, 2nd edn (Calcutta, 1968).

Kayath Lala Babu family from its ill-gotten gains in her ancestral villages, proclaimed her grandson, Kour Himanchal Singh, as the future Raja of Anupshahr, and sought recognition from Bahadur Shah.[34] But if material interest dictated the broad line of separation, communal considerations could in certain critical instances influence political allegiance. The restoration of Mughal authority in Delhi appeared to foreshadow the restoration of the *ancien régime* in the countryside. In determining an acceptable successor authority to the British traditional claims to political ascendancy were clearly important. Where vestiges of the *ancien régime* were still considerable, they supplied the natural framework of authority and all those concerned to repress anarchy and plundering might grant it at least temporary recognition. Bahadur Shah in Delhi, Khan Bahadur Khan in Bareilly, and Tuffuzal Husain Khan in Farrukhabad were raised up in this way by force of circumstance.

In Bulandshahr district no such natural successor authority existed, the country having been parcelled out under several heads for many decades before the British conquest. In terms of actual power and consequence, next to the Kuchchesar raja stood Abdul Latif Khan, taluqdar of the Khanpur estate of some 107 entire villages and 41 portions, besides others in surrounding districts. As head of the Pathans of the famous *Barah Basti* of pargana Ahar and Sayana from which so many of the sowars of the Irregular Cavalry were recruited, he was under considerable pressure to join the revolt. From his father he had inherited a considerable estate and a bitter hereditary feud with the Kuchchesar Jat family. Under the British the struggle for pre-eminence had to be fought out as a struggle for property. Even in the homeland of Gulab Singh, pargana Sayana, Abdul Latif battled with him for control. 'Both vied with each other in getting a footing in every village either as vendors or mortgagees.' In the *huzur* pargana of Baran the alienation of holdings during the currency of the 1839–59 settlement was the highest in the district, amounting to 46 entire villages and 37 portions of others out of a total of 141 villages. Twelve villages were mortgaged owing to the extravagance of their Pathan proprietors and 'the remaining transfers are due to the acquisitive spirit of the great landholders who

[34] K. L. Singh, *Memoir of Zila Bulandshahar*, pp. 43, 128, *Gaz.*, p. 63. *F.S.U.P.*, v, pp. 73–4.

vied with each other in laying baits for getting a footing in the villages'.[35] Clearly the Kuchchesar family came off best gaining 19 villages in the pargana by the purchase of taluqa Bhatwara from the impoverished Pathan family of Manda Kherah.[36]

Abdul Latif supplied the Magistrate with sowars at the outbreak of revolt and was slow to shift his allegiance. The seizure of power by a minor landowner like Walidad Khan on the British withdrawal, even though with the apparent authority of Bahadur Shah, could hardly move him to rapid recognition. As the leading Muslim landowner he played for time, keeping open his communications with the British while seeking a *shuka* of appointment directly from the King in Delhi. By 16 July he was so far successful in obtaining one that Walidad was complaining to the King that 'Abdul Lateef Khan, the Raees of Khanpur, who is an old enemy of mine, is co-operating with the Britishers in causing hindrances in the administration of this place.' He asked especially that 'no royal order be issued in such matters without the knowledge of Your humble servant on mere submission by Raees of the Doab'; otherwise 'chaos and confusion shall prevail in the administration of the territory assigned to me'.[37] Abdul Latif prevaricated fatally. He kept up a correspondence with Sapte, the Magistrate, who issued peremptory demands for him to send in his revenue and at the same time he apparently entertained mutineers and raised contingents from them. On the recapture of Bulandshahr when Walidad fled across the Ganges into Rohilkhand, Abdul Latif started like a guilty thing but then returned to his fort and sent in his revenue. British punishment for his pusillanimity was swift and unrelenting; he was tried, sentenced to transportation for life, and stripped of all his estates.[38]

The other Muslim family of consequence was the Lalkhani Bargujars, but as we have seen, the four sons of Murdan Ali Khan, who had inherited the estates of Chhatari, Pahasu, Dharmpur and Danpur, all adhered to the British cause or stayed quiet. Mahmud Ali Khan of Chhatari and Murad Ali Khan of Pahasu helped to rescue 8 guns from falling into rebel hands in the

[35] *Gaz.*, pp. 121, 176.
[36] K. L. Singh, *Memoir of Zila Bulandshahar*, p. 193.
[37] Walidad Khan to the King, 25 Zigad 1273 (16 July 1857) *transl*: Walidad Khan's letters, no. 15, U.P. State Archives, Allahabad.
[38] Bulandshahr Mutiny Bastas, Files no. 368, 369, 734; U.P. State Archives, Allahabad.

Aligarh district, a few miles to the south, and Murad Ali, before
his death from fever, attacked Indurjit Thakur and successfully
dispersed his forces.[39]

In default of large-scale magnate support Walidad was forced
to rely on lesser men. Chief among these were Muzhur Ali Khan
and his son, Rahim Ali Khan of Khylea, descendants of the great
Bargujar chief, Dandi Khan and the losers of the Lalkhani estate
through the latter's rebellion. These rallied the Sayyids of Shikapur, for whom things had gone ill under the British, their
'extravagance' having cost them a number of their villages. In
Shikarpur the green flag was raised and a holy war preached,
the British noting how deep was the commitment to rebellion by
the fact that so many of the inhabitants fled at their approach.[40]
The leaders Rahim Ali and Muzhur Ali, joined Walidad across
the Ganges, but their degree of prior concert with him is not clear.
Lachman Singh makes no mention of it despite his close personal
knowledge, Shikarpur being his home and as the mortgagee he had
no doubt helped drive such *mafidars* as Kurrum Hoosain, Talib
Hoosain, Musuud Ally, and Shorut Ally into active rebellion.[41] He
merely says: 'They [Rahim Ali and Muzhur Ali] took possession
of the villages owned by Chowdri Lachman Singh, and styled
themselves *Amils* of the king's government for Parganah Shikarpur', and later placed themselves under Khan Bahadur Khan in
Rohilkhand.[42] Walidad found other such pockets of support or
collaboration. One of these was the Nagars of Ahar, a community
of Muslim Brahmins who occupied 4 villages and who helped the
Bareilly mutineers to cross the Ganges at Garmukhtesar towards
the end of May. From among them Sohrab Khan 'set himself up
as Thannadar and had it proclaimed by beat of drum that
whoever mentioned the English should be shot.[43] He appears to
have obtained confirmation of his appointment from Walidad and
followed him later into Rohilkhand. Religion may have been the

[39] B. Sapte to F. Williams, 17 March 1858; Commr. Meerut, Dept. XII,
Special (Revenue) File 58/1858. Also N.W.P. Rev. Proc. no. 106 of 12
September 1859; Range 221/30, India Office Records. *Gaz.*, pp. 67 ff.
[40] C. Currie to F. Williams, 29 Jan. 1859; N.W.P. Rev. Proc. no. 170 of
17 August 1859; Range 221/29.
[41] F. Williams to Sadr. Board of Revenue 13 April 1859; N.W.P. Proc.
no. 168 of 17 August 1859. Range 221/29.
[42] K. L. Singh, *Memoir of Zila Bulandshahar*, p. 42.
[43] C. Currie to F. Williams, 18 June 1858; Commr. Meerut, Dept. XII,
Special (Revenue) File 64/1858.

impelling force behind the action of the 400 or so Nagars of Ahar
and 4 dependent villages, but the fact that some were sowars
in the Oudh Irregular Cavalry and Gwalior Contingent was
perhaps more decisive. One might say the same of the more
important group of Pathan villages known as the Barah Basti.
Walidad drew some of his chief officers from this area along the
Ganges, among them Ismail Khan, his general, and the latter's
uncle, Mohamed Hyat Khan, *risaldar* of the 14th Irregular
Cavalry, both of whom were from Gheesapore. Lachman Singh
states that Ismail Khan a 'near relation' of Walidad, had been
formerly a trooper in Skinner's Horse, and successively kotwal
of Jalandar and Meerut.[44] Ghulam Haider Khan, Walidad's
chief revenue officer, 'a well-to-do man' and proprietor of
4 villages in pargana Baran, may also have been a relative; one
British report stated he was Walidad's 'brother'.[45] Another relative was Mustafa Khan of Jahangirabad who was convicted of
traitorous correspondence with the King of Delhi but later pardoned. In Bulandshahr itself Walidad could count on the support
of the Sheikh and Bahlim revenue-free grantees. Khurja, a key-
road junction, with a strong Pathan element in the town, was also
reckoned by the British 'a hot-bed of disaffection'. Murdan Ali
allegedly 'raised the green flag' and 'directed the Mussulmen to
rebellion', while Azim Khan took office as tahsildar of Khurja
on Walidad's behalf, only later to be caught by Khushi Ram
and hanged.[46] At Gulaothi Gholam Ali acted as Walidad's
thanadar, and even at Sikandarabad Kadir Ali Khan, vakil of
the Munsifs of Bulandshahr, nominally held office as Walidad's
tahsildar.

Walidad began to look more dangerous when at the end of July
he seemed to be extending his authority as far south as Aligarh.
Colvin, the Lieutenant-Governor, and Muir, the head of Intelligence at Agra, grew seriously alarmed at the prospect of Walidad
organising an alternative administration and remitting revenue to
Delhi.[47]

---

[44] Some British reports stated that Ismail Khan was Walidad's nephew;
F.S.U.P., v, p. 807.
[45] List of persons eminent for disloyalty, *op. cit.*; Commr. Meerut, Dept XII,
Special File 79/1858.
[46] List of persons eminent for disloyalty – Bulandshahr district; Commr.
Dept. XII, Special File 79/158. Also C. Currie to F. Williams, 26 June
1858; *ibid.*, File 59/185.
[47] J. R. Colvin to W. Muir and Colvin to H. H. Greathed, 1 August 1857;

These fears were in fact groundless. On the British evacuation of the Aligarh district on 2 July 1857 a *panchayat* took over the administration of the city of Koil to save it from plunder of the Mewatis and lower Muslim orders, but a vakil of the Judge's court, Nasimullah, disappointed in not being given a seat, persuaded Muhammed Ghaus Khan of Sikandra Rao to seize power. The revolutionaries then sought to validate their action by turning to Walidad for formal recognition. But this was empty posturing and in no way a real extension of Walidad's authority and influence. We are told that Ghaus Khan 'never extended his power beyond the city and never collected any revenue'. Walidad's power and formidableness had been magnified out of all proportion. For it should be clear from the analysis we have made that Walidad was unable to establish himself as the successor government. Authority fragmented rather than was seized entire. Admittedly Walidad managed to secure a vague recognition of his claims from outlying collaborating groups or individuals and clearly by August he was the accepted head of the rebellion, maintaining his position persistently while other potential rebels like Abdul Latif Khan had come to nothing. But he had been unable to generalise the revolt and mobilise the resources of the district. At the outset he appears to have sent to Delhi some of the treasure acquired on taking over Bulandshahr, but thereafter it is highly improbable that he was even in a position to send anything further. All his communications with Delhi were pleas for military assistance to enable him to crush the resistance of the Jats and the British, with the expressed intention that when his position was properly secure he would be able to collect and remit the land revenue and then make a push on Meerut.[48] Walidad never overcame the inherent limitations of his position. As a minor landowner he represented the decaying gentry rather than the flourishing magnate class. Only with instant, overwhelming force, could he have enforced his authority over the latter and availed himself of their resources. As it was, they remained effectively neutralised,

---

F.S.U.P., v, pp. 67, 68. Also Colvin to Brig-Gen. Havelock, 22 July 1857; *ibid.*, p. 114.
[48] Cf. Walidad to King, 28 Shawwal 1273 (21 June 1857): 'After dealing a death blow to them in this district I shall proceed to Meerut and turn them out from there as well and along that route I shall present myself before Your Majesty.' Letter no. 19. Cf. also letter no. 12 (n.d.), Walidad Khan's letters, U.P. State Archives, Allahabad.

and ultimately this was bound to tell against him. His hold remained little more than a leader of sepoys with his effective power narrowly circumscribed to the Malagarh area. When the avenging British column under Greathed moved into the district after the capture of Delhi, they encountered an enemy who had failed to push down roots into the countryside and so was unable to deploy its combined resources against them. A quick, sharp blow at Bulandshahr on 28 September 1857 and he was unseated.[49] He withdrew across the Ganges and according to intelligence reports reached Bareilly on 5 October. There Khan Bahadur Khan was said to have placed under his command 4 regiments (paltans), more than a 1,000 cavalry, and 2 guns for the purpose of reconquering Malagarh.[50] Sapte reported him ravaging the country on the other side of the Ganges opposite Ramghat in mid November 1857, but Walidad made no serious effort to cross.[51] Indeed he was reported a little later to have made his way to Farrukhabad, possibly to recruit more troops, but had to withdraw to Bareilly on the British reoccupation of Fatehgarh. For a short time he returned again to Ramghat in March 1858 where a force under Rahim Ali was collecting revenue.[52] In May there was a report that he had gone off to join Nana, and in December 1858 his name appeared among those said to be accompanying Firoz Shah in his break-out from Rohilkhand and subsequent dash across the Doab.[53] The British never managed to run Walidad to ground, and like so many of the leaders of rebellion he vanished silently from history.

Foiled in their desire to see Walidad 'hung on his own bastion' the British blew up his fort at Malagarh on 1 October 1857.[54] The weathered debris still survives on that low bare eminence overlooking the Kali Nadi. The site is strewn with pottery scraps, and here and there great masses of broken masonry. Walidad and his descendants have long since departed; so too have his con-

---

[49] Walidad's force broke after losing only 150 men, Muir, 1, p. 163.
[50] Muir 1, p. 217.
[51] Muir to Sherer, 15 November 1857; cited *F.S.U.P.*, v, p. 119.
[52] *Ibid.*, pp. 381, 387, 907.
[53] Bulletin, Agra, 20 May 1858; *F.S.U.P.*, v, p. 125. Telegram Goodall to Reade, 7 December 1858; *ibid.*, p. 806. But this may have been a case of mistaken identity for Aleedad Khan 'the last of the 3 noted Etawah Mewatee dacoits, a very fine man'; *ibid.*, p. 820.
[54] Sapte's Narrative, cited K. L. Singh, *Memoir of Zila Bulandshahar*, p. 34. Roberts, *Forty One Years in India* (London, 1897), 1, p. 263.

querors. The Hindu ascetic's dream of quiet oblivion that Lyall
recorded in his verse at last belongs to Malagarh.

> When shall these phantoms flicker away?
>   Like the smoke of the guns on the wind-swept hill,
> Like the sounds and colours of yesterday,
>   And the soul have rest, and the air be still.[55]

[55] Alfred Lyall, *Verses written in India* (4th edn 1896).

7

Rural revolt in the Great Rebellion of 1857 in India: a study of the Saharanpur and Muzaffarnagar Districts[1]

In most accounts of the rural uprisings of 1857 the moneylender, whether described as 'sleek *mahajan*' or 'impassive *bania*', is cast as the villain of the piece. It is he who is seen as the principal beneficiary of the landed revolution that occurred in the first half-century of British rule in the North-Western Provinces and gave the non-agricultural classes of the towns a mounting share in the control of land. And his ascendancy is attributed directly to the institutional changes effected by British rule, among the most important of which were the transformation of the immediate revenue-collecting right (*malguzari*) into a transferable private property; the heavy, inelastic cash assessments; and above all, the forced sale of land rights for arrears of revenue or in satisfaction of debt. 'The public sale of land', says Professor Chaudhuri, 'not merely uprooted the ordinary people from their smallholdings but also destroyed the gentry of the country, and both the orders being victims of British civil law were united in the revolutionary epoch of 1857–8 in a common effort to recover what they had lost.'[2]

Professor Chaudhuri elsewhere spells out the consequences of this unwitting partnership of the moneylender and the British revenue laws:

The *baniyas* were mostly outsiders who purchased with avidity the proprietary rights of the zamindars and peasants when they came under the operations of the sale law. By this process a vast number of estates had been purchased by these 'new men' and a large number of families of rank and influence had been alienated. As village

[1] I am indebted to the Nuffield Foundation for a Small Grant to aid in the compilation of the statistics, and to my daughter, Barbara Stokes, for drawing the original map.
[2] S. B. Chaudhuri, *Civil Rebellion in the Indian Mutinies* (Calcutta, 1957), p. 21.

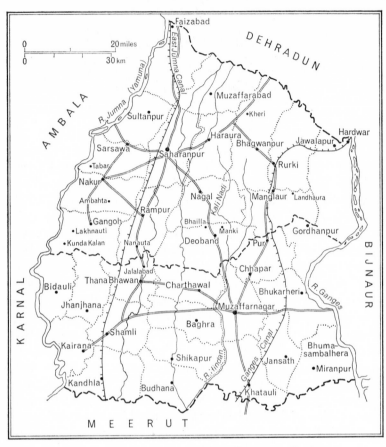

Map 3. Saharanpur and Muzaffarnagar districts

moneylenders they also practised unmitigated usury. The English courts which offered facilities to the most oppressive moneylenders in executing a decree for the satisfaction of an ordinary debt against an ignorant peasantry produced the greatest resentment amongst the agricultural population and a dangerous dislocation of social structure. The protection thus afforded to this class through the medium of the English courts is the sole reason why the peasants and other inferior classes of wage earners to whom borrowing was the only resource were so vindictive and uncompromisingly hostile against the English during the rebellion. It was not so much the fear for their religion that provoked the rural classes and landed chiefs to revolt. It was the question of their rights and interests in the soil and hereditary holdings which excited them to a dangerous degree.[3]

How far does this conventional account stand up to detailed scrutiny? It is instructive to test the importance of the money-lender's role in provoking rural revolt in an area where the statistics suggest that his grip was strongest. Despite the scenic splendour of its Himalayan backcloth the Saharanpur district was the least favoured of the rich Meerut division, whether in soil fertility, irrigation facilities or the agricultural skill of its inhabitants. Edward Thornton's land-revenue settlement of 1838 weighed heavily upon it, and prevented agriculture from making much advance.[4] Substantial landowners were almost non-existent and the *petite culture* of cultivating village proprietors was the dominant form of tenure. These circumstances, together with the prevalence of rent payments in kind among a people scarcely numerate, no doubt helped to deepen dependence on the money-lending castes, and when order began to break down in May 1857 the latter were among the first to feel the popular vengeance. Yet this is far from saying that there was a direct proportional relationship between rural indebtedness and revolt. Indeed, so far as statistics are available and can be relied upon, they tend to show the opposite to be true. The geographical incidence of disturbance varied if anything in inverse proportion to the hold obtained by the moneylending and trading classes. Violence occurred principally in the southern parganas,[5] especially in Nakur, Gangoh and Deoband parganas, which displayed rates of land transfer, mortgage and *mahajan* (i.e. moneylender) ownership that were, generally speaking, markedly below the average (Table 1).

Such a discrepancy can, of course, be explained away on purely tactical grounds. While revolt might on first outbreak be universal throughout the district, it could only survive and flourish in out-

[3] S. B. Chaudhuri, *Theories of the Indian Mutiny* (Calcutta, 1965), pp. 135–6. For other similar interpretations, cf. S. N. Sen, *Eighteen Fifty Seven* (Calcutta, 1957), pp. 32–5; T. R. Metcalf, *The Aftermath of Revolt* (1965), p. 207 *passim*; P. C. Johi, '1857 in Our History' in *Rebellion 1857: A Symposium*, ed. P. C. Joshi (New Delhi, 1957), pp. 141 ff., 195 ff.

[4] Board of Revenue to Govt. N.W. Provinces, 18 Aug. 1871, para. 35; *Saharanpur Settlement Report*, (Allahabad, 1871).

[5] R. Spankie to Commissioner, Meerut, 6 March 1858, Saharanpur Collectorate Pre-Mutiny Records, Judicial Letters issued to Commissioner, May 1856–Oct. 1858 (bk 23*a*, ser. II, 4) U.P. State Archives, Allahabad.

TABLE I. *Saharanpur district: alienations of land and Mahajan holdings during currency of settlement 1839–59*

| Pargana | As % of total cultivation | | | | Chief losers | Percentage of land held by Mahajans in F. 1274 (1868) | Revenue rate per cultivated acre 1839–59 (Rs.) | Revenue rate during 1859–89 settlement (Rs.) |
| | Transfers | | | Total % | | | | |
	Private	By Court decree	Mortgaged					
Saharanpur	20	21	7	48	Hindu Rajputs, Pathans, Gujars, Brahmins	19·5	0–13–3	1–15–7
Faizabad	17	7	18	42	H. Rajputs, Sayyids	22·5	0–9–3	1–7–5
Muzaffarabad	14	11	23	48	Sheikhs, Garas, Brahmins, H. Rajputs	39·3	0–11–4	1–7–10
Haraura	13	17	9	39	H. Rajputs, (⅓ of their land), Sheikhs, Pathans	29·9	1–1–0	1–9–0
Deoband	4	5	3	12	H. Rajputs, Tagas, Gujars	9·6	1–8–0	1–6–2
Nagal	7	12	5	24	Gujars, Tagas	18·2	1–12–0	1–7–5
Rampur	5	6	4	15	Gujars	10·4	1–6–0	1–13–10
Rurki	4	3	0	7	Gujars, Pathans, Brahmans, Rajputs	12·9	1–7–10	1–3–2
Bhagwanpur	10	9	8	27	Gujars, Sheikhs, Pathans, Rajputs	14·9	1–1–0	1–5–7
Jawalapur	7	2	3	12	Gujars	15·3	1–10–10	1–3–2
Manglaur	6	7	2	15	Gujars, Jats	3·1	1–5–0	1–8–8
Nakur	4	7	3	14	Gujars, Jats	12·6	1–4–0	1–3–1
Sarsawa	4	7	18	29	Tagas (nearly all possessions)	19·9	0–14–0	1–7–10
Sultanpur	8	18	11	37	Pathans, Garas	29·5	0–15–0¾	1–3–1
Gangoh	5	10	3	18	Gujars	16·1	1–0–3	1–0–6
District average	9	10	7	26		18·2		

Sources:

Saharanpore Settlement Report N.W.P. (Allahabad, 1871), p. 22, Appx II: 'Abstract Statement of Transfers of Proprietary Right'.
For percentage of land held by Mahajans, *Saharanpur S.R.* (Allahabad, 1891), pp. 50–3. 'Saharanpur District. Area held by each caste.'
For chief losers, Pargana notices in E. Atkinson (ed.), *Gazetteer N.W.P.*, II, Meerut Division, pt I, abstracted from *Settlement Report, 1871.*

lying areas away from the local centre of British power. Many of the initial outbreaks occurred close to Saharanpur city and civil station, but like the Gujar gathering at Malhaipur on 21 May, they were capable of being quickly suppressed.[6] The difficulty of concentrating the revolutionary forces might also be thought to explain the failure of revolt to take a firm hold in the central and northern subdistricts (parganas). The militant communities of Gujars, Rajputs and Rangars were too thin and scattered in these areas to mount a protracted resistance. When H. D. Robertson, the Assistant Magistrate, went north-east into the Kheri region of pargana Bhagwanpur on 23 May to clear the Mohand road of Banjara dacoits he recognised that he was among a people whose loyalties were more than dubious. Indeed the Rangars of Kheri had been deprived of their control of a large number of villages in 1836 and had subsequently lost more through private and public sale. Yet after his visit the area gave no further trouble, a result Robertson thought could be ascribed to 'its being a thinly-peopled tract, cut up by strips of jungle, and separated from the dangerously revolutionary portions of the district by the station of Saharunpore'.[7]

There is a difference in emphasis in the official accounts of the early disturbances, but all acknowledged that resentment at the moneylenders' hold ranked as a prominent incentive for popular violence. Spankie, the Magistrate, tried indeed to argue that rebellion was not initially contemplated:

The plundering tribe of Goojurs was the first affected, and the Rangurs were not far behind them. There was, however, no general outbreak until the disturbances at Muzuffurnaggur occurred [presumably on 21 May]. Then wave after wave of disquiet rolled through the district...The assemblies of Goojurs and others became more and more frequent. Ancient tribe or caste feuds were renewed; village after village was looted; bankers were either robbed of their property or had to pay fines to protect it. The *Zemindars* and villagers took advantage of the general anarchy to obtain from the

---

[6] 'Narrative of Events attending the outbreak of Disturbances and the Restoration of Authority in the District of Saharunpoor in 1857–58.' R. Spankie to F. Williams, Commissioner, Meerut, 26 Sept. 1857, para. 11, in *Narrative of Events regarding the Mutiny in India of 1857–58 and the Restoration of Authority* Calcutta, 1881), 1, p. 468.

[7] Cf. *Narrative*, p. 469, para. 20. H. Dundas Robertson, *District Duties During the Revolt in the North-West Provinces of India* (1859), p. 35. On Kheri Rangars, cf. E. A. Atkinson, *Gazetteer of N.W. Provinces*, 11, Meerut Division, pt 1 (Allahabad, 1875), pp. 198, 261.

Mahajuns and *Buneahs* their books of business and bond debts, etc.
It would appear as if the disturbances in the commencement were
less directed against Government than against particular people and
castes. When the fall of Delhie ceased to be looked upon as imminent,
the agricultural communities began to turn their eyes towards the
local treasures and did not scruple to oppose themselves to Government officers and troops.[8]

Resistance to Government figured early nevertheless. On 22
May Spankie took a force along the Rurki road to Gurhow,
7 miles east of Saharanpur, where a bania's house had been
looted, and then took prisoner the head men (*lambardars*)
of Kunkuri and Phoraur, where the villagers had refused to
pay their revenue.[9] A few days later Robertson, the Assistant
Magistrate, was despatched to Deoband with a detachment of the
4th Lancers in response to a plea for protection from the Hindu
traders of the town. He was startled at the determined hostility
manifested by the nearby Gujar villages, especially Babupur,
Sanpla Bakal and Fatehpur, which bordered the Kali Nadi some
4 miles east of Deoband. Robertson had visited the area in the
course of settlement revision work only six weeks earlier and now
found the transformation bewildering. 'Troops might mutiny,
but I could hardly realize this rapid change among peaceful
villagers.'[10] Their resistance decided him against moving with his
unsteady troops against the formidable Pundir Rajputs of the
Katha, a region immediately west of Deoband: 'the experience
of the previous day had not been lost sight of...It showed me
clearly that the zemindars were one with the lower orders; that
rebellion, not plunder alone, actuated the mass of the population.'[11] The same note of rebellion was struck simultaneously some
12 miles north-east where Umrao Singh of Manikpur (modern
Manakpur Adampur) set himself up as raja, levied revenue, and
became 'the leader of all the disaffected Goojurs in the Pergunnah'.[12]

[8] *Narrative*, paras. 7–8, pp. 467–8.
[9] Gurhow is not given in modern maps, but a point 7 miles east of Saharanpur falls exactly at the junction of the Dehra Dun-Rurki roads just on the
eastern bank of the Hindan river where an unnamed hamlet is marked.
Kunkuri and Phoraur also do not appear on the 1-inch Survey of India
sheet.
[10] Robertson, *District Duties*, p. 43. Cf. Robertson to Spankie, n.d., *Narrative*,
pp. 483–4.
[11] Robertson, *District Duties*, p. 45.
[12] Spankie, *Narrative*, para, 15, p. 469.

Robertson was patently not satisfied with the explanation that the attacks on towns, including the Government offices, were prompted by nothing more than a lust for plunder. To him the attacks were conscious acts of rebellion in which hatred of British rule had developed out of a hatred of the *bania ka raj* – the rule of the moneylender-trader. For he noted that 'the creditors of the poorer class of cultivators invariably inhabit the larger towns, so that these towns naturally enough became a point of attack when the civil power was paralysed'. 'No class', he said, 'seems to have acted with so vindictive a hatred against us as the smaller class of landholders whom the bunyahs had dispossessed through the medium of our courts.'[13]

What is perhaps more remarkable is that Robertson drew his examples from the 'hard core' areas of the southern portion of the district which we have seen were precisely the areas where the grip of the moneylender was weakest. By late June the main centres of disturbance were the wild alluvial valley (*khadir*) of the Ganges to the east, the Gujar villages bordering the Kali Nadi as it described a tortuous arc north and east of Deoband, the Katha (in western Deoband pargana, eastern Rampur, and a small portion of Nagal), and finally the south-west of the district in parganas Nakur and Gangoh. The Ganges khadir was a dacoit affair conducted mainly by Banjaras, a gypsy pastoral people, and not the rebellion of a settled population. The hard-core areas were clearly the Katha and the parganas of Nakur and Gangoh, which formed part of the region traditionally known as Gujarat to mark it out as the Gujar heartland. Here solid clan settlement provided a powerful framework of organisation for revolt. Of particular importance was the cluster of 52 villages in Gangoh and Lakhnauti held by the Batar subdivision (*gotra*) of Gujars.

Disturbances in this western portion of the district first flared up in the Yamuna (Jumna) khadir at Tabar, 4 miles north-west of

---

13 Robertson, *District Duties*, pp. 134–7. Cf. H. le Poer Wynne, Asst. Settlement Officer to H. D. Robertson, Collector, Saharanpur, 17 May 1867, paras. 226–7.
Saharanpur Settlement Report (Allahabad 1871), p. 138: 'At present all such alienations (very numerous they are) fall into the hands of the large money-lenders who congregate in the various towns...he is invariably an absentee, and manages the estate through an Agent. It will be easily imagined how their circumstance tends to keep him disevered from his tenants, and ignorant of what measures their requirements and his own interests alike demand.'

Nakur, where Bukshee (Bakshi), a Rangar, 'had assembled a large body of followers with whom he threatened to attack Nuckoor or Sirsawa'. Driven across the Yamuna into Thanesar on or about 27 May, Bukshee returned to participate in the great Gujar rising that broke out in late June 1857 and began with the sack of Nakur. When Robertson arrived with his troops on 20 June he found the Nakur tahsil offices and thana (police station) in flames and 'all the Government records, with the Mahajuns' accounts, bonds etc. . . . torn up and scattered over neighbouring gardens'.[14] The seat of disturbance clearly lay to the south and after punishing villages in the immediate neighbourhood of Nakur Robertson proceeded in the general direction of Gangoh through the dry upland (*bangar*). 'Revolt had now become universal throughout this tract, and it became a question which body of rebels ought to be first dealt with as the best chance of overawing the rest into submission, our force being too small to entertain a hope of reaching all our enemies.'[15] Ignoring hostile villages like Ghamatpur and several in the vicinity of Ambahta Robertson struck at Budha Khera, a village near the Yamuna escarpment, where 'Futtuah' had proclaimed himself King of the Gujars. Failing to bring the rebel leader to battle, he then passed through Gangoh to encounter and defeat some 3,000 Rangars who were settled about Kunda Kalan in the extreme south-west portion of the district, and who were now threatening to attack Lakhnauti and Gangoh. Robertson's analysis of this chain of resistance is valuable. Like most British officials he believed the revolt to be political in origin, and the product of a widespread Muslim conspiracy but the popular backing it won from the Hindu masses he saw as springing essentially from economic discontent:

---

[14] Robertson to Spankie, no. 241, para. 11, n.d., *Narrative*, p. 485. Cf. later description by Spankie: 'It would be difficult to express the utter ruin that has fallen upon the Hindoo Banias and Mahajuns at Nukoor. Large brick houses and some of them highly ornamental are in ruins. The Bazaar was all but destroyed. The villains concerned in the loot do not appear to have been satisfied with ordinary mischief, but systematically pulled down the houses. Not a Mahomedan's house was touched! The whole lot of Goojurs in the neighbourhood was concerned in this affair – and the Hindoos declare now as they did at the time that the Mahomedans suggested the attack.' R. Spankie, Magistrate, to F. Williams, Commissioner, Meerut, 17 March 1858, para. 4, U.P. State Archives, Allahabad, Saharanpur Collectorate Pre-Mutiny Records. Bk 230, ser. II. 4. Judicial letters issued to Commissioner, May 1856–Oct. 1858.

[15] Robertson, *District Duties*, p. 120.

Such investigations as it was possible to make...proved that the Mahomedans in this tract were throughout the instigators to revolt. They had risen as a body, and the Hindoos who swelled their ranks, rendering the rising universal, were almost all of that class who would gain by anarchy and the destruction of the records of their debts, and that this latter inducement to revolt was one of their keenest relishes it was easy to observe.[16]

The influential Muslims of Ambahta and Nakur, Robertson alleged, 'had excited the Goojurs generally by hopes of plunder, destruction of bunyahs' accounts, bonds, etc., and the more influential amongst them such as "Futtuah" with the chance of regaining the consequence tradition had assigned them in this part of the country, once the principality of their ancestors'. The Kunda Rangars, a Muslim Rajput caste, were prompted, however, by the purely communal motive of re-establishing Muslim supremacy, for he could detect no material grievance; 'unlike the improvident Goojurs their villages are generally populous and wealthy, so that plunder could hardly be their inducement to disaffection, and I could not but admire their bigoted daring'.[17]

Robertson applied the same analysis to the other principal area of disturbance, that of Deoband. In late July while concluding an expedition against the Banjaras in the Ganges khadir he learned 'that the whole country around Deoband had again arisen with the intention of attacking that important place'; and on 22 July he marched to save the town from further assault by the Gujar and Katha Rajput bands, a third of it having already been savagely plundered and sacked.

'The same scenes that had occurred at Nookur had here been re-enacted on a larger scale; the attack having originated from nearly the same motives, viz., plunder and the destruction of banyahs' accounts and bonds.'[18]

All this would appear to give strong confirmation to the notion that hostility to the moneylender played a dominant role, even though his actual hold over landed property was weaker in the 'hard core' areas of resistance than elsewhere in the district. Yet more detailed inspection of the parganas in question sets the rebellion in a totally different light.

[16] Robertson, *District Duties*, pp. 133–4.
[17] *Narrative*, p. 486.
[18] Robertson, *District Duties*, p. 158. Cf. Robertson to Spankie, 4 Aug. 1857: *Narrative*, pp. 481–2.

Firstly, it is to be observed that rebellion was centred in the 'thirsty' tracts, where canal irrigation had not reached and where wells failed to give an adequate water supply. These were precisely the tracts recognised by settlement officers after the Mutiny as severely assessed and in need of relief, and yet curiously they had managed to resist the encroachment of the moneylender more successfully than any other portion of the district. Above all was this true of the main Gujar areas of Nakur and Gangoh parganas, which coincided with what the settlement officers defined as the upland (bangar) and the mixed bangar and river-valley (khadir) tracts (Table 2).[19]

In Nakur pargana as a whole the mahajans had come to possess by 1864–5 some 12% of the total cultivated area, but in the bangar tract (18,510 acres) their holding amounted to no more than 5% against 58% held by the Gujar clan villages. In Gangoh the mahajans had advanced farther but in the bangar still held

TABLE 2. *Gujar (incl. Muslim Gujar) and Mahajan land holdings in parganas Gangoh and Nakur, Saharanpur district 1864–5*

	Pargana	
	Gangoh	Nakur
Canal-irrigated tract		
Total cultivation in acres	9,383	9,281
% held by Gujars	60	37
% held by Mahajans	8	11
Bangar tract		
Total cultivation in acres	25,959	18,510
% held by Gujars	57	58
% held by Mahajans	12	5
Mixed *bangar* and *khadir* tract		
Total cultivation in acres	7,205	7,959
% held by Gujars	Nil	40
% held by Mahajans	36	21
Khadir tract		
Total cultivation in acres	4,426	10,393
% held by Gujars	5	18
% held by Mahajans	45	17
Pargana aggregate		
Total cultivation in acres	46,973	46,143
% held by Gujars	44	45
% held by Mahajans	18	12

Source: Saharanpur Settlement Report, 1871.

[19] Allowing for the fact that the area is in general a level plain, *bangar* refers to the 'upland' and *khadir* to alluvial river lands, in this case of the Yamuna.

only 12% (3,140 acres) against the Gujars' 57% (14,858 cultivated acres, including 5,335 for Muslim Gujars) and against their
own pargana average of 18% of the cultivated acreage. H. le
Poer Wynne in the mid 1860s described the bangar and khadir
tracts of Gangoh as:

held and cultivated by utterly improvident Goojurs who form a compact mass, able and willing to keep any outsider from settling among
them. A few wealthy bankers have ventured to purchase a whole
village here and there, but as a rule all who have ventured to buy
up the share of an impoverished coparcener have been unable to
make their footing good in the new 'purchase'. The warning has
been accepted by moneyed men in general, so that now a Goojur of
these parts can get no credit whatever.[20]

The Gangoh portion had 'long been extremely over-assessed',
15 villages having been actually deserted by their owners. One
must suppose that the pressure of the revenue demand was partly
responsible for the relatively larger extent of land alienation to
the mahajans here. On the edges of this region, however, conditions were different. To the west in the mixed bangar and khadir
tract and in the pure khadir tract Gujar settlement was much
thinner but mahajan gains proportionally much larger. In the
Gangoh mixed bangar and khadir Gujars were not represented
among the proprietary class, but the mahajans had managed to
lay hands on 36% of the cultivated acreage (2,578 out of 7,205
acres); and in the small Yamuna khadir portion of the pargana as
much as 45% (2,009 out of 4,426 acres). In the Nakur pargana
the situation was more explosive, for although the mahajans had
made only the slightest of inroads in the large bangar tract (5%),
they were clearly much more threatening in the smaller and poorer
mixed bangar and khadir tract where they had got hold of 21%
(1,704 out of 7,959 cultivated acres) as against the Gujars who
retained 40%. In the pure khadir tract of Nakur the Gujars were
comparatively minor landholders and their 18% contrasted with
the 17% of the mahajans (in a total cultivated acreage of 10,393).
These figures, of course, were collected nearly a decade after the
mutiny, and cannot provide an accurate picture of the situation
in May 1857; but they would, if anything, probably magnify the

[20] *Saharanpore S.R.* (Allahabad, 1871), H. le Poer Wynne to H. D. Robertson, 17 May 1867, para. 92, p. 100.

mahajan gains since these increased steadily in subsequent years.

They do suggest that it was rather a potential threat than actual loss that prompted Gujar hostility to the mahajans, and a threat mainly acting on the periphery rather than the centre of their clan area (*khap*). The town of Nakur lay on the periphery in the relatively small mixed bangar and khadir tract of the pargana. One must suppose that mahajan acquisition of as much as 21% of the cultivation had a good deal to do with the violence displayed by the Gujar villages in the immediate vicinity of the town. Similarly, in the Gangoh khadir the loss of nearly half the land to the mahajans must have affected sharply the attitude of the Kunda Rangars, however much Robertson might form an impression of their comparative prosperity.

But what really is in question is whether the moneylender was the prime cause of the Gujar uprising or whether he was simply one of the symbols of a new and hated order of things under which the old Gujar mode of life was failing. The evidence, when read together, all suggests that the rebellious Gujars were giving expression to a frustration born of their inability to make good in the new rural economy. Such a supposition gains powerful support from the contrast presented by the Gujar communities of the canal-irrigated tracts even in the violently disturbed Nakur and Gangoh parganas. So far as the evidence goes there would appear to have been no rising in these tracts, and one may reasonably assume that the miracle of transformation upon which Wynne reported so ecstatically in 1867 had already taken effect:

The Gujars to whom by far the bulk of this group belongs, have, like others of Rampore, been reclaimed from the improvident habits and the tendency to cattle lifting which characterize their brethren in the rest of the pergunnah. This happy result is due to the canal. The reward which the use of canal water held out to industry was so great, so immediate, and so certain. that all the traditions of caste succumbed to the prospect of wealth, so that the Gujars throughout the region watered by the canal are the most orderly, contented and prosperous of men.[21]

It is noteworthy that this prosperity had been won without undue dependence on the moneylender, the mahajans owning in the canal-irrigated tract of Nakur in Wynne's time just under 11% (989 out of 9,281 acres) of the cultivated land in comparison

21 *Ibid.*, para. 89, p. 99.

with Gujar holdings of some 37% (3,408 acres), and in the Gangoh canal tract a little over 8% (189 acres) as against Gujar holdings of roughly 60% (5,650 out of 9,383 acres). In Gangoh Wynne felt able to raise the assessment of the 26 villages in the canal tract some 7%, while he lowered it in the 64 villages of the bangar tract by more than 11%. These facts suggest that the grievances of the bangar Gujars were ultimately rooted in a sense of relative deprivation. While their brethren of the canal tracts were adjusting themselves successfully to the new order in which wealth and social precedence were coming increasingly to depend on cash-crop agriculture rather than inherited status and lordship, the Gujars of the dry bangar upland were denied the opportunity for agricultural revolution. They were made to labour under a revenue assessment that was distinctly severe while seeing their brethren in the canal tract enjoy an easy demand in addition to the incomparable advantages of an all-the-year-round water supply.

The same contrast is observable further east in the other hard-core area of rebellion comprising portions of parganas Rampur, Deoband, Nagal and including within it the region traditionally known as the Katha, the homeland of the Pundir Rajputs. Rampur pargana remained relatively peaceful, although the town of Nanauti 'peopled by ill-conditioned Syuds and over-reaching usurers' was excitable and was thought to have been implicated in the disturbances of September 1857 when Inayet Ali Khan (nephew of Mahbub Ali, the Kazi of Thana Bhawan in the Muzaffarnagar district to the south) raised the green flag of Islam and stormed the Government buildings at Shamli.[22] Rampur pargana marched with Nakur and Gangoh, the East Jumna Canal running just within the boundary Rampur formed with them. The Gujars were solidly established here and enjoyed the same prosperity as their brethren in the canal tracts of Nakur and Gangoh, holding just under a third of the total cultivation of the pargana (20,070 out of 63,006 acres). Wynne considered it much too lightly assessed and raised the demand by some 26%. The

---

[22] Cf. R. Spankie to Commissioner, Meerut, 12 March 1858, U.P. State Archives, Allahabad. Saharanpur Collectorate Pre-Mutiny Records. Bk 230, ser. II, 4. Judicial letters issued to the Commissioner, May 1856–Oct. 1858, fo. 206. It must be admitted that Robertson mentions that Rampur was at one stage threatened by the rebels during the main rising in Gangoh and Nakur in June 1857; *District Duties*, p. 133.

mahajan holdings were only moderate, comprising roughly 10%.

Rampur embraced in its south-east corner part of the Katha, a region stretching eastwards into the western part of Deoband pargana and northwards into a small part of Nagal. In the Katha the Pandir Rajputs stood out as the dominant landholders, dwelling together as a formidable clan that had never been properly brought under close administration. A proud, hardy race, who unlike their Rajput caste brethren put their women to work in the fields, they possessed a long history of turbulence, and remained even in the 1860s 'notorious cattle-lifters'. Significantly they had successfully warded off alien intrusion.

Strong, moreover, as the power of combination is among the Goojurs, it is stronger among these Rajpoots, so that they have been able to keep their possessions almost intact, while all around them the ancestral rights of other castes have succumbed to the wealth and acts (arts?) of the usurer. Confident in this power of combination, they used to resist the Police and Revenue authorities by open force.[23]

So formidable did they appear as adversaries before the recapture of Delhi at the end of September 1857 that the British left them severely alone, despite their participation in the attacks on Deoband town and in similar depredations. Although none of their land had the advantage of canal irrigation there was a marked difference in prosperity between the Pundirs of the western and eastern Katha. The western Katha comprised a Rampur portion and a tract east of this reaching to the Hindan River, all of which possessed good, fertile soil and carried a comparatively heavy population.[24] Even in the dozen villages along the Hindan itself where the soil was generally poorer Wynne found a fair measure of prosperity that justified a moderate increase of some 10% in the assessment, an increase somewhat higher, in fact, than that which he imposed on the richer tract to the west between the Hindan and the Rampur border. Mahajan acquisitions were slight, less than 7% in both of these small tracts, and compared with Pundir holdings of 74% and 43% respectively.

In contrast the eastern Katha took in the higher central plateau between the Hindan and the Kali Nadi where conditions were

[23] Wynne, para. 105.
[24] Wynne, para. 107: 'The soil throughout the Katah, as far as the Hindan, is unsurpassed by any that I have seen in the district.'

markedly different, and recalled those of the bangar tracts of Nakur and Gangoh. Population was thin and the land thirsty. The Pundirs held only the western part of this eastern Katha region, their holdings amounting to some 32% of the pargana and the mahajans' some 8%. The settlement was a full one and had to be eased by the settlement officers of the 1860s. It was significantly in this part of the Katha marked by a dry soil and stiff assessment, that violence erupted in 1857, and from which the Pundir raids on Deoband were launched. The main trouble centre appears to have been the large twin village of Bhailaal Kalan and Bhailaal Khurd 'which with its large population and the number of the Rangur khewatdars is a most influential one in the tract of 23 villages comprising what is called the "Kata" and has long been notorious for turbulence and contempt of all authority'.[25] From here sprang the rebel leader Dhuleep who participated in the sack of Deoband and whom the British caught and hanged.[26] Later the persistent recalcitrance of the inhabitants over surrendering their arms moved Spankie, the Magistrate, to make an example of the village, and he ordered its partial destruction.

Deoband also suffered from Gujar attacks, and their provenance demonstrates the same features. The cultivated region in the immediate vicinity of Deoband town was a fertile and prosperous one, the land being owned mainly by Muslim Gujars and by Sheikhs who were 'quite above working for their bread, but prefer to live in idleness on the wretched pittance of rental that they screw out of the actual cultivators'. The mahajan holdings in the neighbourhood of a town of this size naturally ran a little higher than in the more rural areas and amounted to some 14%. The town's trading wealth doubtless provided temptation for plunder, but it is noticeable that the Gujar villages involved in the attacks on Deoband were not situated in the rich agricultural area. On his first punitive expedition at the end of May 1857 Robertson singled out for vengeance Babupur, Sanpla Bakal, and Fatehpur (modern Fatehgarh alias Sanpla Deora); and on his second expedition in

[25] R. Spankie, Magistrate, to Commissioner, Meerut, 11 March 1858, U.P. State Archives, Allahabad. Saharanpur Collectorate Pre-Mutiny Records. Bk 230, ser. II, 4. Judicial letters issued to the Commissioner, May 1856–Oct. 1858.
[26] List of Persons eminent for disloyalty in Zillah Saharanpore, Mag. no. 100 of 8 April 1858; *ibid.*

late July Chota Sanpla (modern Sanpla Khatri?), Bunhera Khas, Dugchara, Salahpur and Manki. All these villages stood close to the Kali Nadi or its tributaries north and east of Deoband and within a 4- to 5-mile radius. They occupied poor sandy soil (*buda*) that bore a stiff assessment, but where mahajan inroads were slight (*c.* 7%).[27] A few miles to the north of this cluster of villages lay Manikpur, where Umrao Singh set himself up as raja. Sited near the banks of the Kali Nadi it fell in the southern tract of pargana Bhagwanpur which Wynne believed had 'suffered much by over-assessment',[28] but admittedly the moneylender gains were greater here, amounting to 12% (or if Borah holdings are added to mahajan, 16%).

The mahajan unquestionably played a significant role in prompting the Mutiny disturbances, but it was different and more complex than generally supposed. It is nevertheless easy to understand how the accepted picture has been constructed. By the mid 1860s the mahajans were in possession of some 18% of the agricultural land in the Saharanpur district, most of their gains having been made by the time of the 1857 outbreak. Among the earliest casualties had been the magnate class. The provincial *Gazetteer* in 1875 looked on them as a thing of the past: 'few of the old respectable families retain their estates which have fallen principally into the hands of the Saharanpur moneylenders'.[29] But these had been neither numerous nor ancient. The hold established over the cultivating communities caused graver concern and by 1854 the Government had been sufficiently alarmed to institute a general inquiry throughout the N.W. Provinces. Ross, the Collector of Saharanpur, emphasised in his reply that the peasantry parted with its land only under extreme necessity and that a widespread sense of grievance was manifest. 'The unjust and fraudulent spoliation thus alleged to be committed through the ready instrumentality of the Civil Court is the theme of loud and constant complaint among the agricultural class', he wrote in March 1855.[30] The officials differed in their analysis of the threat from the moneylender. Robertson and Wynne in the

[27] Wynne's Report, paras. 124–6. For identification of villages, see Survey of India 1-inch sheets 53 G/9, G/10, G/13.
[28] *Ibid.*, para. 140.
[29] *Gaz. N.W.P.*, ed. Atkinson, II, p. 231.
[30] Cited J. Vans Agnew to F. Williams, 28 Jan. 1863, para. 46; *Saharanpur S.R. 1871*, Appx, p. 11.

later 1860s saw the enemy as the large absentee moneylenders, the 'men of large capital' who congregated in the towns. Other officials, like G. Williams a little later, thought the peasantry had become 'to all intents and purposes merely serfs of the petty moneylenders'.[31] All were agreed, however, in recognising that 'the sturdy Rajputs and Gujars' had best resisted the mahajan's encroachment and all were unanimous in absolving the revenue assessment from responsibility for the high rate of land transfers, especially to the non-agricultural classes. Vans Agnew was quick to point out in 1863 that the transfer rate ran highest where the assessment was lightest, parganas Saharanpur and Sultanpur contrasting markedly with the heavily assessed parganas of Gangoh, Nakur and Deoband (Table 1).

All this merely underlines the fact that the principal elements of revolt in 1857 came from castes and areas where the mahajan hold was lightest and the land revenue heaviest. More significantly, perhaps, these were the backward, thirsty tracts.

It would be wrong, however, to suggest that rural rebellion stemmed simply from conservative elements among the clan communities unable or unwilling to adapt themselves to cash-crop agriculture. Events in the Muzaffarnagar and Meerut districts to the south amply demonstrate that the centres of the most advanced and productive agricultural regions, the rich parganas irrigated by the East Jumna Canal, could be the seat of a resistance more determined and formidable than the transient jacqueries of the Gujars. This rebellion of the Jat brotherhoods would seem to stand in economic terms at the other end of the scale, but it shared certain common features with the Gujar risings and throws a sharper light on the workings of rural unrest.

Despite their high farming the Jat communities of the western portion of the Muzaffarnagar district suffered some loss of land to the moneylender in the pre-Mutiny decades, yet their losses were as nothing when contrasted with those of the Sayyid communities in the eastern parganas who remained pointedly quiet in 1857 (Table 3). The rule that areas that had succumbed most to the mahajan were least active in rebellion was also true in Muzaffarnagar district. But in contrast with the Gujar communities of the canal-irrigated tracts of western Saharanpur, the Jats

[31] Cited *Gaz. N.W.P.*, ii, pt 1, p. 227. Wynne, cited p. 233. See Table A.

TABLE 3. *Land holdings and transfers of Sayyids, Jats and Mahajans illustrating the contrast between selected western and eastern parganas of Muzaffarnagar district 1841–61*

Western parganas

		Sayyids	Jats	mahajans	% of zamindari estates	% of bhaiachara estates	% of total area transferred (incl. mortgages)	Revenue rate per cultivated acre (Rs.)
Shamli	(1) % total area, 1841	—	70·8	3·8	2	88	16	2-10-0
	(2) % total area, 1861	—	63·7	11·4				
	(3) % gain/loss on (1)	—	-9·9	+201·8				
	(4) % loss to mahajans on (1)	—	7·6	—				
Kandhla	(1) % total area, 1841	—	37·1	8	13	65	17	2-4-8
	(2) % total area, 1861	—	34·4	14·7				
	(3) % gain/loss on (1)	—	-7·1	+82·7				
	(4) % loss to mahajans on (1)	—	6·6	—				
Thana Bhawan	(1) % total area, 1841	—	10·5	5·9	23	52	12·6	1-13-7
	(2) % total area, 1861	—	9·1	12·6				
	(3) % gain/loss on (1)	—	-12·7	+112·6				
	(4) % loss to mahajans on (1)	—	12·9	—				
Budhana	(1) % total area, 1841	—	20·7	1·4	2	48	11·4	2-3-7
	(2) % total area, 1861	—	19·3	5·0				
	(3) % gain/loss on (1)	—	-6·7	+256·8				
	(4) % loss to mahajans on (1)	—	5·5	—				
Shikapur	(1) % total area, 1841	—	54·7	3·9	5	51	25·8	2-6-7
	(2) % total area, 1861	—	45·8	13·4				
	(3) % gain/loss on (1)	—	-16·3	+241				
	(4) % loss to mahajans on (1)	—	13·6	—				

Eastern parganas

		Sayyids	Jats	mahajans	% of zamindari estates	% of bhaiachara estates	% of total area transferred (incl. mortgages)	Revenue rate per cultivated acre (Rs.)
Muzaffarnagar	(1) % total area, 1841	51·9	1·0	21·6	26	61	27	1–8–2
	(2) % total area, 1861	32·9	1·7	34·7				
	(3) % gain/loss on (1)	−37·8	+62·6	+60·5				
Bhukarheri	(1) % total area, 1841	49·3	—	17·8	53	4	44·2	1–6–8
	(2) % total area, 1861	20·6	—	39·4				
	(3) % gain/loss on (1)	−57·3	—	+120·8				
Jansath	(1) % total area, 1841	79	1·2	8·8	29	10	20	1–4–6
	(2) % total area, 1861	72	3·8	10·2				
	(3) % gain/loss on (1)	8	+213	+14				
Khatauli	(1) % total area, 1841	60	?	9·4	50	35	47	1–11–6
	(2) % total area, 1861	24·4	9·2	22·5				
	(3) % gain/loss on (1)	−56	?	+152				
Bhuma-Sambalhera	(1) % total area, 1841	76	10	5	57	2	50	1–3–2
	(2) % total area, 1861	56·4	9	24·6				
	(3) % gain/loss on (1)	−26	−10	+415				

Sources:

1 For western parganas, *Gazetteer N.W.P.*, ed. E. Atkinson (Allahabad, 1876), III, pt 2, pp. 552–5, and Report of the Permanent Settlement of the Western Pergunnahs of the Moozuffernuggur District, pp. 71 ff. in *Muzaffarnagar Settlement Report*, 1873.

2 For eastern parganas, *Gazetteer*, III, 2, pp. 554–5, and A. Cadell, *Settlement Report on the Ganges Canal Tract in the Muzaffarnagar District* (Allahabad, 1878), p. 12.

NOTE: figures for Jansath, Khatauli, Bhuma and Bhuma are given not in acres but whole villages and *biswas*. These have been roughly verified against 'Statement of Ownership in Caste in acres for 1870' in Cadell, *op. cit*, p. 12, but need to be regarded with particular caution.

were held down by a punitive land-revenue demand. The differential rates imposed on the Jat peasantry in the 1830s and 1840s by Plowden and Sir Henry Elliot in parganas Budhana, Kandhla, Shamli and Shikapur were recognised after 1857 as intolerably oppressive and on any reading stand out as the major grievance of the Jat rebels. But the absolute pitch of the assessment could hardly of itself have been sufficient motive. For the Jats managed to meet it by the admirable skill and industry they displayed as agriculturalists, which in terms of productivity made these parganas some of the finest in the North-Western Provinces. What one suspects rankled deeper than being taxed more heavily than other castes was to find their ancestral lands mulcted so savagely in contrast with their caste brethren to the east, especially in the fertile portions of parganas Khatauli and Jansath.[32] Here a small number of Jat communities flourished unhindered, and so far as the imperfect statistics indicate, were on balance net gainers of land during the 1841–61 settlement, which had favoured these south-eastern parganas so decidedly.[33] The proprietary communities were, of course, nothing like so numerous as west of the Kali Nadi, but there was a substantial Jat cultivating body, particularly in Muzaffarnagar and Bhukarheri parganas, who held as occupancy tenants at what were probably favourable rates.[34] Their condition may well have been more advantageous than that of the smaller coparceners of the overcrowded Jat villages of the west, 'where there was no elbow room left for the superabundant population; every available acre had been utilized when Mr E. Thornton appeared on the scene in 1840'.[35] As with the Gujars and Pundir Rajputs of south-western and southern Saharanpur, the governing motive of the Jat revolt in western

[32] Cf. revenue rates per acre on the cultivation:

Kandhla	Rs. 2–4–8		Khatauli	Rs. 1–11–6
Budhana	2–3–7		Jansath	1–4–6
Shamli	2–10–0		Muzaffarnagar	1–8–2
Shikapur	2–6–7			

[33] For Jat acquisitions see tables, *Gaz. N.W.P.*, III, pt 2 (1876), pp. 554–5, and pargana notices of Khatauli (p. 700) and Jansath (p. 680). For the low revenue rates imposed by Thornton on Khatauli and Jansath, cf. A. Cadell, *Settlement Report of the Ganges Canal Tract of the Muzaffarnagar District* (Allahabad, 1878), pp. 42–5.

[34] On Jat distribution in the eastern parganas and favourable rates for occupancy tenants, Cadell, *Report on Ganges Canal Tract.* pp. 12–13.

[35] S. N. Martin in *Settlement Report on the District of Moozuffernugger* (Allahabad, 1873), p. 157; also p. 70.

Muzaffarnagar may well have been, therefore, relative rather than absolute deprivation.

Even if this hypothesis must remain speculative it is difficult to see the role of the mahajan in provoking violence as more than tangential, or to escape the conclusion that if a single factor can be isolated in the generation of revolt in this region it was the revenue demand. In fastening on the mahajan the British officers were consciously or unconsciously seeking a scapegoat.[36]

There is a further argument to be considered. Revolt cannot be seen purely in terms of economic determinism, for motive is relative not merely to deprivation but to power. Those revolt who are most fit to revolt, and intensity of felt grievance is doubtless always proportionate to fighting and organisational capability.[37] The threshold of tolerability might be lower than 10% for armed Gujar or Jat communities while losses of up to 60% of their land (as in pargana Bhukarheri in Muzaffarnagar) would be borne passively by disorganised Sayyid gentry communities. Even here, however, one must suppose that where transfers to the money-lender were prompted by the pressure of the land-revenue demand, resentment would still fall primarily on the British authorities, and would express itself as rebellion rather than inter-necine caste conflict. But other non-economic considerations complicated the response.

In general terms, landlord or zamindari estates were more numerous in the eastern parganas of the Meerut division, and this feature was at once both symptom and cause of a more extensive revolution in landed rights. While it produced a situation which could facilitate transfers to the moneylending classes, as in eastern Muzaffarnagar district, it permitted at the same time the emergence of a new landed elite whose interests and outlook bound them closely to the British power. In Muzaffarnagar,

[36] Cf. R. M. Edwards, *Narrative of Events*, cited *Gazetteer N.W.P.*, III (1875), p. 626: 'The natural result [of the deliberate inactivity of the police] was that violent crimes of all kinds were daily, almost hourly, committed throughout the district...It is needless naming the chief crimes; it is sufficient to remark that here, as in other parts of the country, the Baniyas and Mahajans were, in the majority of cases, the victims, and fearfully have many of them been made to suffer for their previous rapacity and avarice.'

[37] The formidable Jat clan organisation has been brought out in a modern sociological study, P. C. Pradhan, *The Political Organization of the Jats of Northern India* (Bombay, 1966). For the role of the Baliyan and Gathwala *khaps*, see pp. 107–9.

Alan Cadell noted in the 1870s how despite a huge reduction in the total area held by Sayyids and a dramatic expansion of the area held by the moneylenders a considerable portion of the Sayyid land transferred between 1841 and 1861 was acquired by a few, powerful and expansive Sayyid families, notably Sayyid Husain Ali Khan and his nephews of Jansath, Sayyid Amir Husain and Wazir Husain of Sambalhera, and Gulam Husain of Jauli.[38] Their fortunes were intimately linked with office-holding. In 1857 Husain Ali Khan was not only 'a very extensive landholder' but also tahsildar of Khurja in Bulandshahr district. Another Sayyid, Tufazal Husain of Miranpur, held office as tahsildar at Hapur in the Meerut district while Sayyid Imdad Husain served at Muzaffarnagar. All these exerted themselves to prevent their impoverished Sayyid brethren from resorting to violence.[39] Another Muslim magnate, the Muslim Rajput Nawab of Karnal, had also made large gains of land from the Sayyids, and in 1857 adhered staunchly to the British cause.

In Saharanpur there was no equivalent of a new thrusting landlord class outside the ranks of the moneylenders. But the revolution of property rights produced in the end something of the same political effect in the eastern half of the district. It was a revolution accomplished not by free or enforced sale but by British administrative action in dismantling the great Gujar fiscal lordship (mukarari) bequeathed by Raja Ram Dayal Singh, and comprising on his death in 1813 some 827 villages and 36 hamlets. From these the Landhaura estate of 505 villages and 31 hamlets had been marked out, only to be steadily whittled away and settled with the village communities until in 1854 Landhaura Khas consisted of no more than 38 villages or portions of villages under a minor raja, Raghubir Singh. The remnant was placed under the management of Padhan Sahib Singh, the young raja's uncle, who chose to stand firm for the British in 1857.[40] Although it might be supposed that the Landhaura family, like any decayed chiefly house, would have strong motives for rebellion, it appears

---

[38] A. Cadell, *Settlement Report on Ganges Canal Tract of Muzaffarnagar District* (Allahabad, 1878), para. 59, pp. 53–4.

[39] R. M. Edwards to F. Williams, 3 April 1858; U.P. State Archives, Allahabad, Commissioner, Meerut, Dept. XII, Special File 34/1858. Also F. Williams to G. Couper, 6 Aug. 1859, *ibid.*, File 40/1859.

[40] J. Vans Agnew to F. Williams, 28 Jan. 1863, paras. 64–70, *Saharanpur S.R 1871*, Appx, pp. 17–20.

to have been so drastically reduced beforehand as to have become a creature of the British power, and to have played the role of a collaborating magnate element. Most of the villages of the truncated Landhaura estate fell within Manglaur pargana, where the Gujars still held 48% of the land in 1868. Landhaura village itself broke out in violence and was burned by the British in punishment, but there was no general Gujar rising in this region. The importance of Padhan Sahib's services in placing 'the whole resources of the Raj at the disposal of the Magistrate' and 'by his influence as Goojur' in helping to keep 'this turbulent body in subjection'[41] was subsequently recognised. On the outbreak of the Thana Bhawan rising at the end of August 1857 Padhan Sahib again 'marched with all his followers, some 200 or 300 men and some small guns' to Rampur to prevent any inroad from disaffected villagers in Muzaffarnagar district.[42]

In the south-western portion of the Saharanpur district political influences worked in quite the opposite direction. Here the Batar Gujars, belonging to a different *got* from the Landhaura family, were heavily mixed with Muslim Gujars, interspersed with Turkaman and Sheikh communities, and flanked on the south by the Muslim Rajputs or Rangars of Kunda Kalan. In Gangoh pargana these Muslim elements had fallen into a condition of poverty that provided fertile ground for religious extremism and political disaffection. Lakhnauti was occupied by a Shiah Turkaman colony, the remnants of Tappa Kaini which before the death of their chieftain Barmand Ali Khan had consisted of 21 villages near Gangoh. Gangoh itself was possessed by Sheikhs who were a branch of the Pirzadah house. When Wynne visited the town in the early 1860s he could not comprehend how they managed to eke out an existence, so partitioned was their property and so disdainful were they of working with their hands. He described the place as 'a hot-bed of Wahabeeism'. The Pirzadahs of Ambahta in Nakur pargana were better-off, enjoying 22 revenue-free villages and living in a town that because of the fine minareted tomb of their ancestor, Shah Abul Malli, was a place of pilgrimage. Wynne found them indebted, however, and Spankie and Robertson were convinced at the time that they had been the

---

[41] R. Spankie to F. Williams, 26 March 1858, encl. 2. Saharanpur Collectorate Pre-Mutiny Records, Bk 230. Judicial letters issued to Commissioner, May 1856–Oct. 1858, fo. 222.

[42] *Ibid.* Also Spankie to Commissioner, 18 Sept. 1857, *ibid.*, fo. 129.

principal instigators of the Gujar attack on Nakur, and of the destruction of the moneylenders' houses. There was perhaps a similar connection between the Muslim urban populations of Gangoh and Lakhnauti and the co-religionist Rangars of Kunda Kalan, for Robertson believed the latter were intent on marching on the two towns when he encountered and dispersed their massed array. Certainly materials for an organised *jihad* existed, and the celebrated Deoband school (or *Dar-ul-ulum*) traced its origins and inspiration to the fight against the British organised by Maulana Muhammad Qasim of Nanauta and Maulana Rashid Ahmad of Gangoh in league with the Thana Bhawan insurgents.[43] At the same time it would be wrong to suppose that all Muslims were united in revolt. The Raos of Jalalabad and Lohari refused to join the Thana Bhawan insurgents, and at Shamli Edwards noticed how the attackers had entered the mosque and slaughtered fellow-Muslims within its walls.[44] The adhesion of the Gujars to such heterogeneous Muslim political leadership tended to be loose and short-lived. By the time of the Thana Bhawan rising and the attack on Shamli in September 1857 the Gujars were not prepared to follow, and to the south began actively obstructing Jat attempts to link up with the Thana Bhawan movement.[45] They refused to be cast in a purely ancillary role. However, the British recapture of Delhi at the end of September 1857 prevented the movement from developing and all resistance in the upper Doab quickly collapsed.

One inference that would seem to follow from this analysis is that where proprietary rights circulated most freely, not only could the mahajans gain an extensive hold but also magnate elements could elevate themselves from out of the major losing castes. The latter would be more actively attached to British rule

[43] Z. H. Faruqi, *The Deoband School and the Demand for Pakistan* (Bombay, 1963), pp. 20–1. K. M. Ashraf in P. C. Joshi (ed.), *Rebellion 1857* (Delhi, 1957), p. 92. Aziz Ahmad, *Islamic Modernism in India and Pakistan, 1857–1964* (1967), pp. 28, 104 ff.

[44] R. M. Edwards, Magistrate, to F. Williams, 3 April 1858; Commissioner, Meerut, Dept. XII, Special File 34/1858. U.P. State Archives, Allahabad. Also Edwards to Williams, 1 Sept. 1858, *ibid.*, File 32/1858. Also *ibid.*, 4 March 1859; *ibid.*, File 50/1859. *Ibid.*, 21 Oct. 1859; *ibid.*, File 48/1859. On Shamli massacre, R. M. Edwards, Mutiny Diary, entry 16 Sept. [1857], fo. 87; MSS. Eur. c. 148/2 India Office Library.

[45] Narrative of Events in the Meerut Division by F. Williams, Commissioner, 15 Nov. 1858, para. 113, in *Narrative of Events concerning the Mutiny in India and the Restoration of Authority* (Calcutta, 1881), 1, p. 244.

where as in the case of the Sayyids they owed their rise to office-holding, for indeed much of their land may have been acquired because of the advantages their official position gave them at public sales.[46] Such a group of men could exercise a dispropor-tionately large political influence on their caste or class brethren, even though these may have suffered severe impoverishment. The political decision for or against revolt among the Muslim gentry seems to have been dependent on the occurrence or absence of this internal process of differentiation. While among the failing Sayyid squireens of eastern Muzaffarnagar district a new magnate element emerged, on the western side of the district and in the region abutting it to the north in western Saharanpur district the Muslim Sheikh, Beloch, Afghan and Sayyid communities failed to produce any notables of comparable stature.[47] A decayed Muslim gentry living alongside an impoverished Gujar and Rangar peasantry were combustible materials readily ignited, especially when the powerful Jat brotherhoods of Shamli and the Rajputs of Budhana made common cause with them. Peasant rebellion might originate in the oppressive revenue demand, but the same could not be said of the Muslim gentry, for large numbers of these subsisted on *muafi* or revenue-free holdings, especially in Thana Bhawan pargana. Here admittedly, im-poverished and debt-ridden by constant partition among heirs, they could well nurture a hatred of the moneylender that would pass readily into a general hatred of British rule.

The process of internal differentiation may also have power-fully affected Jat action. On the eastern side of Muzaffarnagar district, not merely were the Jats generally a prospering caste, for whom the opening of the majestic Ganges Canal in April 1854

---

[46] On the discrepancy between the private and public (forced) sale price of land and the irregularities attending public auctions, Cadell, *Report on Ganges Canal Tract*, paras, 21–3, pp. 98–9.

[47] Edwards, the Magistrate, acknowledged the services of Mansur Ali Khan, and his son Muhamed Ali (subsequently appointed *tahsildar* of Thana Bhawan), who 'with the other Raeeses of Jalalabad not only refused to join the Thana Bhown revolt but did their utmost to prevent the out-break, and when they failed they successfully exerted themselves to stop any of their townspeople joining the rebels'; Edwards to Williams, 3 April April 1858, Commissioner, Meerut, Dept XII. Another supporter was Saadulla Khan Afridi, half-owner of nearby Lohari, an elderly man of great influence whose nephew, Ahmad Ali Khan, owner of the other half of Lohari, turned rebel; Edwards to Williams, 1 Sept. 1858, *ibid.*, File 32/1858.

offered splendid prospects, but in the wealthy Jat family of Maulaheri in Muzaffarnagar pargana a new magnate element is evident. By Cadell's time the family were substantial landholders in Muzaffarnagar and Khatauli, owning altogether some 6,000 acres in the Ganges Canal Tract.[48] There is no evidence as to whether they exercised a restraining hand over their caste-brethren, but certainly this was the case still further to the south in the Meerut and Bulandshahr districts. No contrast could be more absolute than that between the ferocity of Jat rebellion in western Meerut (which later spread north into Muzaffarnagar) and the conspicuous 'loyalty' displayed by the Jats of eastern Meerut and Bulandshahr. The only sufficient explanation, apart from the differing incidence of the revenue demand, is that in the western portion the Jats were organised into bhaiachara village communities within a clan organisation, while in the eastern they dwelt as sub-proprietors or occupancy tenants in landlord estates, among which the huge patrimony established by Gulab Singh, the loyalist Jat raja of Kuchchesar, was pre-eminent.[49] But in this contrast the moneylender figured hardly at all. In the mechanism of rebellion he was but the fly on the wheel.

[48] Cadell, *Report on the Ganges Canal Tract*, p. 11. It would appear, however, that many of their gains were post-1857; *ibid.*, p. 54.
[49] See above, pp. 149 ff.

8

Traditional elites in the Great Rebellion of 1857: some aspects of rural revolt in the upper and central Doab

Rural revolt in 1857 was essentially elitist in character. Things may have been otherwise in the cities and towns, where as at Aligarh (Koil) 'the low Muhammedan rabble' could become a potent revolutionary force. But in the countryside the mass of the population appears to have played little part in the fighting or at most tamely followed the behests of its caste superiors. The dominant castes and communities that took the lead in rebellion were a minority of the population, and, of these, the owners of land were a still smaller group. Figures for the classification and enumeration of population have to be treated with reserve, but it is interesting to note, for example, that in Aligarh district in 1872 landowners numbered some 26,551 or $2\frac{1}{2}\%$ of the total population.[1] In Mathura district where cultivating proprietary brotherhoods of Jats were thick on the ground the proportion was higher, some $6\frac{1}{2}\%$. Roughly 47,000 owners (including non-agriculturalists) controlled an adult male agricultural population of 129,000 cultivators; in other words one in three male agriculturalists owned land.[2] It was one in six in the Ganges Canal Tract of the Muzaffarnagar district where the landowning castes – Tagas, Jats, Rajputs, Sayyids, Sheikhs, Gujars, Borahs, Marhals and Mahajans – comprised one-third of the population.[3] In Mainpuri district the Rajputs formed just over 8% of the population and held about one-half of the land.[4] Even, therefore, where 'village republics' owned the land, as in the Jat *bhaiachara* settlements in

---

[1] *Statistical, Descriptive and Historical Account of the N.W. Provinces*, ed. E. T. Atkinson (hereafter referred as *Gazetteer N.W.P.*), II, pt I, p. 390.

[2] *Report on the Settlement of the Muttra District N.W.P.*, by R. S. Whiteway (Allahabad, 1879) (hereafter cited as *Muttra S.R.*), p. 25.

[3] *Settlement Report of the Ganges Canal Tract of the Muzaffarnagar District* (Allahabad, 1878), by A. Cadell, pp. 10 ff.

[4] *Gazetteer N.W.P.*, IV, pp. 386 ff.

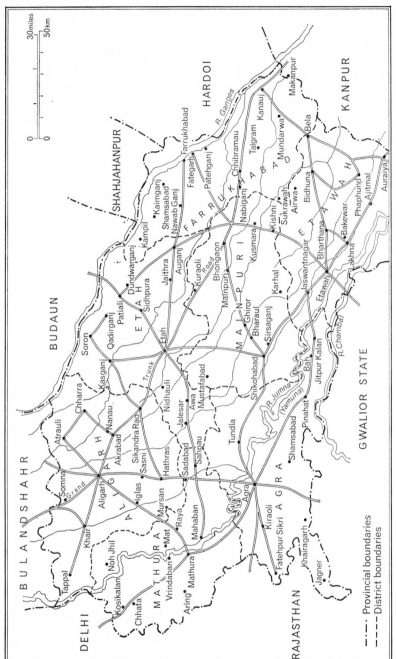

Map 4 The Agra Region

northern Mathura or in the western portions of Meerut and Muzaffarnagar districts, the proprietary body was very much a rural elite. This fact deserves emphasis since it is all too easy to view the peasantry as a rural proletariat.

Most accounts trace the rural rebellion to the revolutionary effects upon the traditional landholding classes of British legal and institutional innovations. The rendering of the *malguzari* right (the right to engage for the government revenue) freely alienable and saleable is held to have resulted in a vast transfer of land rights and the displacement of much of the traditional elite – whether magnate or village zamindars – by the urban trading and money-lending classes and by office-holders drawn from the literate castes.[5] Unquestionably there was a high rate of transfer of proprietary title (though not, of course, of actual cultivating possession), not only in the early fumbling period of British rule but in the later pre-Rebellion decades when the administrative machine was functioning more regularly. In some districts the rate ran as high as 2% per annum, so that, as in Aligarh district, title to more than 50% of the land could change hands in the two decades after 1838.[6] But although the non-agricultural classes made extensive acquisitions, increasing their hold up to as much as 18% of the total cultivation (as in Saharanpur district by 1868), their gains were nothing like proportionate to the transfer rate. As Cohn has found in the Varanasi (Benares) region a large portion of the transfers represented a circulation of property within the traditional elite. The breakdown of British authority so far from throwing this elite wholly on to the side of rebellion split it raggedly down the middle, with the result that, even within the same district, magnate or peasant proprietors of the same caste could react in quite opposite directions. In Meerut district the Jats of Hapur pargana fought stoutly on the British side; to the west on the other side of the Hindan River in Baraut and Barnawa parganas they rose in their thousands, driving off the British columns sent from Meerut and pouring supplies into rebel-held Delhi. In the Muzaffarnagar district the Sayyid communities in the eastern parganas stayed quiet, while on the other side the Muslim gentry rose to support the Thana Bhawan rising

[5] S. B. Chaudhuri, *Civil Rebellion in the Indian Mutinies* (Calcutta, 1957), p. 21. S. N. Sen, *Eighteen Fifty Seven* (Calcutta, 1957), pp. 32–5.
[6] *Aligarh Settlement Report* (Allahabad, 1882), para. 182, p. 65.

of September 1857 when the green flag of Islam was raised and a *jihad* proclaimed against the white infidel. These are complexities that confute generalised *simpliste* accounts but they are still susceptible of historical explanation.

Strong armed clan communities such as the Jat clan settlements in western Meerut and Muzaffarnagar or those of the Gujars in western Saharanpur or the Pandir Rajputs of southern Saharanpur flared readily into rebellion, probably out of resentment at the heavy differential revenue assessment laid upon them.[7] But the critical factor in rural reactions was the presence or absence of a thriving magnate element heavily committed by interest to British rule. Nowhere were objective conditions more ripe for revolt than among the Sayyids of the Ganges Canal Tract of eastern Muzaffarnagar. Their losses of land to the urban money-lender had been on a spectacular scale, rising in some parganas such as Khatauli to as much as 56% between 1840 and 1860. But the danger of revolt was stayed by the leadership of a few thriving Sayyid families who, aided by office-holding under the British, had built up considerable estates. The same phenomenon of magnate leadership is observable in south-eastern Meerut and the Bulandshahr district. Here the Jats unlike their kinsmen near the Yamuna (Jumna) followed the lead of the Jat raja of Kuchesar, Gulab Singh, who held a vast estate of more than 270 villages.[8]

What were the conditions that permitted the emergence of a prospering, collaborating magnate class? A simple answer would be that where zamindari (roughly undivided freehold) tenures were numerous, a market in land titles was more readily created and supplied the conditions of mobility in which a new, active landlord class could emerge. Eastern Muzaffarnagar mirrored such conditions. In contrast, where cultivating proprietary brotherhoods (bhaiachara) held the land, they were not readily ousted by outsiders; mobility of titles was consequently much lower, as the lighter transfer rate in the Jat areas indicate. More important than the tenurial structure of the individual village was perhaps the supra-village organisation of the clan area (*khap* or *ilaqua*), which M. C. Pradhan has shown has persisted tenaciously to the present.[9] Not only did this help to keep outside encroachment at bay, but supplied a powerful political weapon for joint action among village communities. Nevertheless the difficulty which Jats or Gujars faced in revolt was the generalisation of resistance to embrace other clans and groups. In the absence of individual leadership capable of welding, say, a whole district together, the rebellion of peasant communities would remain isolated and confined to their particular localities.

The critical factor remained, therefore, whether for the promotion or suppression of revolt, the action of magnate elements. Impoverished gentry could sometimes fill the gap in leadership, like Khairati Khan of Parasauli in Muzaffarnagar, an old Pindari who apparently placed himself at the head of the Jat rising in late August 1857, but generally such men proved too lacking in scale and resources and themselves looked to magnate leaders. Thus in Bulandshahr district disaffected Muslim gentry like the Sayyids of Shikarpur rallied to the standard of Nawab Walidad Khan of Malagarh, a fallen nobleman who was related by marriage to the Delhi dynasty and well versed in public affairs. For a time Walidad rendered himself formidable, and the British were fortunate that there were few of his calibre in the central and upper Doab. But in this region most of the magnate class in fact stayed quiet or actively assisted the British. The notion that the traditional elite was driven *en bloc* into rebellion needs, therefore, critical re-examination.

Aligarh district makes an interesting study in this respect. Fifty per cent of the land changed hands between 1839 and 1858, spurred by a heavy average revenue demand of Rs. 2-3-1 to the cultivated acre. The moneylending and trading classes registered considerable gains, strengthening their grip from 3·4% of the district in 1839 to 12·3% in 1868. Yet their overall gain of 9% looks modest when viewed against total transfers which evidently in the main took the form of a circulation of proprietary rights within the traditional landholding castes. Circulation took place in two ways: first in the passage of land from village proprietors to magnates, and secondly, among village proprietors themselves.

Now it may seem odd to speak of the gains of the magnate

[9] M. C. Pradhan, *The Political System of the Jats of Northern India* (Bombay, 1966).

class in a district where British administrative action in the pre-Mutiny decades would appear to have been so sharply directed against them. Thornton's settlement of 1839 was notorious for its deliberate attempt to curb the Jat chieftains of Hathras and Mursan by instituting a sub-settlement, wherever possible, with the village communities. The British themselves were agreeably surprised that the magnates should stick by them in the crisis of 1857 in view of the severe mauling the magnates had supposedly received at their hands.

W. H. Smith commented in his settlement report on Aligarh in 1874:

Scarcely one member of any of the old and powerful families of the district joined in the disturbances: on the contrary, some of these gave what assistance they could with undoubted readiness: some like Thakur Gobind Singh, nobly exposed their lives in our cause, while others afforded aid only perhaps because they doubted the policy of refusing. Strangely enough...those of the greater families who had lost most by our rule, turned out our firmest friends in the time of trouble and need. Thakur Gobind Singh, the son of the very man whose fort we had taken and whose power we had crushed (in 1817)...was eminently loyal. He never hesitated from the first, but aided us with his followers, fought in our battles, and kept order on our behalf. Raja Tikam Singh, the son of Bhagwant Singh, whose independence we had forcibly destroyed, assisted us throughout to the utmost of his ability, though his own power had been largely reduced by the policy pursued at the last settlement by Mr Thornton. Without the aid of these two men Hathras would have been plundered, and our footing in the district for the time at least have been lost.[10]

The damage that Thornton's anti-*talukdar* settlement inflicted on the magnate interest in Aligarh was in fact, however, superficial. With the Mursan raja, Tikam Singh, the settlement was a generous one, although he continued to contest it for years afterwards in the courts. He was compensated with a fixed allowance or *malikana* – usually $22\frac{1}{2}\%$ – of the revenue demand paid by the village proprietors (*biswadars*), but Thornton's proposal for allowing him to continue with the work of collection was rejected.[11] Nevertheless the financial arrangement worked to his advantage:

[10] W. H. Smith in *Aligarh S.R.*, para. 55, p. 19.
[11] *Selections from the Records of Govt. N.W. Provinces: Mr Thomason's Despatches* (Calcutta, 1856) i, pp. 19 ff.

instead of a vague title, and an income insufficient for his expenses, especially as it was never fully collected, the former [*viz.* the Raja] has now been recorded as zamindar of more than one-third of the pargana, and as hereditary talukdar with defined rights in the remainder; his income has been considerably increased, and there is every ground for hope that he will fully realise it.[12]

Given the circumstances that the Raja had pitched up the demand to such a height before Thornton's revision that the villages were falling heavily into arrears, there was much to be said from his viewpoint for an arrangement which guaranteed the coercive force of the courts for the collection of his fixed percentage of a punitively heavy demand.[13]

In contrast, so far from stabilising and securing the village communities, Thornton's settlement completely defeated his intentions. Its close definition of landed rights seems to have been the signal for a revolution in proprietary titles, which according to Smith acquired for the first time a saleable value. In this revolution it was the magnate class as well as the moneylending and trading classes that forged ahead.[14] In the Hathras tahsil, where 'a vast revolution of property' took place, the Jats as a caste held their own without loss over the thirty years 1839–68, despite the fact that the transfers in the period amounted to some 66% of the land:

Thirty-four per cent of the land is now in the hands of those who occupied it at last settlement, and the majority of this belongs to Raja Tikam Singh, who has alone remained unaffected by the prevailing changes. . .In fact, the old village occupants, the preservation of whom was Mr Thornton's chief care and thought, have been almost crushed out of the subdivision, and new men, to a large extent Bohras and Banias, have taken their place.

Not all the talukdars, however, were as fortunate as the Mursan raja. Many of the smaller talukdars like Thakur Jiwa Ram of Mendhu and Raja Narain Singh of Husain foundered while Tikam Singh was extending his estates, buying in the biswadars of four villages and so converting his hold to full ownership (zamindari).

The village bodies suffered fearfully. The talukdari settlement,

[12] Cited *ibid.*, para. 335, p. 118.
[13] For Mursan settlement, see Thornton's report in *Allygurh Statistics* by J. Hutchinson (Rurkse, 1854).
[14] Smith, *op. cit.*, paras. 186–7, pp. 67–8.

with its additional increment of malikana, laid on them burdens too grievous to be borne. An assessment that was avowedly based on extracting 80% of the rental assets left them a helpless prey of the Hathras *banias* and the village *saukars*, who now revived old debts they had bought up from European indigo planters after the collapse of the late 1820s. More than a third of the talukdari villages were sold up entirely, and a further third lost more than a half of their land.[15] But the alienation statement for 1838–68 shows the main sufferers to have been the Rajput brotherhoods, who over the period lost 51% of their land, their losses (of 35,284 acres) balancing almost exactly the bania gains.

Other parts of the district illustrate the same transfer of rights out of the hands of the village proprietors. In Sikandra Rao Rajput transfers were again enormous, amounting to some 41% in pargana Akerabad and 57% in pargana Aligarh. But the take-over of the Husain taluk by the moneylending Rajput Jadon family of Mathura (under Raja Pirthi Singh of Awa) from the Porach Rajput family, and other internal caste transfers of this kind, disguise the extent to which property changed hands. In the upshot the Thakur (Rajput) loss appears as no more than 13.4%.

Unfortunately the statistics do not allow us to distinguish with any great clarity the twin processes of circulation within castes which it has been suggested occurred, first the transfer of land from village communities to magnates, and secondly the movement of land within village communities themselves. Where the first process predominated, it seems more than likely that the magnates remained pro-British and were able to smother rebellion. The talukdari parganas, Hathras, Koil, Sikandra Rao, and Atrauli were of this kind. Disturbances, of course, did break out. Mangal Singh and Mahtab Singh, Rajput zamindars of Akrabad (tahsil Silkandra Rao) 'after the plunder of Akrabad Tehseel Treasury by sepoys, permitted the destruction of the records by their own people, refused all aid to the Tehseeldar, and generally lived a life of open rebellion'.[16] Yet they were countered by 'the

15 Smith, *Aligarh S.R.*, para. 340, p. 119. For sales resulting from indigo debts, Revenue Despatch to India, 13 Aug. 1851, India and Bengal Despatches, vol. 72/IOR E/4/811. Also N.W. Provinces Board of Revenue Proceedings, 10 Nov. 1840, no. 12; 16 Octo. 1840, nos. 21–2.

16 W. J. Bramley, Magistrate Aligarh, to A. Cocks, Special Commissioner, 17 Nov. 1858; cited S. A. A. Rizvi (ed.), *Freedom Struggle in Uttar Pradesh* (Lucknow, 1957–61), v pp. 868 ff.

most influential of Pundir Thakurs of Sikandra Rao, Jawahir Singh of Akerabad and Kundam Singh of Nai', who 'behaved remarkably well and afforded continuous and valuable aid'. Kundan Singh at the end of August 1857 was made *nazim* of the pargana, and with a body of 1,500 of his own followers reinstated the tahsildar and maintained him in that position until authority was thoroughly re-established. When he died two years afterwards 'his sons and nephews were left among the most prosperous zamindars in the tahsil'.[17]

On the western side of the district in the thickly settled Jat parganas abutting Mathura district, the two processes were still more confused since the talukdari areas ran cheek by jowl with the Jat clan khaps. While Gobind Singh was raising the Jat Horse for service on the British side, Mohammad Ghaus Khan, who had taken over the leadership of the Muslim revolt in Koil city (Aligarh), was appealing to the Jat peasantry for supplies and promising that the district of Koil would be theirs.[18] Proprietary brotherhoods notoriously stood up better to a heavy revenue demand than single zamindari estates, but, assuming they had also withstood other forms of landlord encroachment by raja or bania, their resentment usually took the form of direct rebellion. This happened at Iglas and Khair. At Iglas the Jat communities 'under the guidance of one Amani Jat, ex-pattidar of Gahon... who had then come to the surface and dubbed himself Raja had the audacity to attack the trained troops of the Gwalior Contingent'. The same body of Jats from the Lageswan region in pargana Hasangarh joined in the attack on the government offices in Khair. Here on 20 May Rao Bhopal Singh, head of the Chauhan Rajputs of the pargana, had deposed the tahsildar, only to be surprised, caught and hanged by Watson, the Magistrate, and his European volunteers on 1 June. The sequence was that 'before the middle of the month the Chohans of the pergunnah, intent on revenge, called in the Jats to their help, attacked Khyr, plundered and destroyed nearly all the Government buildings, as well as the houses of the Bunyahs and Mahajuns'.[19] What bound together Jat and Rajput – hereditary enemies – in fitful alliance?

[17] Smith, *Aligarh S.R.*, para. 55, p. 19; para. 72, pp. 24–5. *Gazetteer N.W.P.*, ed. Atkinson, II, pt i, p. 509.
[18] S. A. A. Rizvi (ed.), *Freedom Struggle in Uttar Pradesh*, v, pp. 668, 686.
[19] Bramley to Cocks, 17 Nov. 1858, para. 10, cited *Freedom Struggle in Uttar Pradesh*, v, pp. 658–9.

In tahsil Iglas small taluks were intermingled with village estates held by Jat proprietary brotherhoods working one of the finest tracts in the district. These taluks, such as Biswan, Kanka, Kajraut, and Gorae, each of a dozen villages or so, had stood up better here than elsewhere, but were probably too small to smother the rebellion of village communities. The severity and, above all, the unequal incidence of the revenue demand placed the village communities under cruel pressure. Where additionally a heavy malikana was exacted by the talukdar the biswadars or sub-proprietors laboured under what was later acknowledged to be 'an almost unendurable burden'.[20] Land rights changed hands freely, as much as 52% of the tahsil being subject to transfer between 1838 and 1868. The industrious Thakurel branch (*got*) of Jats which held the *chauwan gaon* or fifty-four villages of Lagaswan had undoubtedly suffered inroads from the money-lender. But total Jat losses in the tahsil do not appear to have been heavy over the thirty years of the settlement; apparently they parted with some 9,500 acres of their 110,000 acres, 3,500 being confiscated for rebellion in 1857.

W. H. Smith acknowledged that the Jats had put up a 'tough resistance' to the encroachment of the moneylending Brahmin and bania, and in 1868 they still held three-quarters of the land in the tahsil. Their most burning grievance was evidently the inequity of the revenue assessment.

That the Jats of Lagaswan should have sunk their traditional feud and leagued with the Chauhan Rajputs of Khair under Rao Bhopal Singh is testimony to their hatred of British rule. The Chauhan Rajputs had still stronger cause for rebellion. In tahsil Khair as a whole the Rajputs labouring under a revenue rate of Rs. 2-1-3 on the cultivation had lost almost 30% of their land, while the Jats, whose holdings had equalled theirs, lost a mere 5%. In Khair pargana itself the Chauhan Rajputs had in distant times held the whole area together with the neighbouring parganas of Chandaus and Murthal. By 1857 the head of this branch, Bhopal Singh, was reduced to a single village, and, 'urged by the vain hope of recovering the former influence of the tribe', led the attack on the Khair tahsil offices.[21]

All these are instances where land transfers, induced for the

20 *Aligarh S.R.*, para. 250, p. 85.
21 Smith, *Aligarh S.R.*, para. 88, p. 31.

most part by a heavy revenue demand, failed to throw up a rising
landlord element from among the traditional landholding castes.
The fact that the banias made significant gains, largely at the
expense of the unthrifty Rajput communities, sharpened no
doubt the bitterness of loss, and made them a target for vengeance.
But of themselves they hardly supply the main explanation of the
pattern of rebellion. The really violent and persistent disturbances
came from the bhaiachara Jat communities of the western
parganas which continued into the Mathura district up to the
Yamuna (Jumna) River and among whom bania gains were
lowest.

The hard core of Jat settlement lay in pargana Noh Jhil in the
Mathura district among the Nohwar and Narwar gots. Here the
clan community was to be found in its full perfection,[22] and the
strength of its organisation enabled it to withstand a stiff rate of
revenue assessment and keep out the moneylender. In the early
years of British rule (1809) it was remarked 'there is not a
mahajan in the pargana, and the zamindars are so notoriously
refractory that no man of property will become security for
them'.[23] Immediately after the rebellion J. R. Best, the Officiating
Collector, noted that where the bhaiachara system prevailed it
was almost impossible for capital to force its way. Even well after
1857 when confiscations and commercial conditions had promoted
land owning by the trading classes, Whiteway, the settlement
officer, could still report in the early 1870s that 'mahajans and
bankers. . .have much less influence here than in most other parts
of India'.[24]

Mark Thornhill, who had charge of the district at the outbreak
of disturbances, considered Noh Jhil 'perhaps the worst Pergunnah of Muttra. It was the first that went into rebellion and the
last to submit.' From this and other examples of peasant rebellion
he determined on drastic measures:

However paradoxical it may appear it is a matter of fact that the
agricultural laboring class – the class who above all others have

---

[22] Cf. B. H. Baden-Powell, *The Indian Village Community* (London, 1896),
    pp. 281 ff.
[23] *Muttra S.R.*, by R. S. Whiteway, p. 251.
[24] *Ibid.*, p. 249. For Best's comments. J. R. Best to G. F. Harvey, 8 Dec.
    1858; Post-Mutiny Records, Com. (Agra) Revenue 1859, bundle 2 (ii),
    File no 35. U.P. State Archives, Allahabad.

derived the most benefit from our rule – were the most hostile to its continuance, while the large proprietors who have suffered under our rule almost to a man stood by us. As soon as I had realised this fact I brought it strongly to the late Mr Colvin's notice and urged that the Government must reverse its policy and throw itself on the large proprietors and repress the peasantry.[25]

In Noh Jhil he ordered the confiscation of 22 villages and proposed to confer them on the Mathura banking family of the Seths in reward. He carried out similar extensive confiscations elsewhere, but even in the pro-magnate atmosphere of the aftermath of revolt such sweeping proposals produced a reaction. Vansittart, the Special Commissioner, mounted a crusade to reverse the anti-peasant policy not only in Mathura but also in Agra and Etawah districts, resting himself on Burke's argument that he knew not how to draw up an indictment against a whole people. His thesis was simple: 'The main cause of rural rebellion was not the hatred of our rule but a summary adjustment by the sword of those feuds which had arisen out of the action of our Civil and Revenue laws on proprietary rights in land.'[26] Yet British rule could not be so readily exculpated, for 'the money-lenders and the mortgagers or purchasers of land' whom he saw as the enemy were scarcely in evidence in Noh Jhil or other strongly held bhaiachara clan areas. Alienation of land to outsiders was too slight to justify the sack of the Noh Jhil tahsil offices on 4 June by a crowd said to number 20,000 men,[27] which proceeded to destroy the records. One cannot but feel that the swingeing revenue assessment was the root of the matter.

This was to be seen in the parganas to the south of Noh Jhil. In 1881 Robertson, the Secretary to Government, reflecting on the settlement of 1839–69, wondered how the north-eastern parganas of Mathura had stood a revenue rate (Rs. 2-8-3) even higher than that of Aligarh after revision (Rs. 2-6-3). But the rate rose progressively southwards, falling at Rs. 2-3-2 in Mat-Noh Jhil, Rs. 2-8-2 in Mahaban, Rs. 2-13-0 in Sadabad, and Rs. 3-1-8 in Sahpau.[28] Few communities could stand this degree of

[25] Mark Thornhill to W. Muir, Sec. to Govt., 15 Nov. 1858; Post-Mutiny Records, Com. (Agra) Judicial I (iii), File 49 (File 126/1 1857).

[26] Henry Vansittart to Muir, 28 Aug. 1858; *ibid.*, Com. (Agra) Revenue 1859, bundle 2 (ii), File 35.

[27] *Freedom Struggle in Uttar Pradesh*, v, pp. 686, 691. Also Vansittart to Muir, 2 Oct. 1858, Com. (Agra) Judicial I, File 2/1857.

[28] *Gazetteer N.W.P.*, ed. Atkinson, VIII (Allahabad, 1884), p. 127.

imposition, especially when they had not the tight clan organisation of the Noh Jats or their standards of high farming. In Sahpau the village communities crumbled. The alienation statements show 'the frightful extent to which the hereditary zamindars have been supplanted',[29] the majority of the alienations occurring in the twenty-five years between 1833 and the Mutiny. The result was 'the replacement of the hereditary yeomen...by a body of grasping traders and speculators who are not connected with the soil by ancient traditions, and who look upon the land merely as good investment for their capital'. But it is clear from the population figures that Jats were not strongly settled here (they were but 11% of the population in 1872 as against some 53% in Noh Jhil). The major losses during the 1833 settlement were borne by the Rajput communities, much as in parganas Hathras and Khair, to the advantage principally of non-resident Brahmin classes. In pargana Sadabad the position was different. Here the Jats formed the largest caste (some 28%) and still were the most considerable landowners in 1873 (when they held 36%), but the fact that they retained 73% of the total *sir* or demesne lands, as against Brahmins 12% and Thakurs 11%, suggests their losses at some stage had been heavy. McConaghey, the settlement officer in 1873, inferred that the damage had largely been done during the first few years of British rule when Raja Bhagwant Singh of Mursan had been set aside and the revenue engagements taken with the village communities, who then proved unequal to the task of management. By 1873 just under half the land was in the possession of non-resident owners, half again of which can be identified as belonging to non-agricultural classes, Brahmins, Banias and Dhusars.[30]

Sahpau and Sadabad parganas were disturbed in May 1857 during that spontaneous, universal upsurge of anarchy that so flabbergasted Mark Thornhill, the Magistrate. In late June he was able to take punitive measures in the Sadabad area, but on his enforced withdrawal shortly afterwards 'all the country round Sadabad rose, headed by one Deokaran, and plundered the tahsil and police station'. This was a Jat rising, but its details are obscure.[31] Better known are the peasant rebellions in the Mahaban

---

[29] M. A. McConaghey in *Muttra S.R.*, p. 129.
[30] *Muttra S.R.*, p. 138; *Gazetteer N.W.P.*, VIII, p. 227.
[31] Mark Thornhill, *Personal Adventures and Experiences...during...the Indian Mutiny*, 1884, pp. 102 ff.

pargana, which Thornhill's description has made celebrated.[32]
Between 1838 and 1857 some 32% of the land in pargana
Mahaban was subject to transfer, the greater part going to
strangers rather than other sharers. McConaghey estimated that
in 1808 the Jats held at least three-fourths of the parganas; by
1874 their possessions had been reduced to one-third, that is, a loss
of a half. The chief gainers were Brahmins, who extended their
possessions from roughly 16% in 1808 to some 32% by 1874, and
also banias who acquired some 15%. It is not possible to date
these gains, and, since a further 25% of the pargana was alienated
between 1858 and 1874, the extent of Jat losses needs to be kept
in proportion. Now it is true that many of the Brahmin acquisitions as in Sahpau went to the non-agricultural class in Mathura
and other towns, but in Mahaban it would appear that the
principal beneficiary was the Brahmin Pachauri family of Mahaban itself 'whose importance dates from the time of Puran Chand,
whose son Mukand Singh and grandson Ballab Singh were
tahsildars in this district'.[33] Ballab Singh was recorded as a
loyalist in 1857 who 'accepted the tahsildarship of P[h] Muhabun
and with the aid of sowars he was authorized to raise managed to
restore order in the P[h] in his own estates'.[34] The Jats traditionally
made provision for their Brahmin priests by the grant of land, and
the Pachauri family had claims to gentility, unlike that of
Jagdispur (pargana Mahaban) or Salahpur Chandwara (pargana
Sadabad) or Chhatari (pargana Mat), who advanced through
moneylending.

After a punitive expedition to depose the celebrated Devi Singh
of Tappa Raya who set himself up as raja and sacked the tahsil
offices, it was possible to restore and maintain order in this and
neighbouring parganas through the use of collaborating agents.
Thornhill appointed Raja Pirthi Singh of the Jadon family of
Awa, to the office of nazim of Sadabad,[35] while Raja Tikam Singh

[32] *Muttra S.R.*, p. 155.

[33] Statement of persons who have rendered valuable services to Govt. dated
19 May 1858, signed J. R. Best; Com. (Agra) Judicial 1 1857, File 1.

[34] *Muttra, S.R.*, p. 31.

[35] Prithi Singh is a representative figure of a new entrepreneurial magnate
class emerging from the ranks of the traditional elite. By the 1880s the
rajas of Awa's estates were 'reputed to be among the wealthiest in Upper
India', paying some Rs. 3,75,000 in revenue; *Gazetteer N.W.P.*, VIII,
p. 72, and *Aligarh S.R. 1882*, para. 7, p. 25. For services in Rebellion,
G. Couper to Officiating Commissioner, Agra, 2 Mar. 1859; Com. (Agra)
Revenue Dept. 1860, bundle 3 (ii), File 40.

of Mursan was given charge of pargana Mahaban where he still retained rights as talukdar in the small taluks of Ar, Sonkh, and Madim. According to Thornhill the recipe of governing through the great landholders worked the charm: 'the position from perfect anarchy was brought to perfect order and the entire revenue collected' even in the absence of British authority, except from parganas Noh Jhil, Kosi and part of Sahar.[36]

Here again then, in parganas Mahaban and perhaps Sadabad, the Jat colonies were too interspersed with magnate elements prepared to rally to the British to sustain a protracted resistance.

It should not be supposed, of course, that the traditional magnate class always rallied to the British. Where it did so, as in the person of the Mursan raja or the Lalkhani Bargujar house of Chhatari whose possessions spilled over from Bulandshahr into Aligarh district,[37] one may reasonably assume that it had successfully adjusted itself to the novel conditions of landholding introduced by British rule. Such adjustment was far from automatic. It is a remarkable feature of the central Doab that, while on the Jumna side the magnates largely sided with the British, on the Ganges side they went over to the rebels. In some measure they were undoubtedly influenced by their proximity to the stronghold of rebellion across the Ganges in Rohilkhand and Oudh, with bridge-heads across the river at Farrukhabad and Kanpur; but this supplies no sufficient explanation of why the rajas of Etah and Mainpuri threw in their lot with the cause of revolt. A detailed examination would be out of place here, but a brief examination of Mainpuri district and a quick glance at Etah may offer some pointers.

Between 1840 and 1857 some 32% of the cultivated areas of Mainpuri district changed hands, although the proportion lost by the original owners was probably nearer 25%. The transfers effected, however, a much smaller displacement of caste. Rajputs, easily the largest landholders, held 48% of the villages in 1840 and still retained 44% in 1870; while Brahmins rose from 14% to 18% and banias from $1\frac{1}{2}$% to $3\frac{1}{2}$%. The value of land remained low and the settlement officers concluded that it was only

---

[36] M. Thornhill to W. Muir, Sec. to Govt. 15 Nov. 1858, *Gazetteer N.W.P.*, VIII, p. 170.
[37] For the Chhatari family, see above pp. 151, 153.

after 1858 that 'capitalists' entered the land market. Assuming
that Brahmin and other gains could be accounted gains of the
trading classes, during the whole term of settlement between 1840
and 1870 the latter rose no more than 10%.[38] There would
therefore seem to be little that was typical of the classical revolutionary situation in Mainpuri. Yet Tej Singh, the raja, declared
against the British and actively participated in military operations
against them.

It is usual to suppose that, as one of the most sorely stricken
victims of the anti-magnate policy of the Thomasonian era of the
1840s, Tej Singh had every justification.[39] But, as we have seen
in Aligarh, this policy by no means spelled disaster to the magnate
class. There high cultivation and a high revenue demand had
generated a quasi-commercial market in land titles, while at the
same time part of the traditional elite had transformed itself into
a successful magnate element and more than kept its footing
alongside the trading classes.

Conditions were clearly different in Mainpuri district. Tej
Singh did not hold sway over densely settled cultivating brotherhoods, as may be seen from the very low numbers of bhaiachara
estates. The Rajputs while holding a half of the district as late as
the 1870s formed but 8% of the population, and constituted more
of a gentry or 'sturdy yeoman' class. Absentee ownership was
high, characterising three-fourths of the villages, and cultivating
proprietors worked only 14% of the total cultivated area as *sir* or
home farm, Rajputs holding some 7%. Apart from the Raja of
Mainpuri and the Raja of Eka (heading the Pratabner branch),
the Chauhan Rajputs, who played the critical role in the 1857
rising, were most strongly entrenched in small estates in the fertile
central tracts of the district. The question before 1857 was
whether they could hold their traditionally dominant position
against other Rajput clans as well as other castes. The evidence
suggests that they were forced to give ground on the western side
of the district while maintaining their hold elsewhere. In what
became Mainpuri pargana in the central region, for instance,
the Chauhan proprietors (outside the twenty-three villages owned
by large landholders) jostled for room. Property was extensively
subdivided owing to the number of shareholders who traditionally

---

[38] *Mainpuri S.R.* (Allahabad, 1875), pp. 17, 51–2.
[39] Cf. J. W. Kaye, *History of the Sepoy War*, II, 1864, pp. 161 ff.

took to military service to supplement their income. But no more than some 8% of the cultivated area was subject to transfer, and the Rajputs still held 61% (Chauhans 55%) in 1879 as against 62% in 1840. In Bhongaon pargana, further east, the transfer rate was higher, with about a quarter of the cultivation changing hands between 1840 and the rebellion, but the Rajput holdings remained steady from 1840 to 1870 at 39%. The Brahmins increased their hold from 17% to 25% but mainly at the expense of the Kayaths and Lodhas. In Kishni pargana, bordering on Farrukhabad, the Chauhans in fact managed to increase their hold from 44% to 50% over the settlement period.

On the western side of the district the story was different. The Mustafabad pargana marched with Agra and Mathura districts. Over the settlement period Rajputs dropped from 53% to 48%, but Chauhan losses were more severe, their holdings falling from 46% to 36%. Even Brahmin holdings dropped slightly from 9% to 8%. The principal gainers were of the Marwari caste, a sure sign of intrusive commercial forces whose activity was so much more marked on the Yamuna side of the Doab. Transfers in this rich pargana ran extremely high, as much as 40% of the land changing hands in a single decade between 1840 and 1850, while the revenue demand fell sharply on the cultivation at Rs. 2-3-2.

In Ghiror pargana, which stood between Mustafabad and Mainpuri, the Chauhans had again suffered, losing land to the moneylending Rajput Jadon family of Awa and to Brahmins from Kanauj, mainly it seems before 1857.

The Chauhan Thakurs still form the largest body of proprietors although their possessions have been sadly curtailed since the commencement of our rule. The members of the Partabner branch have suffered most severely, and the splendid estates of Usnida, Pachawar, Karaoli, Harhai, half Himmatpur, and Nahal Katengra with its six subordinate villages have passed away from them for ever for a mere song, before they were thoroughly acquainted with the rigid working of our system. It is distressing to see such men reduced to the position of cultivators when they might have been saved by more careful and lenient treatment. The Jadon Kunwars of Awa and Chaudhri Jai Chand of Binsiya now own their ancestral properties and are their masters.[40]

[40] *Mainpuri S.R.*, p. 145.

British officials later took the view that there was no mass rising of the agricultural community in Mainpuri as in Mathura district, but rather a struggle for the mastery between two landholding castes, the Chauhans and the Ahirs.

In this District there seems to have been no such thing as a national attempt at the subversion of the Government authority. No sooner did the mutiny commence, the Ahir tribe resumed their predatory habits and were followed by the Chowhan Rajpoots...All restraints were cast off and every malcontent found an opportunity for avenging old wrongs or recovering former possessions. Then followed the struggle for the mastery between the two tribes, and ended in the subversion of the Ahirs by the Chowhans. It was owing in great measure to these incessant commotions that so many estates were ruined, and the prevalence of anarchy and suspension of authority were prolonged for so long a period.[41]

On this western side of the district, opposing the British presence at Agra, rebellion presented a ragged front. There was no clean division among the major caste groups; instead they fractured internally into collaborating and hostile elements. The Ahirs of Bharaul in Shikohabad pargana successfully repulsed Tej Singh, the Mainpuri raja, while their caste brethren, Ram Ratan and Bhagwan Singh of Rampur village, 'kept the whole pergunnah [of Mustafabad] in a state of rebellion and fought against British rule'.[42] Similarly, on Tej Singh's behalf 'the famous Ristee Ram of Khynuggur...with Soondar Singh, his uncle, headed several marauding expeditions into Furozabad and Moostufabad which contributed in no small degree to the anarchy and disorder which prevailed in these Perghunnahs'. Yet other Chauhans of Mustafabad pargana remained faithful to the politics of collaboration. It is noticeable that those like the Uresar family under Kunwar Gajadhar who 'did good services during the mutiny' were also those who had been 'more provident' than their Chauhan caste brethren and 'succeeded in retaining their ancestral land intact'. Bijai Singh, head of the Milauli family, was a similar 'shrewd and intelligent native gentleman, who, while most of his fellow caste-men were squandering away their

---

[41] E. J. Boldero, Collector, to W. H. Lowe, Sec. Sudder Board of Revenue, 17 Dec. 1858; Com. (Agra) Revenue 1859, bundle 2 (ii), File 35.
[42] Report by H. Chase, Joint Magistrate, 27 May 1859; Com. (Agra) Rev. Dept. 67/I of 1859, bundle 2 (iii). File no 44.

hereditary lands, has succeeded in amassing considerable wealth and in acquiring fresh property'.[43]

It is against this background of Chauhan fearfulness for their traditional dominance, that Tej Singh's defection from the steadfast fealty of his ancient house to the British Raj must be judged. Apparently nature and circumstance had not lent him the capacity of adjustment that magnates nearer the Yamuna (Jumna) displayed. Edmonstone's picture of the Mainpuri house in 1840 as sunk in illiteracy, incompetence and corruption was a loaded one, but even a more favourable view would hardly suggest the dynasty had bred up a race of improving landlords. The talukdari sub-settlement struck an irretrievable blow. Although framed on terms similar to those of the Mursan raja in Aligarh, it had far less favourable results. It appears to have left the raja heavily dependent on his talukdari income rather than that derived from the small number of his estates recognised in full zamindari. Devoid of commercial aptitude or opportunity his position necessarily rested on his powers of lordship, of which he was deliberately stripped. He was left to draw his malikana from the district treasury and at a blow lost all power to intervene in 133 out of his 184 villages. Given the fact that his estates were situated in the portion of the district least given to cash-crop farming, with lower transfer and lower revenue rates, there was little prospect of his riding the blow.[44]

The Etah raja, Dambar Singh, was similarly placed. He was left with but 19 of his 147 estates in zamindari possession, and

[43] *Mainpuri Settlement Report*, p. 61. Also G. E. Lance, Officiating Collector to G. F. Harvey, Commissioner Agra, 1 Feb. 1859; N.W. Provinces Political Proceedings, 10 Mar. 1859, no 147.

[44] Tej Singh's defection was also prompted by personal factors. The young raja had been installed in 1851, but his right to succeed was disputed by his uncle, Bhawani Singh, whose appeal was pending before the Privy Council at the outbreak of revolt. Tej Singh was reputed weak and dissolute, and had been placed under check by A. H. Cocks, the district officer. Bhawani Singh was thought to have been loyal, but informed official opinion in the district later came to the conclusion that he had persuaded Tej Singh to revolt and then played a clever double game. See on the question *District Gazetteer of United Provinces*, x, *Mainpuri*, ed. E. R. Neave (Allahabad, 1910), pp. 174–5. Also N.W.P. Pol. Progs. 13 May 1859, no. 116; 11 Aug. 1850, nos 68, 69, 24 Sept. 1850. nos. 199, 218. For the financial position of the Mainpuri raja compared with the Mursan raja, see N.W.P. Pol. Progs., 13 May 1859, nos. 116, 119; 1 Sept. 1859, nos. 12, 13; 8 June 1861, no. 29. Also N.W.P. Rev. Progs., 18 July 1842, no. 3, cited *Parliamentary Papers, 1857–8*, xlii, pp. 297 ff.

from the rest was given what appeared to be a generous malikana of 29%. Yet by 1852–3 he was being compelled to mortgage 97 villages, so serious was his financial disarray.[45] When the British were evicted from the district in June 1857 he faltered into rebellion. Etah was again a comparatively backward region with a relatively low standard of agriculture. It too presented no favourable milieu for the emergence of an enterprising magnate element able to adapt successfully in face of the institutional pressures being exerted against the old forms of lordship. As we have seen elsewhere, it was the presence or absence of such an element that appears to have been critical in determining political allegiance in 1857. In large areas of Mathura and Aligarh districts it was able not merely to hold down tumultuous peasant revolt but to forward valuable sums in land revenue to the beleaguered British authorities in Agra. Where it had failed to emerge and a declining, aggrieved aristocracy held sway, districts smarting much less severely from the economic and social dislocation of British rule could be carried into rebellion.

[45] Com. (Agra) Judicial I (ii) 1857, File 13. Statement of Debts filed on Estates of Raja Dambar Singh.

9

The structure of landholding in
Uttar Pradesh, 1860–1948

At the end of British rule, with a population swollen to some 63 million, the land of the United Provinces was found to be in the ownership of just over two million persons (2,016,783).[1] Of these the vast proportion, or some 85% (1,710,530), were small men falling in the category of revenue-payers of less than Rs. 25. Their average revenue payment was, in fact, only some Rs. 6. Probably more than half paid Rs. 1 or less, the proprietary share of each being well under one acre. Meeting only some 15% of the total land revenue, these 1,710,530 proprietors must have owned (allowing for the favourable differential assessment for the small owner) no more than a fifth of the agricultural land. A further $13\frac{1}{2}$% (276,111) of revenue-payers paid between Rs. 25 and Rs. 250. The remaining $1\frac{1}{2}$%, a mere 30,142 persons, were responsible for meeting 58% of the land-revenue demand. On any reckoning these constituted the economic elite. But as an elite it was far from homogeneous and spanned vast disparities of wealth. Somewhat more than half (16,758) paid under Rs. 500 each, a further quarter (7,491) between Rs. 500 and Rs. 1,000. Of the remaining 5,893 persons paying over Rs. 1,000 each, there were 804 who paid over Rs. 5,000, the membership qualification for the Agra Province Zamindars' Association.[2]

Taking the United Provinces at large, the landownership structure can be described, therefore, as a pyramid possessed of an extremely broad base but tapering rapidly to a tall, narrow elite

[1] *U.P. Zamindari Abolition Committee Report* (Allahabad, 1948) (cited hereafter as *Z.A.C.R.*), II. On the reliability of the Report's statistics, see the comments of W. C. Neale, *Economic Change in Rural India* (1962), pp. 250 ff.

[2] The number of large revenue payers had probably been reduced sharply before 1947 in anticipation of zamindari abolition. Cf. figures for Meerut district: *Meerut Settlement Report 1940*, 19 over Rs. 5,000; 6 over Rs. 10,000; *Z.A.C.R.* 12 over Rs. 5,000; 4 over Rs. 10,000.

pinnacle. Despite large differences in other respects the width of this elite pinnacle remained more or less constant throughout the province, the number of revenue-payers over Rs. 250 rarely exceeding a thousand in any one district (ranging from the extreme of 140 in Bahraich to 1,594 in Moradabad). But the height of the pinnacle and the size of its pyramidal base varied enormously. For example, Meerut and Etawah districts both possessed elite pinnacles of almost equal size (in Meerut 1,035 persons raising some 8½ lakhs, in Etawah 875 persons raising some 9 lakhs). Yet in Meerut the pinnacle rose from a huge base of 20,000 or so 'yeomen' farmers (paying between Rs. 25 and Rs. 250 in revenue and raising over 14 lakhs)[3] and 145,000 petty proprietors (paying under Rs. 25 and raising some 7 lakhs). In Etawah by contrast the base was of diminutive proportions, the 'yeoman' farmer class numbering only 4,452 (and raising nearly 3½ lakhs) and the petty proprietors, 19,328 (raising just over 1 lakh). A still more arresting contrast was to be seen in the Oudh (Avadh) district of Sitapur where a very considerable revenue (of some 21 lakhs) was raised by a handful of taxpayers, as much as 18 lakhs being found by only 749 persons (paying over Rs. 250 each), and the remaining 3 lakhs by fewer than 10,000 persons (see Table 4).

It might be supposed that the elitist character of landowning was sharply exaggerated by the *taluqdari* system of Avadh. Yet when the Avadh figures are subtracted, those for the remainder of the territory (in practice, the province of Agra) show little variation in the distribution of proprietary rights. Revenue-payers under Rs. 25 formed 85·5% of the total and met 17·6% of the land revenue; revenue payers between Rs. 25 and Rs. 250 amounted to 13·2% of the total and met 31·3% of the revenue: revenue payers over Rs. 250 formed 1·3% of the total and met 51·2% of the revenue.

All this was the end-product of a century or more of British rule. How far had the ownership pyramid altered? On the face of things, very little. Until 1921 population remained remarkably

---

[3] The category of 'yeoman farmer' as one paying revenue up to Rs. 250 was proposed officially in 1896. *Selections of Papers on Agricultural Indebtedness*, III, Govt. of India (Simla, 1898), p. 1. Insofar as it denotes a social rather than economic category it has to be used cautiously in the knowledge that some proportion of this group would be members of the trading classes.

stable, increasing by no more than 10% in the previous half-century, but leaping by some 37% in the next three decades.[4] The numbers of landowners would also appear to have remained fairly constant, the census reporting them as 1,196,876 in 1881 and 1,275,432 in 1931. The figures of land-revenue payers returned for franchise purposes in 1919 and for the Zamindari Abolition Committee in 1947 were much higher – 2,270,664 and 2,016,783 respectively – but observed the same constancy. The discrepancy between the two sets of figures is readily explicable. Among the revenue payers of 1919 was a vast mass of some one and a half million persons paying under Rs. 1, over half of whom in the census of 1931 failed to qualify for classification as primarily landowners by occupation, and the great bulk of whom must have been inextricably intermixed with the tenantry through holding tenant land in addition to their proprietary shares.[5] For all the precautions enjoined there may also have been a considerable element of double-counting of the same persons, given the extraordinarily complex and fragmented nature of ownership rights at this level.[6] Even so, there seem strong

[4] U.P. population:

1872	42,780,292	1921	46,669,865
1881	45,034,574	1931	49,776,754
1891	47,844,299	1941	56,531,848
1901	48,625,310	1951	63,215,742
1911	48,152,273		

SOURCE: *Census of India, 1951*, II. *Uttar Pradesh, Part I–A Report* (Allahabad, 1953), p. 25, Table 27.

[5] Cf. In Gorakhpur district the smallest fraction in use for coparcenary tenures was 1/1,105,920,000. H. R. Nevill (ed.), *U.P. District Gazetteer*, XXXI (Allahabad, 1909), p. 109.

[6] I am greatly indebted to Professor P. D. Reeves for information and criticism on the number of landowners. The 1919 figures are taken from *The Reforms Committee (Franchise). Evidence Taken before the Reforms Committee (Franchise)*. I (Calcutta, 1919), Table VIII, p. 90 (India Office Library, J & P (Reforms) ser. 427). Comparison with the *Z.A.C.R.* figures gives the following results:

Statement of persons paying land revenue:

		1919	*1948*
over	Rs. 100	120,073	81,706
	Rs. 50–100	87,790	81,657
	Rs. 25–50	125,503	142,800
under	Rs. 25	1,937,298	1,710,530

The figure of one and a half million persons (*viz.* 1,489,246) paying less than Rs. 1 in land revenue is arrived at from the figure of 2,270,664 as the total number of landholders given in 1926 (*U.P. Legislative Council Proceedings, Official Report*, XXX, 1 July 1926, pp. 196–7), less the figure of 781,418 persons paying over Rs. 1 given in 1919. (Professor Reeves

grounds for believing that the multiplication of proprietary interests was accelerating from the end of the nineteenth century and that the subdivision of ownership rights proceeded much farther than the Zamindari Abolition Committee's Report suggests. In almost any district selected at random the number of co-sharers recorded in the roughly contemporaneous settlement reports is far in excess of the report's figures (see Table 5). No doubt the liability to double counting was higher here, the records for settlement purposes being concerned with the number of shares into which estates were divided rather than the actual number of sharers who were physically present in a tahsil or district and who might own multiple shares in different estates. The percentage of absentee co-sharers, a portion of whom would be town-dwellers or reside outside the district, was often well over 50% and probably accounts for the wide discrepancy between the figures of the settlement reports and that of the Zamindari Abolition Committee. Some of the increase in the numbers of recorded co-sharers was artificial, in the sense that men who had previously been content to share informally and allow one or more of their brotherhood to be recorded as the proprietors wished increasingly from the later decades of the nineteenth century to have their interests registered officially. The same growing sense of individual rights lay behind the partition of estates so that these multiplied along with the number of co-sharers. In Bijnor, the settlement officer in 1939 wrote of 'the immense increase in the number of mahals as a result of partition'; certainly since 1872 it had almost trebled.[7] If the figures are to be believed the increase was as much as eightfold between 1860 and 1921 in Muzaffarnagar district. Yet, when all allowances have been made for subdivision among existing sharers there can be little doubt that their numbers also increased absolutely through natural increase and partition among heirs. In Bareilly district the settlement officer in 1942 noted that 'the number of co-sharers has almost quadrupled since the settlement of 1870'. In Meerut the increase was some two and a half fold between 1865 and 1940; in Mainpuri two and a quarter between 1824 and 1944; in Unao twofold between 1895 and 1930 (see Table 5, p. 226).

considers the 1926 Legislative Council answer to be framed on the 1919 statistics.)

[7] *Bijnor S.R. 1939*, pp. 7, 45; *Bijnor S.R. 1899*, p. 13.

This fragmentation of ownership rights and the subdivision of proprietary holdings occurring at the base of the landholding pyramid was associated with another process, that of land transfer. The two, however, by no means marched hand in hand; indeed, the rate of land transfer appears to have slowed down as the multiplication of proprietary rights gathered pace during the present century.[8] While land transfer bore most directly on the social composition of the proprietary classes, the subdivision of proprietary rights affected the size of 'estates' (*mahals*). Yet all were not affected alike. There seem good grounds for believing that the economic elite in possession of large estates was kept insulated from the general process of subdivision and transfer partly because of economic and partly because of institutional forces. The main casualties were instead the intermediate and the peasant proprietors. In 1907 H. K. Gracey, the settlement officer of Kanpur (Cawnpore), shrewdly observed:

The fact is that the only zamindar for whom the Indian economy has a proper place is either the big talukdar governed by the law of primogeniture and owning so large an estate that he can afford to be generous or the peasant proprietor cultivating his own land. For the small middleman who tries to live on his rents and whose property is being constantly split into smaller and smaller shares under the ordinary rules of Hindu or Mohammedan heirship, there is no niche.[9]

Contemporaneously, W. J. D. Burkitt was commenting that in Aligarh over the previous thirty years 'the rich Zamindars have on the whole gained, [and] nearly all the loss [of land] has fallen on the small men and the [village] communities'.[10] In Mainpuri conditions were also unpropitious to middle-sized estates: 'the big zamindars are few and are mostly absentees from the district while the mass of petty proprietors, who own, and with their fellow castemen cultivate, the bulk of the district, are at all times impecunious and living up close to the critical margin of subsistence'.[11] In Azamgarh the same levelling process appears to have

[8] In Etah district the number of co-sharers in *pattidari* and *bhaiachara* tenures doubled between 1904 and 1944, while one-third of the land of the district changed hands (*Etah S.R. 1944*, p. 6, paras. 20–2). The slowing down of the transfer rate is seen most vividly in Mainpuri where between 1870 and 1904 some 25% of the district land was transferred outright, and between 1905 and 1942 only 9%, *Mainpuri S.R. 1944*, p. 8, para. 21.

[9] *Cawnpore S.R. 1907*, para. 25.

[10] *Aligarh S.R. 1903*, p. 7, para. 11.

[11] J. E. Lupton, *Mainpuri S.R. 1906*, p. 15, para. 30.

been at work: 'where the area held by any clan [of Chattris] has materially diminished, the decrease is due to the losses of those individuals who have had estates of more than usual size'.[12] Two decades later A. A. Waugh was observing the persistence of the same phenomenon in Budaun: 'The zamindar who is content to live on his rents and to use neither his brain nor his hands has lost ground.'[13] Yet, in effect, the fractionalisation of 'land control' did not stop short at the cultivating proprietor.

In the immediate post-Mutiny decades the price rise from the late 1860s, the swing to cash rents, and the expansion of cash-crop agriculture had appeared to give reality to British institutional arrangements for reducing Indian tenures to a landlord-tenant basis. In Saharanpur district it was found as late as 1867 that there was 'hardly any distinction between the rent-paying tenant and the rent-paying proprietor', except on estates bought up by moneylenders where competition rents had begun to appear. By 1890 L. A. S. Porter could report that apart from a small number of estates held by cultivating communities where a certain amount of land was let out at revenue rates, 'the old equality of landlord and tenant has given way to competition'.[14] But counter-vailing forces were already at work to whittle away landlord advantages as the legal recognition of occupancy rights began to take practical effect.

In Budaun it is possible to trace their action distinctly. Between 1850 and 1870 no difference existed between occupancy and yearly tenants, according to Waugh's estimate, both continuing to pay on average some 20% of the produce value despite the background of rising prices. By 1900, however, occupancy rents represented only 13% of the produce value while yearly tenants still paid 20%. The decisive change came after 1900. Between 1900 and 1926 prices rose roughly 100% and yearly tenant rents by 110%, but occupancy rents rose no more than 25%. At the same time the occupancy tenant area increased rapidly, amounting to 70% of the total tenant area by 1928. The effect was to strike at the income of the small non-cultivating proprietor proportionately. While his cost of living had risen 100% his income had risen by under 25%. 'In other words, the profits arising from

[12] C. E. Crawford, *Azamgarh S.R. 1908*, p. 12.
[13] *Budaun S.R. 1930*, p. 7, para. 29.
[14] *Saharanpur S.R. 1890*.

the rise in prices of grain has gone to the cultivator and not to
the proprietor.' The combined effects of the subdivision of holdings and of the sluggishness of occupancy rents was, therefore,
'to leave the majority of zamindars in no position to dominate
either the tenant or the money lender.'[15]

The comparative prosperity of the occupancy cultivator had
been observed in Saharanpur as early as the 1860s. Wynne, the
settlement officer, noted at that time that Gujars whose proprietary rights had been confiscated for rebellion and transferred
to outsiders were in consequence in a much more thriving
condition. By 1921 the settlement officer in Saharanpur was
reporting that 'the occupancy tenant appears to be even more
prosperous than the cultivating proprietor' and on average possessed a larger holding.[16]

The position in Saharanpur may have been somewhat extreme,
but the absence of any sharp gulf between the cultivating proprietor and his tenant was general, at least in the western U.P.
where *bhaiachara* tenures were common and caste differences
were not marked. Inevitably it engendered conflict from the
time the discrepancy between occupancy and competition rents
became apparent in the 1890s. For both economic and social
reasons cultivating proprietors found difficulty in resisting the
accrual of occupancy tenant rights, but their own pressing need
for subsistence as their numbers proliferated could well force them
into what the board of revenue described in 1905 as 'a struggle
for existence: the landholders [in the eastern districts] require the
land more and more for themselves to meet their growing necessities, and it would be hard if they are in any way prevented from
getting it into their own hands'.[17] Hence in Azamgarh the area
under proprietary cultivation (*sir* and *khudkasht*) could increase
at the same time as the area under occupancy tenancy was

[15] *Budaun S.R. 1930*, p. 7, para. 29.
[16] D. I. Drake Brockman, *Saharanpur S.R. 1921*, pp. 21, 25.
Average size of holding:

	Cultivating proprietors	Occupancy and ex-proprietary tenants	Non-occupancy tenants
	(in acres)	(in acres)	(in acres)
1830–8	16·5	10·6	7·5
1860–2	9·5	7·5	5·8
1920	8·4	11·3	4·6

[17] *Board of Revenue, Revenue Administration Report U.P. 1903–4* (Allahabad, 1905), p. 18, para. 42.

growing, even though the tenant-at-will land and the total tenancy area as a whole was being reduced.[18] In Meerut it was not un-known for a small proprietor to have to rent his own land from his occupancy tenant at twice the rental he received for it.[19] The occupancy tenant had in effect become a sub-proprietor.

Now this situation obtained not only in small mahals but also in some of the larger estates of the older landholding families. On the Kuchchesar estate which was spread over the northeast portion of Bulandshahr district and the southeastern portion of Meerut, the occupancy tenant had become almost independent by the turn of the century: 'the occupancy tenant feels that he has no concern with his landlord except to send him a money-order for his rent and commonly refers to his occupancy land as 'hamari' [ours]'.[20] On the estates of the Mainpuri raj there was also a long tradition of indirect management which kept rents low and tenants independent.

The sum of these conditions vitally affected the position of the rural elite. On the one hand, middling-sized properties held by a gentry-farmer class tended to disappear and to leave little between the large estate owner and the cultivating proprietor. On the other hand, the growth of sub-proprietary rights meant that the elite was confronted not by a body of tenants who could be welded into coherent economic units or estates in the more modern sense, but by a mass of petty proprietors with whom their relations tended to be those of absentee rent-receivers.

What held the properties of the higher elite together? In Oudh, if we accept Dr Metcalf's explanation, it was government action that shored up the great talukdari estates. But outside Oudh he acknowledges that the old magnate class was deprived of such institutional buttresses as encumbered estates acts and faced a hostile tradition that consistently opposed the landlord class throughout the nineteenth century.[21] Dr F. C. R. Robinson has underlined the distinction between Oudh and the eastern districts on the one hand, and the Doab and the western U.P. (including Rohilkhand) on the other. It was in this latter region, which

[18] *Azamgarh S.R. 1908*, p. 14, para. 6.
[19] S. W. Gillan, *Meerut S.R. 1901*, p. 19, para. 32.
[20] *Ibid*.
[21] T. R. Metcalf, 'Social Effects of British Land Policy in Oudh', in R. E. Frykenberg (ed.), *Land Control and Social Structure in Indian History* (Madison, Milwaukee & London, 1969), pp. 157–8.

possessed in 1911, according to Robinson, 45% of the population but enjoyed 72% of total U.P. trade, that the corrosive action of commercial forces on the position of the traditional landholding classes exerted really serious effects:

Thus the old elite of the Mughal Empire, Muslims, Rajputs and their Kayasth servants who owned 60 to 65 per cent of the land in the province were losing land, and social, economic and political power to those characterised [by Sir Auckland Colvin] as the 'mere rubble of the political building', the trading and moneylending castes, Vaishyas, Khattris, Kalwars, and in some cases Brahmins whose gains in land had been immense over the nineteenth century, particularly in its last 30 years.[22]

Robinson appositely points to Kanpur district where money-lending castes, according to him, extended their hold from 15·7% of the land in 1802 to 41·7% in 1900.[23] Although Robinson has exaggerated the timing and extent of this alienation, his thesis blends readily with the notion that while the social composition of the elite may have altered, large-scale landholding persisted. In other words, economic forces tended to sustain the size of the estate at the upper levels and countered the tendency towards subdivision.[24] At the top there was a shift towards plutocracy rather than a change of scale. A glance at the larger landholders of the western U.P. would seem to confirm this impression. In the Saharanpur district in 1920 there were 13 landholders paying over Rs. 5,000 in revenue, of which 6 are clearly identifiable as Vaishya; in Muzaffarnagar in 1921, 5 of the 15 can be similarly identified. In 1940 in Meerut 8 of the 26 leading proprietors

22 F. C. R. Robinson, 'Some Themes in U.P. Politics, 1883–1916', a seminar paper read at the Centre for South Asian Studies, Cambridge, in May 1969. Cf. also his article 'Municipal Government and Muslim Separatism in the U.P., 1883 to 1916' in J. Gallagher, G. Johnson and A. Seal (eds.), *Locality, Province and Nation: Essays on Indian Politics, 1870–1940* (Cambridge, 1973) pp. 81 ff.

23 Robinson has counted all Brahmins as members of the moneylending castes whereas they formed an important part of the agricultural class in Kanpur, see later footnote *infra* for table of landownership changes in Kanpur district.

24 The 'estate' in this sense was no more than an aggregate of revenue-paying lands. How far estates were consolidated into effective social and economic units and how far they became mere bundles of scattered rent properties is another and most important question. Cf. P. Musgrave, 'Landlords and Lords of the Land: Estate Management and Social Control in U.P. 1860–1920', *Modern Asian Studies*, VI (3), 1972, pp. 257 ff.

(paying over Rs. 5,000) are described explicitly as Vaish.[25]

What evidence is there that estates of intermediate size were being steadily squeezed out of existence? For the most part one must rely on inferences to be drawn from the details of land transfers. These point strongly to a long, secular decline of traditional 'gentry' elements, Muslims in particular. In Aligarh Muslim landholding fell from 22% in 1874 to 19.3% in 1903, and to 15.7% in 1943. It is noticeable that the loss fell lightest (4%) on the Pathans who held substantial properties, especially the Sherwani Afghan family in Atrauli tahsil; and heaviest among the smaller Muslim landholders, particularly the Sheikhs who parted with 36% of their land between 1874 and 1903. This tendency for the large men to prosper and the small men to decline, which Burkitt remarked upon in 1903, evidently persisted, for in 1943, S. Ahmad Ali, the settlement officer, could still observe: '[Among the Muslims] the Pathan zamindars of Atrauli, and the bigger Musalman zamindars elsewhere have done well on the whole, and the loss is generally restricted to the small zamindars who are poor.'[26] The same features are visible in the neighbouring district of Bulandshahr where total Muslim holdings fell between 1891 and 1919 from some 33% to 29%. But while the broad-acred Naumuslim Lalkhani proprietors increased their holdings slightly, Sayyids lost 28% of theirs. Their fate was general. In Meerut they lost some 10% of their meagre possessions between 1870 and 1900, and in Muzaffarnagar where they had once been the dominant landholding community they lost over 20% between 1890 and 1920.[27]

Whether traditional 'gentry' losses were almost wholly absorbed by Vaishya gains and middling-size estates thus reconstituted is unclear, but as absentee rent-receivers without natural ties with the local community Vaishyas could never act as a rural

[25] *Saharanpur S.R. 1921*, Appx III, p. 48; *Muzaffarnagar S.R. 1921*, Appx VIII, p. 36; *Meerut S.R. 1940*, Appx VIII, p. 56.

[26] *Aligarh S.R. 1943*, p. 5, para. 14.

[27] *Bulandshahr S.R. 1901*, p. 9, para. 35; Appx VIII A. *Meerut S.R. 1901*, p. 10, para. 26: 'Between the rent-collecting landlords and the cultivating zamindars are several communities chiefly Musalman, who partake of the qualities of both. They resemble the second in the number of sharers, but like the first, let out their land instead of cultivating. Some of these communities, like the Sayyids of Abdullahpur, have an extensive property, but the shares are constantly being subdivided, and generally the conditions of such proprietors is less satisfactory than that of other classes.' *Muzaffarnagar S.R. 1921*, p. 7, para. 35; Appx VIII B.

elite. Notions of drastic social and economic change must, however, be regarded with caution. While it is true that land transfers
remained brisk in the period after 1860 it is questionable whether
the rate of inter-class or inter-caste transfer was sufficiently pre-
cipitous to effect a social revolution. F. C. R. Robinson points to
the Kanpur district as a striking example of the rapid passage of
land from the traditional to the commercial castes, and superficially there is much to corroborate such a view. H. K. Gracey,
the settlement officer in 1907, lamented:

reviewing events from cession downwards the salient feature in the
situation is the progress and success of the bankers and speculators
and the commercial men, irrespective of caste, and the downfall of
the orthodox zamindar...While there are in the district several
properties of considerable size and importance, the owners are in the
great majority of cases new or comparatively new men, and nothing
is more striking in the district than the disappearance of the old
estates, especially those of the Rajputs, whose Rajas, Rawats and
Raos have either disappeared or have been reduced to the greatest
straits. Even the most important Rajput property in the district, that
of the Gaur family of Khanpur Dilwal in the Derapur tahsil, is in its
present form of recent origin, the bulk of the land having been
acquired by purchase or as the reward of the loyalty during the
rebellion of 1857.[28]

Yet the statistics make it quite plain that the major losses on the
part of the Thakur communities and the major gains on the part
of the commercial Brahmin and moneylending castes were accomplished before 1873–4, and that changes after that period were on
a very much reduced scale.[29] The same can be said of other districts

[28] *Cawnpore S.R. 1907*, para. 21.
[29] Kanpur district.

PERCENTAGE OF TOTAL LAND HELD

	Rajputs (Thakurs)	Brahmins	Money-lending castes	Muslims	Kayasths
1802	50	11·2	1·5	12·6	7·8 (10·84?)
1840	38·4	18·8	3·7	15·7	6·1
1873–4	31·6	29·6	6·3	12·4	6·8
1907	30·3	33·2	5·2	6·8	4·5

SOURCES: E. A. Atkinson (ed.), *Gazetteer N.W.P.*, VI; *Cawnpore S.R. 1970*, Appx X.

The protagonists for restricting the power of hereditary agriculturalists to
alienate land tended to exaggerate the extent of transfer to the non-
agricultural classes, but even the inflated figures cited in the Memorandum
on the Restriction of the Power to Alienate Interests in Land, Calcutta,

which were supposedly most susceptible to intercaste transfer. In Aligarh the Vaishya element strengthened its grip from 3·4% in 1839, 12·3% in 1868, 12% in 1903, to 13·6% in 1943. Brahmins, who included some commercial men among their numbers, rose from 9% in 1839, 9·2% in 1868, 13·5% in 1903, to 14·5% in 1943. Thakur holdings fell from 38% in 1838, 28% in 1868, 23·3% in 1903, to 22·1% in 1943. In Meerut, purportedly one of the most highly commercialised districts, Vaishya gains were slow and modest – 7% in 1865, 7·8% in 1900, 14·7% in 1940. To the north in Muzaffarnagar and Saharanpur districts they look more startling. Vaishya holdings in Muzaffarnagar rose from 16·5% in 1891 to 24% in 1921; in Saharanpur, from 19% in 1866, 25·1% in 1890, to 27·9% in 1921. But much of their earlier gains in these districts were made in uncleared jungle grants in the Siwalik terai or in *khadir* land in the Ganges valley.[30] The dramatic loss of Sayyid land in Muzaffarnagar was also primarily a pre-1870 phenomenon.[31] U.P. society in these western districts – where change was supposedly most intense – seems in fact to have been slowly evolving on lines laid down in an earlier period. The decisive revolution in land control had occurred before the Great Rebellion of 1857, in a pre-commercial era, the product of institutional rather than economic change.

Nothing is more striking in this respect than the stability of the great estates in the post-1860 period. A list drawn up in 1860 and 1940 would display remarkably few changes; in Saharanpur the Landhaurah raj, in Muzaffarnagar the Jansath Sayyids, in Bulandshahr the Kuchchesar and Lalkhani estates (including Chhatari), in Aligarh the Mursan raj, the Awagarh estate, and the Sherwani properties. Doubtless they had suffered many vicissi-

---

1895 (India Office Library List 10.2362/1), purportedly written by Denzil Ibbetson, support the notion that the major phase of transfer occurred before 1873. In ten districts taken at random moneylenders held in 1873 27% of the total area, as against 10% 30 years earlier. *Ibid.*, p. 10, para. 33.

The figures cited by Robinson from the District Gazetteers in no way support percentage rates of 27%; Gallagher, Robinson and Seal, *Locality, Province and Nation*, pp. 83–4.

[30] *Aligarh S.R. 1874*, p. 66; *Aligarh S.R. 1943*, p. 5, para. 14; *Meerut S.R. 1901*, p. 10, para. 27; *Meerut S.R. 1940*, p. 13, para. 2: *Muzaffarnagar S.R. 1921*, p. 35, Appx VIII-B; *Saharanpur S.R. 1891*; *Saharanpur S.R. 1921*, p. 47, Appx II.

[31] Alan Cadell, *Settlement Report of the Ganges Canal Tract in the Muzaffarnagar District* (Allahabad, 1876).

tudes and some had carried in their time a heavy load of debt and litigation, but nevertheless they remained the great revenue payers of their districts. They differed, of course, considerably in their internal management. Where a traditional magnate was of the same caste as his 'tenant' and held a position of quasi-lordship, he was unlikely to exact high rents. This was the position on the Gujar Landhaurah family's lands in Saharanpur and Meerut, on the Kuchchesar estate in Bulandshahr, and Meerut, and on the Mainpuri raj estate in Mainpuri district.[32] But where caste homogeneity was lacking, traditional landlords could be severe and grasping. The Lalkhani estates in the 1890s acquired 'a general and unenviable reputation for oppressive management, exorbitant demands from tenants, including all sorts of nazarana'. Although these abuses had greatly diminished by 1919, it was reported that 'Lalkhani management indeed is still exacting, rents are high and rigidly collected, occupancy rights are prevented by leases, and the proprietor's authority is stoutly maintained.'[33] If caste could ever have been overtaken by class it was from here that a great landlord interest might have been organised, and it is perhaps significant that the despairing attempt to mobilise the landlords in a political sense should have been led by the head of the Lalkhani estates, the Nawab of Chhatari.[34] Whether such heterogeneous magnate elements constituted more than an economic category is a specifically socio-historical question towards whose answer an investigation of the history of the Zamindars' Association (founded at Muzaffarnagar in 1896) and of the Agra Province Zamindars' Association (1914) would make a valuable contribution.[35] Still more significant, perhaps, would be the history of opposition to the magnate class, culminating in zamindari abolition. And here we return to our starting point. The 1947 figures of the Zamindari Abolition Report show that the critical

---

[32] *Meerut S.R. 1901*, pp. 12–13.
[33] *Bulandshahr S.R. 1919* p. 7, para. 29. For details see *Bulandshahr S.R. 1891*.
[34] P. D. Reeves, 'Landlords and Party Politics in the United Provinces, 1934–7', in D. A. Low (ed.), *Sounding in Modern South Asian History* (London, 1968), pp. 267 ff.
[35] Cf. T. R. Metcalf in Frykenberg, *Land Control and Social Structure*, pp. 157–8, basing himself on P. D. Reeves 'Landlord Associations in U.P. and their Role in Landlord Politics, 1920–37', a working paper of the Institute of Advanced Studies, Department of History, Australian National University, 4 May 1961.

differences among districts concerned, firstly, the number of large estates in any one district paying over Rs. 10,000 and, secondly, the number of petty and yeomen proprietors and the proportion of revenue they raised. In Meerut district large estates were few, but there were an enormous number of petty proprietors (145,126) paying under Rs. 25, as well as the largest number of yeomen farmers in the whole of the U.P., 20,603 each paying Rs. 25–150. Together these two groups raised 31·2% and 40·8% of the large district revenue respectively, or a total of 72%. It was appropriate that one of the centres of the zamindari abolition campaign should have been Meerut under the Jat leader, Shri Charan Singh.[36] The most dangerous enemy of the great landlord was the small cultivating landlord who here was the Jat peasant proprietor.

But in some districts the process of land transfers appears to have prevented this expansion of the pyramidal base, the area under peasant proprietorship appearing to suffer marked contraction. Kanpur district was the most extreme example. Here large estates assessed at over Rs. 10,000 were also negligible, but the petty and yeomen proprietors were by 1947 remarkably weak in numbers and, above all, in the proportion of revenue they provided. The two latter groups numbered 31,160 and 7,189 and raised only 8·5% and 29·6% of the revenue respectively. The predominant feature of Kanpur district had become the medium-sized landlord 'estates', owned by some 1,229 men who paid between Rs. 250 and Rs. 5,000 and who met 49·5% of the revenue demand (see Table 4). The absence of large traditional estates and the long history of commercial investment in rent rights had apparently resulted in the reconstruction of land proprietorship on a new social base. Yet the artificiality of the distinction between landlord and tenant warns us against facile conclusions drawn solely from the statement of proprietary rights. In a district like Kanpur, which suffered extensive tenurial derangement in the early years of British rule, a gap was opened

---

[36] Cf. P. Brass, *Factional Politics in an Indian State: The Congress Party in Uttar Pradesh* (Bombay, 1966), pp. 139 ff. Charan Singh, *Abolition of Zamindari. Two Alternatives* (Allahabad, 1947). Shri Charan Singh was an active member of the Zamindari Abolition Committee set up in 1946. It is noticeable that among the 26 revenue-payers of over Rs. 5,000 in 1940 only six were Jat, and that five of these were magnates from the Kuchchesar estate; *Meerut S.R. 1940*, p. 56, Appx IX.

between revenue-engagement rights (*malguzari*) and the proprietary dominion of the soil itself (*milkiyat-i-zamin*) that was probably never closed. Almost at the outset a substantial portion of the dominant cultivating castes were legally transformed into tenants while in practice they continued to exercise effective proprietary control, so that the Famine Commission of 1881 could single out as a typical cultivator a Brahmin occupancy tenant with a 21-acre holding.[37] The effect of British tenancy laws was, as we have seen, to reinforce the artificiality of the distinction. While for land-revenue purposes a category of revenue payers was separated out and called landowners these remained for the most part proprietors of a rent charge on the effective owner, the protected tenant, to whom as a result of rent control and social forces the bulk of agricultural profits increasingly passed. The greater value of tenant right over proprietary right was first visible in the permanently-settled districts of the east. The settlement officer of Ballia district reported in 1881: 'The value of the tenant right is very much greater than that of the proprietary right in most instances. The proprietary right is a multiple of the rent less the revenue, generally 16 times. The tenant right value is a much greater multiple of the rent 20, or 30, or 40 times, and is particularly valuable since no occupancy right can accrue under it.' Consequently agricultural incomes bore little direct relationship to the list of proprietors or revenue payers. 'It is a matter of purely technical and litigious interest whether a given individual is a zamindar, or a fixed-rate tenant, or an occupancy tenant. The material point is whether he holds his land at favourable or unfavourable rates, and whether he has got enough of it.'[38]

The crucial economic and social divide was, therefore, not between landlord and tenant, but between the man who derived his income from rents and the man who depended on agricultural profits. At its widest extent – and in practice there were many intermediate positions – the divide corresponded with that between the absentee rent-receiver and the cultivating landholder, whose holding was composed of land held under various tenures

[37] *Parliamentary Papers 1881*, xxi, pt 2, p. 265.
[38] D. T. Roberts, *Reports of the Board of Revenue on the Revenue Administration of the N.W. Provinces, 1882–83* (Allahabad, 1884), Divisional Reports, p. 26.

ranging from full proprietary right to tenancy at will. The profitability of rent ownership was by no means as large as the traditional image of the landlord supposes. If illegal cesses on the one
hand and shortfalls in collections on the other are discounted,
proprietary incomes look distinctly modest even at the higher
levels. After meeting management and other expenses the net
income from rents of most proprietors by 1949 was distinctly
below half rental assets. Only 13,384 enjoyed an annual net
income of Rs. 1,162 or more; and of these only some 1,500 paying
revenue in excess of Rs. 3,000 were in receipt of more than
Rs. 5,000.[39]

Yet in ordinary circumstances there was little prospect of the
gap between the rent receiver and the agriculturalist being closed.
The fact that in the most thriving districts like Meerut the largest
cultivating holdings averaged no more than 40 acres set an in-
exorable limit to enlarging the scale of production and so obtaining substantial farm incomes. No doubt under conditions of high
prices, as in 1921, a holding of 50 acres of Jungle Wet I soil in
Muzaffarnagar district could produce crops to the value of
Rs. 200 per acre and so reap a handsome profit, even after meeting rent at Rs. 13 per acre and the living costs of as many as ten
cultivators and their families at Rs. 280 each.[40] Even in impoverished eastern Gorakhpur (later Deoria district) the net profit
in 1919 after meeting all expenses was reckoned at Rs. 40 per
acre.[41] But such conditions were doubtless exceptional and could
not in any event have been repeated again until the high prices of
the Second World War. The Provincial Banking Enquiry Committee of 1929–30 conducted its proceedings in the onset of the
great slump, and reported that an economic holding to support one
cultivator and his family in Meerut district must be regarded as
5 acres or so.[42] On this basis there was little profit beyond subsistence for cultivators on all but the largest holdings. Hence the
pursuit of agriculture threw up at the top a substantial peasant
elite rather than a farmer class that could rival economically the
larger rent-receiving landlords. The gap was closed only by the

[39] Neale, *Economic Change*, p. 252 and Table 19.
[40] *Muzaffarnagar S.R. 1921*, p. 9. Cost of cultivation is estimated from *U.P.
Provincial Banking Enquiry Committee Report* (Allahabad, 1930), I, p. 25.
[41] *Gorakhpur (Padrauna, Hata and Deoria tahsils) S.R. 1919*, pp. 20–1.
[42] *Report of U.P. Provincial Banking Enquiry Committee 1929–30* (Allahabad, 1930), I, p. 25.

relatively few men who filled both roles and combined direct cultivation with a significant income from rental property.

The pattern of cultivating holdings seems to have been analogous in evolution and structure to the pattern of proprietary rights. The Zamindari Abolition Committee failed to obtain accurate figures of cultivating holdings, presumably because of the difficulty encountered by village record keepers (*patwaris*) in tracing all the holdings of an individual and recording them under a single name. The consequence of double-counting was not only to inflate grossly the numbers of cultivators but to exaggerate the numbers of smaller holdings. Yet the progressive subdivision of cultivating holdings was a process that had long been observed and formed a subject for official concern many decades before the crisis of the 1930s when the sharp increase in population growth and fall in crop prices brought to public attention the full gravity of the agrarian problem. Concern to ensure that cultivators did not fall below the minimum 'economic holding' necessary for adequate subsistence led successive commissions of inquiry into an obsession with the average size of holdings, seemingly oblivious to the unrepresentative nature of the arithmetical mean.[43] There seems good reason for believing, however, as we have observed already in the case of proprietary holdings, that population pressure did not operate to reduce the size of cultivating holdings equally. Instead the latter appear to have remained stable at the upper level but to have undergone the most marked subdivision and fragmentation at the bottom. The strongest influence at work was the increase in the rural proletariat. The myth of the rise of the landless labourer has helped to obscure the fact that only a very small minority of the rural population was without cultivating rights of some kind, even though such plots were hopelessly inadequate without another source of livelihood. In 1919 D. M. Stewart estimated that only 11 % of the population in one of the most crowded parts of the U.P., Western Gorakhpur, were agricultural labourers pure and simple, and that the vast bulk of the rural poor crowded into the ranks of the lower tenantry.[44] The U.P. Provincial Banking Enquiry Committee of 1929–30 estimated 'allotment holders' at some 5 % of all U.P. cultivators, but the

[43] These commissions of inquiry are briefly reviewed in *Z.A.C.R.* i, pp. 10 ff. Cf. Sir Manilal P. Nanavati and J. J. Anjaria, *The Indian Rural Problem* (Bombay, 1944), pp. 39 ff.
[44] *Gorakhpur (Western Portion) S.R. 1919*, p. 13.

category needs considerable extension. The Zamindari Abolition Committee went to the other extreme and estimated that 37·8% of cultivators had holdings of less than one acre (occupying 6% of the area) and 81·2% under five acres (occupying 38·8% of the area).[45]

According to the Committee's figures, in Gorakhpur 91·6% of the cultivators possessed holdings of under five acres and occupied as much as 54·5% of the area. This contrasted with 79% of such cultivators in Meerut occupying 36·6% of the land.[46] The degree of exaggeration in these figures can be judged from contemporary settlement reports. In 1940 it was estimated that in Meerut only 32% of cultivators had holdings under five acres and occupied no more than 12% of the area.[47] For Gorakhpur there is no contemporary evidence, but the settlement report of 1919 is not without significance. In 1919, K. N. Knox abandoned the use of patwari returns because of the enormous extent of double-counting and attempted an estimate of holdings based on plough areas. In the most crowded area of Deoria he found that only 16% of the area was taken up by cultivating holdings of less than four acres, and even in the worst *tappas* the figure rose no higher than 27%.[48] Despite these findings, J. K. Mathur 12 years later used the patwari returns noted by Knox in his report to state the average size of tenant holdings in Deoria as 0·65 acres;[49] 30 years later the Zamindari Abolition Committee gave figures showing that 53·7% of the new Deoria district comprised holdings of less than four acres. Even allowing for the worsening of the position since Knox made his estimates, it is difficult to believe that his personal observation of conditions could have been so wildly astray.

The Zamindari Abolition Committee stood at the end of a long tradition of U.P. Congress politics on the agrarian question. For its special purposes the Committee chose to give prominence to the extremes of the landholding structure – at one end the large revenue-paying landlords and at the other end the mass of petty agriculturalists struggling for existence on minute holdings. It

[45] *U.P. Provincial Banking Enquiry Committee Report 1929–30* (Allahabad, 1930), I, p. 22. Neale, *Economic Change*, p. 272, Table 27.
[46] *Z.A.C.R.* II, pp. 34–9.
[47] *Meerut S.R. 1940*, p. 17.
[48] *Gorakhpur (Tahsils Padrauna, Hata and Deoria) S.R. 1919*, p. 19.
[49] J. K. Mathur, *The Pressure of Population: Its Effects on Rural Economy in Gorakhpur District*, Department of Agriculture Bulletin (Allahabad, 1931). See also below, pp. 235–6.

passed over in silence the intermediate peasant elite. Exaggeration (through double-counting) of the number of cultivators at more than 12 million led to the calculation of the average holding (in the 41 million acres odd of the cultivated area) at no more than 3·37 acres.[50] Yet even without such double-counting the calculation of the average holding as an arithmetic mean was a wholly unreal process since it ignored the pattern of distribution. For the average was completely thrown out by the mass of small holders occupying a relatively small portion of the land. Even on the Committee's swollen figures 67·4% of cultivators held under three acres and occupied 22·8% of the cultivated area. If these are excluded then the average holding over 77·2% of the area rose to over eight acres for the remaining 4 million cultivators. There is good reason to believe that it was in practice bigger than this. In Meerut in 1940 the settlement officer estimated that 36% of cultivators held over ten acres apiece and commanded 60% of the area. Even in overcrowded Deoria one may question how far the 31% of the land cultivated in 1919 by families with two pairs of plough bullocks (8–10 acres), or as much as 55% in such holdings north of the Gorakhpur-Hata-Kasia road in the Haveli pargana and possessed mainly by Saithwar (Kurmi) families, had been substantially reduced by 1948.[51] Zamindari abolition in 1951 left this peasant elite without serious rival in the countryside.

[50] Cf. Neale, *Economic Change*, p. 272, Table 27.
[51] *Gorakhpur (Tahsils Padrauna, Hata and Deoria) S.R. 1919*, p. 19.

TABLE 4

Classification of zamindars (proprietors) in U.P. 1946–7 according to categories of land-revenue payments

| | Numbers of zamindars and percentage of total district land revenue paid by each category | | | | | | | | | | | | Total land revenue Rs. |
| | Rs. under 25 | | Rs. 25–250 | | Rs. 250–1,000 | | Rs. 1,000–5,000 | | Rs. 5,000–10,000 | | Rs. over 10,000 | | |
	Nos.	%	Nos.	%	Nos.	%	Nos.	%	Nos.	%	Nos.	%	
DOAB													
Saharanpur	95,812	29·0	9,549	34·8	613	15·3	126	11·9	5	2·5	4	6·5	17,16,032
Muzaffarnagar	83,919	26·3	10,702	37·9	603	15·2	141	14·0	7	2·4	4	4·3	18,61,321
Meerut	145,126	31·2	20,603	40·8	862	13·8	157	9·6	12	2·8	4	1·9	30,33,203
Bulandshahr	65,761	13·2	8,382	25·9	838	18·2	206	15·5	24	7·9	18	17·5	22,24,563
Aligarh	47,336	14·7	8,451	24·0	954	17·2	244	18·0	24	7·3	23	18·9	25,57,422
Mathura	55,058	22·4	6,749	29·6	507	16·6	105	14·6	12	5·3	6	11·8	13,87,904
Agra	44,833	14·1	7,490	31·2	904	24·0	162	16·9	14	6·1	6	7·7	16,98,919
Mainpuri	25,987	11·9	5,203	32·4	610	23·8	91	15·0	8	5·0	7	12·0	11,71,671
Etah	34,855	11·4	4,449	23·7	435	15·4	90	13·0	7	2·9	9	33·7	13,80,626
Farrukhabad	39,072	13·4	5,884	32·0	493	18·4	97	16·5	12	6·0	2	14·6	11,84,206
Etawa	19,328	8·0	4,452	25·2	706	25·4	141	19·0	19	9·4	9	13·2	13,46,233
Kanpur	31,160	8·5	7,189	29·6	1,001	25·7	228	23·8	23	9·2	5	3·5	19,04,777
Fatehpur	21,631	12·2	4,709	32·6	557	24·6	124	23·2	3	2·4	3	4·9	10,23,561
Banda	30,443	23·2	5,576	36·1	349	15·7	74	16·0	6	4·3	4	4·7	9,64,533
ROHILKHAND													
Bareli	39,628	11·0	8,982	39·7	822	22·2	172	20·8	6	2·3	4	4·0	16,83,675
Bijnor	52,469	13·6	5,169	25·6	642	19·0	174	22·4	4	1·9	9	17·6	15,71,385
Philibhit	6,165	5·7	1,812	23·0	364	23·4	95	24·6	3	2·7	7	20·6	7,05,962
Budaun	50,546	17·6	7,179	35·5	786	24·2	143	17·7	9	4·3	1	0·9	14,31,450
Moradabad	70,632	14·3	8,056	28·0	1,353	27·5	225	20·3	10	3·2	6	6·9	22,42,275
Sahajahanpur	39,945	12·8	4,879	30·7	566	21·6	120	20·4	12	6·6	4	8·0	11,68,726

OUDH												
Kheri	5,395	2·7	9·6	1,575	6·5	167	11·1	65	4	2·6	13	67·6	12,14,996
Lucknow	8,346	5·4	23·5	3,522	22·8	581	18·0	111	8	4·7	10	25·7	11,21,015
Unnao	22,868	13·9	34·8	6,118	19·6	538	16·7	111	10	6·9	6	8·4	12,34,594
Rae Bareli	8,044	3·2	9·9	22,225	8·0	295	11·8	94	11	4·7	27	62·5	16,33,985
Sitapur	6,249	2·4	12·2	3,232	12·2	544	16·8	171	14	4·8	20	51·5	21,07,720
Hardoi	28,469	15·0	34·8	8,136	14·8	570	9·5	90	9	3·9	10	22·1	16,50,900
Faizabad	15,451	5·3	10·3	2,933	4·6	186	8·4	64	13	4·4	15	67·0	18,56,162
Sultanpur	24,256	11·4	22·0	5,152	8·5	282	6·2	48	7	3·4	14	48·6	14,76,430
Partapgarh	9,476	5·1	8·0	1,436	11·3	333	7·0	42	15	8·8	14	60·0	12,45,097
Bara Banki	13,861	6·2	19·0	4,792	14·4	596	9·9	104	16	17·6	21	43·1	19,48,746
Bahraich	1,507	0·9	3·8	536	4·0	91	5·8	35	3	1·9	11	83·6	11,12,990
Gonda	20,742	5·8	11·2	2,866	6·1	170	7·9	59	7	2·6	10	66·4	16,46,543
EASTERN DISTRICTS												
Allahabad	36,613	7·5	20·4	7,419	15·0	835	17·7	215	14	3·7	24	35·7	25,84,583
Banaras	16,169	7·3	19·0	3,650	16·5	492	15·4	110	7	3·7	4	38·3	13,67,382
Jaunpur	31,508	18·3	31·7	5,539	15·6	380	10·7	74	1	0·4	5	23·2	11,32,042
Ghazipur	37,013	27·0	43·3	5,644	16·7	292	11·9	53	2	1·3	0	0·0	8,15,005
Ballia	31,596	28·4	31·6	3,121	14·9	216	8·3	30	0	0·0	1	16·8	6,18,233
Azamgarh	89,681	31·0	41·4	14,084	11·9	553	7·3	76	4	1·2	3	7·3	19,83,690
Gorakhpur	67,154	24·0	30·0	7,250	14·7	497	18·3	138	8	3·6	9	9·4	15,27,354
Basti	95,587	24·3	34·9	13,802	13·8	783	10·1	133	16	4·2	13	12·6	24,83,063
Deoria	64,611	22·4	31·4	8,379	14·2	541	9·7	94	4	1·8	11	20·6	16,84,280

Source: Report of the United Provinces Zamindari Abolition Committee, II (Allahabad, 1948), pp. 12–17.

TABLE 5

Table showing increase in number of estates (mahals) and of proprietors or co-sharers in selected U.P. districts as recorded in land-revenue settlement reports contrasted with Zamindari Abolition Committee's figures

AGRA	1880	1905*	1930		Z.A.C. 1948
mahals	1,703	6,208	6,907		
total co-sharers	43,551	53,869	75,847		53,409
ALIGARH	1882	1903	1943		
mahals		3,316	5,271		
total co-sharers	44,840	61,014	86,921		57,032
BAREILLY	1874	1911*	1942		
mahals	3,236	6,486	7,328		
total co-sharers	23,122		77,812		40,614
BIJNOR	1872	1899	1906*	1939	
mahals	2,229	3,547	5,853	6,485	
	(3,364)	(5,260)			
total co-sharers				113,515	58,647
non-resident co-sharers				77,335	
BUDAUN		1901	1930		
mahals		4,408	1,709		
total co-sharers		61,946	99,185		58,664
non-resident co-sharers			60,390		
ETAH	1874	1905	1944		
mahals	1,499	3,065	3,850		
total co-sharers	13,531	46,193	75,087		39,845
non-resident co-sharers		21,366	38,541		
ETAWAH	1875	1911*	1915		
mahals	1,813	4,446	4,807		
total co-sharers	15,523		18,873		24,655
GORAKHPUR	1891	1909*	1919		
mahals	8,463	14,586	14,661		(incl. Deoria)
total co-sharers	100,249		332,134		148,696
non-resident co-sharers			228,100		
KANPUR	1848	1881*	1907		
mahals		2,550	5,771		
total co-sharers	16,542		36,572		39,606
MAINPURI	1875	1906	1944		
mahals	1,435	2,600	3,417		
total co-sharers	21,295	37,143	53,868		31,906

TABLE 5 (*contd.*)

	1883	1903*	1926		Z.A.C. 1948
MATHURA	*1883*	*1903**	*1926*		*Z.A.C. 1948*
mahals	1,375	2,684			
total co-sharers			82,793		62,437
MEERUT	*1874*	*1901*	*1940*		
mahals			7,795		
total co-sharers	105,237	153,668	251,665		166,764
MUZAFFARNAGAR	*1860*	*1890*	*1921*		
mahals	1,061	2,992	8,033		
total co-sharers			144,215		95,376
SHAHJAHANPUR	*1875*	*1901*	*1907**	*1943*	
mahals	3,063	3,558	3,783	4,584	
total co-sharers			88,288		36,526
UNAO	*1895*		*1931*		
mahals	2,784		5,366		
total co-sharers	28,455		57,963		29,651

SOURCE: *U.P. Land Revenue Settlement Reports.*
Years indicate date of publication of settlement report not year of verification.

*H. R. Nevill (ed.), *District Gazetteers of U.P., 1903–11* (Allahabad), 48 vols. or E. A. Atkinson (ed.), *Gazetteer N.W.P., 1874–86* (Allahabad), 14 vols according to date.

Except in case of Gorakhpur these figures take no account of district boundary changes between given dates.

IO

Dynamism and enervation in North Indian agriculture: the historical dimension

> *In the west, when they talk of a* Purbi (literally someone
> from the east, an inhabitant of the middle or lower
> Ganges) *they automatically add the adjective* dhila
> *meaning rather unenterprising. One cannot but agree
> with the epithet. We are a long way from the robust
> northern castes –* Gilbert Etienne, *Studies in Indian Agri-
> culture: the Art of the Possible.*

One of the well-worn problems which have long engaged observers of the agrarian scene has been the uneven growth performance of Indian agriculture in different regions. In the north of
the subcontinent there is the obvious contrast between the eastern
and western portions of the Indo-Gangetic plain. While Bangladesh, Bengal, Bihar, and eastern U.P. have apparently remained
sunk in stagnation and depression, western U.P., Haryana and
the Punjab exhibit all the untidy signs of entrepreneurial activity
and dynamic growth. Is not the expansion as straightforward as
the phenomenon itself? The agriculturally secure regions were the
first to enjoy prosperity and the first to fall victim to over-population, so that the centre of dynamic growth moved progressively
away from the deltaic and lower riverine areas to the more thinly-
held tracts of upper India, where the *Pax Britannica* and canal
irrigation acted like a forced draught behind agricultural expansion. In this way, over the course of the nineteenth-century
Lakshmi, the fickle goddess of fortune, betook herself with uneven
tread westward from the lush verdure of Bengal until she has
come to fix her temporary abode on the Punjab plain between
Ludhiana and Lyallpur. The explanation has been applied over
a narrower geographical span. Historians have become accustomed to tracing back the decisive east-west shift in economic
power and activity in the U.P. region to the railway age of the
1860s and 1870s.[1] It was then that the thriving economy of the

[1] Cf. F. C. R. Robinson, *Separatism among Indian Muslims* (Cambridge,
1974) pp. 59 ff.

Benares region, founded on the export of cash crops like sugar, indigo, opium, and rice, and backed by an important handloom textile industry and a great entrepôt trading centre at Mirzapur, began to lose out to the new centres of manufacture like Kanpur and to the wheat and sugar producing regions of the upper Ganges-Jumna Doab.

Overpopulation remained the favourite explanation of the contrast. In the wake of his labours on the U.P. Provincial Banking Enquiry Committee of 1928–30, the celebrated Professor Radhakamal Mukerjee commissioned a series of village and district studies by his M.A. pupils at Lucknow. In a foreword to one of these officially published monographs, Bholanath Misra's *Over-population in Jaunpur,*[2] Mukerjee employed the biological analogy of the 'fruit fly' effect to argue the recessive effects of overcrowding. From 1891 numbers in Jaunpur district had remained stagnant, the result of high disease mortality rates and emigration as population pressed up against the fearful natural limits Malthus had postulated. The pressure of numbers had lowered the size of the average cultivating holding to 3·5 acres and had resulted in a *petite culture* increasingly turned back towards subsistence rather than export cash crops. Sugar cultivation had declined progressively since 1841, and stood in 1929 at half the former level, an illustration, Mukerjee declared, of 'the agricultural adjustment of a district which has now more mouths to feed than the existing system and standard of cultivation can afford'.

Mukerjee contrasted Jaunpur with the most thriving district of the western U.P., Meerut. Here the average cultivating holding was more than twice as large (7·8 acres), a clear proof that the proportion of poor subsistence cultivators was much lower. Yet in other respects the contrast with Jaunpur was difficult to press. Compared with Jaunpur's population density of 797 per square mile, Meerut ran at the high figure of 702, and in the western portion the land carried as many as 1,000 per square mile, almost the equal of some of Jaunpur's most congested tahsils. Was it, then, the opening of the Ganges Canal in 1855 and the steady

---

[2] B. Misra, *Overpopulation in Jaunpur,* Dept. of Agriculture Bulletin, no. 59 (Allahabad, 1932). For a striking exposition of the difference between East and West U.P., see also *Report on the Present Economic Situation in the U.P.* (Govt. of U.P., Naini Tal, 1933); Hailey Collection, India Office Records, MSS Eur. 1. 230/29C.

subsequent expansion of the irrigated area that had endowed
Meerut with the dynamism of self-reinforcing growth equivalent
in its effects to the presence of an expanding frontier into fertile
virgin land? Yet, curiously, the double-cropped area in Meerut
was no more than 22% of the cultivation by 1908, less than
Jaunpur had achieved (26.5%) by its elaborate, though doubtless
more labour-intensive system of well irrigation. The cropping
pattern, of course, differed. One contrasting feature was the proportion of the cultivated area devoted to sugar by the turn of the
century, Meerut's (11%) being nearly double that of Jaunpur
(6%). At this time sugar yielded in Meerut the relatively good
profit of Rs. 15 per acre. By the 1940s both districts had each
devoted a further 2% of the cultivated area to sugar. The most
striking difference, however, lay in the main crop. Meerut put
30% of the cultivated area under wheat, yielding an estimated
average of Rs. 15 per acre, while Jaunpur had 26% under rice,
which yielded roughly only Rs. 9 per acre in 1908. But one
advantage of lowering the acreage under sugar was that it extended double-cropping; when rice or maize was substituted in
the *kharif* the land could be used again for a *rabi* crop.[3]

What, then, was the secret of Meerut's far higher living
standard, and, even more important, of the thrust and drive in its
economic life that contrasted so glaringly with the listless stagnation of Jaunpur? Mukerjee had one principal explanation but
half suggested another. The most obvious was the development of
urban and industrial occupations in Meerut district which had
not only boosted income but also relieved the dependence of the
population on agriculture significantly. The more extensive
urbanisation of Meerut was no recent feature. Edmund White,
the census commissioner, had as long ago as 1882 drawn attention
to the marked contrast between the eastern and western districts
of the province. The most striking difference lay between Gorakhpur and Saharanpur, with the most agricultural and the least
agricultural population, respectively. But Jaunpur and Meerut
fell only shortly behind, Jaunpur having 75.77% of its population
classified as agricultural and Meerut only 52.2%. The gap continued to widen after 1882, the 1901 census figures being 77.4%
and 49%, respectively. By the time Mukerjee wrote in 1932, he

[3] *U.P. District Gazetteers*, IV, *Meerut* (Allahabad, 1904) pp. 37 ff.; XXVIII,
Jaunpur (Allahabad, 1908) pp. 31 ff.

reported that 76% of the Jaunpur population were supported by agriculture, 10% by industry, and 5% by commerce, while in Meerut the figures were 42% agriculture, 21% industry, and 6% commerce. This contrasting situation had not been created because of the population of the eastern districts multiplying more rapidly and more recently. So far as the imperfect census statistics indicate, the population of the province increased only slowly from 1853 to 1881. But the increase was far greater in the west than the east, 15·8% in the Meerut division as against 7·2% in the Allahabad and Benares divisions. 'The Meerut Division, as might have been expected', commented White, 'shows the greatest increase. In no part of the province is agriculture so flourishing, and the wealth of the urban population so marked.' Apart from the Benares district itself, the Benares division was purely rural. 'The agricultural classes must have long ago multiplied up to the limits permitted by the size of their holdings.'[4] Temporary emigration provided, of course, an important access to secondary occupations, in Jaunpur a net figure of some 80,000 emigrants being returned at the three censuses of 1901, 1911 and 1921.

Mukerjee believed that, because of fractionalisation and fragmentation of holdings, there was chronic under-employment and idleness in Jaunpur. 'Low agricultural income and agricultural idleness thus often go together and as a result either the non-cultivating money-lending classes or the landless labourers, or both, grow at the expense of small properties and tenants.' In terms of non-agricultural pursuits, the people of Jaunpur had shown far less initiative to strike out new lines than their brethren in Meerut.[5] This was the nearest he got to half suggesting another explanation and to touching on a question others had treated much more boldly and confidently – the issue of caste.

The British administrative mind had always reverted in its consideration of the agrarian problem to the mental shorthand expressed in the notion of fixed ethnic types. Agricultural performance, it believed quite simply, could be directly predicated of the 'tribe' or caste of the agriculturalist. Such a belief constituted the staple argument of such a leading authority as Malcolm Darling in his *The Punjab Peasant in Prosperity and Debt* (1922)

---

[4] *Census Report N.W. Provs. and Oudh, 1881* (Allahabad, 1881), pp. 27, 31, Table XII.

[5] R. Mukerjee in Misra, *Overpopulation in Jaunpur*, p. 7.

and the numerous subsequent books he published describing his peregrinations on horseback through the old Punjab province. The argument survived in Meerut down to the time that C. Cooke, in 1940, revised the settlement of the district in the expiring days of the Raj.[6] Since independence, mention of caste has, understandably, been more muted; and, for sound political reasons, the Indian Government struck out caste as a category from the decennial censuses. It became for a time as impolite and impolitic to raise the matter as it once was to mention national work characteristics in the discussion of the stagnation of the British economy compared with the German or French. Economists dislike such irrational and unquantifiable factors: witness Morris D. Morris's attempt to banish caste from economic history in his well-known article in 1967.[7] Agronomists have also been taken up with the revolutionary potential of the new technology in agriculture, with pump sets, fertilisers, and high-yielding varieties, and believe that whatever problem remains may be resolved into one of class and not caste.

Yet, there have always been voices raising the old cry. Professor Etienne, in his book *Studies in Indian Agriculture: the Art of the Possible*,[8] has contrasted the superior energy and purposiveness of the agriculturalists in his sample village in Bulandshahr district with their dispirited counterparts in the Benares district. Like Darling and generations of European observers before him, he ascribed the dynamic informing the agriculture of the western region to the dominance of the Jats and their fighting traditions, so that even in agricultural economics it would seem that the biblical adage holds true: the kingdom of heaven suffereth violence until now and the violent take it by force. Etienne drew on a long tradition testifying to the superior capacity for toil in the west. In 1892 the settlement officer (J. O. Miller) of Muzaffarnagar, the district in the upper Doab immediately to the north of Meerut, commented on how the people 'shrank from a descent to the level of the Purbiyas or inhabitants of the most easterly districts'.[9] They accepted that their higher living standards de-

[6] *Meerut Settlement Report 1940*, pp. 15 ff.

[7] M. D. Morris, 'Values as an Obstacle to Economic Growth in South Asia', *Jl. Econ. Hist.*, XXVII, 4 (1967) pp. 588 ff.

[8] G. Etienne, *Studies in Indian Agriculture: the Art of the Possible* (London, 1968). First published in French, 1966.

[9] *Muzaffarnagar S.R. 1892*, p. 23.

pended on uninterrupted hard work. In this joy in labour the Jat took the palm, yoking his oxen to the plough before the coming of dawn and returning to the village long after the sun had set. William Crooke gave the Jat cultivator pride of place in the frontispiece photograph of his book, *The North Western Provinces*; 'in the whole of India', echoed Darling for the Punjab, 'there is no finer raw material than the Jat'.[10]

Yet, the very men who constructed their analysis out of such solid images proved strangely qualified in their detailed application. Even in the early days John Lawrence, Jat panegyrist though he was, found himself bound to conclude in 1838 that it was the nature of the land rather than innate caste characteristics that appeared to determine the character of agriculture and the mental attitudes of the people. The easily won crops of the sandy rain irrigated (barani) soils of the Bahora tahsil in the later Gurgaon district rendered even the Jat careless, while the stiffer loam of neighbouring Palwal not only brought out the Jat's sturdiest characteristics but also transformed the thriftless cattle-keeping Meo.[11] It was the same in the Doab districts. The change in human attitudes worked by the profitability of canal irrigation was noted by Thomason along the Eastern Jumna Canal well before the Mutiny. Most prominent were the Gujars, traditionally addicted to 'grazing their own and stealing their neighbours' cattle, and leading the idle life they love'. As R. W. Gillan, the settlement officer of Meerut, observed in 1901,[12] 'The Gujars are creatures of circumstance. Give them a canal and teach them the profits of agriculture, and they work their villages like Jats. Put them in a tract like the Loni Khadir and they pay their revenue by stealing cattle and committing burglaries in Delhi.' The same was true of higher castes like Rajputs, Tyagis, and Brahmins, who were important as owners and cultivators, the Jats farming, in fact, only 30% of the Meerut district. When reporting on the revised settlement of the Jalalabad pargana of Meerut in 1868, W. A. Forbes remarked: 'Jats are always a busy pushing race, but Tagas and Rajpoots curiously enough seem always influenced

---

10 W. C. Crooke, *The North Western Provinces* (London, 1897).
11 *Reports of Revision of Settlements under Regulation IX of 1833 in the Delhie Territory* (Agra, 1846), pp. 25–6.
12 *Meerut S.R. 1901*, p. 10. Also J. Thomason, Minute on E. Jumna Canal, 1 Mar. 1848, *Selections from the Records of Govt. N.W. Provinces, Mr. Thomason's Despatches* (Calcutta, 1856), 1, p. 390.

by any example they may have beside them.'[13] Etienne noted how, in Bulandshahr district, Brahmins scorned no form of field work.[14] Caste distinctions in the west had always been relatively weak. In the 1870s Charles Elliott, the celebrated revenue authority, found that as far east as Farrukhabad caste had no influence over rent rates. Pradhan has noted how, in the 1950s, in the Jat villages of Muzaffarnagar the Jats engaged for sport in wrestling matches with the lowly sweeper.[15]

How far was this malleability of caste type and responsiveness to economic stimuli absent in the eastern district? Denzil Ibbetson, in his classical treatise on Punjab castes, argued that the people and culture of the Punjab and the contiguous western districts of the U.P. had never come under the influence of Brahmanical religion, and hence caste distinctions had never been ritualised among them, as in the eastern districts. Blunt, in the 1911 Census, used a related argument borrowed from Risley, that, as hypergamy was practised westwards, so caste distance increased eastwards. Did this mean that the higher castes' disdain for agriculture and hence their dependence on a socially inferior tenant and predial labour class, increased as one proceeded eastwards? Here, again fixed stereotypes collapse on closer inspection. C. E. Crawford, the settlement officer of Azamgarh in 1908, found that, while castes with a secondary occupation like Kayasths, and in some measure Brahmins, made indifferent cultivators, 'the Chhattri and the Bhuinhar are on the other hand both industrious and capable'. But to the north, in Gorakhpur district, Brahmins were so numerous that they had been driven much closer to the soil, owning a quarter of the district in 1891 and, together with Bhuinars, cultivating some 18% (almost exactly the same proportion as Brahmins and Tyagis in Meerut). In Azamgarh it was found that the caste prohibition against Brahmins handling the plough had been relaxed so far as to apply only to the actual operation of ploughing itself. Brahmins carried out every other agricultural task, even to yoking the oxen to the plough.[16] Plainly, to employ again Edmund Leach's well-known

---

[13] *Meerut S.R. 1874*, p. 39.

[14] Etienne, *Studies in Indian Agriculture*, p. 80.

[15] C. A. Elliott in *Sels. Recs. Govt. N.W.P.*, 2nd ser., II, no. 4 (Allahabad, 1869). M. C. Pradhan, *The Political System of the Jats of Northern India* (Oxford, 1966), p. 50.

[16] E. A. H. Blunt citing authority of H. H. Risley in *Census of India, 1911*,

tag, the constraints of economics were prior to the constraints of morality and law.

If human nature proved adaptable to circumstance in this fashion was there perhaps some constraint it could not overcome? The most obvious was the pressure of population on the soil, causing excessive subdivision and fragmentation of holdings. Mukerjee, in 1931, pointed to the fact that the average cultivating holding in Jaunpur was half that in Meerut. The position in Gorakhpur looked even worse. In the Deoria subdivision (later district), where population clustered at 1,100 to the square mile, tenant holdings averaged apparently only 0·65 acres, according to the figures reproduced by another student of Mukerjee.[17] In practice, however, it was impossible to discover actual cultivating holdings out of the multitude of scattered plots into which they were fragmented, and extensive double-counting clearly occurred in census taking. Using plough areas or units, the settlement officer for eastern Gorakhpur in 1919 had a very different story to tell. Even in the overcrowded Haveli pargana of Deoria, he estimated that as much as 55% of the cultivation was made up of holdings of 8–10 acres or more. In the very worst *tappas* of Deoria no more than 27% of the cultivation was taken up by holdings of 4 acres and under, while the average for the subdivision came out at only 16%.[18] This impression that the larger part of the cultivated area comprised holdings of an economic size received striking confirmation thirty years later in the All-India Rural Credit Survey carried out in 1951–2, on the eve of zamindari abolition. In the Survey's *District Monograph on Deoria*[19] a sample of eight villages showed that, although the average cultivating holding was 3 acres and 66·9% of families held under this amount, nevertheless as much as 69·5% of the holdings area consisted of holdings averaging 8·5 acres[20] and families cultivating more than 8·5 acres held over 40% of the sown area. Of course, holdings in Meerut were unquestionably larger, but the dispro-

xv, U.P., pt 1 (Allahabad, 1912), p. 21. C. E. Crawford in *Azamgarh S.R. 1908*, p. 16. J. R. Reid, *Azamgahr S.R. 1881*, p. 86.

[17] J. K. Mathur, *The Pressure of Population: its Effects on Rural Economy in Gorakhpur District*, U.P. Agric. Bulletin, no. 50 (Allahabad, 1931), p. 9.

[18] *Gorakhpur (Tahsils Padrauna, Hata, and Deoria) S.R. 1919*, p. 19.

[19] *All-India Rural Credit Survey: District Monograph on Deoria* (Bombay, 1958).

[20] *Ibid.*, pp. 15–16.

portion with the eastern districts was nothing like so great as the misleading statistical averages used by Mukerjee and his pupils (in company with many eminent authorities) suggested. The closest comparable figures we have for Meerut show that in 1940 32% of cultivators had possessed holdings of under 5 acres and occupied some 12% of the cultivated area, while 36% of cultivators held over 10 acres and occupied 60% of the cultivated area.[21] The Jats were far from exempt from the problems of fractionalisation and fragmentation of holdings resulting from their inheritance customs; and even in the Jat homeland the Government of the Punjab took legislative powers in the 1920s and 1930s to effect consolidation of holdings.

Was there, then, some institutional constraint inherent in the system of tenure itself? Here one might venture an hypothesis. Parallel to the much stronger grasp of the higher castes over ownership and cultivating rights in the eastern districts was the contrast in tenures. As late as 1940 52% of proprietary holdings in Meerut were classified as *bhaiachara*, while in the eastern districts joint zamindari and imperfect *pattidari* prevailed overwhelmingly. The vagaries of official classification and the distortions which sale and partition had inflicted on the fundamental tenurial forms made such comparisons valuable merely as broad indicators of the contrast in underlying structure. Even then it may be urged that the distinction among different forms of joint tenure is immaterial, merely signifying whether the land revenue was paid according to ancestral shares (joint zamindari and pattidari) or according to the amount of land held (bhaiachara). But this was not the really vital distinction. For the essence of true bhaiachara was the exclusion of landlord forms within the village or neighbourhood community. Theoretically speaking, the tenure admits of no tributary tenant or quasi-tenant body, and proprietor and cultivator are identical.[22] Baden-Powell

---

[21] *Meerut S.R. 1940*, p. 17.

[22] In practice there was, of course, always a minority of temporary and hereditary 'non-proprietary' cultivators, who usually held land at the same rates as members of the proprietary body. In 1827 in Khanda, a village in the Kharkhaudah pargana of Rohtak district, G. R. Campbell classified the population as follows:

Proprietors	Hereditary cultivators and new settlers	Engaged in 'industry'	Trade	Labourers
1,273	204	74	71	6

I.O.R. Board's Collections, L/4/1215, fo. 414.

noted that bhaiachara peculiarly characterised Jat communities, and that except for the sense of supra-village 'tribal' union the tenure was indistinguishable from ryotwar. Now there seem good grounds for believing that ryotwar tenures throughout India were the tenurial form natural to regions of insecure agriculture where land was plentiful and hands few, just as landlord forms, whether zamindari, pattidari, or 'landed *mirasi*', were the products of regions of secure agriculture where population pressed on the land and generated a quasi-rental surplus.[23] Bhaiachara was the dominant tenure of Haryana, and it is reasonable to suppose that the Jat communities brought the tenure with them into the richer Ganges-Jumna Doab. When Sir Henry Elliot settled Meerut in the mid 1830s he found nothing in the nature of a tenantry existing in the western or Jat parganas, and hence found it impossible to construct standard rent rates on which to frame the assessment, and in the 1860s W. A. Forbes encountered the same difficulty.[24] Whiteway also found this condition persisting among the Mathura (Muttra) Jats at the end of the 1870s, at least in the insecure tracts west of the Jumna. In the Rohtak district (of Haryana) Martin Gubbins had reported in 1839: 'Rent rates do not exist in this district – land being in greater abundance than hands to cultivate it – proprietors are generally glad to let their free lands to nonproprietors at the same rates of revenue which they pay themselves.' As late as 1910 two-thirds of the arable land in Rohtak was still being cultivated by proprietors and the remaining one-third was only notionally held by tenants. The settlement officer said that many of the latter 'were in the position of villagers who subsisted by taking in each other's washing. There is no real tenant class. Owners who exchange plots for temporary convenience in cultivation, and men who take a little free land from their fathers are all recorded as tenants.'[25] Sixty per cent of land ownership remained in Jat hands, a proportion that rises still higher if the non-Jat area of Jhajjar, added after the Mutiny, is excluded. In Haryana, the word for farmer and Jat was synonymous, suggesting that the economic basis for the social and ritual distinc-

---

[23] See above, pp. 7, 54, 88.
[24] *Meerut S.R. 1874* Resolution, Revenue Dept., 10 June 1880, p. 8. Also H. M. Elliot in *Selections from the Reports of the Revenue Settlement of the N.W. Provinces under Regulation IX, 1833* (Benares, 1862–3), I, pp. 179 ff. Also *Meerut S.R. 1901*, pp. 15 ff.
[25] *Rohtak S.R. 1910*, p. 11.

tions of caste did not exist within the cultivating communities. At the same time, agricultural conditions were such as to require and reward unremitting labour, neither breeding the fatalism of the semi-desert nor the careless indolence that Malcolm Darling believed had corrupted the Jats of the fertile Naraingarh tahsil of the Ambala district, where landlordism and Rajput life-styles had crept in.[26] In Rohtak, there was no weakening of the fibre. Here Darling thought human toil could be carried no further, even the Jat women rising before 5 in the morning, grinding the corn, performing all manner of field work, and not ceasing their labours until 10 at night.[27]

How did the bhaiachara form survive in the Doab? Sir Henry Elliot noted in 1836 how, in the Meerut district, Rajputs, Pathans and Sayyids, 'being too indolent and proud to cultivate much themselves, inclined to pattidari tenures'.[28] In other words, over-lord castes, whenever opportunity offered, tended to retain a portion of the village lands in their own hands as their *sir* or home farm and to leave the remainder to be cultivated by others in return for tributary payment or rent. Landlord forms were repressed among the Jat communities by the high pitch of the differential revenue assessment imposed upon them by the Begam Sumru and the successor British power down until the 1860s. When at length the demand was eased and the railway and canal irrigation gave promise of a new prosperity, the balance of advantage between rental income (or, more strictly, *mal-guzari* profits) and the profits of direct farming swung decisively in favour of the latter, assisted no doubt by the increasing rent restrictions of British tenancy legislation. Hence, there was little temptation to develop a rentier landlord class among the Jats.

In the eastern districts the regression of the proprietary castes back into cultivation probably began much earlier. Indeed, Buchanan Hamilton commented on the direct participation of Brahmin groups in agriculture at the beginning of the century.[29] The later decades of the nineteenth century witnessed a general quickening of the movement of proprietary castes to extend their

[26] M. Darling, *Rusticus Loquitur* (Oxford, 1930), p. 68.
[27] *Ibid.*, pp. 98, 103.
[28] H. M. Elliot, *Sels. Reps. Rev. Settl. N.W.P. Reg IX, 1833*, II, p. 190.
[29] Cited Montgomery Martin, *The History, Antiquities, Topography, and Statistics of Eastern India* (London, 1838), II, p. 452.

cultivation by the enlargement of sir as well as by taking up land on tenancy.[30] At some points, overswollen Rajput proprietary communities reproduced the outward lineaments of the bhaia-chara tenure, the most remarkable examples being the bighadam *mahals* of the Dobhi taluq in Jaunpur and of the neighbouring Deogaon and Belhabans parganas of Azamgarh, where the entire village lands were claimed as sir. Yet the slow, enforced descent from lordly status and the gradual shift from close joint landlord forms towards a type of ryotwari (bighadam) were hardly the conditions to breed dynamic entrepreneurship in agriculture. The old tenurial forms proved obdurate, not simply because of the struggle that had to be fought with lower-level cultivators to regain cultivating possession but because, for the higher castes, the old landlord tenures continued to possess considerable short-term social and economic advantages. Wherever possible Rajput, Brahmin and Bhuinhar remained a petty landlord class, driven close to the soil but still continuing to exploit it through lower caste sub-tenants and predial labourers.[31]

These tendencies were not absent from similar castes in the west. Not all Rajput groups in the upper Doab had improved themselves out of recognition. Mukerjee's M.A. students readily resorted to the old stereotypes of thakur ease and indolence when they came to examine Rajput villages like Khiwai in the Meerut district.[32] Nor, because of the almost equally intense pressure of population on the land, did the Jats wholly escape landlordism and preserve the pristine character of their bhaiachara tenures unimpaired. In the Doab, unlike much of Rohtak, the Jats had always made use of substantial Chamar predial labour and had never enjoyed the same almost exclusive tribal monopoly of population.[33] Moreover, there was not a straight choice between

---

[30] *U.P. Board of Revenue Administrative Report 1903–4* (Allahabad, 1905), p. 18, para. 42. Also *ibid. 1882–3* (Allahabad, 1884), Divisional Reports, p 26, quoted above in Paper 9, p 211.

[31] See above, p. 79.

[32] Report of Kunwar Bahadur, *U.P. Provincial Banking Committee Report 1929–30*, II (Allahabad, 1930), p. 228.

[33] Pargana caste statistics, given in *Meerut S.R. 1874*, Introdn. pp. 6–7, show that in the district as a whole Chamars (197,273) outnumbered Jats (145,524) in the total district population of 1,273,676, but in the western Jat parganas (Baraut, Chaprauli, Kotana, and Barnawa) Jats outnumbered Chamars more than two to one (56,152 to 23,408). In Rohtak at this time there was still no proper agricultural labour class and Chamar numbers remained proportionately small: Chamars in 1881 numbered 50,081

the roles of rentier and farmer. The fact that the largest average cultivating holding was 40 acres meant that the ownership of malguzari rights continued to offer itself as a means of obtaining additional income as well as of social and political consequence. (The estimated rental assets of the U.P. doubled between 1899 and 1929 while the revenue demand rose by only 12%). The bhaiachara tenure, despite appearances, had never been an egalitarian structure and had always spanned large discrepancies in the size of holdings. In formal terms, it could readily break up into a scatter of small zamindari properties. Evidently, in some villages Jats were demoted to become tenants of others, as in Edalpur in Mathura district.[34] Ownership was also intimately linked with the system of cash-crop production, marketing, and the provision of credit, in a skein so complex and variegated that commissions of inquiry never succeeded in disentangling it. How far this complex structure, along with greater urbanisation and a more substantial agriculture-based industry, supplied one of the keys to Meerut's superior economic drive must remain an important but unanswered question. One fact seems clear. In the eastern districts landlords and superior agriculturalists constituted the main source of agricultural credit, whereas in Meerut the professional money-lender and trader held a large share of the business. No doubt rural credit and usury remained an important buttress for landlord elements to shore up their position in the east.[35]

Ingrained attitudes associated with caste cannot be swept aside, but as a local kinship system caste was, in Leach's words, merely another way of talking about a system of property relations. What is suggested in this paper is that, while in the agrarian domain pressure of population and subdivision of holdings were tending to approximate conditions in the eastern and western U.P. more closely, the traditional tenurial expression of property

compared with Jats, 182,776 in a total district population of 553,609. *Punjab Gazetteers, Rohtak District 1883–4*, pp. 81, 125, 128 and Tables IX and XV. But in the rural population Jat preponderance was even more striking. In the Gohana pargana in 1839 the crude census showed Jats as forming as much as 80% of the population. *Sels. Reps. Rev. Settl. Reg. IX, 1833, Delhie Territory*, no. 1 (Agra, 1846), p. 81.

34 *U.P. Prov. Banking Enqu. Rep.*, ii, Evidence, p. 250. For increase of rental assets, A. A. Waugh, *Rent and Revenue Problems* (30 Aug. 1934). Hailey Collection, I.O.R., MSS. Eur. E. 220/29C.

35 Written evidence of Mohan Lal Sah, *ibid.*, p. 51. Also pp. 153, 162, 175.

rights was one of the factors helping to keep them on different paths. The owner-cultivator holding was the form natural to the Jats and the bhaiachara the most readily adaptable tenure to maximise production under Indian *petite culture*.[36] In the east the joint zamindari and imperfect pattidari tenures proved atavistic devices, landlord structures that had outlived their role but survived because even a minute fractional share in the joint patrimony validated caste status for other purposes.[37] Among the Dobhi *thakurs* the joint rather than the nuclear family remained overwhelmingly predominant. Among congested communities conditions inexorably drove the dominant castes into similar *de facto* owner-cultivator holdings (though ownership in this sense might mean the beneficial ownership equated with occupancy tenant right), but generally the slower institutional descent from landlord status failed to generate an answering entrepreneurial drive in the newer role of farmer.[38] In caricature it produced the

---

[36] The British classification of tenures was necessarily crude and inconsistent. Rarely did tenures conform to their 'ideal types' and the imperfect *pattidari* villages of the Punjab bore only the most superficial resemblance to those of the U.P. eastern districts just as did the western *bhaiachara* to the bighadam. The real test was the extent to which owner and cultivator diverged or coincided. Cf. the despairing cry over the confusion of terms by B. H. Baden-Powell, *The Indian Village Community* (London, 1896), pp. 353 ff. Also H. M. Elliot, 31 Aug. 1836: 'The fact is, whatever definition may be given, it will not apply equally to every Zillah. Some little peculiarity will, perhaps, be found which would exclude each tenure from the limits which had been assigned to it; what one man includes under *zemindaree* another calls *putteedaree*, and one includes under *putteedaree*, what another calls *bhyachara*.' *Sels. Reps. Rev. Settl. N.W.P., Reg. IX, 1833*, I, p. 186.

[37] S. P. Sharma, 'Marriage Family, and Kinship among the Jats and Thakurs of Northern India: some comparisons', *Contributions to Indian Sociology*, new ser., 7 (1973), pp. 81 ff. Also see above, p. 42.

[38] The extent of owner-cultivation varied considerably in the eastern districts. In Jaunpur *sir* and *khudkasht*, *viz.* proprietary cultivation, was estimated at 18·59% in 1906 compared with 42·78% in Meerut in 1901. Yet in Azamgarh, the district adjoining Jaunpur on the north, the area of sir and khudkasht ran as high as 41% in 1908, of which rather more than one-quarter was sublet. *Azamgarh S.R. 1908*, pp. 14–15. The difference lay in the extent of cultivating rights relative to proprietary rights. In Meerut at the turn of the century Jats owned some 27% of Meerut district and cultivated 30%. There are no strictly comparable figures for Azamgarh, but in Belhabans pargana, for example, where the dense Bais Rajput communities owned 89% of the land and sir amounted to 46·2% 'the Rajputs hold less of the land than might be anticipated; for Ahirs hold nearly as large an area [as cultivators], and Brahmans, Lunias, and Chamars all cultivate a large acreage'. *District Gazetteers U.P.*, XXXIII, *Azamgarh* (Allahabad, 1911), p. 206.

squireen rather than the green revolutionary. S. P. Sharma has concluded,[39]

Some of the social differences between Rajput and Jat groups can still be found if we examine the Thakurs of Senapur [in the Dobhi taluq of Jaunpur] and the Jats of Basti [pseudonym of a village 15 miles south west of Delhi on the Gurgaon border] in contemporary context. Until the later part of the nineteenth century the Thakurs of Senapur, though they were the undisputed landlords of the village, did not personally cultivate the land because they thought of themselves as rulers rather than as workers of the land. All the agricultural land in their possession was worked by hired labour. It is only during the past two or three generations that the Thakur has been shamefacedly involved in agriculture. The Jats on the other hand have always been farmers, deeply rooted in the soil. In Basti Jat women and children work with their menfolk in the fields. According to a local saying: 'The Jat's baby has a plough handle for a plaything.'

[39] S. P. Sharma 'Marriage, Family and Kinship', p. 83.

II

Peasants, moneylenders and colonial rule: an excursion into Central India

It is still widely supposed that the introduction of modern transferable title destroyed or fundamentally distorted peasant land
rights in India and allowed the moneylender and middleman
trader to gain a novel and portentous hold over the countryside.
This hold, it is urged, was largely parasitic, direct investment in
farm production being scorned for the easier and richer profits of
rack-renting, usury, and the marketing of crops obtained at
'distress' prices. Middleman agency thus siphoned off the enhanced value of agriculture which resulted from increased cash-
cropping and the price rise from the late 1860s. So far from
peasant farming developing, a 'depeasantisation' took place that
reduced the mass of agriculturalists to cultivators working for the
barest subsistence return under a form of debt peonage. This
picture is not one original to latter-day Marxists but was drawn
by the British colonialists themselves. In essentials it was already
complete by 1852 when Sir George Wingate wrote bitterly of the
moneylender in the Bombay presidency being intent on reducing
the ryot 'to a state of hopeless indebtedness in order that he may
be able to appropriate the whole fruits of his industry beyond
what is indispensable to a mere existence...should the present
course of affairs continue it must arrive that the greater part of
the realised property of the community will be transferred to a
small monied class, who will become disproportionately wealthy
by the impoverishment of the rest of the people'.[1] Now at first
glance it might be supposed that the grip of the moneylender-
trader would be strongest in the richer agricultural regions where
the market economy was most fully developed. But the extent of
the agriculturalist's dependence was not to be equated with the

[1] G. Wingate, 24 Sept. 1852, *Deccan Riots Commission. Appx A. Papers re
the Indebtedness of the Agricultural Classes in Bombay* (Bombay, 1876),
pp. 88–9. I.O.R. (71) 2043/2.

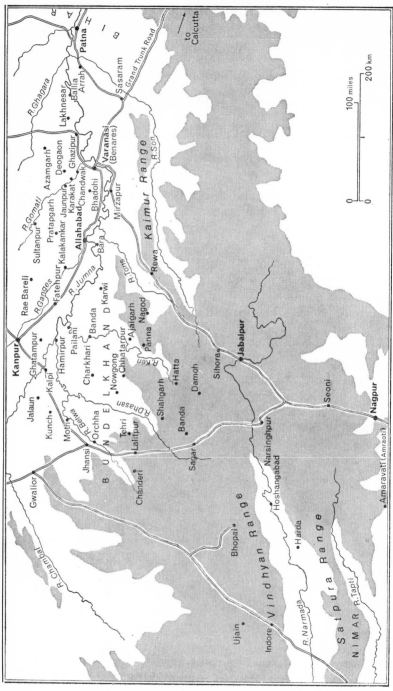

Map 5. Central India and E. Upper Gangetic Plain. For adjoining regions to the north see Maps 1 & 6.

sheer volume of indebtedness. That dependence was highest where the professional moneylender exercised a virtual monopoly of credit and hence where the agricultural community was backward and lacking in a substantial rich peasant or gentry class with financial resources of its own. Such regions were marginal to the market economy or had only recently been brought into close connection with it. They were typically characterised by uncertain rainfall, insecure agriculture, and low population density. Their natural propensity was towards subsistence farming and a ryotwar or owner-cultivator form of land tenure, since the land-man ratio was generally too low to generate the rental surplus which formed the basis of single or joint landlord villages. Debt servitude was deepest and often socially most explosive where the moneylender appeared as an alien intruder, and resentment against him boiled over most readily into violence among tribal peoples like the Bhils, Santals and (to a markedly less extent) the Gonds. Yet the relations of the peasant cultivators of the Bombay Deccan and Central India with the Marwaris, and of the West Punjab Muslim peasantry with the Kirars or Arora moneylenders worried the British much more seriously.[2]

In Central India the moneylender's grip predated British rule and sprang from the tax system rather than the credit needs of market-orientated agriculture. Under a severe revenue administration like that of the Marathas the absence of a powerful village landlord class capable of managing the revenue responsibility threw the peasantry into peculiar dependence on the resources and expertise of the 'outside' financier. The extent of private debt incurred for revenue purposes and carried over from the Maratha period struck officials most forcibly in the central Indian region between the Jumna and Narmada when between 1803 and 1854 it came piecemeal under British administration.

[2] On the threat of the saukar to the Bhils c. 1870, cf. *ibid.*, pp. 21 ff. For the Santals, cf. K. K. Datta, *The Santal Insurrection 1855–57* (Calcutta, 1940). On West Punjab as well as connection between indebtedness and agricultural insecurity, cf. M. Darling, *The Punjab Peasant in Prosperity and Debt* (Oxford, 1925), p. 107 *passim*. On Marwaris in Deccan cf. *Selections from Records of the Government of India Home Dept.*, no. cccxlii (Calcutta, 1897), 'Papers re Deccan Agriculturalists Relief Act 1875–94', II, p. 256, '[At the time of the Deccan Riots of 1875] the moneylenders were chiefly foreigners, different in religion from their clients, entirely out of sympathy with them, and accustomed to retire with their profits after a sufficiently long course of business to their homes in Rajputana.'

A scrutiny of the later history of this region, which has lain off the beaten academic track, permits the time-honoured question of the effects of British rule on Indian agrarian structure to be looked at anew. For here the derangement of indigenous tenures and the onset of land control by the outside moneylender appears to have proceeded more rapidly and extensively than in the remainder of the North-Western Provinces, which exercised administrative control of the region until 1862, and whose settlement system continued to exert a powerful influence. The northern portion comprising the Banda district and parts of what later swelled to become the Hamirpur and Jalaun districts came under the British revenue system as early as 1803. The fertile but disaster-prone black soils of British Bundelkhand gave not only to their cultivation but to their revenue management an uncertain speculative quality, which was enhanced in the first four decades of the century by the financing of cotton as an export crop. The cotton culture had relied traditionally on advances from the East India Company's agents or private traders and moneylenders. At one time the Company made purchases of 40 lakhs a year in the Kalpi cotton market and private individuals 18 lakhs. From 1830 the Company's purchases ceased and private investment dwindled until by 1842 it amounted to barely 7 lakhs.[3]

The prospect of gains to be made from gambling in revenue farms and auction purchases on the basis of the wealth brought by cotton undoubtedly must have been the main incentive for the disproportionate rush of speculators into Hamirpur and Banda districts in the first two decades of British rule. Many of these speculators failed to survive the periodic agricultural failures and commercial slumps.[4] Yet in Banda they not only overturned the old tenurial system but established themselves permanently. The black *mar* 'cotton soils' flanking the Jumna, Ken and Chambal were inhabited by strong Rajput cultivating communities organised into extensive *bhaiachara* village groups. After the first experimental settlements they were quickly recognised as the natural claimants to the proprietary title, but overassessment and the sale process soon stripped this from them over large areas. Rajput

[3] [Sir] William Muir, Report on Assessment of Calpee Pergunnahs. *Reports of the Revenue Settlement of the N.W. Provinces under Regulation IX, 1833* (Benares, 1863), II, p. 825.
[4] Cf. *Hamirpur Settlement Report 1842*, pp. 791–2, *Banda S.R. 1881*, pp. 109, 112, 114, 120 *passim*.

communities, which were estimated to have held some three-fifths of Banda district in proprietary right at the outset of British rule, were reduced to a quarter by 1874. They were superseded by a group of substantial auction purchasers composed very largely at first of Muslim service families connected with the British administration. But behind these stood men like the notorious Khandeh Brahmin, Hate Lal Dube, and the Kanpur *bania*, Salig Ram Sona, to whom the leading Muslim (and later rebel) magnate, the Nawab of Banda, was heavily indebted. In the wake of the Mutiny the monied element bought up confiscated estates extensively, and generally strengthened its grip so as to become the dominant landholding class.[5]

Jhansi did not come under permanent British administration until 1854, but already by 1867 the settlement officer was lamenting 'what a vast change has taken place in the constitution of these village communities since the time when the district passed into the hands of the British Government'.[6] In the absence of strong coparcenary communities the British invested the village headman with the proprietary right and so reduced all other village landholders to the formal status of tenants. But this internal derangement of the village appeared as nothing to the effects of 'the fatal gift of proprietary right'. By the early 1870s in the wake of the severe local famine of 1868–9 there was intimidating evidence of the rapid strides being made by the Marwari moneylender in gaining control of the land. It is true that British officials believed that a condition of total serfdom prevailed already under Maratha rule in Jhansi. 'The advances of seed and food being invariably made by local moneylenders and grain merchants and the Government demand being practically realised from them also, all the profits of agriculture were diverted into the pockets of the traders from the tillers of the soil, who were furthermore thrown hopelessly into debt, if such a term can be applied to those whose labour went no further than to support life'; such was the historical appraisal of Maratha rule by the Jhansi settlement officer in 1863.[7] The grant of proprietary title and the accompanying power of mortgage vastly extended

[5] *Banda S.R. 1881*, pp. 31–4. On Nawab Ali Bahadur's indebtedness to Salig Ram Sona etc., cf. N.W. Provinces Political Proceedings, 27 Jan. 1860, no. 123; 28 April 1860, no. 200.
[6] *Jhansi S.R. 1871*, p. 115.
[7] *Jhansi S.R. 1871*, p. 49.

the security for loans so that, whatever the position under the Marathas, by 1864 even in Moth, the richest pargana of Jhansi district, it was found that 'the whole of the profits are taken by the Marwarees, and no yearly settlement of accounts takes place between them and their creditors'.[8]

Yet Bundelkhand was no moneylender's elysium. By the 1870s he was finding himself bound to the soil by the silver chains that he had fastened on the peasant producer. The Bundelkhandi cultivator was by nature a subsistence farmer, growing millet crops for the *kharif* (or autumn monsoon harvest) even on the fertile dark mar soils. He practised an extensive rather than intensive agriculture under the notion that a large scattered holding only roughly tended was the best insurance against crop failure. In these conditions the development of cash-crop agriculture was an artificial and forced activity, pushed by the revenue demand and the creditor's pressure. 'Wheat is grown mainly for the bania and revenue collector; and the predominance of wheat soil in a village is frequently referred to, in seeming paradox, as a serious hardship', reported the Jhansi settlement officer in 1893.

The willingness of the bania to extend credit on the security of the new proprietary title compounded the effects of the inelastic revenue demand in a region where nature produced violent fluctuations in the size of the harvest. It meant that the engine of debt was driving the expansion of the cultivated area and of cash-cropping to artificially high levels, and in consequence left the peasant economy dangerously exposed and unbalanced. Severe drought or excessive rainfall, which elsewhere caused only temporary distress, could pull Bundelkhand down into prolonged depression because it lacked the power of rapid recuperation. Crop failure, followed by loss or distress selling of plough oxen, destroyed the peasant's credit with the moneylender and at once reduced him to a subsistence farmer, who concentrated his cultivation, abandoned wheat, and used the mar soils for growing the *juar* necessary for survival. The substitution of a light scratching of the soil for the deep and frequent ploughing required for wheat cultivation opened the way for the scourge of *kans* grass which often put the land out of use for ten to fifteen years.

[8] *Jhansi S.R. 1871*, p. 142; cf. also Minute of Sir J. W. Muir, 9 Aug. 1872, *Deccan Riots Commission Report. Appx B. Action of the Civil Courts and the Law on the Agricultural Debtor* (Bombay, 1876), p. 282. Also *Census of N.W. Provinces, 1965*, 1, General Report (Allahabad, 1867), p. 101.

The typical Marwari moneylender was not by nature a land-holder, his Jain faith and distinct life style marking him out as an alien who was as unassimilable outside his own profession as the medieval Jew. The proprietary title held out little attraction for him, since in thinly populated and calamity-stricken Bundelkhand the proprietary right – or more strictly, revenue-collecting right (*malguzari*) – yielded only management profits and not a rental income. Moreover, with land freely available the cultivators were all too ready to abscond rather than live under an alien landlord. As late as 1906, H. C. R. Hailey was warning of the consequences of alienation to non-agriculturalists in the Jalaun district.

It may be said without exaggeration that for every member of an agricultural community sold up, a cultivator of the soil is lost. For him has usually been substituted a Marwari – an alien to the soil whose last idea is to till it. In other parts of the province [of Agra] where the zamindar is merely a rent-collector, it is not very material whether he is an agriculturalist by profession or a money lender. But in Jalaun a Marwari who has ousted the old proprietor has often no means of finding cultivators in their place.[9]

This natural deterrent to moneylender landholding was modified in some parts of the Jhansi district where the new proprietor could look cheerfully on the departure of the cultivators. For with the growth of the market in clarified butter (*ghi*) in Kanpur and else-where later in the century, there were profits to be made out of putting land down to pasture and selling grass for fodder. But in general the move of the monied and trading classes into land-holding after 1870 was more often a signal of distress than an index of mounting prosperity.

Faced with the agricultural crash and widespread default on loans that followed the 1868–9 Bundelkhand famine the money-lender *faute de mieux* began to foreclose mortgages and fasten on the proprietary title to ensure himself of at least the rental income. The danger that such dispossession would drive the impoverished Bundela *thakur* gentry deeper into dacoity prompted the eventual

[9] *Jalaun S.R. 1906*, p. 15; cf. also *Jhansi S.R. 1889–93*, p. 81: 'The money lenders (all of them local [Marwaris] for outsiders will have nothing to do with the country)...have hitherto showed a marked unwillingness to become proprietors. *Zamindari* is not their profession, they say, and they drive a much better business by making the landowners their bond slaves... than by taking their place and entering into direct relations with an independent and possibly migratory tenantry.'

passing of the Jhansi Encumbered Estates Act of 1882. This had some effect. Between 1864 and 1892 a fifth of the Jhansi district (discounting repeated transfers of the same land) was subject to sale, not a high rate on any comparative reckoning. But as much as half the district was transferred by temporary mortgage.[10] Administrative policy helped check further outright alienation in Jhansi, but in Banda, with an additional half century of British rule behind it, the transfer process had been allowed a freer course and had been accelerated by serious and prolonged overassessment. In 1874 Cadell, the Banda settlement officer, was lamenting over the gains of the grasping monied men who had stepped into the proprietors' ranks in place of the bankrupted coparcenary village communities. It was noticeable, however, that their hold became dominant only when the famed cotton cultivation of Bundelkhand began to fall into serious decline. As late as 1842 cotton still covered a quarter of the cultivation in Banda; by 1878 it was down to 15%, and by 1907 to 10%.[11] Moving into landholding on an extensive scale proved to be no royal road to salvation for the banker and bania. Firstly the estates of Seth Kishan Chand went to the wall, and then in the wake of the 1896–7 Famine the estates of the Khandeh Brahmins, founded by the famous Hate Lal Dube, had to be partially sold off.[12] By 1906 H. C. R. Hailey in the nearby Jalaun district was commenting on the inefficiency of Marwari management. Having locked up money unprofitably in land, a considerable number of Marwari firms, he reported, were unable to finance their ordinary moneylending and banking business and so had come to grief.[13]

Any further tendency to move into direct landholding was repressed by the Bundelkhand Alienation Act of 1903 which forbade alienation to non-agriculturalists. In Jhansi the fears of administrative officers seem in retrospect to have been exaggerated. Between 1864 and 1945 bania proprietary holdings rose from 0·2% to 6·3%, while Brahmins, of which a proportion must be set down to Marwari Brahmins, rose from 20% to no more than 24·66% of the district.[14] Compared with the gains made by so-called 'non-agriculturalists' castes in other parts of the U.P.,

---

[10] *Jhansi S.R. 1889–93*, pp. 73–5.
[11] *District Gazetteers U.P.* xxi, – *Banda*, p. 49.
[12] *Ibid.*, pp. 108–10. *Banda S.R. 1907*, pp. 11, 23–5.
[13] *Jalaun S.R. 1906*, p. 15.
[14] *Jhansi S.R. 1947*, p. 6.

these figures look decidedly modest.[15] That did not mean that the moneylender had faded out, only that he had fallen back into his more indirect role. What is not clear is the extent to which agricultural and other credit had come to be financed internally within the landholding community and relieved it of total dependence on the extraneous agency of bania and banker. Certainly in the backward tracts of Bundelkhand when the British came to bid their farewell to India the story appeared to end as it had begun. 'The bunyas have been content to keep the cultivator permanently in their "jajmani" ', observed H. T. Lane in the Jhansi Settlement Report of 1947, 'and the logical conclusion of this in Lalitpur has often been a kind of economic serfdom.'

How far had traditional tenures been affected? In a region where lands were plentiful and hands few the bonds of dependence *within* rural society had always been political rather than economic. In the absence of conditions for landlord rents all cultivators of whatever status paid at revenue rates. The village elite realised the economic benefits of their political lordship by a commission on the revenue collections and 'service tenures' of rent-free or rent-privileged land.[16] The British constituted the revenue-collecting right (malguzari) a separate and alienable property, but overassessment was so general before the Mutiny in British Bundelkhand that, as R. N. Cust described the position in Banda in 1855, 'in a tightly-assessed estate the zemindaree profits are but the *profits of management.* Pure rent has been reduced to a cypher. We cannot wonder then if a property has become valueless.'[17] Theoretically, therefore, a revolution could occur in the revenue-collecting right without the cultivator being affected – at least in his purse. Before 1857 the sale or alienation of the

---

[15] Figures produced for 1873 purported to show that in the previous 30 years non-agricultural proprietors in the N.W.P. had increased their holdings from 10% to 27% of the revenue-paying area in 10 districts. *Deccan Riots Commission Report. Appx A. Paper re Indebtedness* (Bombay, 1876), p. 54. These figures probably exaggerated the position cf. above pp. 215–16.

[16] Before Jalaun District came under revenue survey in 1854, there were already 34,922 *muafi* claims on file of which only 7,864 had been decided, and the survey was expected to bring many more claims to light; N.W.P. Rev. Progs. P/220/34 no. 533.

[17] R. N. Cust, 26 Jan. 1855, *Selections from the Records of the Government of the N.W. Provinces,* new ser., IV (Allahabad, 1868), p. 346. On overassessment of Hamirpur, cf. *Reps. Rev. Settl. N.W.P. Reg. IX, 1833,* ii, pt 2, p. 797. Also *District Gaz. U.P.* XXII – *Hamirpur,* pp. 100 ff.

revenue-collecting right away from the village meant usually no more than the installation of an agent (*karinda*) of an absentee purchaser, although such agents had made themselves sufficiently unpopular in 1857 to suffer wholesale ejection in the Mutiny uprising in the Banda district.[18]

Internal change within the village is more difficult to trace. The derangement of the bhaiachara communities in northern Banda and Hamirpur in the early decades of British rule was a familiar theme.[19] The British broke up many of them for contumacy in resisting the revenue demand. Others were transformed by internal struggles among members of the brotherhood. By 1874 only 25 out of the 890 revenue-paying units or 'estates' in Banda were classified as bhaiachara, although together with imperfect and perfect *pattidari* estates cultivating communities still continued to own some 45% of the total.[20] Nevertheless the political and revenue management of the brotherhoods had been displaced in the remainder largely by outsiders. This transformation probably remained essentially micro-political in character. Although by 1874 Rajputs had been reduced in their proprietary control of the occupied area from three-fifths to one-quarter, they still worked – as owner or tenant cultivators – a third of the cultivated area (which formed little more than half the occupied area because of the extensive amount of arable out of cultivation). In other words it would appear that on balance Rajputs lost most of their proprietary control over 'tenants' of other castes and were forced back roughly to the limits of the land they cultivated whether as owners or tenants. This was a loss, we have argued, largely of management profits rather than of valuable rental property. With proprietary cultivation continuing to run up to 40% in the northern and western parganas, there is

18 In Bhadawur village, Darsenda pargana, the *karinda*'s attempts to collect rents (allegedly with the aid of Government *chaprasis*) led to violence in 1850; N.W.P. Rev. Progs. 11 May 1854, no. 311. For rural uprising in Banda in 1857, cf. *Banda S.R. 1881*, pp. 81 ff.; also F. O. Mayne, *Narratives of Events re Mutiny*, 1, pp. 250 ff.

19 See above, p. 84. As late as 1842 (Sir) William Muir reported that the *bhaiachara* tenure prevailed widely over Bundelkhand; *Reps. Rev. Settl. N.W.P. Reg. IX, 1833*, 11, pt 2, p. 867.

20 *Banda S.R. 1881*, p. 41. Bhaiachara survived better in Hamirpur, especially in the predominantly Brahmin and Rajput parganas of Hamirpur and Sunapur, where in 1908 they still formed 39% of tenures compared with a district average of 12%. But the difference from Banda may well have resulted from different criteria of classification.

reason to think that the main Rajput proprietary losses occurred in the south and the east, outside the main area of bhaiachara settlements.[21] Hence the economic or financial dislocation was probably far less grievous than in a heavily populated district like nearby Kanpur where proprietary rights despite overassessment were more valuable. The loss in political consequence is another matter and may well have played a large part in the spontaneous agrarian rising of 1857 that so flabbergasted Mayne, the Collector. Forming less than 10% of the district population of Banda the Rajputs had enjoyed unnatural pre-eminence in land control in comparison with their numbers. The mass of the cultivating classes outside the ranks of labourers were Kurmis, Lodhis, and Ahirs, who lacked the supra-village organisation of the Rajput clans and whose tenurial customs were much nearer to those prevailing in the rest of Bundelkhand.

In Jhansi, we have already observed, the British officials were quick to believe that a vast tenurial revolution had occurred within little more than a decade of annexation in 1854. Proprietary title had been conferred on the village headman except in the considerable portion of the district (one-quarter in Jhansi proper and one half in Lalitpur) where the Bundela thakur had fought successfully to translate his *ubari* or quit-rent lordship into zamindari right. So limited were proprietary profits and so little did the people appreciate the new arrangements that it was found easier to distribute the profit arising from the limitation of the Government demand in the shape of a lower assessment rate on the cultivation of headman families. Hence in practice the old method of remunerating the headman for managing the collections by a monetary commission (*haq mehat*) or a reduced assessment on his personal holding appears to have altered little. Where there was derangement the cause was the carelessness in ascertaining claims to headman rights. The relative paucity of population and comparative abundance of cultivable land meant that there was little prospect of the customary lump revenue payments on holdings giving way to competition field rates and of a more modern landlord-tenant relationship emerging. In 1907 the settlement officer found that in Jhansi 'the zamindar, promoted from among his fellows by British administration, is still only *primus*

[21] *Ibid.*, p. 38.

inter pares [first among equals], and the legal distinction between landlord and tenant is more marked than the social'.[22]

In a subject in which it is notoriously unsafe to make generalisations, one may conclude that the institutional arrangements of colonial rule were relatively powerless to bring about decisive tenurial change in the absence of a decisive expansion of agricultural production. The decline of cotton and wheat as commercial staples left Bundelkhand in a backward condition.

The artificiality of the tenurial system imposed by British law appeared at its most open and avowed in the Saugor and Nerbudda Territories. These had been acquired in 1818 and loosely administered as part of the North-Western Provinces until amalgamated with the Nagpur territories to form the separate administration of the Central Provinces in 1861. Because of this early connection the system of village 'estates' was to be carried far to the south.

The districts forming the comparatively narrow valley of the Narmada (Nerbudda) enjoyed reasonable agricultural security, especially Hoshangabad, Narsinghpur, and part of Jabalpur (Jubbulpore), while their dark soils constituted a natural wheat plain. Charles Elliott called it with pardonable exaggeration 'the richest and most fertile valley in India'.[23] Inhabited before the sixteenth century almost exclusively by the animist Gonds, it was a thinly-peopled marcher region into which Hindu colonists had steadily migrated from all quarters until they outnumbered and pushed back the Gonds into remote hill and jungle country. For the first twenty years the assessment imposed by the British proved ruinously excessive and the settlements were constantly breaking down. In Hoshangabad in the 1820s the demand was pitched up threefold on the Maratha figure, and only in 1835 was some element of moderation introduced when short-term settlements were at last abandoned in favour of a twenty-year period. The paucity of population and the abundance of cultivable land meant an absence of true landlord tenures, and the British were constrained to assess their demand on the cultivator in ryotwar fashion. Both on grounds of expediency and principle they were determined, however, to avoid a formal ryotwar system.

[22] R. W. Gillan, Preface to *Jhansi S.R. 1907*, pp. 2–3.
[23] Cited *Narsinghpur S.R. 1923–26* (Nagpur, 1927), p. 5.

The Marathas had laid responsibility for detailed collection on a host of temporary malguzars drawn indifferently from village headmen, moneylender-traders, and petty officials alike. The British continued the practice, allowing the malguzar an estimated profit of 15% on the collections. Ultimately in 1854 in the Saugor Proclamation the Government announced its intention of conferring full proprietary title on the malguzars, and this was carried into effect in the settlements of the 1860s.

In districts of insecure rainfall like Sagar (Saugor) and Damoh, which covered part of the eastern Malwa plateau north of the Narmada valley, overassessment persisted until the 1860s with a high, inflexible demand. As late as 1867 J. N. H. Maclean could report that in the Banda tahsil of Sagar district 'notwithstanding continuous reductions the Government demand presses so heavily that all enterprise has been crushed, and there is not the slightest attempt at improvement. The widespread misery and distress throughout this division must be seen to be appreciated. The impression conveyed to me on inspecting these tracts was *the Pergunnahs were dead*, so vast was the desolation, and so scarce the signs of life or of human beings.'[24] Yet in more favourably situated districts like Hoshangabad and Narsinghpur the greater moderation of the twenty-year settlements of 1836 gave happier results. (Sir) Charles Elliott estimated that in thirty years from 1832 the cultivated area of Hoshangabad had doubled and large areas of the plain had been transformed into 'an illimitable expanse of waving corn'.[25] On the face of things the result was an artificially created system of village landlords. It was artificial because the economic conditions for a true landlord rent had not emerged and the malguzar's profit resided simply in a commission for managing the State revenue demand. Even when Elliott resettled Hoshangabad for thirty years in 1865 he could find nothing in the shape of competition rents. Land was still too abundant and cultivators too few, the population falling at no more than 150 to the square mile compared with the average of 460 in the N.W. Provinces. Hence despite the doubling of the cultivated area Elliott found it impossible to raise the overall demand in line with the obvious increase in 'rental assets', for even with the informal aid of Government officials the malguzars

[24] *Saugor S.R. 1867*, p. 40.
[25] *Hoshangabad S.R. 1865* (Allahabad, 1867), p. 5.

were unable to secure a commensurate increase in the 'rents' cultivators paid to them. That was the penalty of renouncing a ryotwar system in which State power could be wielded to raise all cultivators' payments irrespective of the land-man ratio. While Elliott put up the Government demand on malguzars by 43%, tenant rents rose by only 32%. This still left malguzars in Hoshangabad with an estimated profit of 54% on the revenue engagement (before cesses), but in absolute terms revenue rates remained so low that 'rental profits' provided only a subsidiary motive for landholding. Direct cultivation proved conversely a much more remunerative activity, 'for with the present high prices the profits of cultivators are very high and the rent bears a proportion to them so ridiculously low that it would hardly be believed in the older Provinces'.[26] Elliott estimated in 1865 that after deducting all expenses of cultivation the direct profits of agriculture ran at Rs. 4-8-0 per acre compared with a return of Rs. 1-4-0 per acre in rental income. Hence the malguzars were prominent as agriculturalists. A fifth of the cultivation was held sir (or proprietor's cultivation), a high proportion for so small a proprietary body, in which no more than 632 recorded holders shared the 218,705 acres under 'home farm' among themselves. Many of the malguzars (or zamindars as they were alternatively called) owned ten or twelve ploughs and cultivated 140 acres apiece. One of their number, Tulsiram Shukul of the Harda pargana, had 'no less than 150 ploughs and occupies actually 4,500 acres of cultivated land'.[27]

This seemed a contradictory phenomenon for a region where land rights were supposed to have passed wholesale to the non-agricultural classes. In Hoshangabad, Elliott reported that non-agriculturalist Brahmins alone held as much as 29% of the land. In Jabalpur, Marwaris and 'banias' gained early prominence as malguzars, and their increasing hold over the land was occasion for an official inquiry by the 1870s. The Commissioner of Jabalpur reported in 1874 that 211 villages were in the hands of the mahajans, the greater part of the Jabalpur Tahsil owned by Seth Gokal Das.[28] Yet such appearances were deceptive, or rather, reality was more complex, for no real distinction could be ob-

26 *Ibid.*, p. 188.
27 *Ibid.*, p. 95.
28 *Sels. Recs. Govt. India*, no. CIV, 'Correspondence re Law of Land Sale' (Calcutta, 1879), p. 402.

served between agricultural and non-agricultural classes: 'There is hardly a single moneylender in the district who is not a landlord, and many of the landlords, even of the agricultural castes, combine the business of money and grain dealer with that of a cultivator'.[29]

Traditionally the malguzar in the Narmada valley fulfilled a much more important role than that of a petty revenue contractor or lessee. In a country of recent colonisation the provision of credit was all important, and Elliott put down the heterogeneous character of the malguzari class in Hoshangabad exclusively to this cause:

So far as a cultivating clan possesses capital, it can, when it immigrates, become proprietor of the land it settles on; but if it is unable to pay the rent and support itself for a year till the crops are ready, it, or at least the weaker members of it, must rely on loans from someone else; and the same man who lends the money becomes the Malgoozar, and interposes between them and Government. It is a mere accident whether this man is an old Malgoozar, who has saved money from the village he already holds, or a Brahmin who has made money by astrology and prayers, or a wealthy merchant, or a follower of some man in authority; whoever, having money by him, came forward with it at the right time when the cultivators were ready to break up the jungle, if fed and clothed, that man became the Malgoozar.[30]

While there was undoubtedly a strong element of artificiality in turning the malguzars into a landlord class, it has again to be stressed that the prevailing social structure qualified the grant of proprietary rights in an important way. The relative affluence of malguzars was much less prominent where the land had been brought into cultivation without substantial aid from creditors and where the village patel families had retained the malguzari right. In Nimar – outside the wheat zone – the position of the ordinary ryot had been too strong to be ignored, and under a ryotwar-minded official a high proportion of cultivators were recognised as plot proprietors (*malik mabhuza*) and the remainder

[29] *Hoshangabad S.R. 1905*, p. 34. Cf. a similar statement by H. R. Crosthwaite, *Hoshangabad S.R. 1919*, p. 27. *Jubbulpore S.R. 1912*, p. 18.

[30] *Hoshangabad S.R. 1865*, pp. 64–5. Cf. conditions in Jabalpur district soon after cession, as reported later, where 'cultivators scarcely ever pay money-rents, that the Malgoozar takes all the produce and feeds them, furnishes seed and generally bullocks also; they are thus in reality mere labourers'; *Jubbulpore S.R. 1869*, p. 23.

given occupancy rights. The result was little different from a ryotwar settlement, and the malguzar was unable to raise himself much above his fellows: 'he is still as a patel, as he was before, primus inter pares, but like his neighbours in his mode of life'.[31] This capacity to adjust to circumstances was sufficient to give the malguzar a degree of mobility powerful enough to overcome the occupational limitations of caste. In the wheat zone the malguzar seemed possessed of all the qualities of a capitalist entrepreneur, able to lead and exploit the unparalleled material development that ensued during the thirty-year settlement from 1865. The completion of the railway in 1870 was followed by an immense acceleration in exports,[32] the wheat boom reaching its height in the 1880s. The malguzars took a leading role, their proprietary cultivation rising by a third to become 23% of the occupied area. By 1893 the ordinary Hoshangabad malguzars constituted a plainly visible 'rich peasant' or gentleman farmer class: 'They have almost without exception good *pucca* houses built with an elaborate main entrance (darwaza) which is easily distinguishable from the houses of the tenants, and around which cluster their cattle sheds and granaries. They practically never do any manual labour, the majority employing bailiffs to do even the supervision of their cultivation.'[33] What was significant was that despite a steady increase in their income from rents it still remained true in 1893 that two-thirds of their total net income (after payment of the Government revenue) came from the agricultural profits reaped from their direct cultivation.[34] There could be no stronger testimony to the success of the 'green revolution' in wheat in the Narmada valley. Even on the Malwa plateau to the north there were twenty good years after 1870 to relieve its habitual insecurity. In Sagar (Saugor) district between 1865 and 1895 population increased 18%, the cropped area rose by 48%, and wheat exports by rail leapt from 40,000 maunds in 1887 to 758,000 maunds in 1897.[35]

The extensive commercialisation of agriculture (though it must be remembered that in the valley wheat remained the staple food

[31] *Nimar S.R. 1895–1899* (Nagpur, 1903), p. 17.
[32] Hoshangabad's exports almost trebled between 1872 and 1891, *Census of India 1911*, x. *C.P. & Berar. Pt I Report* (Calcutta, 1912), p. 16.
[33] *Hoshangabad S.R. 1891–96* (1905), p. 35.
[34] *Ibid.*, p. 61.
[35] *Saugor S.R. 1911–16* (Nagpur, 1918), p. 23.

grain) was inevitably accompanied by an expansion of credit. Malguzars who had never lost the role of moneylender, or just as easily acquired it, lent freely to their fellows and to the more substantial tenants, especially in Hoshangabad. Even before the long boom finally collapsed certain types of indebtedness were already causing more serious alarm. Just how much weight must be given to the anxiety of British officials like Bamfylde Fuller is problematical. Fuller joined readily in the chorus orchestrated by Denzil Ibbetson and other Punjab officials who formed the ruling official clique at Calcutta against the nefarious activities of the rural usurer and the danger he posed to continued peasant contentment with British rule.[36] In the Central Provinces it so happened that he could point to an area where indebtedness took the shape of a direct confrontation between the humble toiling peasant and the professional Marwari and Parwar moneylender. It is evident that a rural entrepreneur would be most readily diverted from direct exploitation of the soil in areas where high farming and population pressure on the most fertile soil enabled rents to be driven up to a competition or rack-rent level. This happened earliest in the Jabalpur haveli (the region containing the district capital) where, as we have seen, circumstances had allowed the leading house of Seth Gokal Das, the Marwari, to gain an early and decisive hold. In the C.P. Revenue Administration Report for 1889–90 Fuller wrote that in the Jabalpur haveli rents had been run to cruelly high limits frequently ranging from Rs. 6 to Rs. 7 per acre for unirrigated land, and the tenants 'have been chained down by debt into a position but little removed from that of servitude'. Analogous conditions, although prompted originally by high revenue pressure, were observed in the Sagar and Damoh havelis where the Kurmi malguzars struggled in the bania's grip. Yet apart from special instances the major move of predominantly moneylending families into landholding did not occur until the great agrarian crisis and collapse of the decade 1893–1903 when, because of alternate flood and drought, famine even swept the Narmada valley districts. Before this disaster only some 16% of villages had been transferred in Jabalpur during the whole thirty-year settlement, the losses falling mainly on 'old

---

[36] Cf. C. J. Dewey, 'The Official Mind and the Problem of Agrarian Indebtedness in India, 1876–1910', unpublished Cambridge Univ. Ph.D. thesis, 1973, pp. 61, 182.

feudal families many of whom parted with their villages to the moneylenders'.[37] In the eighteen years that followed 1889 some 40% of Jabalpur villages changed hands, more than half going to the moneylenders. It was the same story as in Bundelkhand; the creditor was seeking to limit his losses by closing on his security rather than moving acquisitively into landholding as some supposed. He could not escape unscathed from his debtors' widespread default and huge sums had to be written off under debt concilation proceedings.[38]

Unlike the fortunes of the cotton country of Berar to the immediate south the vicissitudes of the wheat zone seem to have had their origin more in fluctuations of weather than price, but the risks of overextension in wheat were sharply exposed. The Narmada valley districts experienced a savage setback in which their population fell off sharply for a time; but their much higher degree of agricultural security endowed them with a power of recuperation denied to the Malwa plateau on the north. There conditions resembled Bundelkhand more closely. The black mar soils which prevailed in the haveli tracts had led to them being devoted entirely to the monoculture of wheat (or wheat and gram grown together, viz. *birra*) for the rabi harvest. Crop specialisation had so taken over that despite repeated crop failure the cultivators felt bound to go on borrowing seed grain and plunging themselves ever more deeply into debt. The Damoh settlement officer noted in 1914:

The Haveli...is a one-crop tract, and if the wheat is ruined it may be said that for that year all is lost...The Haveli tenant is noted for borrowing the same amount of rabi seed when he is in temporarily reduced circumtances as when he is prosperous. He knows that if wheat land is let go for a single year it may be lost to him for a decade. He thinks that he cannot afford to concentrate and in his reluctance to lose a little he has often lost all.[39]

Indebtedness in the entire Sagar and Narmada region exhibited those characteristic features that Darling observed later in the Punjab province. The problem was most severe at the two extremes – the intensive and the extensive margins. In the Punjab these proved to be firstly, the densely settled zones about the

[37] *Central Provinces Gazetteers – Jubbulpore*, p. 190.
[38] Cf. *Damoh S.R. 1908–13* (Nagpur, 1914), p. 20.
[39] *Ibid.*, p. 10.

capital, Lahore, and the overpopulated submontane tract of Hoshiarpur and Gurdaspur, and, secondly, the insecure and thinly populated south-western districts of Dera Ghazi, Mianwali, Multan, and Muzaffargarh. In the Central Provinces these extremes were given emphasis because of the strong hold which the Marwari and Parwar bania moneylenders had established at both margins, both in the close-settled Jabalpur, Damoh or Sagar havelis and in the thinly-held insecure Khurai tahsil in the north of Sagar district. This latter tract suffered severely from drought and kans was never absent. Forty-one per cent of the tahsil was transferred between 1896 and 1916, the big moneylenders (including Diwan Bahadur Seth Ballabdas of Jabalpur) taking over shares equivalent to nearly a quarter of the tahsil. It was here that the *gallia* or debt serf was observed by the settlement officer in the late 1880s, and though subsequent inquiry failed to substantiate the charges Khurai tahsil continued to cause anxiety.[40] The Provincial Banking Enquiry Committee which reported in 1930 and which sought to put a good face on things confessed to concern over these marginal areas. Yet it insisted that these were exceptional. Despite bad seasons in the 1920s debt had not risen significantly in the secure tracts of the wheat zone taken as a whole. Only 5% of cultivators were hopelessly indebted while 31% were entirely free from debt.

If, therefore, we accept that the seriously indebted tracts were exceptional, what happened to the promise of capitalist agriculture that had looked so favourable in the 1880s? The boom conditions never returned after the series of unparalleled disasters. That conjuncture of a revolutionary advance in output led by a single leading crop, wheat, combined with high agricultural and low rental profits, was part of the pioneer age. The old single-mindedness of wheat monoculture was abandoned in favour of a greater measure of mixed farming, in which kharif crops and cattle products figured more prominently. The malguzar spread his risk. Proprietary cultivation fell back, subletting of sir increased, and with even the tenant able to sublet at two-and-a-half to three times the rent he himself paid, rental incomes took on a new importance.[41] Moneylending was also given a fresh lease of

[40] *Saugor S.R. 1911–16* (Nagpur, 1918), pp. 33 ff. *Saugor S.R. 1887–97*, pp. 41–2.
[41] Cf. *Hoshangabad S.R. 1913–18* (Nagpur, 1919), pp. 19, 25, 40.

life. The Banking Enquiry Committee found that while some
20% of rural credit in the wheat zone was supplied by landlords
the latter also played an increasingly profitable intermediary role
as sublenders between the professional moneylender-bania and
the tenant cultivator. Rai Sahib Pandit Laxinarayan of Noni told
the Committee that only those malguzars and cultivators now
accumulated wealth who combined moneylending with agriculture and that the former was the more paying business.[42]

Now it may be said that this 'advance towards vagueness', which
Geertz argued was characteristic of Asian society,[43] this diffusion
of economic roles and the obstinate refusal of the social and
economic order to evolve on clear, determinate lines of class differentiation, all this was a return to the Indian norm. Charles
Elliott had pardoned the low out-turn per acre in Hoshangabad
on the analogy of the opening of the American prairies.[44] But the
malguzars of the Narmada valley were no Texans. Their attachment to a traditional life style was not to be shaken. Lordship and
its attendant display were still dear to their heart. In Narsinghpur,
where monied men had made least headway into the landlord
ranks, the malguzar as late as the end of the 1920s was still fond
of purchasing an elephant to mark his wealth and social ascendancy.[45] Even in Sagar, a Jain cult centre, the Parwar banias vied
with each other in profuse public spending, lavishing often more
than a lakh on the costly temple car (*rath*) ceremony in order to
raise themselves through the honorific degrees of Singhai, Sawai
Singhai and Seth.[46] Was it not an illusion to look on such men as
capitalist entrepreneurs in a system of 'federated grain factories'?[47]
Might it not be said that the exceptional profitability and expansion of wheat cultivation between the 1860s and 1890s was bound
to end once the land was taken up, population grew, rents rose,
and advancing prosperity made moneylending increasingly advantageous? Natural disaster in the 1890s merely hastened this
inevitable conclusion. Yet this would be to misread the situation.

---

[42] *Report of C.P. Provincial Banking Enquiry Committee 1919–30* (Nagpur,
1930), I, p. 45.
[43] Cited above, p. 38.
[44] *Hoshangabad S.R. 1865*, p. 107.
[45] *C.P. Provincial Banking Enquiry Committee Report, Appxs* II, p. 680.
[46] *Saugor S.R. 1887–97* (Nagpur, 1902), p. 39. *C.P. District Gaz. – Saugor*
(Allahabad, 1906), pp. 48–50.
[47] Professor M. M. Postan's description of thirteenth-century English
monastic estates.

Like so many regions that had earlier experienced the surge of commercialised agriculture, whether it was the Patna region, Bundelkhand, or Benares and the eastern U.P., permanent disappointment and frustration succeeded to the first spring hopes of constant dynamic growth. Yet it was underpopulation rather than overpopulation that appears to have kept back the economic development of the Narmada valley. Practising a careless agriculture and relying for labour chiefly on the massive seasonal migration of Gonds and others from the hills, even the most fertile tracts remained thinly occupied. Cultivators were under no pressure of population to abandon their careless mode of agriculture more suitable for pioneer days.[48] Yet just as Bundelkhand discovered after recovering from the famine of 1868–9 that the cotton market had permanently altered its sources of supply, so the Narmada wheat cultivators discovered that the highly volatile export market had gone. India's position as a major world wheat supplier began in any event to fade away after 1900 and dwindled to nothing by 1930. Yet almost the whole of this declining export trade fell from the turn of the century into the hands of the Punjab. More seriously Punjab and western U.P. took up between them from the 1890s pretty well the entire increase in the much larger domestic wheat market.[49] Up to the end of British rule the area under wheat and wheat-gram in the Central Provinces never permanently recovered the figure of $3\frac{1}{2}$ million acres which it had attained by 1879.[50] What is more noticeable is that while the insecure districts like Saugor and Damoh recovered their peak wheat acreage by 1923, the major wheat-producing district of Hoshangabad rarely again rose above 70% of the old 1891–2

---

[48] For seasonal migration of 15,000–20,000 Gond labourers to Jabalpur, cf. *Census of India 1891, XI, C.P. pt 1 Report* (Calcutta, 1893), p. 48. *Census of India, XIII, C.P. pt 1 Report* (Nagpur, 1902), p. 215.
   F. J. Plymen, the C.P. Director of Agriculture, said total annual migration for harvest labour was up to 120,000 for the wheat zone, *Royal Commission on Agriculture in India* (London, 1927), VI, p. 5.

[49] For decline of India's overseas wheat exports and growing Punjab share, cf. *Report on Marketing of Wheat in India* (Simla, 1937), p. 48. For increase of domestic wheat production and Punjab's share cf. *ibid.*, p. 3. Punjab wheat acreage rose from $6\frac{3}{4}$ million acres in 1870 to nearly $9\frac{1}{2}$ millions (as a ten-year average) in the decade 1925–35.

[50] 'The Wheat Production and Trade of India', *Sels. Recs. Govt. India* (Home, Rev. & Agr. Dept.), no. clx (Simla, 1879), p. 16; and also G. Blyn, *Agricultural Trends in India, 1891–47* (Philadelphia, 1966), Appx, pp. 260–1, Table 3A. See also above, pp. 13–14.

peak production, and by 1935–6 after the slump was still only 64%.[51]

Plymen, the Central Provinces' Director of Agriculture, acknowledged to the Banking Enquiry Committee that the low return of 800 lb an acre had allowed the Punjab to beat the Central Provinces in costs of production.[52] At the critical point when the high profitability of wheat cultivation could only be sustained by high farming with its more intensive capital inputs of irrigation facilities and manure, the Hoshangabad cultivators turned away to the more certain returns from mixed cropping, dairy-farming and rentier landlordism. The more dynamic element among the monied men fixed their attention increasingly on the development of industrial enterprise in the city of Jabalpur. Here the Marwari house of Seth Gokaldas made its most significant contribution towards the future.[53] The second Green Revolution in the Narmada valley is only now struggling painfully from the planner's drawing board.

[51] *Annual Season and Crop Reports of C.P.* from 1919–20 to 1935–36 (Nagpur, 1920 etc.).
[52] *Royal Commission on Agriculture in India* (London, 1927), vi, p. 72.
[53] On the growth of Jabalpur and the Marwari contribution, cf. *C.P. District Gazs. – Jubbulpore*, pp. 224, 354, 356.

12

The return of the peasant to South Asian history

No platitude could be more trite than that the balance of destiny in South Asia rests in peasant hands, yet no platitude has been grasped with more laggardliness by political scientists and historians. Part of the explanation is perhaps the split level at which South Asian society appears to operate. Charles Metcalfe and Karl Marx long ago gave vivid formulation to the notion of an underlying discontinuity between the political superstructure and the agrarian base.[1] No doubt this insulation of the peasant world from the state is in some measure typical of all pre-modern autocracies, but in the Indian subcontinent it seemed to receive particular reinforcement from the brittle foreign-conquest character of the larger political systems and from what appeared to be the peculiar economic and social self-sufficiency of a village society regulated by the institutions of caste. As a result even the periodic irruption of the peasantry into politics through rebellion looks strangely absent in Indian history, unless one follows Irfan Habib in regarding the rise of the Maratha, Sikh and Jat powers in the later seventeenth and eighteenth centuries as essentially peasant movements, or believes with Kathleen Gough that constant peasant rebellion under colonial rule has been deliberately over-looked.[2] It has, therefore, seemed natural to treat politics as a self-contained activity and relegate rural India to the role of a dim,

This paper originated as an undergraduate lecture given at the Universities of New South Wales and Western Australia in March 1976. I am grateful to Dr John Harriss of the South Asian Studies Centre, Cambridge, for guiding my further reading.
[1] The argument and sources are summarised in Paper 1, pp. 19–21.
[2] Irfan Habib, *The Agrarian System of Mughal India* (London, 1963). ch. ix. Kathleen Gough, 'Indian Peasant Uprisings', *Economic and Political Weekly* [hereafter referred to as *EPW*], IX (1974) [special no. Aug. 1974] pp. 1391 ff.

shadowy backcloth to the political stage.[3] This attitude survived the ending of colonial rule. At independence not merely was power transferred from white to brown hands but the historical study of the subcontinent was transferred from amateurs to professionals. The latter turned at once to investigate the political processes by which the displacement of the Raj had been accomplished. For this they ransacked the records of the legislative assembly, the council chamber, and the party *pandal*, burst open the ballot boxes and rifled the correspondence of the dead. Yet it is only to rediscover the truth long since trumpeted metaphorically by Kipling in his uproarious barrack-room ballad, *Loot*, that in history's many-storied pagoda the most precious treasures are buried out of sight in the good strong earth of the foundations. To what T. S. Eliot called 'the life of significant soil' the historians of the French, Russian, and even English revolutions have long ago resorted, fired by the conviction that in all pre-industrial societies the river of historical change issues from rural springs, and taught by modern experience that while cities may go up in revolt it is the countryside that makes or breaks revolutions. Now too among the students of the colonial revolution in South Asia the city slickers are at last quitting town.

One may be surprised at their laggardliness, but that would be to underrate the difficulties. Spengler roundly declared that the peasant is without history, meaning that he leaves no trace of his own in the form of the written word. We usually come at him only by external observation, and in the case of India by external observation of a peculiarly precise, distorted, and forbidding kind. Our intelligence is overwhelmingly desk-bound and official, the product of clerk and tax collector, of men of the office and not the spade, whether their faces have been white or brown. Their purposes were essentially fiscal and legal, their data overwhelmingly impersonal and statistical. Despite the wealth of government records, the phenomena of rural life were lumped crudely into general categories irrespective of their manifold and bewildering variety, and they have remained entangled in a fearsome thicket of technicality. These circumstances made them peculiarly vulner-

[3] Barrington Moore, Jnr discusses 'the apparent political docility of the Indian peasants' in *Social Origins of Dictatorship and Democracy: lord and peasant in the making of the modern world* (London, 1967), pp. 330 ff.

able to the distorting simplifications of the modern intelligence. Unreachable through the intimacy of shared experience and its accompanying intuitive understanding, the peasantry has to be approached through mental surrogates, through generalisations, concepts, models and theories. No class outside the so-called primitive societies has been so totally struck down as the hapless victim of the academic interpreter.

This tendency for abstract presupposition to rush in to cover up the absence of direct experience has remained to this day, and in turn has rendered South Asian history, itself one of the most literal-minded branches of historical study, the unwitting prey of intellectual fashion. Nowhere has this been more marked than over the notion of the Indian village community.

So powerfully did the image of a traditional India composed of a myriad of self-contained village republics stamp itself upon the educated consciousness of the nineteenth century that the influence of modernity was read invariably as a disintegrative one. Had not the traditional forms of local self-government resting on the village *panchayat* and the village headman been rapidly drained of life by the judicial and administrative machinery of the modern state? Had not the monetisation of the land-revenue demand and the pressure for cash-cropping been followed by an invasion of the closed village economy by foreign manufacturers with the resultant overthrow of traditional handicrafts? Had not the novel introduction of modern proprietary title deprived the peasant of his essential property in the soil, and in law or practice reduced him to a mere tenant or labourer of an outside purchaser, usually an urban moneylender? Crude, simple, powerful ideas like these were shared alike by British administrators and Indian nationalists by the later nineteenth century.[4] They resulted in fitful latter-day efforts to resurrect village institutions, to stem

---

[4] Cf. William Cunningham, the Cambridge economic historian, on a visit to India, writing on 8 March 1882: 'Each village was self-sufficing when the simple necessaries of life were manufactured by the village carpenter, potter, and weaver who were supported by common contributions from village resources. Manchester mills are now underselling the local weavers...domestic spinning is dying out. The more prosperous men are withdrawing from the responsibilities of village life, the authority of the *patil* is disappearing, and the village artisans are no longer supported...Trade is the great solvent which breaks up social organization...we really are nihilists, overthrowing the institutions of society, and helpless to develop anything in their stead.' E. Homberger, W. Janeway and S. Schama, *The Cambridge Mind* (London, 1970), pp. 22, 24.

further alienation of peasant land to outsiders, and to introduce village cooperatives.

Indian nationalists found it still harder to resist sentimentality and the Gandhian school shaped their soaring political ideals on the revival of a golden past in which *panchayati raj* and an autonomous village economy symbolised by the spinning wheel would re-emerge triumphant.[5] Down to the Second World War almost every school of historical interpretation, Marxist or non-Marxist, was agreed that whatever the novel degree of physical unity imposed, the main effect of British rule on traditional Indian agrarian structure was one of dissolution.[6] To Nehru it was axiomatic that despite India's stormy history 'the village self-governing community continued. Its break-up began only under British rule.'[7] The one novel social formation that emerged to counter this trend was (what could still unblushingly be called) the modern English-educated Indian middle class, from whose ranks the reintegrative force of nationalism was destined to spring.

The powerful simplicity of this historical imagery was lost in the post-War decades. Two contradictory currents of academic interpretation converged to form a new view of the past, which renounced the concept of foreign rule as the agent of massive structural change and berated the arrogance behind the assumption that a few thousand white men held India's millions in the hollow of their hands. Colonial rule was shown to be a much weaker form of dominion and one essentially dependent on the internal cooperation of the ruled. Firstly, in Western academic circles the neo-Machiavellian school of Ronald Robinson and John Gallagher insisted that imperialism so far from constituting an all-powerful impulse was always exerted with maximum economy of effort, and was, therefore, dependent on finding appropriate sets of collaborators among rival local elites. In this intellectual climate Robert Frykenberg demonstrated how in the

[5] For the persistence of the village community ideal and its present influence, cf. H. Maddick, *Panchayati Raj* (London, 1970), pp. 22–8. On the economic side, cf. I. Klein 'Indian Nationalism and Anti-Industrialization: the Roots of Gandhian Economics', *South Asia*, 3 (1973).

[6] Radhakamal Mukerjee, *The Rural Economy of India* (London, 1926); D. R. Gadgil, *The Industrial Evolution of India* (Calcutta, 1924, 1929, 1933, 1942). The fifth edition, *The Industrial Evolution of India in Recent Times, 1860–1939* (1971), retains the original 1924 account of the self-sufficient village community on pp. 9–12. L. S. O'Malley. *Modern India and the West* (Cambridge, 1941), pp. 85, 259–60.

[7] J. Nehru, *Discovery of India* (Bombay, 1961 edn), p. 263.

districts – or at least, in Guntur district in Madras – the British reigned but did not rule.[8] The shifting district officer danced unwittingly to the tune called by the local official service class. In the towns no modern middle class emerged, as Marx and others had prophesied, for economic change was far too limited in extent to cause structural social change. Already at the colonial take-over India possessed a sophisticated economy and a complex, articulated society that could readily accommodate itself to the increased volume of commercial activity under colonial rule without undergoing fundamental internal alteration. Hence there was simply some lateral adjustment and internal circulation of elites. The most successful collaborators with the British were the old clerisy or literate service castes, a section of which took as readily to English as their fathers to Persian, Urdu or Modi. Modern nationalism could be explained purely in terms of the internal dynamics of this group. While they derived their political and social strength from their role as a broker class capable of interpreting and manipulating the impulses and discontents moving other sections of traditional Indian society, the main motor force behind nationalism stemmed from their own internal divisions and competitiveness. Competing interests as well as pure factionalism drove them to exert upward pressure on the British overrulers for a greater place in the sun of official power and patronage and to thrust downwards to mobilise support among aggrieved elements in traditional society beneath. Such, put crudely, was the substance of Anil Seal's conclusion in *The Emergence of Indian Nationalism*, published in 1968, but which first saw the light of day as a fellowship dissertation in 1961. Oddly it came curiously close to the old Colonel Blimp view that modern nationalism was an artifact, the projection of the ills and ambitions of a swollen intelligentsia in no way representative of the country at large. In such a scenario the peasantry remained an inert mass.

This neo-Machiavellian interpretation had taken wing in the 1950s when elite theory, Namierism, and the 'end-of-ideology' mood were current in Western academic circles. As an intellectual tradition its roots ran back to Pareto, Mosca and Michels.[9]

[8] R. E. Frykenberg, *Guntur District 1788–1848: A History of Local Influence and Central Authority in South India* (Oxford, 1965).

[9] Among the influential works of the 1950s concerned with elitism and neo-Machiavellianism were C. Wright Mills, *The Power Elite* (1956), J. H.

Unwittingly it was aided and abetted by the neo-Marxist school of economic history and sociology of the post-War generation. This too saw colonialism in a different light, not as the brutal but progressive force envisaged by Marx but as a parasitic blood-sucking vampire that left its victim enervated but unchanged. Its function was to skim cash crops off a stagnant agrarian base, or as Clifford Geertz has argued (for the argument has currency outside purely Marxist circles) 'the central desire of all imperialist countries was the wish to bring people's products into the world economy but not the people themselves; to have one's economic cake and eat it too by producing capitalist goods with precapitalist workers on precapitalist land'.[10] Capitalism had struck a local bargain with feudalism. Such an argument allowed no room for the conception of a modern, populist nationalism producing a groundswell from below. It gave no place to the peasantry as an active component, and so curiously reinforced the elitist interpretation of the neo-Machiavellians.

Yet this new double mirror held up to historical nature has already been badly cracked. Even the neo-Machiavellians following the argument whithersoever it led are now foremost in proclaiming that the Congress movement was a mere coalition of provincial associations and that the ultimate power base of politics is to be discovered in the countryside in the person of the local political 'boss'. This migration from the capital to the *mofussil* finds one of its most striking exemplifications in the work of two younger Cambridge historians, Christopher Baker and David Washbrook.[11] But other more powerful influences have, of course, been principally responsible for shattering the elitist image. The

---

Meisel, *The Myth of the Ruling Class* (1958), H. Stuart Hughes, *Consciousness and Society* (1959), Daniel Bell, *The End of Ideology*. For useful summaries see T. B. Bottomore, *Elites and Society* (London, 1964) and J. H. Meisel (ed.), *Pareto and Mosca* (Englewood Cliffs, N.J., 1965).

[10] C. Geertz, *The Social History of an Indonesian Town*, p. 45, cited in M. Adas, *The Burma Delta: economic development and social change on an Asian rice frontier 1842–1941* (Wisconsin, 1974), p. 209.

[11] C. J. Baker, *The Politics of South India, 1920–1937* (Cambridge, 1976); 'The Rise and Fall of the Madras Village Officer', unpublished paper in SSRC Conference on Indian Economic and Social History, St John's College, Cambridge 23–5 July, 1975. D. A. Washbrook, 'Country Politics: Madras 1880–1930' in J. A. Gallagher *et al.*, *Locality, Province and Nation: Essays in Indian Politics 1870–1940* (Cambridge, 1973). C. J. Baker and D. A. Washbrook, *South India: Political Institutions and Political Change 1880–1940* (Delhi, 1975).

ideological and political shock waves released by successful peasant war and rebellion in China and Vietnam, the impact of the Green Revolution and the echoing impulses from South Asian agricultural economics and Western peasant studies have together shaken the foundations of the old learning. The result is a conceptual revolution that has run far ahead of empirical inquiry. Even in the more readily accessible terrain of political history the shift in the angle of vision is seen by Anil Seal as having transcendent importance.[12] But in the immensely diverse and intractable domain of peasant society the advance of theory without adequate empirical definition and support has led to an analysis that is often as rudimentary as the older generalisations about the internal structure of the self-sufficient Indian village community. In pre-Independence days the Congress and Marxist Left defined the comprador or collaborating elements as the princes, the big landlords, and the merchant usurers; these were the allies of imperialism and the upholders of reaction in the countryside.[13] Now that these elements have been cut down or severely pollarded, the true culprit has been discovered. He is, of course, none other than the kulak, the 'rich peasant', supposedly the mainstay of the Congress Right throughout most of the subcontinent and the unyielding opponent of genuine land reform and true democracy. Here the old picture of 'changeless change' or 'static expansion', or whatever paradoxical term one uses to describe the involution rather than evolution of the Indian village community,[14] has to be modified to accommodate a measure of structural change – sufficient at least for a 'rich peasant' or kulak class to be separated out.

Not that stratification within the village has not always existed. The reports of all first-hand observers even at the beginning of the nineteenth century – particularly the careful observations of Buchanan-Hamilton in Bengal and Bihar – testify to the importance of a dominant peasant elite.[15] Yet from 1860 or so this elite

---

[12] A. Seal, 'Imperialism and Nationalism in India' in J. A. Gallagher *et al.*, pp. 1 ff.

[13] Cf. R. Palme Dutt, *India Today* (London, 1940), p. 390.

[14] C. Geertz, *Agricultural Involution: the Process of Ecological Change in Indonesia* (Los Angeles and Berkeley, 1963), pp. 90, 102–3.

[15] Buchanan-Hamilton, cited in R. and R. Ray, 'The Dynamics of Continuity in Rural Bengal under the British Imperium', *Indian Economic and Social History Review* [hereafter referred to as *IESHR*], x, 2 (1973), pp. 111 ff.

was armed with special advantages because of its ability to benefit from the bursting of the price dam and the enhanced profits to be made from cash crops like jute, cotton, wheat, sugar and tobacco. The struggle of the resident village land controllers against the superior rent owners and landlords for the appropriation of the new 'surplus value' sometimes took violent forms. K. K. Sen Gupta has interpreted the Pabna disturbances of 1873 in this fashion, the fight for the new wealth from jute taking the form of a struggle over occupancy rights between zamindars and jote-dars.[16]

There was scarcely time for a 'rich peasant' class to separate itself out in northern India before the great explosion of 1857, although the later 1840s and early 1850s saw a great expansion of cultivation and other signs of an agricultural boom. It would seem that the major agrarian violence did not come from peasant groups most closely involved in cash-cropping. Rather it came from traditionally superior clan communities for whom British rule had meant loss of political consequence and relative economic deprivation. The western parts of the rebellion zone, around Delhi and in modern Haryana, had in pre-British days been dominated by cattle-keeping peoples of Rajput and quasi-Rajput status who scorned the plough. Such were the Bhattis and Ranghars of Haryana and the Gujars of the upper Doab, looked upon by the British as naturally turbulent. The British land-revenue system had pressed hard against them, weighted as it was in favour of the thrifty agriculturalist by its taxation of all land as arable rather than pasture. Yet they had suffered more than the heavy hand of the tax collector. The Bhattis of Hissar had found themselves pushed off their extensive grazing grounds and the land marked out in blocks for the industrious Jat immigrants. In the Doab the Gujars had lost their old predominance formerly exercised from the *mukararis* of Landhaura and Parikshitgarh. Gujar village *maliks* had seen their *malguzari* (or revenue engagement)

The division into wealthy, comfortable, and poor peasants was made by G. R. Campbell even among the so-called egalitarian *bhaiachara* Jat villages of Rohtak in 1826 and 1827. See his settlement reports, Board's Collections, vol. 1214, no. 30954.

[16] K. K. Sen Gupta, *Pabna Disturbances and the Politics of Rent, 1873–85* (New Delhi, 1974). Also 'The Agrarian League of Pabna, 1873' and 'Agrarian Disturbances in the Nineteenth Century', *IESHR*, vii (1970), pp. 255 ff., viii (1971), pp. 192 ff. 'Peasant Struggle in Pabna, 1873', *Nineteenth Century Studies* (Calcutta), 3 (July 1973), pp. 328 ff.

rights pass extensively into the hands of their urban creditors in towns like Sikandarabad, which they sacked with fanatical ferocity. Yet the most determined resistance to British authority and the best organised rural uprisings came from groups least penetrated by the urban usurer and least affected by the sale of land-control rights in satisfaction of debts. They usually inhabited riverine tracts or little alsatias where the writ of government had at best run with difficulty. Such were the tracts close to the Jumna river throughout its length from the Siwaliks to where it joined the Ganges at Allahabad. The Gujars of the Gangoh region and the Pandir Rajputs of the Kata, the Jats of Noh Jhil in the Mathura district, the Bhadauria Rajputs of Agra, the Chauhan Rajputs of Chakkarnagar in Etawah are merely a few examples of such embattled communities. They largely stood on the periphery of the high-farming area, and worked under traditional forms of leadership which leaned either to 'republican' or 'monarchical' forms. Even in a high farming sugar-growing district like Shahjahanpur the Chandel Rajputs of the Khundur *ilaqa* refused to cultivate sugar from fear of losing their land-control rights. The first care of these and similar communities like the Jhangara Rajputs of Bareilly or the Ahars of Budaun was apparently to maintain their local quasi-autonomy, and they stood ready to resist central bureaucratic authority whether it was that of the British or of the successor rebel power of Khan Bahadur Khan.[17] Yet to warn us against using all this as a form of negative evidence in favour of the turbulence of declining 'middle peasant' groups and the docility of 'rich peasants' is the remarkable rebellion of the Jat communities of western Meerut and Muzaffarnagar districts. These had long been famous for their advanced cash-crop farming and had been the primary beneficiaries of the re-opening of the old Mughal East Jumna Canal in 1830. The British were totally at a loss to understand the Jat uprising. '[W]ithout the slightest cause or the slightest excuse...these thriving agriculturalists became rebels,' was the judgement of Fleetwood Williams, the Meerut Special Commissioner, 'the whole population threw themselves heart and soul into the combination against Government, and to this in great measure the

---

[17] *Shahjahanpur Settlement Report, 1874*, p. 26. *Narrative of Events regarding the Mutiny in India of 1857–58 and the Restoration of Authority* (Calcutta, 1881), I, 371 ff., 449, 459 ff.

protraction of the seige of Delhi may be ascribed, and a great deal of the disaffection in the Meerut and neighbouring districts'.[18] What stands out in all these instances is the supra-village organisation of the clan community and its capacity to unite against what was conceived as an external threat whether coming from Government, rebel, taxman, or urban creditor. One may suggest that even in the altered conditions of the twentieth century this capacity for local combination on clan or caste lines remained an important ingredient in all important peasant agitations. Of course some form of 'crisis' leadership and organisation was required to compose internal factions and extend political scale. In 1857 it was provided either by lineage 'rajas' or in the 'republican' Jat areas by self-made leaders like the old Pindari warrior, Khairati Khan, in the Muzaffarnagar district and before him 'Shah Mull' in the Meerut.[19] In the twentieth century this function fell to political parties or religious organisations

Fearing renewed upheavals the British authorities in zamindari territories like Bengal and the North-Western Provinces moved from the 1870s to protect the superior peasantry through tenancy laws. By rent control and fixity of tenure they gradually brought about a virtual 'transfer of ownership' to the village maliks.[20] In the ryotwar provinces, especially where railway communications or irrigation had lent an impulse to cash-cropping, the peasant elite had little in the way of a superior landlord class to contend with, and surged ahead. Everywhere in India the more thrusting peasant benefited from stricter provision against differential land assessments on the more industrious agricultural castes. The rise of the rich peasant, we are told, was balanced by the decline of the poorer peasant. For the latter was left to feel the full weight of dearer prices without himself being able to move effectively into the market economy because of his inadequate command of land and credit. Hence he was either forced back on subsistence farming, or, if he produced cash crops, was reduced to the dependent status of a sharecropper and debt peon. Dependence on the rich peasant was particularly marked in Bengal where the jotedar increasingly let out the greater part of his land to *bargadars* or *adhiars*, cultivators who as their name implied

---

[18] N.W. Provinces Revenue Proceedings, 221/30. Nos. 309–11 of Sept. 1859.
[19] See above, pp. 15 ff., 175 ff.
[20] W. C. Neale, *Economic Change in Rural India: Land Tenure and Reform in U.P.* (New Haven, Conn., 1962).

paid over half their crop as rent and were left with a bare subsistence wage in kind.[21] Hence we are to suppose that agrarian
society was not blown apart by market forces as Marx and others
had foretold, but instead it was taken hold of and stretched out
elastically from either extremity.

The progress of the rich peasant was subject to much regional
variety even within the confines of a single province like Bombay,
and Ravinder Kumar has claimed to observe a newly rich elite
ensconced on the Deccan plateau by the 1840s. Reports on parts
of Gujarat in the 1850s observe the same phenomenon taking the
shape of a drive by the lesser Kunbi peasants for Patidar status.[22]
Yet there seems general agreement that the 'golden age' of the
rich peasant in India spanned the period 1860–1900 – at least in
areas like Gujarat and the Narmada valley where prosperity went
unchequered by famine.[23] In the Hoshangabad district of the
Narmada valley the wheat boom had created by the 1890s a
clearly recognisable class of rich peasant farmers:

They have almost without exception good *pucca* houses, built with
an elaborate main entrance (*darwaza*) which is easily distinguishable
from the houses of the tenants, and around which cluster their cattle
sheds and granaries. They practically never do any manual labour,
the majority employing bailiffs to do even the supervision of their
cultivation.[24]

Elsewhere the golden age was shorter and more fitful. Traditionally D. R. Gadgil sees the all-India halcyon phase as a brief one
running from 1880–95 when there was no real failure of the rains
in the whole of the subcontinent and 'a phenomenal expansion in
the export of the raw Indian produce took place'.[25]

---

21 Cf. R. and R. Ray, 'The Dynamics of Continuity'.
22 Ravinder Kumar, 'The Rise of the Rich Peasants in Western India' in
   D. A. Low (ed.), *Soundings in Modern South Asian History* (London,
   1968). Ravinder Kumar, *Western India in the Nineteenth Century* (Oxford,
   1968). Neil Charlesworth, 'Rich Peasants and Poor Peasants in late
   Nineteenth Century Maharashtra' and 'Economic and Social Stratification
   among the Bombay Peasantry: Some more reflections', unpublished
   seminar papers, Institute of Commonwealth Studies, London University,
   7 May 1963 and 6 April 1976. D. F. Pocock, *Kanbi and Patidar* (Oxford,
   1972), pp. 58–9.
23 D. Hardiman, 'Peasant Agitations in Kheda District, Gujarat, 1917–
   1934', Sussex D.Phil. 1975, p. 55 says the 'golden age' for the lesser
   Kunbis lasted from 1855 to 1899.
24 *Hoshangabad Settlement Report 1891–96* (1905), p. 35.
25 D. R. Gadgil, *The Industrial Evolution of India* (5th edn, OUP India
   1971), p. 64.

The boom came to an end in the later 1890s when it slowly became evident that India had entered an agrarian 'crisis' whose nature ran deeper than the effect of famine and plagues extended over more than a dozen years (1895–1908) and affecting hitherto secure tracts. Not only did the period coincide with the thirty-year revision of the land-revenue demand in northern, central and western India, and with the attempt of governments and landlords to obtain their share of the increase in rental values since the 1860s and 1870s; but the communications revolution and increased competition for labour began to loosen the hold of rich farmers over predial labour in significant fashion.[26] The 'rich peasant' began to feel himself under pressure from above and below. For the first time there was a significant questioning of the discretionary and authoritarian character of British district administration, whether this concerned framing the revised revenue assessment in Gujarat and parts of the Central Provinces, or prescribing new canal rates and new conditions of tenure and agricultural practice in the Punjab canal colonies. The result was to bring the better-off peasant into politics often at first as part of a movement of decorous protest on the part of all landholders great and small, such as the movement to which R. C. Dutt's *Open Letters to Curzon* (1900) gave publicity.[27] The flare-up in the lower Chenab Canal Colony in 1907 showed, however, that protest could easily get out of hand and assume serious proportions.[28]

---

[26] Substantive economic and social change in village society beginning around 1900 is argued by sociologists in many areas: cf. K. Gough, 'The Social Structure of a Tanjore Village' in McKim Marriot (ed.), *Village India* (1969 edn), p. 41; B. Cohn, 'The Changing Status of a Depressed Class' [Jaunpur District, U.P.], in *ibid.*, pp. 67–8; A. Béteille, *Caste, Class and Power* (Los Angeles and Berkeley, 1965), p. 131.

How far the institution of predial labour declined through growing scarcity of labour or through changes in the cropping pattern and consequent labour abundance is discussed in Jan Breman, *Patronage and Exploitation: Changing Agrarian Relations in South Gujarat, India* (Los Angeles and Berkeley, 1974). For the effects of higher wages and decline of deference on the part of the Baraiya (Koli) labouring class in Kaira from c. 1900, D. Hardiman, *op. cit.*, p. 81 and *passim*.

[27] R. C. Dutt took up the issue as President of Congress at the Lucknow Sessions in 1899 and publicised the decorously-couched protests of Indian members of the Viceroy's Legislative Council in *Open Letters to Lord Curzon* (London, 1900).

[28] N. G. Barrier, 'The Punjab Disturbances of 1907', *Modern Asian Studies* [hereafter referred to as *MAS*], 1 (1957), pp. 353 ff.; 'The Arya Samaj

The First World War and its aftermath vastly accentuated these tendencies. The thriving Punjab peasantry was caught between the expansive pull of rising crop prices and the incentive these gave to use every available hand on the land and the constrictive counter-pull of the British authorities forcing recruitment for war service and rationing consumer goods. The Punjab disturbances of 1919 of which the Amritsar massacre was the dramatic centre-piece reflected the temporary loss of the rich peasant's collaboration with Government. In the Chenab Canal Colony Basil Poff has shown how the British were constrained to switch rural collaborators and find their new ones among the traditionally turbulent Kharral and Bhatti groups whom the original colonisation by Jat peasant groups was intended to pacify.[29]

In 1917 Gandhi mounted the first of his *satyagrahas* in the indigo-growing district of Champaran in Bihar. Jacques Pouchepadass has recently sought to dispose of the myth that Gandhi and his associates had a monopoly of political activism while 'the peasants themselves remain[ed] as a pathetic downtrodden mass in the background'.[30] He has concluded that the main agent in peasant political mobilisation was the 'richer peasants' who found the European plantocracy a rival to their ambitions for dominance in landholding and the supply of credit. In the Kheda (Kaira) satyagraha in Gujarat in the same year, where the issue was remission of the revenue demand because of poor seasons, Judith Brown has similarly concluded: 'Kaira's wealthiest farmers were Patidars, and it is logical to assume that they were the core of the satyagraha'.[31] The same generalisation can be applied to the Kisan Sabha and Eka movement centred on Rae Bareli and the eastern districts of Avadh from 1920 onwards.[32]

and Congress Politics in the Punjab, 1893–1908', *Journal of Asian Studies* [hereafter *JAS*], XXVI, 3 (1967), pp. 373 ff.

29 Basil Poff, 'Rural Control and Imperial Violence in the Punjab in 1919', unpublished seminar paper Centre of South Asian Studies, Cambridge University, January 1975.

30 J. Pouchepadass, 'Local Leaders and the Intelligentsia in the Champaran Satyagrahas (1917): a study in peasant mobilization', *Contributions to Indian Sociology*, new ser., 8 (1974), p. 68.

31 Judith M. Brown, *Gandhi's Rise to Power* (Cambridge, 1972), p. 107.

32 P. D. Reeves, 'The Politics of Order: 'Anti Non-Cooperation' in the U.P., 1921', *JAS*, XXV, 2 (Feb. 1966); W. F. Crawley, 'Kisan Sabhas and Agrarian Revolt in the U.P., 1920–1921', *MAS*, V, 2 (1971); M. H. Siddiqi, 'The Peasant Movement in Pratapgarh, 1920', *IESHR*, IX, 3 (1972), cited in Gyanendra Pandey, 'A Rural Base for the Congress in the

The next round of agrarian-based political crises coincided with the onset of the world slump after 1928. They began in Bardoli in Gujarat where the Congress leaders determined to renew the anti-Government campaign hastily broken off by Gandhi in 1922 after news of the resort to violence at Chauri Chaura in the U.P. Again, as Ghanshyam Shah has recently emphasised, this was a movement conducted avowedly in the interests of superior landowning peasantry who were contesting an enhancement of 22% in the land-revenue assessment announced in 1927.[33] Following on the success of the Bardoli agitation Congress launched its Civil Disobedience campaign in the U.P. in 1930 with a special emphasis on mobilising peasant discontent. But constantly this was directed towards the superior peasantry and attempts to push the movement into a more radical stance were firmly repressed.[34] Parallel but separate was agrarian unrest in Burma. Here, as Michael Adas has sought to demonstrate, the gathering disaffection which characterised Lower Burma after 1900 can be directly related to the ending of the rice boom of the later nineteenth century and to the onset of new difficulties over land and labour supply which tended to polarise and stratify the peasant communities even more sharply. The old view, fostered by J. S. Furnivall and others, was that the commercialisation of agriculture left the peasantry an inert and disintegrating mass while the benefits of rice production were siphoned off by the mechanism of a 'plural society' in which almost all the modern 'capitalist' and service roles were filled by European, Indian and Chinese immigrants. Michael Adas now argues that it simply was not true that imperialism skimmed cash crops off a stagnant agrarian base as Geertz has suggested. In fact the colonisation of the Irrawaddy delta rice bowl had brought about a high degree of social mobility and the emergence of a thrusting rich peasant class among the Burmese. It was the frustration of this class, anxious to push its sons into the professions, and finding its advance blocked by the expatriate grip over

---

U.P., 1920–39' in D. A. Low (ed.) *Congress and the Raj* (forthcoming);
D. N. Dhanagare, 'Congress and Agrarian Agitation in Oudh, 1920–22 and 1930–32', *South Asia*, 5 (1975).

[33] Ghanshyam Shah, 'Traditional Society and Political Mobilization: the experience of the Bardoli Satyagraha (1920–1928)', *Contributions to Indian Sociology*, new ser. 8 (1974), pp. 89 ff.

[34] G. Pandey, *op. cit.*

the economy and employment opportunities, that sparked off the troubles of the 1920s. Race riots in Rangoon in 1922 and again in 1928 were followed by the much more serious agrarian rebellion of Saya San in 1928–30. As in India much of the cause could be traced to the thwarting of rising expectations:

Insofar as it was economically inspired, the Saya San rebellion was a product of frustrated hopes rather than hopeless oppression. Although the problems of Burma's economy were very serious by the 1920's, few, if any, persons in the province starved even when the slump was at its worst in the early 1930's. In the boom decades of the late nineteenth century and early 1900's, however, the classes engaged in agrarian production had come to expect rather high standards of living and levels of consumption and considerable upward mobility. In the decades of transition social and economic realities increasingly fell short of these expectations. By the time of the Depression the social and economic arrangements that had once brought the Burmese cultivator prosperity no longer seemed to work in his favour. Consequently thousands of agriculturalists allied themselves with visionaries and *pongyis* who promised to destroy the institutions that had evolved under alien rule and to bring about a return of an idealized golden age in the past.[35]

All these instances suggest a groundswell coming up from within peasant society which was decisive in loosening the political hold of colonial rule and promoting the nationalist cause. Without the rural dimension the urban politician would have remained ineffectual. Yet the mechanism by which the politicisation of the countryside was accomplished is all-important, for it defines the locus of historical initiative. Christopher Baker and David Washbrook have continued the tradition of the Cambridge school in giving primacy to political action and the role of central authority. Their main theme is that before 1920 the old Madras Presidency remained a stable, if not stagnant, society, almost unaffected (except in a few exceptional areas) by the limited extent of economic development that had occurred under British rule. At best there was a strengthening of the economic position of the rich peasant. Yet between 1900 and 1920 politics came to the countryside. The effective agent of political mobilisation was Government itself, which found it expedient for the solution of its own besetting financial problems to extend administration and

[35] M. Adas, *The Burma Delta*, pp. 202–3.

introduce some measure of local self-taxation and self-govern-ment. The use of electoral machinery produced in turn the rise of political parties, caste associations, and a range of other associational activities. Their emergence in this period 'can hardly be ascribed to a sudden alteration in the socio-economic base'.[36] Politicisation brought about in this fashion proceeded from the top downwards; and we are given to suppose that it remained firmly under the initiative and control of the rich peasant 'boss'. That is, at least until 1930, when the full force of the world depression struck Madras. The price fall caught the 'village elite' with particular severity, but the tenant and landless classes were also sharply affected.[37] Rural society became the scene of violent agitations which the Congress leaders orchestrated in the Civil Disobedience campaign and subsequently utilised to unseat the ruling Justice Party. It may be, therefore, that in the south we are dealing with a more slow moving time scale in which the cli-macteric date was 1930 rather than 1900 or 1917. Until then the 'rich peasant' can be viewed as remaining largely prosperous and so loyal to the Raj, and only subsequently was he turned by economic change into more radical political courses. In Baker's final account the role of economic forces in effecting structural social and political change would thus seem to have gained ultimate recognition. Yet he still leaves in play the central political initiative of the Raj in withdrawing British authority from the provinces and in introducing a 'mass' franchise under the 1937 India Act. We are left with a philosophy of historical conjuncture rather than of economic determinism.

One of the inherent difficulties of the 'rich peasant' or kulak concept is that it bears a pejorative rather than a scientifically neutral connotation. Even non-Marxist historians lean instinc-tively to the assumption that the political influence of the rich peasant must by definition be thrown into the reactionary scale. Those more Marxist-inclined see this reactionary influence ex-tended to the economic field. The Bengali jotedar has been in-dicted by Ratna and Rajat Ray as the buttress both of 'imperialism' and 'underdevelopment' in the countryside throughout the nine-teenth century.[38] Sumit Sarkar has smelled out the jotedar as the

---

[36] C. J. Baker and D. Washbrook, *South India*, p. 43.
[37] C. J. Baker, *The Politics of South India*.
[38] Cf. R. and R. Ray, 'The Dynamics of Continuity'.

prime historical agent of communalism. When Curzon promulgated his partition of Bengal, Hindu and Muslim students in Calcutta expressed the natural unity of the intelligentsia by marching hand in hand in demonstration in September 1906 to hymn the common mother country and hurl defiance at the Raj. But the united front was shattered by the Muslim jotedars of eastern Bengal who used the opportunity under the cloak of religion to prosecute their economic war against the largely Hindu zamindars and called in the *maulavis* to their aid.[39] In this way responsibility for sundering the seamless web of the Bengali 'nation' and propelling it towards the luckless state of modern Bangladesh and West Bengal can be laid firmly at the door of the rich peasant. As the story is told by Sunil Sen, so reactionary did the rich peasant become that even before the ending of colonial rule the bargadar sharecroppers rose up in the Tebhaga rebellion of 1946–7 against his parasitic exactions.[40]

The distrust of the 'rich peasant' infects the account of less politically-committed historians. It is easy to interpret the limited and controlled nature of peasant agitation in the Kisan Sabha movement of 1920–1 and 1930–1 and of the contemporaneous anti-Government campaigns in Gujarat as an indicator of the fears of the more substantial peasantry, worried lest the landless and petty cultivators whom they had mobilised should get out of hand and mount a general campaign for land redistribution, or loose off mindless pillage of haves by have-nots. In this interpretation the Leninist and Maoist analyses of peasant society, as mediated through the writings of Eric Wolf, have exercised a compelling influence.[41] The triple division of the peasantry into rich, middle, and poor is now taken as axiomatic. In this teaching it is, of course, the middle peasant, the truly marginal man, partially enmeshed in the market economy but partially still retaining the independence of the subsistence farmer, who is the essential soul of anticolonial resistance and revolution. In contrast

[39] Sumit Sarkar, 'Hindu; Muslim Relations in Swadeshi Bengal, 1903–1908', *IESHR*, IX, 2 (1972), pp. 161 ff. Also *The Swadeshi Movement in Bengal, 1903–1908* (New Delhi, 1973).
[40] Sunil Sen, *Agrarian Struggle in Bengal, 1947* (New Delhi, 1972).
[41] Eric Wolf, *Peasant Wars of the Twentieth Century* (London, 1971). The literature is surveyed *inter alia* in Hamza Alavi, 'Peasants and Revolution', in K. Gough and H. P. Sharma (eds.), *Imperialism and Revolution in South Asia* (London, 1973), pp. 291 ff.

the rich peasant remains the natural upholder of the *status quo*, being all too closely integrated in the market economy and the established political order to make anything more than careful reformist gestures.

So powerfully has this theoretical analysis carried conviction that historians fall over themselves to discover the radical middle peasant at the centre of disturbance. David Hardiman has gone so far as to say that in the Civil Disobedience movements in Gujarat, 'the rich peasants, who often acted as village leaders, had to be forced in many cases to join in and lead the agitation. As a result, we can say that although the lesser Patidars were not a class of middle peasants as such, they tended to act in the interests of the middle peasantry'.[42] Hardiman is so impressed with Wolf's model that he has taken over Wolf's explanation of the radicalism of the 'middle peasantry' for India and put it down to the loss of their rights as small proprietors. 'In the past, the middle peasants had held sharehold rights in the villages, but under a capitalist economy they were demoted to the ranks of the proletariat as mere tenant farmers. Unlike the poor peasants, the middle peasants have often refused to accept this menial role.'[43] Yet this theoretical argument has to be reconciled with the contradiction that the Kheda (and Bardoli) agitations centred almost entirely on the protest against land tax pressure on *owners*. The middle peasants in the Charotar, the richest part of the Kheda district, so far from having been 'proletarianised' were the largest land-owning group. But how is a 'middle peasant' to be defined? Hardiman adopts the standard mode of definition according to size of land-holding, a rich peasant owning in the Petlad Taluka (Charotar) more than 25 bighas (16 acres), a middle peasant 5 to 25 bighas ($3\frac{1}{2}$ to 16 acres), and a poor peasant less than 5 bighas.[44] Taking an all-India basis for the period 1945–55 T. J. Byres defines the middle peasant as one holding between 5 and 15 acres, the rich and poor peasant categories falling respectively above and below

[42] D. Hardiman, 'Peasant Agitations', p. 318.
[43] D. Hardiman, 'Politicisation and Agitation among the Dominant Peasants in Early Twentieth Century India', *EPW*, ix, (28 Feb. 1976), p. 369. I am indebted to Peter Mayer of Adelaide University for drawing this thoughtful and stimulating article to my attention.
[44] D. Hardiman, *op. cit.*, pp. 316–18. This is a table of proprietary and not cultivating rights. Such a table of landownership is a less meaningful index than a table of operational holdings viz. the actual amount of land, whether owned or leased in, that a farmer commands.

these amounts.[45] Inevitably any definition remains imprecise, even more so since the Marxist classification is not seeking to measure the scale of income polarisation but to define a distinct economic and social role for each category.[46] Now, under colonial rule the rich peasants on the Marxist definition 'were a class of capitalist farmers in embryo, in the womb of the old order',[47] men who marketed the bulk of their crop and employed a preponderance of hired rather than family labour. The middle peasant in contrast used almost entirely family labour and consumed the larger part of his production. Size of holding may be a crude indicator of peasant category but more important, it has been argued, is the input of capital and labour. To establish viable economic class-groups is, therefore, difficult enough; to identify such groupings in a given historical or contemporary setting sets up serious logical strains. Hardiman found in Kheda that social and political action was primarily conducted within the framework of extended lineage or caste groups. 'The distinction between a superior and lesser Patidar was not a class distinction. Within each superior and lesser Patidar village it was possible to find rich, middle and even poor Patidar peasants.' Hence he felt obliged to analyse the peasant agitations historically according to 'precise cultural distinctions' rather than 'imprecise class distinctions'.[48] Sociologists have refused to accept the concept of separate and discordant hierarchies of wealth and status within the confines of a local community, and have resolved the dilemma by the idea of the summation of roles in a dominant caste.[49] Where a single caste is dominant the relations among its leaders are likely to be those of factional competition based on vertical cross-caste alliances with 'followers'. It has been argued, however, that social

---

[45] T. J. Byres, 'Land Reform, Industrialization and the Marketed Surplus in India' in David Lehmann (ed.), *Agrarian Reform and Agrarian Reformism* (1973), p. 235.

[46] This point is argued most trenchantly by Utsa Patnaik, 'Capitalist Development in India: A Note' and 'Further Comment', *EPW*, VI (1971) (*Review of Agriculture*, Sept. 1971), pp. A–123 ff. and Dec. 1971, pp. A–190 ff.

[47] T. J. Byres, *op. cit.*

[48] D. Hardiman, *op. cit.* (1975).

[49] The main authorities remain F. G. Bailey, 'Closed Social Stratification in India', *Archiv. Europe. Sociol.*, IV (1963), pp. 107–24, and M. N. Srinivas, 'The Dominant Caste in Rampura', *American Anthropologist* (Feb. 1959), pp. 1 ff. The argument is summarised in R. Kothari (ed.), *Caste in Indian Politics* (Bombay, 1970), pp. 6 ff. 133 ff.

organisation in the dominant caste at a lower level occurs by way of horizontal mobilisation within the caste group. This is the level of the middle peasantry, and caste organisation, though acting in the interests of the middle peasantry, pulls in rich and poor peasants alike. This thesis utilised by Hardiman propounds that despite the outward appearance of moving on caste lines local society operates in fact in class terms. Such a thesis also appears to be implicit in Ghanshyam Shah's analysis of the Bardoli agitation of 1928.[50]

In discussing the 1942 Quit India disturbances in Bihar and eastern U.P., M. V. Harcourt is equally at pains to find the locus of agitation in the middle peasantry. From police and Congress reports he concludes that 'the statistics on caste certainly do not indicate a rising of "the wretched of the earth" in status terms. They show rather a predominantly middle and high caste crowd.' Indeed some 44·5% of the 'crowd' were drawn from the Brahmin and Rajput-Bhuinar castes. Yet Harcourt finds no difficulty in calling the movement primarily a *kisan* rebellion, and in defining 'kisan' as belonging to the bottom of the tenurial hierarchy. For him the kisans are 'either "dwarf cultivators" from the bottom strata of the jotedar category or sharecroppers'.[51] It is a bold semantic leap.

Yet the notion – in Hamza Alavi's words – that 'poor peasants are *initially* the least militant' and 'middle peasants. . .are *initially* the most militant'[52] is not borne out by observers in the south. While D. N. Dhanagare rejects it for India as a whole[53] Robert Hardgrave has found that in the Mappila Rebellion of 1921 in Kerala the main rebellion zone lay in the Ernad and Walluvanad talukas of South Malabar where militancy came from the poorest tenant cultivators of Kerala who were sharply differentiated economically and socially from their landlords. The area of north Malabar dominated by middle and rich peasant owner cultivators lagged well behind.[54] D. N. Dhanagare comments on the Telan-

[50] Ghanshyam Shah, 'Traditional Society', pp. 89 ff.
[51] M. V. Harcourt, 'Kisan Populism and North Indian Politics: The Context of the 1942 Rebellion in Bihar and eastern U.P.' in D. A. Low (ed.), *Congress and the Raj* (forthcoming).
[52] Hamza Alavi, 'Peasant Revolution' in K. Gough and H. P. Sharma (eds.), *Imperialism and Revolution in South Asia*, pp. 333–4.
[53] D. N. Dhanagare, 'Peasant Movements in India, 1920–1950' (Sussex Univ. D.Phil., 1973).

gana 'insurrection' of 1946–51 in the Andhra delta and neighbouring Hyderabad that 'the poor peasants and the labourers
were the backbone of the resistance from the beginning till the
very end'.[55] Joan Mencher has concluded from her study of
Chingleput that 'organised movements have occurred in areas
where there is a strong polarisation between the landless and all
others. . .Small or middle peasants have not been the ones to
organise or lead revolts of any kind. This is strongly opposed to
the situation described by Wolf. In the South Indian peasant
context it has been the landless labourers, unconstrained by
possible ties to the land, who have been the main agitators or
strikers.'[56]

Mencher's attempt to classify rural society in Chingleput
according to primary occupation – landlord, capitalist farmer,
independent farmer, small holder, and landless farmer – comes
to nothing. The multiplicity of roles exercised by individuals and
the constant shifting from one to another leave the lines of demar-
cation too broken and blurred to be of service. It is precisely this
overlapping of functions, she concludes, that inhibits class conflict.
Although in the 1971 census some 43% of male rural workers
were classified as agricultural labourers by primary occupation,
some of these in any one year would become sharecroppers. Even
the smallest landholders, instead of conforming to the image of
the poor peasant, were employers (perhaps because of the peculiar
labour requirements of wet rice cultivation), and the small 2-acre
men identified themselves with the landed rather than the landless.

The same difficulty in finding a clearly articulated class structure is evident elsewhere. In Bengal the jotedar eludes precise
definition. Basically he was the possessor of a 'home farm' or
'demesne' irrespective of overlord rights he might have held in
other land. But the size of the jotes could differ so enormously
that it is idle to pretend that all jotedars can be lumped together

54 R. L. Hardgrave, Jnr, 'Peasant Mobilization in Malabar: the Mappila
Rebellion, 1921' in R. L. Crane (ed.), *Aspects of Political Mobilization in
South Asia* (Syracuse Univ., 1976).
55 D. N. Dhanagare, 'Social Origins of the Peasant Insurrection in Telangana
(1946–51)', *Contributions to Indian Sociology* new ser., 8 (1974), p.
129.
56 Joan M. Mencher, 'Problems in Analysing Rural Class Structure', *EPW*,
IX (1974), pp. 1495, 1502.

in a single class. Even in the Rays' account they are constrained to acknowledge that, in Rangpur, Buchanan-Hamilton found giant jotedars with 500–6,000 acres, middle jotedars with 50 acres, as well as the normal range of villagers with much smaller amounts.[57] Moreover the saleability of title resulted in absentee rentiers of the professional and service castes intermingling in the jotedar ranks with the traditional agricultural castes (Mahisiyas, Sadgops, etc.). It is only the force of modern political slogan-mongering that has tempted scholars to create a class out of such heterogeneous material, and it is difficult to see how the concept can survive André Béteille's powerful essay in critical demolition.[58]

In any event, according to the lights of the academic left, the case of the jotedar is symptomatic of the tendency of the rich peasant to avoid capitalist farming and to fall back on the 'semi-feudal' exploitation of leasing out to sharecroppers. In this way cash-cropping has failed to transform economic and social relations and consequently class formation and conflict have been held back. While more traditionalist Marxist economists like Utsa Patnaik valiantly argue that a capitalist sector is becoming established in agriculture and that productivity of landholding observes the ordinary rules of economies of scale,[59] there is a strong neo-Marxist school which believes in making a virtue of necessity and formulating a theory of 'underdevelopment' to explain the absence of capitalist relations. Djurfeldt and Lindberg have carried this tendency farthest. Despite the appearance of capitalist modes the rich peasant producing for market by means of wage labour is not in their view earning a true return on capital investment but simply exploiting his monopoly of a scarce means of production in a country where the ordinary man must raise a subsistence from the land or starve. This is a twentieth-century extension of Richard Jones' theory of peasant rents in which, as stated by J. S. Mill, the landholder's return is determined directly

[57] R. and R. Ray, 'The Dynamics of Continuity', p. 115.

[58] A. Béteille, 'Class Structure in an Agrarian Society: the Case of the Jotedars' *Studies in Agrarian Social Structure* (Oxford, 1974), ch. 4.

[59] Utsa Patnaik, 'Economics of Farm Size and Farm Scale: Some Assumptions Reexamined', *EPW*, VII (1972) (Special No. Aug. 1972), pp. 1613 ff. Mrs Patnaik here contests the prevailing assumption that productivity increases in inverse ratio to the size of holding, cf. M. Lipton citing authorities in D. Lehmann, *op. cit.*, pp. 288–9, and T. J. Byres, *op. cit.*, pp. 244–5.

by the ratio of population to land rather than to capital. In India this ratio drives wage rates so low that for Djurfeldt and Lindberg the rich farmer's profit is in fact a form of land rent.[60]

Despite overlapping roles a clear theoretical line can be drawn through village society between exploiters and exploited and income polarisation has increased drastically. Nevertheless the two authors are forced to conclude that 'despite all poverty and suffering, Thaiyur is a coherent and even harmonious formation: there are few dissidents, and few conflicting world-views. This conclusion tallies with our spontaneous and most frustrating experience in the field: there is so little which augurs revolt, or even a protest.'[61]

Their final explanation is one of economic and social dualism. The village survives as a pre-capitalist formation at the periphery of the system but through its external links via the market and the state it is subordinate to capitalism at the centre. In this way the ghost of the old notion of the self-contained Indian village community remains alive. In practice Marxists and non-Marxists record a more or less identical situation in which caste organisation and values tend to dominate in the village while at a wider territorial level the solidarities of class make their intermittent appearance. The account given by Djurfeldt and Lindberg differs little – once the academic top-structure has been cut away – from the balanced and sensible purview taken by Béteille in *Caste, Class and Power* (1965) and reaffirmed in his more recent *Essays in Agrarian Social Structure* (1974). A historian would comment that the one general agrarian movement which superficially bears the imprint of class was the campaign for zamindari abolition. But looked at more closely it represented an alliance of village leaders achieved through the political system to oust an alien or non-resident element from the village community. Even in the south where the evidence for class conflict among the peasantry is much more compelling, one may ask whether the movement against the Brahmin *mirasdars* did not follow on from their gradual withdrawal from the direct supervision of cultivation into

---

[60] G. Djurfeldt and S. Lindberg, *Behind Poverty: The Social Formation in a Tamil Village*, Scandinavian Institute of Asian Studies Monograph, no. 22 (Lund/London 1975), p. 172. For the influence of Richard Jones' theory in the nineteenth century, see Paper 4, pp. 94 ff., 107 ff.

[61] Djurfeldt and Lindberg, *op. cit.*, p. 316.

absentee public service employment and an increasingly rentier role.[62]

In conclusion, we may say that agrarian agitation formed an increasingly important element in politics after 1900; that such agitations were scattered, intermittent, and short-lived; that they usually occurred either in 'high-farming' areas where agrarian society was peculiarly open to market forces or in peripheral areas that had been subjected to recent economic disturbance; that they took hold where supra-village caste organisation remained strong. Marxists acknowledge that the division of the peasantry into rich, middle and poor is a rough and ready heuristic device and that a much more refined instrument of classification is necessary for modern economic sociology. For the historian used to working with blunt tools the threefold division is probably adequate for the scantier evidence on which he has to work in peasant studies. Yet even if non-economic elements in social organisation could be brushed aside and a 13-point classificatory scale be employed as Linz has recently sought to use for European peasantry, the complexities of political response in Europe would warn of the difficulty of constructing some handy ready-reckoner on which the student of Indian political history could happily rely.[63] Indeed whether it is valid to view the peasantry as divided internally into opposed economic and social classes remains a matter of contention even among Marxists. Chayanov's argument of a cyclical mobility preventing any such permanent class formation continues to carry weight, and the débâcle which the *ujamaa* 'anti-kulak' policy in Tanzania has met with has drawn cries of protest from those who argue within the rounded circle of Marxist thought:

The relationship between progressive farmers and peasants is much more usefully understood as one between different strata of the same

[62] Cf. Béteille, *Caste, Class and Power*, pp. 111 ff, and *Studies in Agrarian Social Structure*, p. 152.

J. Harriss, 'Implications of Changes in Agriculture for Social Relationships at the Village Level: the Case of Randam', in B. H. Farmer (ed.), *Green Revolutions: Technological Change in Rice Growing Areas of Tamilnadu and Sri Lanka* (Macmillan, London, 1977). The eastern taluks of the Old Delta in Thanjavur (Tanjore) present an exceptional case. Here Brahmin *mirasdars* have turned to commercial farming, tenancy has been almost eliminated, and the vast bulk of the Harijan population are employed as agricultural labourers. The naked congruence of caste and class has brought about an explosive situation.

[63] Juan J. Linz, 'Patterns of Land Tenure, Division of Labor, and Voting Behavior in Europe', *Comparative Politics*, VIII, 3 (April 1976), pp. 365 ff.

social class. From a Marxian perspective the progressive farmers are not a discrete social class separate from the peasantry: they are simply the most well-off section of the peasantry. Insofar as the concept of a peasantry can be understood to apply to that segment of the rural population characterised by (1) a dependence upon land husbandry for its principal source of livelihood, and (2) occupancy and cultivation of the land on the basis of family units, poorer peasants and progressive farmers belong to a common category in class terms. Whatever the dissimilarities in the sizes of their land-holding, both groups are composed of individuals who possess land and earn their living by investing their labor in it. The differential patterns of land occupancy demonstrated by Van Hekker and Van Velzen are evidence that processes of rural class formation are well under way, and not, as these authors assume, that economically opposed social classes have come into being.[64]

If even the Marxist trumpet sounds so uncertain a note, who else will prepare for the battle? In the present age the historian must content himself with the role of humble camp follower to the sociologist and economist. But like the sweeper in my regiment who carried the thunder-box of the sahibs through the Arakan campaign there is the hope that in the end it is he and not they who will be awarded the decoration.

---

[64] Michael F. Lofchie, 'Agrarian Socialism in the Third World: the Tanzanian Case', in *ibid.*, p. 493. For Chayanov, see D. Thorner, B. Kerblay, and R. E. F. Smith (eds.), *A. V. Chayanov on the Theory of Peasant Economy* (Homewood, 1966), and Charlesworth's perceptive comments, 'Economic and Social Stratification among the Bombay Peasantry', seminar paper, *op. cit.*

GLOSSARY

(Alternative or archaic spellings are given in brackets)

agraharam   Village or part of a village occupied by Brahmins and usually held on privileged tenure (S. India).

amil   Pre-British district revenue official.

bach (baach)   A money rate fluctuating with the demand, and paid by all the sharers according to the quantity of land in the possession of each and without reference to his hereditary share of the estate.

ballotadar (balutadar)   A village officer or member of service caste, traditionally 12 in number (W. India).

bangar   Upland, as distinct from *khadir* or riverain land.

bania (banya, bunneah)   Hindu trader, often also a moneylender.

barah   Lit. twelve. A group of 12 mutually dependent villages.

bargadar   Sharecropper, metayer (Bengal).

bargdar   A village co-sharer (Gujarat); cf. *pattidar*.

basti   Village, town, inhabited place.

batisa   A group of 32 mutually dependent villages.

bhaiachara (byachara, bhaeechareh)   Lit. custom of the brotherhood. Under British revenue law denoted a form of tenure in which the land-revenue demand was apportioned among the village proprietors on some principle other than ancestral shares.

bigha   Land measure standardised by the British at $\frac{5}{8}$ths of an acre.

bighadam   Apportionment of revenue demand at so much per *bigha*; cf. *bach*.

biswa   Lit. a twentieth. A twentieth share of a village or estate.

biswadar	A coparcener. In taluqdari estates the term used under British revenue law in N.W. Provinces for a village sub-proprietor.
Borah (bohra)	Member of a Gujarati trading and banking caste. Used loosely to denote village banker.
chak	A separate parcel or tract of land.
chali	Land bearing highest rate of assessment, a share of which each permanent cultivator was required to cultivate (W. India).
Chamar	Member of a caste traditionally associated with tanning hides and menial labour tasks.
Chattri (Chhattri, cf. *Kshatriya)*	Term commonly used in eastern U.P. to denote member of a Rajput caste.
chaudhuri	Local headman or petty notable.
chaukidar (chowkidar)	A watchman.
chaurasi	A tract containing nominally 84 villages usually controlled by one particular dominant clan.
des	Country, local district, homeland.
desi	Local, locally-produced.
desmukh	Hereditary local headman or petty notable of a district.
despande (despandiya)	Hereditary revenue accountant of a locality (W. India).
dharra (dhar)	Faction.
doul (daul, dowl)	Estimate of amount of revenue an estate might be expected to yield.
ghair maurusi	Lit. without hereditary land rights. A cultivator holding by lease or custom without hereditary rights.
got (gotra)	Exogamous kin group or clan.
gram	Type of pulse or grain.
grassia (grasia)	Military or predatory chieftain claiming portion of revenue of certain villages as protection money (W. India).
haq (huk)	Prescriptive fee or allowance.
haq mehat	Village headman's perquisites or allowance.
haveli	Tract adjacent to capital town of a district.
huzur	Lit. pertaining to authority. Used often to denote chief or leading, as the chief *pargana* of a district in which the capital is situated.

ilaqa (ilaka)   Dependency, property, or estate.

inam   Grant of land held rent- or revenue-free (S. & W. India).

istumrari   Land held in revenue farm or leased on a perpetual rent.

jaedad (jaidad)   Life grant of revenue from a tract for the maintenance of troops.

jagir (jaghir, jageer)   The assignment to a person of the State revenue due from a specified area or estate.

jagirdar   The holder of a *jagir*.

jama (jumma)   Aggregate revenue payable by a cultivator or estate.

jamabandi   Detailed rent roll or revenue statement of a village or estate.

jemedar (jamadar)   Most junior commissioned officer in the Indian army.

jihad (jeehad)   Muslim holy war.

jodi   An easy or quit-rent.

jote (jot)   Tillage, cultivation. Often used to denote *nij-jot*, or proprietary cultivation; cf. *sir*.

jotedar   A superior cultivator and *de facto* sub-proprietor, often with land leased out to share-croppers; cf. *bargadars* (Bengal and Bihar).

juar (jowar, joar)   Type of millet used extensively as food grain.

kanungo (qanungo)   Hereditary local revenue accountant of *pargana* or group of villages.

kapu   Principal cultivator or headman (S. India).

karinda   An agent or manager.

karnam   Hereditary village accountant (S. India).

kazi (qazi)   A Muslim judge in matters of religious law.

khadir   Low or alluvial lands; cf. *bangar*.

khalsa   Lands held immediately of Government, not alienated in *jagir* or *inam*, and paying land revenue directly to the State.

kham   Term used when Government itself has temporarily set aside proprietor or other revenue engager and collects revenue from immediate cultivators.

khap   Area held or controlled by a clan.

kharif   The autumn crops or harvest reaped in October–November.

khudkasht	leased-in land cultivated by a proprietor
kisan	Cultivator, husbandman, peasant.
koli (*kuli*, hence 'coolie')	Tribal people who migrated to plains in Gujarat and formed bulk of labouring class in some areas, but in other areas through turbulence had obtained local village dominance.
kotwal	Chief police officer of town or city.
kulkarni	Hereditary village accountant (W. India).
lakh	One hundred thousand.
lakhiraj (*lakharaj*)	Land exempt from payment of revenue.
lambardar	One who has a number on the revenue roll. Hence a person who pays land revenue on behalf of a number of small proprietors. One of a number of village headmen.
lathi	A stout stick or stave often ringed and ferruled.
mahajan (*mahajun*)	A village or small town banker.
mahal	An estate or proprietary holding as defined in the revenue accounts. In upper India it often coincided originally with *mauza*, or lands pertaining to a single village.
mahalwari	The system of village land-revenue settlements in which the demand was levied on the *mahal* or *mauza* (N.W. or later United Provinces).
malba (*malbah*)	Village expenses, including entertainment and payment of minor functionaries.
malguzar	Person engaging for land revenue.
malik	Lit. master, lord. Term used to describe a proprietor in a village; cf. *pattidar*.
malik mabhuza	A ryot recognised as having a proprietary right; a plot proprietor (C.P.).
malikana	Under British revenue law the allowance paid to a proprietor temporarily excluded from the revenue engagement.
mamlatdar	Revenue officer in charge of a *taluka* (W. India).
mar	A rich black loam soil.
maulavi (*maulawi*)	A Muslim scholar or divine.
milk(*i*)	Property. In Rohilkhand used to refer to revenue-free grants held by Muslims.

milkiyat-i-zamin	Property in the soil equivalent to freehold right.
miras	Property (W. & S. India).
mirasdar	Person having hereditary ownership of land.
mirasi	Single or joint village landlord right (W. & S. India).
makassa (mukhasa)	Land held rent-free or at privileged rent in return for service (W. India).
Marwari	Lit. a person from Marwar (part of Rajasthan). Used of banking and trading castes from this region.
muafi (mafi)	Grant of land free of revenue.
mukarari	Tract of land or fiscal lordship held at a fixed revenue payment.
muqaddam (mukaddam, mocuddum)	One of the managers of a village proprietary body.
naidu	Title or surname used by a person of the Telegu Kamma caste; hence loosely a headman (S. India).
nankar	Lit. subsistence. An assignment of revenue or land made as a reward for undertaking revenue-management rights, or as compensation for being deprived of them.
Naumuslim	A Muslim convert.
nayakar	Military chieftain (S. India).
nazim	Governor of a province or vicegerent.
nikasi	An account of the revenue assessed upon an estate.
pahi	A temporary or non-resident cultivator without tenurial rights or formal lease: a tenant-at-will.
paltan	A regiment or battalion of infantry.
panchayat	A caste or village council.
pandal	Temporary covered arena or pole and cloth building designed for meetings.
pargana (pergunnah)	A revenue subdivision of a *tahsil*. A group of mutually connected villages.
patel	A village headman (W. & S. India).

patta (pottah)	Written agreement or lease.
patti	Division or share.
pattidar	One who holds land on which the payment of the revenue demand is apportioned by the proprietary kin group according to ancestral shares.
pattidari	System of tenure in which the land is farmed in severalty but in which the revenue demand on the estate is apportioned by the kin group on ancestral shares.
peishkar (peshkar)	Deputy or manager in revenue affairs.
poligar (poliyagar)	Small warrior chief (S. India).
pucca (pukha)	Lit. ripe, cooked. Substantial, permanent, well-finished.
rabi	Spring crops, or harvest reaped in February–March.
rais (raees)	A notable, a man of position.
raj	Kingdom, principality. Used loosely to denote the British Indian Empire.
reddi	Name of a principal caste of Telegu cultivators; loosely a chief cultivator or headman.
risala	A troop of horse.
risaldar	Indian officer commanding a troop of horse.
rusoom (rusum)	A commission or allowance on a transaction.
ryot (raiyat)	Cultivator or farmer, as distinct from labourer.
sadr (sudder)	Leading or chief (adj.).
satyagraha	Lit. truth- or soul-force. Used to denote a non-cooperation or civil disobedience campaign led by Gandhi.
saukar (sahukar, sowcar)	A banker, moneydealer.
sawar (sowar)	An armed horseman or cavalryman.
shikmi	A dependent or subordinate cultivator who pays revenue through a superior but whose name is not recorded in the settlement register. Often used to denote an unrecorded tenant cultivating a proprietor's *sir* or home farm.
shuk (shooqa)	Royal letter or missive.
sir (seer)	Personal or home farm; land under owner cultivation.

sirdar (1) A holder of *sir* land. (2) Under U.P. Zamindari Abolition Act, 1951, a former hereditary tenant who now pays his rent to the State instead of to a private landlord. (3) Corruption of *sardar*, a chief or leading man.

tahsil (tehsil, tehseel) Administrative subdivision of a district (N. India).

tahsili Administrative headquarters of a *tahsil*.

tahsildar Indian officer in charge of a *tahsil*.

taluk(a) (ta'alluq, talooq) Lit. dependency, connection. (1) Fiscal lordship or estate, in which the holder is responsible for the revenue collection from a number of dependent villages (N. India). (2) A group of villages held in mutual dependence by lineage ties among the proprietary bodies. (3) Administrative subdivision of a district (W. & S. India); cf. *tahsil*.

talpad Land paying the full revenue assessment (Gujarat).

talukdar (taluqdar) Holder of a *taluk*. Under British revenue law in N.W. Provinces a superior proprietor drawing a fixed percentage on revenue payments made by village sub-proprietors or *biswadars*. In Oudh a full proprietor of a number of villages; cf. *zamindar* in Bengal.

tappa Cluster of villages acknowledging the supremacy of one among them, and often connected by lineage ties. Used more frequently in West U.P. and Haryana; cf. *taluk* in East U.P.

thakur Lit. lord, master. Usually denotes Rajput landholder (N. India).

thana A police station, or area under jurisdiction of a local police station.

thika A private lease or private revenue farm.

thikadar One who receives the rents from the cultivators and pays a stipulated amount to the proprietor.

ubari (oobari) An overlord tenure in Bundelkhand.

umul (amal) Share or portion of revenue after expenses have been defrayed (W. India).

Vaish(ya)   Broad occupational caste classification for any person belonging to a trading or moneylending caste.

vaita   Land of superior quality and most highly assessed (Gujarat).

zail   Subdivision of a *tahsil* in the former Punjab province.

zaildar   Officer in charge of a *zail*.

zamindar   Lit. landholder. Under British law designated a person recognised as possessing the proprietary right.

zamindari   An estate held in full proprietary right (N. India). Used adjectively to describe system of land-revenue settlement in which notables responsible for collection from a considerable number of villages were recognised as proprietors of such 'estates' (Bengal).

INDEX